MW00994994

Turkish Germans in the Federal Republic of Germany

As the largest national group of guest workers in Germany, the Turks became a visible presence in local neighborhoods and schools and had diverse social, cultural, and religious needs. Focusing on West Berlin, Sarah Thomsen Vierra explores the history of Turkish immigrants and their children from the early days of their participation in the postwar guest worker program to the formation of multigenerational communities. Both German and Turkish sources help to uncover how the first and second generations created spaces of belonging for themselves within and alongside West German society, while also highlighting the factors that influenced that process, from individual agency and community dynamics to larger institutional factors such as educational policy and city renovation projects. By examining the significance of daily interactions at the workplace, in the home, in the neighborhood, at school, and in places of worship, we see that spatial belonging was profoundly linked to local-level daily life and experiences.

Sarah Thomsen Vierra is an assistant professor of history at New England College in Henniker, New Hampshire. She received her doctorate in European history from the University of North Carolina at Chapel Hill, and was granted the Fritz Stern Dissertation Prize by the Friends of the German Historical Institute, Washington, DC, in 2012. She has published on West Berlin's Turkish community, the influence of the Cold War on the guest worker program, and migration in modern German history more broadly. Her research interests include migration, ethnic and religious minorities in European society, and everyday history.

Publications of the German Historical Institute

Edited by

Simone Lässig

with the assistance of David Lazar

The German Historical Institute is a center for advanced study and research whose purpose is to provide a permanent basis for scholarly cooperation among historians from the Federal Republic of Germany and the United States. The Institute conducts, promotes, and supports research into both American and German political, social, economic, and cultural history; into transatlantic migration, especially during the nineteenth and twentieth centuries; and into the history of international relations, with special emphasis on the roles played by the United States and Germany.

A full list of titles in the series can be found at:

www.cambridge.org/pghi

Turkish Germans in the Federal Republic of Germany

Immigration, Space, and Belonging, 1961–1990

Sarah Thomsen Vierra

New England College

GERMAN HISTORICAL INSTITUTE

Washington, DC

and

 CAMBRIDGE
UNIVERSITY PRESS

CAMBRIDGE
UNIVERSITY PRESS

University Printing House, Cambridge CB2 8BS, United Kingdom

One Liberty Plaza, 20th Floor, New York, NY 10006, USA

477 Williamstown Road, Port Melbourne, VIC 3207, Australia

314–321, 3rd Floor, Plot 3, Splendor Forum, Jasola District Centre, New Delhi – 110025, India

79 Anson Road, #06–04/06, Singapore 079906

Cambridge University Press is part of the University of Cambridge.

It furthers the University's mission by disseminating knowledge in the pursuit of education, learning, and research at the highest international levels of excellence.

www.cambridge.org
Information on this title: www.cambridge.org/9781108427302
DOI: 10.1017/9781108691475

First published 2018

Printed and bound in Great Britain by Clays Ltd, Elcograf S.p.A.

A catalogue record for this publication is available from the British Library.

ISBN 978-1-108-42730-2 Hardback

Contents

Figures

Maps

Acknowledgments

I had very little idea at the outset of the journey that would end with this book just how many people and institutions would play such an important role in its making and my life, and it makes me very glad that I can use these first pages to acknowledge their formative contributions.

First, I would like to thank Konrad H. Jarausch for his enthusiasm for my project, his invaluable guidance during graduate school, and his continued support beyond. At the University of North Carolina at Chapel Hill, Christopher Browning, Karen Hagemann, Claudia Koonz, and, especially, Don Reid gave time, support, and thoughtful feedback at various stages of the dissertation and helped bring that stage of the project to a successful completion, for which I am grateful. My Turkish language professors, Erdağ Göknar and Cangüzel Zulfikar, and my conversation partners, Şeyma Kayman and, in Berlin, Filiz Güngör were instrumental in helping me realize my goal of learning and using Turkish. They offered their expertise, patience, and good humor, even in the face of their slow and at times impatient student, and were invaluable in my learning the language and being introduced to Turkish history and culture. Yekta Zulfikar sailed in and aided in translations when time was at a premium. To all of you, *çok teşekküler*!

The generous support of the Alexander von Humboldt Stiftung made my field research possible and my time in Germany a joy. From the staff of the foundation to my fellow "Bukas," the people I came to know through my participation in the German Chancellor Scholarship Program enriched my experience of living in Germany, and made it much more than a research trip. While in Berlin, I was generously hosted by Humboldt Universität's Institute for European Ethnology, at the time directed by Professor Dr. Wolfgang Kaschuba. The intellectually rigorous and socially informal atmosphere of the institute, as well as Professor Dr. Kaschuba's own hospitality, were among the highlights of my time in Berlin. Many thanks also to Perrin Saylan for her painstaking work on interview transcriptions.

From professional, well-established archives to the dusty basements of secondary schools, the staffs of numerous institutions aided in my research, and I am grateful to each of them. In particular, at Berlin's Mitte Museum, Sigrid Schulze rendered invaluable assistance and expertise, which continued long past my return to the United States. The archivists at the Dokumentationszentrum und Migration über die Migration in Deutschland in Cologne and the Siemens Corporate Archive (then in Munich) helped me make the most of my regrettably quick visits to their institutions. Many thanks also for the assistance of those at the Amt für Statistik Berlin-Brandenburg, Bezirksmuseum Friedrichshain-Kreuzberg Archiv, Bundespresseamt Archiv, Deutsches Technikmuseum Historisches Archiv, Herbert-Hoover-Schule, Landesarchiv Berlin, Staatsbibliothek zur Berlin, Zeitungsabteilung, and Theodor Plievier Oberschule.

Individuals also played a significant role in the success of my research in Germany. Historian Ursula Trüper's fascinating interviews, as well as her personal accounts and assistance, were a determining factor in my choice of Sprengelkiez, and I am in her debt. In Sprengelkiez, I had the very good fortune to connect with the director of the Büro für Stadtteilnahe Sozialplannung, Engin Günükutlu. Engin's enthusiasm, energy, and helpfulness knew no bounds, and without him, local research would have been less rich and considerably less fun. Dr. Eduard Ditschek offered his time, his memories, his personal archives, and his "Vitamin-B" to the project, both during and after my stint in Berlin, and the book is much richer for his contributions. Finally, I would like to express my deepest thanks to my interview partners, who set aside their time and privacy to help a curious American who wanted to know about Turks in Germany. Thank you for your time, your sharing, and your good humor!

At five critical points in the research and writing process, I was able to take part in workshops and seminars that helped me to form my questions, refine my methodology, and clarify my conclusions. In June 2008, I participated in the Trans-Atlantic Summer Institute in European Studies, headed by Donna Gabaccia and Barbara Wolbert; in January 2009 the Technical University's Center for Metropolitan Studies' Second Generation Research Dialogue, coordinated by Viola-Donata Rauch and Philipp Schnell; in May 2010 the German Historical Institute's Transatlantic Doctoral Seminar convened by Roger Chickering, Norbert Frei, and Richard F. Wetzell; in fall 2010 to spring 2011 the Andrew W. Mellon Sawyer Seminar "Diversity and Conformity in Muslim Societies," headed by Sarah Shields and Banu Gökarıksel; and in July 2015 "Berlin in the Cold War – The Cold War in Berlin," convened by

Konrad Jarausch, Martin Sabrow, Stefanie Eisenhuth, and Scott Krause. I am very grateful to all the conveners and my fellow participants, whose intervention along the way was vital in the development of my ideas and the way that I communicated them on paper.

The transition from dissertation to book was an intense and rewarding process. I was honored to receive the Fritz Stern Dissertation prize from the German Historical Institute (GHI), and thank the GHI as well as committee members Ann Goldberg, Maria D. Mitchell, and Ulrike Strasser for the recognition. The GHI's invitation to publish as part of their series with Cambridge University Press brought me to editor Liz Friend-Smith, who made the crooked path smooth and easy to tread, and copyeditor Alison Auch, whose keen attention to detail caught and polished numerous rough patches. Many thanks also to David Lazar at the GHI for providing insightful feedback as I revised chapters and for answering many, many questions along the way. I am deeply grateful to the two anonymous readers, whose insightful criticisms gave the revision process concrete direction and resulted in, what I hope they would find, a much improved final product. Earlier versions of sections of Chapters 4 and 5 were published previously, and I thank the GHI and IB Tauris respectively for the permission to include those in this book. My thanks also to Meral and Lena Kurt for the permission to use their father's photographs, so that readers could put faces and places to names.

Bill Smaldone showed me that historians could be just as passionate about the present as the past, and is always in there swinging. Brittany Lehman's and Brian J. K. Miller's ongoing enthusiasm and well-informed suggestions for this project have been a great encouragement. Nathan Swanson sailed in with his mapping expertise, saving me time and frustration. Sarah Summers read and gave insightful feedback on multiple drafts, and cooks a mean Thanksgiving goose. Julia Osman's generosity is as boundless as Mary Poppins's carpetbag; everyone should have a friend so steadfastly in their corner. A team of capable, giving women cared for my daughters so that I could sometimes enjoy a relatively undivided brain when working – my heartfelt thanks to Ginger Ehmann, Julie Ault, Jean LaPointe, and, especially, Bonnie LaPointe!

I am deeply grateful for my parents, Gary and Sandy Thomsen, whose love and support are a constant in my life, and who always seem calmly confident in my ability to take on new challenges. I am grateful for my daughters, who demand my life be more fun than it would be if left to my own devices. Kathryn, born when I was in the middle of writing my dissertation, taught me time management like nothing else had or could. She is now a voracious reader herself, and keen to see my book on our bookshelves. Laurel came three years later, as I waded ever deeper into revisions, and has made me laugh every day since. My last and greatest thanks are to Ben, who is my partner in all things, has been with me through every step in this years-long process, and is likely even more relieved than I am that it is finished.

Abbreviations

ASBB   Amt für Statistik Berlin-Brandenburg, Berlin
BFKA   Bezirksmuseum Friedrichshain-Kreuzberg Archiv, Berlin
BPA   Bundespresseamt Archiv, Berlin
DLSA   "Die Leute vom Sparrplatz" Ausstellung
DOMiD   Dokumentationszentrum und Museum über die Migration
            in Deutschland, e.V., Cologne
DTHA   Deutsches Technikmuseum Historisches Archiv, Berlin
EDF   Dr. Eduard Ditschek, personal files pertaining to
            Volkshochschule Wedding, Berlin
HHS   Herbert-Hoover-Schule (Realschule), Berlin
LAB   Landesarchiv Berlin
MMA   Mitte Museum Archiv und Bibliothek, Berlin
SCA   Siemens Corporate Archives, Munich
SBZ   Staatsbibliothek zur Berlin, Zeitungsabteilung, Berlin
TPO   Theodor Plievier Oberschule (Hauptschule), Berlin

Introduction

Eren Keskin was born in 1960, one year before representatives from the Federal Republic of Germany (FRG) and the Republic of Turkey signed the bilateral labor contract that would change the course of his life. Thirty-three years later, in a bar in the Berlin district of Wedding, he sat across the table from a German historian to tell her his story of the intervening years. His parents had seen the recently signed contract as an opportunity to improve their family's financial situation, and became two of the eventual hundreds of thousands of Turkish *Gastarbeiter*, or guest workers, who moved to the Federal Republic to work for West German companies. Young Eren, however, was initially left behind and spent most of his childhood in the family's small home village in rural Turkey. At age thirteen, his parents brought him to live with them in West Berlin. Although he described that transition as a "trauma," the teenaged Keskin was quickly distracted by the excitement of living in a big city. But the veneer, he told the historian, soon wore off, and at age sixteen he was already working to earn money for his family. By twenty-two, Keskin had married and started his own family, later becoming the owner of the small *Kneipe* (pub) where the interview was taking place.

But Keskin was not interested in talking about his experiences as an immigrant or his success as a business owner. Instead he focused on changes in his neighborhood that made him uneasy. His neighborhood of Sparrplatz, in Wedding's Sprengelkiez quarter, had been more ethnically mixed when he was younger, and he had known all of his neighbors. In the last few years, though, the population had become majority Turkish. There used to be a lot of work before the Wall fell, Keskin explained to the German interviewer, but when the Wall came down, unemployment shot up. And people from the East work for cheap! To add to it, most of the kids that hang out at the park across from his business, Keskin complained, are doing drugs. Despite these changes, however, he insisted that "we are satisfied with Sparrplatz."

The clatter of games in the background abated slightly as some of his customers paused to give their own opinions. One patron contended that the kids were doing drugs because they didn't have any work; another blamed the drug use on boredom. Keskin agreed that unemployment, boredom, and drug use were connected, but no one could agree which was the cause and which the effect. Talk shifted to asylum seekers – Germany needs to tell them, "We're full," Keskin posited, but they can't because of *Menschenrechte* (human rights). At this point in the discussion, apparently wanting to bring the conversation back to the men's own experiences, the interviewer interjected a question: What about getting German citizenship? Keskin replied dismissively, "Ha! We have black heads, and everyone knows that we're not Germans. You know?"[1]

The interview with Keskin and the debate among his customers provide a revealing snapshot of the complex and often conflicting forces at play in the settlement of Turkish immigrants and their children in West German society. In one moment, he expresses sentiments common among many former West Germans in the wake of reunification, while in the next, he sets himself unequivocally outside that community. What does it say about the situation of the Turkish population in Germany that a man like Keskin, after twenty years of living in the country, could simultaneously feel himself to be both a part of and apart from that society? How did that conflicted sense of belonging come about? That question is the focus of this book. In the pages that follow, I examine the history of first-generation Turkish immigrants and their children in the Federal Republic of Germany, primarily from Turkey's inclusion in the guest worker program in 1961 to German reunification in 1990. In particular, I explore the ways they experienced and constructed belonging in the course of their daily lives in order to better understand the complicated and dynamic process we call integration.

The formation of a Turkish minority population in Germany began as a consequence of postwar labor policy in the Federal Republic. During the rebuilding efforts after the Second World War, the West German government began in 1955 to enter into a series of temporary labor contracts with southern and southeastern European countries. The migrant workers came to be called *Gastarbeiter*, or "guest workers," both to distinguish them from the term *Fremdarbeiter* (foreign workers), most recently used by the Nazi regime, as well as to emphasize the intended temporary nature of their stay.[2] The majority of these migrant laborers

---

[1] Eren Keskin (pseudonym), "Wirt einer Kneipe am Sparrplatz", interview with Ursula Trüper, audiocassette, side A, "Die Leute vom Sparrplatz" Ausstellung (DLSA), Mitte Museum Archiv (MMA), Berlin, 1993.

[2] The term *Gastarbeiter* was the result of a radio contest held to find a different name for these new foreign workers. See Ernst Klee, "Ein neues Wort für Gastarbeiter" in Ernst Klee, ed., *Gastarbeiter: Analysen und Berichte* (Frankfurt am Main: Suhrkamp, 1981), 149–157.

worked in semiskilled or unskilled positions in industry, manufacturing, and agriculture; lived in dormitory or barrack-style housing; and
intended to return to their homes after completing their term of service
or accumulating a certain amount of savings. Historians such as
Ulrich Herbert and Klaus Bade have shown how the *Gastarbeiter* program built on preexisting patterns of foreign labor employment, including the types of work for which migrant workers were hired, the areas of
the country where they were employed, and the social and political
separation of native Germans and foreign laborers.[3] More recently,
scholarship has uncovered startling similarities between Nazi Germany's
and the Federal Republic's treatment of foreign workers, including the
methods of transportation used to bring workers to Germany and the
vocabulary West Germans used to describe those "transports."[4] These
studies have begun the critical work of integrating the postwar labor
program and its resultant ethnic minority communities into the broader
narrative of German history, an effort this book continues.[5] Yet this
earlier historical scholarship has primarily approached postwar immigration from a German perspective, a focus heavily influenced by its
German-language sources and reflected in the questions asked of these
sources. In addition, these earlier studies often conceived of the guest
worker program as "a history of men," discussing women almost solely in
connection with later family reunification.[6] As we will see in the coming

---

[3] See Ulrich Herbert, *A History of Foreign Labor in Germany, 1880–1980: Seasonal Workers, Forced Laborers, Guest Workers*. Translated by William Templer (Ann Arbor: University of Michigan Press, 1990), 211–253; Klaus Bade, ed., *Auswanderer-Wanderarbeiter-Gastarbeiter: Bevölkerung, Arbeitsmarkt und Wanderung in Deutschland seit der Mitte des 19 Jahrhundert* (Ostfildern: Scripta Mercaturae Verlag, 1984); Klaus Bade, *Europa in Bewegung: Migration vom späten 18. Jahrhundert bis zur Gegenwart* (Munich: C. H. Beck, 2000), 314–330.

[4] Jennifer Miller, "On Track for West Germany: Turkish 'Guest-worker' Rail Transportation to West Germany in the Postwar Period," *German History* 30, no. 4 (December 2012): 528–549.

[5] On the need to locate the history of postwar immigrants to Germany within German history, see Konrad H. Jarausch, "Unsettling German Society: Mobility and Migration," in Konrad H. Jarausch and Michael Geyer, eds., *Shattered Past: Reconstructing German History* (Princeton: Princeton University Press, 2003): 197–220.

[6] Ulrich Herbert and Karin Hunn, "Guest Workers and Policy on Guest Workers in the Federal Republic: From the Beginning of Recruitment in 1955 until Its Halt in 1973," in Hanna Schissler, ed., *The Miracle Years: A Cultural History of West Germany, 1949–1968* (Princeton: Princeton University Press, 2001), 199. Here, Herbert and Hunn are specifically addressing the 1960s, arguing that more than two-thirds of participants in the guest worker program in 1962 were single men. While true, this position overlooks the fact that even in the 1960s and especially in Berlin, women were actively recruited by West German companies, and that, by 1962, there were already approximately 220,000 *Gastarbeiterinnen* (female guest workers) in the Federal Republic. See Monika Mattes, "*Gastarbeiterinnen*" in der Bundesrepublik: Anwerbepolitik, Migration, und Geschlecht in den 50er bis 70er Jahren (Frankfurt am Main: Campus Verlag, 2005), 9. More recent scholarship, such as Jennifer Miller's study mentioned in note 4, work to correct this incomplete perspective of the guest worker program.

chapters, West German companies recruited both male and female guest workers, all of whom played an active role in shaping their work and living environments.

In 1961, when construction of the Wall halted the flood of people pouring in from East Germany, the Federal Republic looked to Turkey for labor, and thousands of Turks took advantage of the opportunity, becoming the largest national group of guest workers in the country by 1972. As Karin Hunn has demonstrated, German and Turkish migration politics; the state of, interests, and actions of business; and the attitudes of German society as well as Turkish immigrants all affected the shape and character of Turkish participation in the program and experiences in West Germany.[7] Although many early Turkish guest workers returned home after a stint in West Germany,[8] increasing numbers of these migrant laborers began renewing their work and residence permits and bringing their families from Turkey to live with them.[9] Due to their larger numbers and to Germans' perceptions of them as particularly "foreign" culturally, Turks became more visible and controversial than any of the other *Gastarbeiter* groups.

This important development coincided with two others in the history of the *Gastarbeiter* program. First, by the early 1970s, family reunification prompted many in West Germany to realize that these so-called guest workers were transforming into immigrants. Second, the global oil crisis of 1973 and the resulting economic downturn gave West German politicians, already considering the possibility, a clear opportunity to stop recruitment for the *Gastarbeiter* program.[10] That action had the opposite effect to the one intended; seeing the waning opportunity to return to West Germany to work at a later point, many guest workers – and especially Turks – responded by bringing their families to live with them and settling into established multigenerational immigrant communities. Whereas earlier scholarship argued that, until after 1973,[11] the Federal

---

[7] Karin Hunn, *"Nächstes Jahr kehren wir zurück..."*: *Die Geschichte der türkischen "Gastarbeiter" in der Bundesrepublik* (Göttingen: Wallstein Verlag, 2005), 21.

[8] Brian Joseph-Keysor Miller, "Reshaping the Turkish Nation-State: The Turkish-German Guest Worker Program and Planned Development, 1961–1985," (PhD dissertation, University of Iowa, Iowa City, 2015), 165–203.

[9] In Chapter 1, we will see how West German companies, contrary to the initial aims and stipulations of the guest worker agreements, facilitated and encouraged renewal of work and residency contracts in order to retain their now-trained workforce.

[10] Herbert and Hunn, "Guest Workers and Policy on Guest Workers in the Federal Republic," 187–218; Marcel Berlinghoff, *Das Ende der "Gastarbeit": Europäische Anwerbestopps 1970–1974* (Paderborn: Schöningh, 2013).

[11] See Herbert, *A History of Foreign Labor in Germany*, 193–254; Stephen Castles, "Migrants and Minorities in Post-Keynesian Capitalism: The German Case," in Malcolm Cross, ed., *Ethnic Minorities and Industrial Change in Europe and North America* (Cambridge, UK: Cambridge University Press, 1992), 36–54.

Republic did little to nothing to help guest workers and their families integrate into West German society, more recent studies, including this one, demonstrate that what might have been the case on the federal level was not uniformly consistent on the city level. Sarah Hackett's comparison of the city-state of Bremen with Britain's Newcastle upon Tyne reveals authorities in that West German city (as well as the British one) were actively concerned with the integration of their growing population of foreign residents long before the official recruitment halt in the early 1970s.[12]

The growth of substantial ethnic minority populations, a direct consequence of the *Gastarbeiter* program, contributed to two major developments in postwar Germany and Europe more broadly than this book addresses. First, it has spurred debate and examination of dominant political and cultural identities. In the case of the Federal Republic, cultural and intellectual interventions of minority-background writers have compelled a significant rethinking of that perennial and problematic question, "What is German?" Historian Rita Chin's groundbreaking book *The Guest Worker Question in Postwar Germany* examines the formative role of minority elites in this debate, and is critical to our understanding of the political and cultural history of the guest worker question. In particular, it explores the postwar histories of concepts such as integration, multiculturalism, and German identity.[13] Yet, with its focus on cultural elites, Chin's study does not give us a clear picture of the extent to which the lives of "ordinary" Germans, immigrants, and second-generation youth matched these ideological debates. Nor does it explore how those without access in wider realms of discourse and power – a situation shared by the majority of Turkish immigrants and their

---

[12] Sarah Hackett, *Foreigners, Minorities and Integration: The Muslim Immigrant Experience in Britain and Germany* (Manchester, UK: Manchester University Press, 2016), 9–10.

[13] Rita Chin, *The Guest Worker Question in Postwar Germany* (Cambridge, UK: Cambridge University Press, 2007). Similarly, Alexander Clarkson has written an excellent book on interactions between homeland-oriented immigrant activists and the West German state during the Cold War, which argues, in part, that such activism was "at the core of this process of community building, adaptation and paradoxically, integration" (186). Clarkson demonstrates how collective action and building networks with the West German government worked to both integrate immigrant activists within West German political spaces and prompt the FRG to engage with the idea and reality of diversity. Yet such activists, as with the cultural elites of Chin's work, represented a minority within West Germany's immigrant population. In addition, the large immigrant communities formed as a result of the guest worker program arguably forced the West German state to deal with issues of diversity, and the long-term implications of that diversity for German identity and society, to a greater and more lasting extent. See Alexander Clarkson, *Fragmented Fatherland: Immigration and Cold War Conflict in the Federal Republic of Germany, 1945–1980* (New York: Berghahn Books, 2015).

children – shaped understandings of belonging in their own spheres of influence. In this sense, what I am doing here is shifting the focus from broader level debates about belonging to the more mundane efforts to construct it, and thereby demonstrating the agency of "ordinary" individuals in and the importance of everyday life to that process.

The debates surrounding German identity and the meaning of integration have taken on a particularly sharp tone in regard to perceived cultural differences stemming from the fact that the majority of people of Turkish background in Germany identify as Muslim. In retrospect, it is somewhat surprising to us now that both the West German and Turkish governments gave the religious lives of Turkish guest workers so little thought. Partly as a consequence of this oversight, practicing Muslims initially observed their religious duties relatively informally and largely outside the attention of the broader West German public. Then, in the 1970s, two developments dramatically influenced the character and perception of the Turkish immigrant community and, in particular, its Muslim members: the *Anwerbestopp* (recruitment halt) and the Iranian Revolution. The halt of the guest worker program in 1973 and the regulations on foreign residency that followed had the unintended consequence of speeding up the rate of family reunification among guest workers who decided to stay in West Germany. Now a growing multi-generational community with more diverse social, cultural, and religious needs, Turkish immigrants, including observant Muslims, became a more visible presence in local neighborhoods and schools.

The Iranian Revolution and the founding of the Islamic Republic were international events with distinct domestic ramifications in the Federal Republic. What began as a series of protests against the rule of Mohammad Reza Shah Pahlavi in the fall of 1977 grew into a full-scale revolution that ended in his ouster in January 1979. Although the participants in the revolution had come from diverse religious and political backgrounds, the new government that assumed control instituted a theocratic state that strictly regulated all areas of life based on its fundamentalist interpretation of Islamic law. News coverage of these events shocked the Western world and gave Islam a revolutionary political character that caused great unease. West German politicians and media, and by extension the West German public, started to look at their local Muslim communities with new and increasingly suspicious eyes, imagining the radicalism they witnessed in Iran flourishing in Turkish immigrant mosques.[14]

---

[14] I will address the role of the West German media in the construction of Muslim identities in Chapter 5.

In this environment, family reunification and the seeming hostility of West Germans toward Turkish immigrants contributed to an increasing importance of Islam among elements of the immigrant community[15], and feelings of insecurity prompted some parents to emphasize more conservative religious and cultural values that reinforced a patriarchal family structure.[16] Yet, just as the presence of ethnic minority communities have prompted Germans to reconsider their national and cultural identity, so, too, has immigration to and settlement in West Germany led Turkish and Turkish-German Muslims to reexamine what it means to be Muslim, particularly in the European context.[17]

Critical to these identity-based debates is the issue of gender.[18] From the inception of the guest worker program, gender played an important role both in the motivation for employing foreign laborers and the types of work given to male and female *Gastarbeiter*.[19] Earlier scholarly attention to first-generation working migrant women found that their participation

---

[15] See Andreas Goldberg, "Islam in Germany," in Shireen T. Hunter, ed., *Islam, Europe's Second Religion: The New Social, Cultural and Political Landscape* (Westport: Praeger Publishers, 2002), 30–47; Yasemin Karakaşoğlu, "Turkish Cultural Orientations in Germany and the Role of Islam," in David Horrocks and Eva Kolinsky, eds., *Turkish Culture in German Society Today* (Providence: Berghahn Books, 1996), 157–179.

[16] See Shireen Hunter, ed., *Islam, Europe's Second Religion: The New Social, Cultural and Political Landscape* (Westport: Praeger Publishers, 2002); Barbara Freyer Stowasser, "The Turks in Germany: From Sojourners to Citizens," in Yvonne Yazbeck Haddad, ed., *Muslims in the West: From Sojourners to Citizens* (Oxford, UK: Oxford University Press, 2002); Dursun Tan and Hans-Peter Waldhoff, "Turkish Everyday Culture in Germany and Its Prospects," in *Turkish Culture in German Society Today*, eds. David Horrocks and Eva Kolinsky (Providence: Berghahn Books, 1996).

[17] Peter P. Mandaville, "Muslim Youth in Europe," in Shireen Hunter, ed., *Islam, Europe's Second Religion: The New Social, Cultural, and Political Landscape* (Westport: Praeger Publishers, 2002), 219–229; Ruth Mandel, *Cosmopolitan Anxieties: Turkish Challenges to Citizenship and Belonging in Germany* (Durham: Duke University Press, 2008).

[18] Scholars such as Helma Lutz and Nira Yuval-Davis have stressed the importance of gender as a category of analysis in migration and ethnic studies, showing it to be a constitutive element of both the self and subjected identities of ethnic minorities and a central factor of how immigrants experience migration and settlement. See Mirjana Morokvasic, "Birds of Passage Are also Women..." *International Migration Review* 18, no. 4, Special Issues: Women in Migration (Winter, 1984): 886–907; Caroline B. Brettell and Patricia A. de Berjeois, "Anthropology and the Study of Immigrant Women," in Donna Gabaccia, ed., *Seeking Common Ground: Multidisciplinary Studies of Immigrant Women in the United States* (Westport: Greenwood Press, 1992), 41–64; Helma Lutz, Ann Phoenix, and Nira Yuval-Davis, eds., *Crossfires: Nationalism, Racism and Gender in Europe* (London: Pluto Press, 1995); Annie Phizacklea, "Gendered Actors in Migration," in Jacqueline Andall, ed., *Gender and Ethnicity in Contemporary Europe* (Oxford: Berg, 2003), 23–37.

[19] Monika Mattes, *"Gastarbeiterinnen" in der Bundesrepublik: Anwerbepolitik, Migration, und Geschlecht in den 50er bis 70er Jahren* (Frankfurt am Main: Campus Verlag, 2005).

in the workplace and economic contribution to their families had an emancipatory effect.[20] Yet, as the second-generation Turkish Germans began coming of age in the later 1970s and the 1980s, researchers argued that conflicting expectations from both immigrant communities and West German society hampered their integration.[21] Women, and especially women's bodies, have been a measuring stick against which German politicians, the public, and researchers have evaluated the success of integration, but the focus shifted in the 1970s and 1980s from socioeconomic issues to concerns about perceived religious or cultural differences in the 1990s and 2000s. During these decades, public attention in Western Europe grew increasingly focused on Muslim women's head coverings (known in Germany as the *Kopftuch*, or headscarf) as a symbol of Islam's incompatibility with modern Western, democratic values. Historian Joan Scott argues convincingly that, in France's case, this idea of incompatible cultures was not the cause of "differences between France and its Muslims" but rather "the *effect* of a very particular, historically specific political discourse."[22]

While France's headscarf debate began in 1989 with the rights of schoolchildren, Joyce Mushaben locates the origins of its German version in 1997 Baden-Württemberg when Fereshta Ludin, the daughter of an Afghani diplomat, found herself barred from completing her teaching degree and obtaining a position due to her wearing a headscarf. A series of legal actions and political debates ensued about whether civil servants, as employees and representatives of the state, were or should be allowed to wear a headscarf, which opponents argued constituted a form of proselytizing.[23] Both Scott and Mushaben argue that the headscarf debates create false dichotomies that proscribe the belonging of Muslims in European society and obscure the deeper political and socioeconomic

---

[20] Nermin Abadan-Unat, "Implications of Migration on Emancipation and Pseudo-Emancipation of Turkish Women," *International Migration Review* 11, no. 1 (Spring 1977): 31–57; Ayse Kudat, "Personal, Familial, and Societal Impacts of Turkish Women's Migration to Europe," in UNESCO, ed., *Living in Two Cultures: The Socio-Cultural Situation of Migrant Workers and Their Families* (Paris: UNESCO Press, 1982), 291–305.

[21] Umut Erel, "Gendered and Racialized Experiences of Citizenship in the Life Stories of Women of Turkish Background in Germany," in Jacqueline Andall , ed., *Gender and Ethnicity in Contemporary Europe* (Oxford: Berg, 2003), 155–176.

[22] Joan Wallach Scott, *The Politics of the Veil* (Princeton: Princeton University Press, 2007), 7.

[23] Joyce Marie Mushaben, *The Changing Faces of Citizenship: Integration and Mobilization Among Ethnic Minorities in Germany* (New York: Berghahn Books, 2008), 294. The Berlin Assembly's response to the headscarf debate in connection with the civil service was the 2005 Neutrality Law, which banned the head covering for officials serving in schools, legal professions, and law enforcement. See Mushaben, 303.

challenges that hinder immigrants and their children from becoming full members of the receiving society. It has been easier, in other words, to point to the headscarf and claim it as evidence of essential and incompatible cultural difference than to address basic assumptions of political membership and national belonging. Interestingly, debate about the headscarf was scarce in West Germany before reunification. Instead, focusing on the local level prior to reunification reveals how behaviors and expectations served as the primary markers of perceived cultural differences.

The rising discourse of cultural difference was not limited in focus to Muslim women who both began and continued to wear a headscarf, however. Public debate and political attention expanded to include growing concern about the assimilability of Turkish and Muslim men (those two identities often being conflated). The headscarf as a symbol reflected equally on Muslim women and men. Anthropologist Katherine Pratt Ewing explores how German society has used specific definitions of Turkish and Muslim masculinity as a tool of publicly accepted xenophobia, a way to exclude and justify the exclusion of certain identities from being "German."[24] Ewing's approach to the post-reunification period is especially effective in illuminating the "new racism" focused on cultural difference, but it is also critical to consider the impact of the Iranian Revolution and the formation of the Islamic Republic as well. As noted earlier, in the period between the beginning of postwar Turkish immigration and German reunification, the FRG's perception of these developments significantly influenced the conflation of Turkish and Muslim identities and the characterization of Islam as an internal threat.[25]

Related to the reexamination of "German" and "Muslim" identities is the second challenge to the Federal Republic that emerged from the guest worker program: the place of immigrants and their children in relation to German society. This second challenge clearly interweaves with the first, as identity constitutes the critical determinant of belonging, yet it also contains a spatial element. Where and how have immigrants fit? Spatial belonging – fitting in – has both abstract and practical implications. In regard to public discourse, use of the word and image of a

---

[24] Katherine Pratt Ewing, *Stolen Honor: Stigmatizing Muslim Men in Berlin* (Stanford: Stanford University Press, 2008), 2–17.
[25] Ibid., 27–55. Ewing thoughtfully mines "the genealogies of contemporary representations of Turkish and Muslim manhood" (27) from nineteenth-century European travelers to the Ottoman Empire to twenty-first-century Turkish feminists and scholars, and produces an insightful analysis for how those representations converged, but that representation needs to be expanded to account for the impact of the Islamic Revolution. See Chapter 5.

"ghetto" to describe particular locations associated with immigrants has reduced Turkish-German places of belonging to specific urban sites, thereby emphasizing difference and foreignness and ignoring the transnational spaces of Turkish Germans that make them a part of Berlin beyond their ethnic or religious ties.[26] Such urban sites have often been viewed as part of a *Parallelgesellschaft* (parallel society), a separate space hindering the integration of Turkish immigrants and their children into larger German society. This perspective often conceives of integration as a linear journey with an endpoint where one essential identity (Turkish) converts to another (German). In the context of daily life, however, the Turkish-German community has often utilized those physical spaces to localize their identity and enable themselves to engage with the host society on their own terms in ways that have challenged commonly held understandings of "integration."[27] Connected to this, examination of how members of the Turkish-German community shaped and understood "home" more abstractly gives insight into the impact of gender and generation on immigrants' sense of belonging.[28]

By bridging these three themes resulting from the *Gastarbeiter* program – the impact on postwar German history, the implications of a growing Muslim population, and the place of immigrants in a host society – this book examines the history of Turkish immigrants and their children from the beginning of Turkey's participation in the guest worker program to German reunification in a way that recognizes their integration as a process that is historical, reciprocal, and spatial in nature. The Turkish-German community actively made a place for themselves within, and at times alongside, West German society by constructing spaces of belonging within the context of their daily lives. A number of factors influenced that process, from individual agency and community dynamics to larger institutional factors such as educational policy and city renovation projects, but it was profoundly linked to local-level daily life and experiences.

"Integration" is a word assigned many meanings, some at odds with each other, that seek to describe the relationship between immigrants and host societies. Earlier, both policy makers and scholars used "integration," or its antecedent "assimilation," to describe the endpoint of

---

[26] Ayşe S. Çağlar, "Constraining Metaphors and the Transnationalisation of Spaces in Berlin," *Journal of Ethnic and Migration Studies* 27, no. 4 (October 2001): 601–613.

[27] Patricia Ehrkamp, "Placing Identities: Transnational Practices and Local Attachments of Turkish Immigrants in Germany," *Journal of Ethnic and Migration Studies* 31, no. 5 (March 2005): 345–364.

[28] Esin Bozkurt, *Conceptualising "Home": The Question of Belonging Among Turkish Families in Germany* (Frankfurt: Campus Verlag, 2009).

a process through which an immigrant shed those attributes that distinguished him or her significantly from the host society and became identified with it. That linear conception of migration, settlement, and assimilation no longer fits (if it ever truly did) in an era of increasing ease of travel of people, ideas, and goods, and with the proliferation of transnational spaces. Being integrated has meant being a full member of society, and that is determined by a set of diverse but interrelated elements inherent in a particular historical context. Given these changing contexts and its consequential nature as a moving target, the meaning of integration shifts, making it a process without an ultimate endpoint.

Understanding integration as a spatial process allows us to investigate it as the interaction between people, ideas, and environment over time. This approach takes into account not only what integration meant to the host society but also to the immigrants – those of whom it was being asked. By exploring integration spatially, we can chart how immigrants and their children took an active role in making space for themselves in their "new" home (which, in some cases, had been home for decades), how those spaces exerted their influence within and beyond the immigrant communities, and the impact of spaces and space-making on identity formation. Integration is a process directly linked to identity and to how a given identity allows (or precludes) belonging to a society or a nation. Just as the spaces that immigrants create and inhabit can and do have conflicting influences on their relation to the broader society, so, too, are place-based identities subject to the constant flux of both internal dynamics and connections to external networks. And so, for this book, integration is understood and deployed as a space-making process that reflects the relationships within immigrant communities and between those communities and the broader host society within given historical contexts. Although the primary focus of the study is between the beginning of Turkey's participation in the guest worker program and German reunification, given this conceptualization of integration I will also examine briefly how the spaces that developed during that period extended into the 1990s and early 2000s.

The nature of this type of investigation requires a marriage of sorts between the disciplinary approaches of history and geography, in particular social and cultural geography. The geography side brings to the union a key theoretical understanding of space-making and the methods required to read those spaces. As defined by philosopher and sociologist Henri Lefebvre, a space represents a place of convergence of meaning, routines, geography, and built environment. It is produced through the interaction among three processes over time: (1) representations of space, (2) the ideals or imaginations contained within, and (3) daily practice.[29] Geographers employ this framework to explore how societies use and are influenced by spaces, in addition to focusing on how groups form an "everyday landscape" of meaning through material objects.[30] Yet the connection between space, social relations, and meaning "inherently implies the existence in the lived world of a simultaneous multiplicity of spaces: cross-cutting, intersecting, aligning with one another, or existing in the relations of paradox or antagonism."[31] While Doreen Massey was primarily interested in space in terms of class and gender relations, her conception of space, particularly its role in "the production of the social," is highly relevant to the study of immigrant communities.[32] It allows us to investigate both how the diversity of spaces that immigrants and their children encountered, created, and inhabited shaped their own self-understanding, or identity, as well as how these spaces can have conflicting effects. Further, by understanding how place-based identities – which are formed through spatial interactions – are impacted by internal dynamics and connections with external networks, the dependency of these geographical functions of integration on historical context comes to the fore.

The history half of the study makes its own important contributions, namely in terms of time frame and scale. Turkish *Gastarbeiter* began arriving in West Germany in the early 1960s, and certainly the community has undergone significant changes in the intervening half century. Understanding those developments requires a long view that takes into account how their experiences – and the process of integration – have been shaped by the historical contexts in which they lived and operated. In addition, to learn how members of this relatively marginalized community created space for themselves, one needs to look at the level where they could and did exert the most influence: at the local level in the course of their everyday lives.[33] A local-level perspective allows us to see

---

[29] Henri Lefebvre, *The Production of Space*. Translated by Donald Nicholson-Smith (Oxford: Blackwell, 1991).

[30] For a historiography of cultural geography's use of place in migration studies, see Rachel Silvey and Victoria Lawson, "Placing the Migrant," *Annals of the Association of American Geographers* 89, no. 1 (March 1999): 121–132.

[31] Doreen Massey, *Space, Place, and Gender* (Minneapolis: University of Minnesota Press, 1994), 3.

[32] Ibid., 4.

[33] As a historian studying marginalized communities, I use space as a way to examine how certain groups circumvented their political or social disadvantage through activity in various physical and social spaces. In doing so, I draw on the examples set by historians of minority and/or marginalized communities: Donna Gabaccia, *From the Other Side: Women, Gender, and Immigrant Life in the U.S., 1820–1990* (Bloomington: Indiana University Press, 1995); George Chauncey, *Gay New York: Gender, Urban Culture, and the Making of the Gay Male World, 1890–1940* (New York: Basic Books, 1994);

immigrants' participation in the host society as a series of nuanced and active negotiations that challenge authority even as they operate within it.[34] As Joyce Mushaben has argued, the connection between integration and national identification is considerably weaker than it is between people's everyday experiences in their local contexts.[35]

A concentration on daily life, or *Alltagsgeschichte* (everyday history), necessitates a sharp focus to uncover and understand the historical significance of seemingly mundane and ordinary actions. As such, this book primarily examines the history of one Turkish-German community in the Berlin-Wedding neighborhood of Sprengelkiez in order to take an in-depth look at how its residents created spaces of belonging for themselves in places they lived and operated on a daily basis. Although this study cannot be taken as representative of all Turkish Germans in the Federal Republic (nor is it intended to be), it is important to remember that these smaller building blocks construct the larger pictures that come to form our understandings of those broader developments and narratives.[36] In addition, as Massey has argued, places are sites of "intersecting social relations," some of which are contained within a given place, but others of which "stretch beyond it, tying any particular locality into wider relations and processes in which other places are implicated too."[37] In stretching beyond its own porous borders, the local both reflects and impacts developments at different levels of society.

For immigrants, part of the process of integration is the construction of a sense of belonging in one's everyday life. Belonging, here, is related to the process of integration, but not synonymous with it.[38] Rather, it

---

Sarah Deutsch, *Women and the City: Gender, Space, and Power in Boston, 1870–1940* (Oxford: Oxford University Press, 2000); Bronwen Walter, *Outsiders Inside: Whiteness, Place and Irish Women* (London: Routledge, 2001).

[34] Michel de Certeau, *The Practice of Everyday Life* (Berkeley: University of California Press, 1984).

[35] Mushaben, *Changing Faces of Citizenship*, 54. Mushaben argues that a city-level analysis is necessary to understand the dynamics of integration, but I contend here that an even tighter focus – that of the district and neighborhood level – is necessary in order to analyze the agency of first-generation Turkish immigrants and their children as well as to chart how integration as a reciprocal process occurred on a more subtle but fundamental level.

[36] For an excellent explanation and defense of *Alltagsgeschichte*, see Andrew Stuart Bergerson, Paul Steege, Maureen Healy, and Pamela Swett, "The History of Everyday Life: A Second Chapter," *The Journal of Modern History* 80, no. 2 (June 2008): 358–378.

[37] Massey, *Space, Place, and Gender*, 120.

[38] "Belonging," here, is connected to the concept of home, which Esin Bozkurt reminds us "is a multi-dimensional and dynamic concept that refers to emotional, spiritual, social, cultural, territorial and political self-location over time and space." See Esin Bozkurt, *Conceptualising "Home": The Question of Belonging Among Turkish Families in Germany* (Frankfurt: Campus Verlag, 2009), 25.

encompasses both the feeling of "fitting in" to one's surroundings and of having a degree of authority or legitimacy within them, by creating spaces of belonging or "a sense of place, a structure of feeling that is local in its materialization, while its symbolic reach is multilocal."[39] In this sense, immigrants created a home for themselves, "a place not only where they belonged but which belonged to them, and where they could afford to locate their identities."[40] The integration of Turkish immigrants and their children needs to be understood through their efforts to create belonging within their everyday landscapes and social spaces embedded therein. In this case, spaces of belonging are ones that the Turkish-German community constructed, came into contact with, operated within, shaped, and were shaped by on a daily basis. These spaces were affected by the composition, motivations, and activities of their participants; the physical sites in which they were located; and the reactions of those "outside" the spaces. Whether they helped connect immigrants to the broader host society, estranged them from it, or a complex combination of the two, the spaces were embedded in and drew legitimacy from the local environment.

In order to chart the complex dynamics of these spaces of belonging, this book pulls from materials produced across the various levels of society, from the individual to the institutional. To include the voices and experiences of the people most directly involved in the daily lives of Turkish immigrants and their children, I conducted a series of oral history interviews with former *Gastarbeiter*, second-generation Turkish Germans, German residents of Sprengelkiez, teachers and administrators, representatives of local religious institutions, and neighborhood activists.[41] I also utilized a collection of interviews of Sprengelkiez residents

---

[39] Anne-Marie Fortier, *Migrant Belongings: Memory, Space, Identity* (Oxford: Berg, 2000), 163.

[40] Massey, *Space, Place, and Gender*, 166. Here, Massey writes about the different meanings of "home" for the colonizers and the colonized. The colonized, she points out, do not have the same nostalgic relationship with the concept of home. Her clarification of home in this context, however, resonates with my efforts here to break down the multifaceted concept of integration.

[41] I met my interview partners through a variety of means. Some I contacted directly based on their official role in the district, such as school principals, religious leaders, and government officials. Others I met through referrals from mutual acquaintances and other interview partners. All interviews were conducted primarily in German at a place of the interview partner's choosing, most often in their home, workplace, or a neighborhood site. In one case, the adult child of one of my interview partners joined us, and occasionally assisted in translating a phrase or idea for her mother and me.

The "recovering" of experience is problematic, as people, whether wittingly or unwittingly, craft the way they remember and relate their experiences. Interview subjects, especially those given the open space of an oral history, often present their lives as a cohesive story, fitting their experiences into an overarching narrative. To interrogate the

by historian Ursula Trüper, whose work on a 1995 exhibit at the Mitte Museum first introduced me to the rich history of one neighborhood in that quarter.[42] Trüper's interviews, conducted in the early 1990s, are a fascinating resource through which to investigate the perspectives of local residents, and her interviews with children and youth, in particular, provide a rare opportunity to hear voices not often present in historical research. Finally, I draw on unpublished and published interviews as well as memoirs of individuals from other cities to use as points of comparison and evidence of the broad spectrum of experiences in the Turkish-German community silent within the borders of Sprengelkiez.[43] Hackett similarly focuses migrants' integration in the context of their daily life experiences with work, housing, and education, and reveals the approaches German officials in Bremen took to help their foreign residents more effectively integrate into local life. Yet her source base includes little generated from Bremen's Turkish Muslim community,

---

narrative as well as its constitutive parts, I draw on the work of Joan Scott, Helga Lutz, and others, who address the challenges and opportunities of deconstructing experience and of examining migrants' own "biographical work." See Joan W. Scott, "Experiences," in Judith Butler and Joan W. Scott , eds., *Feminists Theorize the Political* (London: Routledge, 1992), 22–40; Helma Lutz, "Hard Labour: The 'Biographical Work' of a Turkish Migrant Woman in Germany," *The European Journal of Women's Studies* 7 (2000): 301–319; Umut Erel, "Gendered and Racialized Experiences of Citizenship in the Life Stories of Women of Turkish Background in Germany," in Jacqueline Andall, ed., *Gender and Ethnicity in Contemporary Europe* (Oxford: Berg, 2003): 155–176.

[42] Trüper, a Berlin-based historian and author, worked at the community center Sparrladen in the early 1990s, and met her interview partners through the connections she made while there. The backgrounds of her interview partners represented the diversity of the neighborhood, and included long-term native German residents, neighborhood activists, local government officials, first-generation immigrants, businesses owners, blue-collar workers, and second-generation youth. She conducted her interviews in a variety of sites around the neighborhood: the Sparrladen, schools, a local business, and her partners' homes. Her interviews with second-generation youth were conducted in German, and interviews with first-generation immigrants took place in both German and Turkish, the latter with the assistance of one of two translators, Hatıce Renç and author Kemal Kurt.

[43] Published biographies and memoirs are often not considered representative of the "normal" experience, as they are written by people whose lives are extraordinary enough to garner widespread interest and consumption. In addition, the author often has a specific purpose in writing the book, a particular agenda that shapes their narrative. In my use of memoir literature, I take into account the motivations of the author, while at the same time taking seriously the events and situations they feel shaped their lives. I also bear in mind that the experiences of the authors or subjects were embedded in their own particular everyday landscapes, not in the same places as Trüper's and my interview subjects. While these particular features of published memoirs and interviews understandably cause one to be mindful in their use, they still represent a valuable, though not central, source.

and therefore restricts her from making an equally compelling assessment of the immigrants' perspectives.[44]

This book also makes use of German- and Turkish-language print media, from local- and city-level newspapers such as *Vis-á-Vis* and the *Berliner Morgenpost* to nationally circulated periodicals, including *Die Zeit* and the European edition of *Hürriyet*. These sources help trace the development of the Turkish-German community at the local, state, and federal levels. At the same time, analysis of both German- and Turkish-print media demonstrates their active role in shaping public versions of the Turkish experience abroad and reveals how the media itself helped form these spaces of belonging. Institutional-level sources include documents from German businesses that employed *Gastarbeiter*, archival materials from local schools, and employment and demographic reports from governmental organizations at all levels. This broad and diverse source base gives critical insight into the dynamics of Turkish immigration, settlement, and integration at the local level in Sprengelkiez. But why is Sprengelkiez itself particularly useful in understanding those dynamics?

Sprengelkiez, the focal point of this study and the neighborhood Eren Keskin called home, is situated in the formerly West Berlin district of Wedding. Although a relative latecomer to the *Gastarbeiter* program, West Berlin quickly attracted large numbers of guest workers, and by 1968 its Turkish population exceeded the other guest worker groups in that city.[45] Most of the city's *Gastarbeiter* moved into apartments in the districts of Tiergarten, Kreuzberg, and Wedding, whose locations bordering East Berlin made their real estate unappealing to West Berliners who could afford to live elsewhere in the city. Although boisterous and dynamic Kreuzberg has received more scholarly attention, the seemingly more mundane Wedding also attracted large numbers of guest workers from early on, experiencing similar challenges. As a result, the district today is home to a well-established and ethnically diverse community.

Located at the southern edge of Wedding and bordered on one side by the north bank of the Spandauer Canal is the neighborhood of Sprengelkiez. As with its parent district, the good transportation connections and relatively accessible housing attracted foreign workers and their families, particularly Turks, to the neighborhood beginning in the 1970s. Although its immigrant population grew gradually, by the 1980s

---

[44] Hackett, *Foreigners, Minorities and Integration*, 12–14. In addition, Hackett does not describe her own definition of "integration," nor is she explicit as to what it meant to officials and immigrants in Bremen and Newcastle at different points in time.

[45] Statistisches Bundesamt, Germany (West), *Statistisches Jahrbuch für die Bundesrepublik Deutschland* (Stuttgart: W. Kohlhammer, 1968), 151.

their numbers reached a point at which some of the native German residents felt their neighborhood had "suddenly" become Turkish. The longevity of its Turkish community enables us to see how the first and second generations interacted with and influenced the local environment, and its size provides internal diversity and a broad spectrum of experiences. Longtime German- and Turkish-background residents of Sprengelkiez contribute their personal accounts and perspectives of daily life there over the past decades, while local organizations – schools, community centers, places of worship – provide institutional history and memory of neighborhood life. Finally, in addition to these critical perspectives on the everyday, Sprengelkiez's history contains events around which local memory coalesces that provide an enlightening glimpse into its past.

Within the settings of Sprengelkiez and broader West Berlin, this book explores the connections between daily life, the construction of belonging, and space in five sites within the everyday landscape of Turkish immigrants and their children: (1) workplaces, (2) homes, (3) the neighborhood, (4) schools, and (5) places of worship. These sites represent both exterior spaces produced by and shared with Germans (workplaces and schools) as well as interior ones created by the Turkish-German community to address their own needs (homes and places of worship). The neighborhood as a built environment was originally constructed and inhabited by Germans, but as more Turkish immigrants moved in, their influence created a hybrid space that blurred the line between exterior and interior. Taken together, these sites were settings in which members of the Turkish-German community interacted both with each other and with native Germans and German institutions on a regular basis.

Each chapter follows the unfolding map of the physical sites that Turkish immigrants, and then their children, inhabited as they moved to West Germany for work, brought their families to live with them, and settled into communities. Within each chapter, I trace how particular spaces developed over time, often starting with the influences and activities of the first generation, and then exploring how those sites changed in response to the increasing participation of the second generation. As Turkish immigrants were originally brought to the Federal Republic as part of the *Gastarbeiter* program, I begin in Chapter 1 with the workplace, and examine how Turkish guest workers used the site to further their own needs or agendas, what connections and relationships were forged that tied them to their new environment, and how their experiences in that site shaped their perception of their place in broader German society.[46]

[46] See Appendix for a map of Berlin with the referenced workplaces.

Chapter 2, which focuses on the home, looks at the transition from single-sex company-dormitory living to the family-centered households of Turkish guest workers and their children. Here, I examine the practical challenges to setting up and running a household in a new environment as well as the changing and conflicting meanings of home in the first and second generations. Directly connected to the construction of belonging in the home are the experiences of the Turkish-German community in the neighborhoods where they lived. In Chapter 3, Wedding, and especially Sprengelkiez, come to the fore both as a setting and as a character in the broader story of Turkish integration as I investigate the ways generational conflict, gender expectations, and inter-neighborhood dynamics shaped belonging on a local, daily level.[47]

As Turkish immigrants moved into German neighborhoods and established families, their children joined other local youth at school. Chapter 4 explores the reciprocal influences between Turkish-German children and the German schools they attended, from the primary and secondary schools up through the local *Volkshochschule*.[48] School brought the second generation into direct contact not only with other school-aged Turkish and German children but also with German authority figures and institutions, playing a critical role in the formation of belonging. Chapter 5 focuses on places of worship – prayer rooms and mosques – and the ways in which they have served as religious, social, and cultural spaces for Muslims in the Turkish-German community. It also gives context to Sprengelkiez residents' experiences by including the debates in local and national media regarding the growing Muslim population and how these shaped Turkish-German belonging.

Although this book is primarily a study of Turkish-German belonging in West Germany, the spaces that the first and second generation created and inhabited continued to grow and change past the historical marker of German reunification. So, in Chapter 6, I consider the fall of the Berlin Wall and reunification, briefly examining their influence through the 1990s and early 2000s on the people, developments, and trends that formed the basis for this book. In addition to tracing postreunification developments in Sprengelkiez, I broaden the focus to the city of Berlin, where the repercussions of reunification – both in regard to the political

---

[47] See Appendix for maps of Sprengelkiez and important local sites in and around the neighborhood.
[48] A *Volkshochschule* is similar to the U.S. community college. It is an educational institution that offers a wide range of courses to members of the community. The *Volkshochschule* of Berlin-Wedding played an important role as a cultural educator and mediator, and will be discussed more fully in Chapter 4.

and economic climate as well as debates about the nature of German identity – became especially sharp.

When *Kneipe* owner Eren Keskin described his rootedness in his local community in one sentence and retorted that his "black head" separated him from native Germans in the next, he captured the complex and fluid nature of Turkish integration in the Federal Republic. In the pages that follow, this book investigates how Keskin and others, through their daily experiences, came to feel they belonged in Germany, if not always in German society.

1   Settling In at Work

Sevim Özel was just seventeen years old when she left her home in a village in Turkey to work at a Siemens factory in West Germany. According to the contract's stipulations, she was supposed to be at least eighteen to take part in the labor program that took her so far from home. Her father, though, felt it was an opportunity not to be missed, so they lied to the official at the recruitment center about her age. After an eight-month wait, an invasive medical screening, and a taxing three-day train trip, Özel arrived in West Berlin on a rainy October day and started her new job with Siemens. But what began as a temporary measure to make some good money and return home gradually turned into permanent change. Özel settled into her new life in Berlin, met and married her husband, raised her children, and eventually retired. Nowadays she vacations in Turkey, but she lives in a second-floor apartment in Berlin with her husband and youngest daughter.[1]

Sevim Özel is one among hundreds of thousands of Turkish workers who came to West Germany in the 1960s and 1970s as part of a guest worker, or *Gastarbeiter*, program instituted by the Federal Republic to continue fueling its miraculous postwar recovery. In the early 1950s, the newly formed Federal Republic of Germany faced acute labor shortages in industry, agriculture, and mining. Not only was the often dirty, dangerous, and physically taxing nature of these positions unattractive to unemployed German workers, companies also had difficulty convincing them to move to the newly industrialized zones.[2] The temporary, regulated employment of a foreign, mobile workforce seemed the most appealing solution to this labor problem. Similar to the United States' employment of Mexican workers under the Bracero Program (1942–1967), the Federal Republic entered into a series of bilateral labor contracts,

---

[1] Sevim Özel (pseudonym), interview by author, 30 June 2009, transcription by Perrin Saylan, Berlin.

[2] Deniz Göktürk, David Gramling, and Anton Kaes, *Germany in Transit: Nation and Migration, 1955–2005* (Berkeley: University of California Press, 2007), 9.

beginning with Italy in 1955 and extending to Turkey in 1961. Both the sending countries and the FRG intended these guest workers to be temporary cogs in the German economic machine. The migrant laborers, too, considered their work away from home to be a short-term measure. Yet in the years that followed, it slowly became apparent to the government, German society, and the *Gastarbeiter* themselves that this provisional workforce was becoming a permanent population.

Scholars' analysis of the guest worker program historically centered around the motives and mechanizations of the state in regard to internal foreign populations. Sociologists led the first scholarly inquiries with studies about immigration policy and the socioeconomic effects of foreign labor employment, among them Stephen Castles, who analyzed the employment of foreign workers in light of European class structure and the stratification of the working class. The Federal Republic was not alone in its use of temporary foreign workers; many countries in Western Europe sought to address labor shortages and elevate the status of their working-class populations with a disposable, external workforce.[3] Although part of a broader European trend, historian Ulrich Herbert pointed out that the FRG's reasons for and practical use of foreign labor were also reflected in the country's historical experience with foreign workers, from Imperial Germany through the Third Reich.[4] At the same time, the guest worker program was not simply an issue of labor market politics but also of gender politics.[5] Monika Mattes challenged the existing narratives of earlier studies by demonstrating how the German government and businesses recruited *Gastarbeiterinnen* (female guest workers) deliberately and employed them in jobs that would enable German women to maintain or return to their primary social role in the home.[6] Thus, scholarship concerning the postwar employment of guest workers has done much to show the continuities in state treatment of foreign laborers as well as to highlight contemporary political and social attitudes toward gender roles.

As scholars turned their attention to specific national groups of guest workers, their studies both reinforced and complicated these earlier findings. For example, Jennifer Miller has shown how, when the FRG

---

[3] Stephen Castles and Godula Kosack, *Immigrant Workers and Class Structure in Western Europe*, 2nd ed. (Oxford: Oxford University Press, 1985), 2.

[4] Ulrich Herbert, *A History of Foreign Labor in Germany, 1880–1980: Seasonal Workers, Forced Laborers, Guest Workers*. Translated by William Templer (Ann Arbor: University of Michigan Press, 1990), 3–4.

[5] Monika Mattes, *"Gastarbeiterinnen" in der Bundesrepublik: Anwerbepolitik, Migration und Geschlecht in den 50er bis 70er Jahren* (Frankfurt: Campus Verlag, 2005).

[6] Mattes, *"Gastarbeiterinnen" in der Bundesrepublik*, 11.

expanded the guest worker program to include Turkey in 1961, it also extended practices from earlier uses of foreign labor under previous regimes, including both the methods of transporting workers to their new jobs and housing them.[7] But it was also affected by the Turkish state's motives and lack of membership in the European Economic Community (EEC) as well as the attitudes of German society toward Turkish workers and vice versa. Focusing on Turkish guest workers, as historian Karin Hunn has done, also required a focus on Islam, which played an increasing role in German perceptions of Turkish guest workers and their self-identities.[8] More recently, Sarah Hackett has argued that the existing historiography has overemphasized the extent to which discrimination influenced Turkish guest workers' participation in the labor force, contending instead that the desire for economic independence shaped their efforts and experiences.[9] This focus on the broad spectrum of players and perspectives involved in the employment of Turkish workers in West German companies lays a solid foundation for our understanding of what first brought Turkish immigrants to the country and shaped the first generation's early experiences there.

In this chapter, I build on this foundation by examining the experiences of Turkish *Gastarbeiter* in the workplace, the space the Federal Republic had brought them to occupy and where they began to make themselves at home, while taking into account the critical influence of the Cold War both in their recruitment and their employment. The workplace was a space formed and reformed by the daily interactions of the West German state's and companies' intentions, German workers' actions, and Turkish guest workers' interventions. To understand the dynamics of that process, particularly in its early stages, this chapter asks three questions: First, what kind of workplaces were West German companies trying to create? Second, how did Turkish guest workers experience these spaces and begin to use them in ways unintended by their employers? And third, how did the workplace change in response to

---

[7] Jennifer Miller, "On Track for West Germany: Turkish 'Guest-worker' Rail Transportation to West Germany in the Postwar Period," German History 30, no. 4 (December 2012): 528–549.

[8] Karin Hunn, *"Nächstes Jahr kehren wir zurück...": Die Geschichte der türkischen "Gastarbeiter" in der Bundesrepublik* (Göttingen: Wallstein Verlag, 2005), 448–449.

[9] Sarah Hackett, *Foreigners, Minorities and Integration: The Muslim Immigrant Experience in Britain and Germany* (Manchester, UK: Manchester University Press, 2016), 33. Although Hackett frames her comparative work as a study of Muslim immigrants, she points out that, in the case of Bremen, the overwhelming majority of the city's Muslims were from the Turkish immigrant community, Hackett, 34. Hackett's discussion of Turkish Muslim self-employment in Bremen provides an interesting comparison to the Berliner counterparts, but as her sources about Bremen entrepreneurs come from 2001, I address them later in Chapter 6, where I discuss Turkish-owned businesses in reunified Berlin.

the presence and actions of the Turkish employees and, eventually, owners? To answer these questions, I focus primarily on companies and workers in West Berlin but also take into account developments in the national context. I argue that Turkish guest workers, by their presence as well as their active negotiations and circumventions, created spaces within West German businesses that mediated their permanent settlement in a country that officially maintained its nonimmigration identity. In other words, the site that defined Turkish "guest workers" as temporary ended up facilitating their long-term settlement.

Attracting and Preparing Turks for Work in West Germany

The postwar *Gastarbeiter* program was not the first time Germany turned to foreign workers to fill the gaps in its own labor force. From Polish women harvesting sugar beets in eighteenth-century Prussia to the forced and slave labor on German farms, in factories, and in concentration camps in the Third Reich, Germany already had a long history of migrant workers. This latest iteration drew on those past experiences in both its ambitions for a temporary, cheap labor force, and its regulations enforcing those ambitions.

Several factors influenced the Federal Republic's decision to initiate a series of bilateral labor contracts. At the end of the Second World War, growing tensions between the Allies, more particularly between the Soviet Union and its Western Allies, found a physical outlet in the partition of Berlin. The four zones of occupation in the capital city increasingly coalesced into two: the one administered by the United States, Great Britain and France; the other under the authority of the Soviet Union. Likewise, the official split of Germany into West and East in 1949 resulted in a divided Berlin, part of which remained under Western control but was now located deep within East Germany's borders. West Berlin's location made it a key entry point for Germans from the eastern side fleeing to the Federal Republic. The East German government took steps to curtail the embarrassing and damaging emigration, including the closing of the inner German border in 1952 and the institution of a new passport control system at the end of 1957. These actions resulted in further concentration of East Germans through Berlin, and around three million people used the city's unique status and location to leave the German Democratic Republic (GDR) for the political freedoms and career prospects the West offered.[10]

---

[10] Mary Fullbrook, *The Divided Nation: A History of Germany, 1918–1990* (New York: Oxford University Press, 1991), 184.

The fledgling West German state welcomed the influx both because of the migrants' symbolically significant choice and because of the Federal Republic's acute labor shortage. Reconstructing the West German economy in the wake of the Second World War required a vast and diverse labor force, one that could not be fully staffed by that country's population, as much of the manufacturing was highly labor intensive. Although much of the state's labor needs were initially met by the East German émigrés, the labor crunch became even more acute in 1961 when the East German government sought to stop the damage to its economy and political image through construction of the Berlin Wall, effectively halting potential workers from leaving the East.

Yet the loss of labor was not the only influence Cold War relations had on West Germany's decision to institute a guest worker program and to eventually extend it to Turkey. Gender politics also became a significant ideological marker of difference between the two Germanys. With the East promoting the image and reality of the working mother and collectivizing childcare, the Federal Republic reinforced its ideological commitment to traditional gender roles, which emphasized the role of women as wives and mothers, not workers.[11] Employing foreign workers on a temporary basis would allow West Germany to solve its own labor shortcomings without having to compromise its commitment to the male-breadwinner family model. Finally, Turkey's geopolitically strategic position in the Cold War and its membership in the North Atlantic Treaty Organization (NATO) made further connections between the West German state and the Republic of Turkey an advantage from a foreign policy standpoint.[12]

Whatever the West Germans' motivations, their overtures found a ready audience in both the Turkish government and its citizens, and by 1974 Turkish *Gastarbeiter* outnumbered their fellow foreign workers.[13] Whereas earlier scholarship has credited Turkey's slow industrialization and lagging economic development, paired with high population growth, for Turks' willingness to immigrate to West Germany for work, social scientist Ahmet Akgündüz argues instead that the mechanization of

---

[11] Karen Hagemann, "A West-German '*Sonderweg*'? Gender, Work, and the Half-Day-Time Policy of Child Care and Primary Education," in Karen Hagemann, Konrad H. Jarausch, and Cristina Allemann-Ghionda, eds., *Children, Families and States: Time Policies of Child Care, Preschool and Primary Schooling in Europe* (Oxford: Berghahn Books, 2011), 298–300.

[12] For more on the foreign policy aspect of the guest worker program, see Heike Knortz, *Diplomatische Tauschgeschäfte: "Gastarbeiter" in der westdeutschen Diplomatie und Beschäftigungspolitik 1953–1973* (Cologne: Böhlau Verlag, 2008).

[13] Statistisches Bundesamt, Germany (West), *Statistisches Jahrbuch für die Bundesrepublik Deutschland* (Stuttgart: W. Kohlhammer, 1974), 144.

agricultural production resulted in a surplus working population in rural areas and increased pressure on small landowners. "Moreover," Akgündüz writes, "economic development and change and increasing linkages with the West also affected values, cultural perceptions and the taste of consumer goods particularly among youngsters in urban and capitalised areas."[14] As a result, working in Western Europe became an acceptable and even preferred means for many middle- and lower middle-class Turks to solve their own labor problems and achieve their financial and lifestyle goals.

The Turkish government, too, had high hopes for participation in a temporary labor program with the Federal Republic. The short-term absence of rural and unskilled workers would benefit Turkey's economy through the easing of unemployment and the boon of workers' remittances, but the government also reasoned that the returning, newly skilled workforce would accelerate the country's industrialization and modernization processes. At the same time, the political and bureaucratic demands of the *Gastarbeiter* program, such as intergovernmental and interbusiness communication and coordination, along with the experience of Turkish workers in West Germany and other European countries, would "stimulate the idea of integration of the country into the European political and economic community."[15] With these potential benefits in mind, the Turkish government set up the administrative framework, including labor recruitment agencies, for Turkish nationals to work in Western European countries, making the process predictable and affordable for even the poorest of its citizens and setting into motion a large-scale labor migration.

Both the Turkish and West German governments employed recruitment strategies at the federal level, but business leaders mounted their own efforts to win over potential workers not just to West German industry but specifically to Siemens, AEG-Telefunken, and other such leading companies. When these companies began hiring Turkish workers for their factories in West Berlin, they set out to create and propagate an idealized workplace that would be attractive to potential employees. This was particularly important in the period directly following the initiation of the labor contract between the Federal Republic and Turkey, as West German businesses could not yet rely on word of mouth to spur interest. In addition, companies had discovered that West Berlin itself, deep within communist East Germany and often considered a likely

[14] Ahmet Akgündüz, *Labour Migration from Turkey to Western Europe, 1960–1974: A Multidisciplinary Analysis* (Aldershot, UK: Ashgate, 2008), 47.
[15] Ibid., 94.

battleground should the Cold War grow hot, proved a difficult sell to West German workers. Siemens' efforts to recruit foreign workers reflect how West German companies promoted an image of West Berlin directly influenced by the city's Cold War identity as much as the jobs themselves.

One such recruitment brochure, published by Siemens (a global German engineering company) in the mid-1960s and full of glossy pictures of a vibrant West Berlin, describes a stroll down Kurfüstendamm, where "a thousand illuminated advertisements glow," and one could see how so many of their compatriots "have found a well-paying workplace in this capital city of the free Western world." The brochure goes on to list the many opportunities for enjoyment in the city: large department stores, modern squares and transportation, rivers, parks, restaurants, cafés, churches, theater, movies, dance halls, and so on.[16] The twin messages of freedom and prosperity echo throughout the words and images, and the stress on progress, consumption, and leisure emphasized the benefits of life in Cold War West Berlin. The city's unique situation in the Cold War provided the economic conditions for expanding the guest worker program, and it gave companies such as Siemens the West Berlin identity that helped them sell it.

Yet West German companies such as Siemens still needed to convince potential recruits of the attractiveness of the jobs they were seeking to fill. Siemens' recruitment literature from the mid-1960s, therefore, also sought to describe the reader's potential workplace as at once historic, modern, and familiar. With more than forty thousand employees manu-facturing the latest in machinery and home appliances, Siemens was world renowned. Recruitment brochures reassured prospective Turkish employ-ees that the company was familiar to "your countrymen," who "work happily at Siemens and are accommodated in cozy and beautiful rooms." "Some compare us to a large family," the brochure continues, and "we do a lot to lighten the living and working stresses of our foreign co-workers."[17] In the pictures that follow, the recipient of the brochure is treated to images of efficient foreign workers operating large, gleaming machines in spotless factories. Men and women, Germans and *Gastarbeiter*, work

---

[16] "In Berlin bummeln" in "Deutscher Text für Broschüre zum Anwerben von Arbeits-kräften aus Griechenland und der Türkei," p. 2, Rundschreiben zur Beschäftigung von Ausländischen Arbeitnehmern, Sig. 10585–1, Schlüssel 04610585, SCA. Although the document is not dated, the content, language, and placement in the file suggest publica-tion in the mid-1960s.

[17] "Das Haus Siemens" in "Deutscher Text für Broschüre zum Anwerben von Arbeits-kräften aus Griechenland und der Türkei," p. 2, Rundschreiben zur Beschäftigung von Ausländischen Arbeitnehmern, Sig. 10585–1, Schlüssel 04610585, SCA. While the document is not dated, the content, language, and placement in the file suggest publication in the mid-1960s.

together harmoniously, with management and foreign consuls looking on approvingly.[18] The message of the brochure is clear: a job at Siemens means working for an important company, doing interesting work, and enjoying pleasant coworkers –all while earning a "good wage."

The brochure illustrates the idea of a modern, attractive workplace, but the company's internal memoranda reveal the steps Siemens took to control workplace conditions before the guest workers even left their country of origin. Such concerns about control over the workers and workplace environment, and the tactics used to address those concerns, were also common to other West German businesses. In addition to the efforts Siemens made to attempt to ensure that the presence of Turkish guest workers in their factories would be temporary, the company also sought to create a workplace as unencumbered by human frailty and social distraction as possible. To this end, they required extensive medical screenings of all potential foreign employees, both in the country of origin[19] and immediately after their arrival in West Berlin.[20] Determining that young women applicants were not pregnant was both a normal part of the medical screening process and part of Siemens' effort to keep workers from being distracted by caring for family members. In this vein, Siemens initially banned guest workers from bringing any family member with them who was not also employed, and sought to discourage women from getting pregnant in West Germany by stressing the difficulties pregnancy would raise.[21] The workplace was to be an efficient, harmonious space with healthy, productive workers unencumbered by familial distractions. That, at least, was the goal.

Between West German businesses' recruitment efforts, the Turkish government's facilitation, and the growing role of social networks, Turkish guest workers soon became a significant portion of the foreign worker population in the Federal Republic. Between 1960 and 1974, more than one million people migrated from Turkey for work in West Germany.[22] Of those, more than 50 percent emigrated from urban

---

[18] "Έναν περίπατο στήν λεωφόρο Κονρφίρστενταμ του Βερολίνου" in "Deutscher Text für Broschüre zum Anwerben von Arbeitskräften aus Griechenland und der Türkei," p. 2, Rundschreiben zur Beschäftigung von Ausländischen Arbeitnehmern, Sig. 10585–1, Schlüssel 04610585, SCA. The brochure corresponds to the German translations from the document in footnote 16 and is the Greek-language version of a brochure designed for recruitment in Greece and Turkey.

[19] "Beschäftigung von Gastarbeitern: Bisherige Ergebnisse des Arbeitskreises Ausländerfragen im Berliner-Siemens-Bereich," pp. 1 and 4, 2 October 1970, Rundschreiben zur Beschäftigung von Ausländischen Arbeitnehmern, Sig. 10585–1, Schlüssel 04610585, SCA.

[20] Özel interview, 4.   [21] "Beschäftigung von Gastarbeitern," pp. 1 and 4.

[22] Akgündüz, *Labour Migration from Turkey*, 96.

centers.[23] Although Turkish migration to West Berlin was not significant in the first few years of Turkey's participation in the *Gastarbeiter* program, by the end of 1966, Turks made up 27 percent of the 17,817 guest workers in that city. Both those considering the guest worker program and those already in West Germany learned via official recruitment efforts as well as by word of mouth that West Berlin was a place that could satisfy their financial motivations and desire for adventure. Leyla Sezer and her friend traveled to Istanbul to sign up for the guest worker program. When asked by a taxi driver why they would go to West Berlin for work, Sezer, whose husband was already in West Germany, answered, "Because in Berlin there's the Wall, there's a lot of money."[24] While working construction in Düsseldorf, Mehmet Korkmaz met a Turkish engineer who ran a construction firm in West Berlin. The engineer confirmed the rumor that Korkmaz and his friend could earn almost twice their wage in West Berlin, and offered to pay their train fare. "The Germans themselves weren't interested in going to Berlin," Korkmaz recalled, "but for us, it didn't matter. We wanted to make money." Korkmaz and his friend became two of the first fifty Turkish guest workers to officially enter the city.[25]

The number of guest workers in West Berlin, including Turkish workers, grew rapidly in the coming years; by the end of 1974, 49 percent of the 87,593 of its guest workers were from Turkey.[26] The shift to large-scale employment of *Gastarbeiter* in West Berlin occurred at a time when Turks began to increasingly outnumber their fellow guest workers, and this change was reflected in the growing number of Turkish workers in that city. Their jobs brought Turkish workers onto the factory floors of large companies such as Siemens, AEG, and Osram, and into contact with fellow *Gastarbeiter*, German coworkers and supervisors, and with a new, initially bewildering, work environment.

Turkish Workers on the Job

West German companies generally employed *Gastarbeiter* in jobs that were unattractive to German workers, and the experience of Turkish

[23] Ibid., 163.
[24] Leyla Sezer (pseudonym), interview by Hatice Renç and Ursula Trüper, 28 January 1993, translation and transcript by Hatice Renç, "Die Leute vom Sparrplatz" Ausstellung, Mitte Museum Archiv, Berlin, p. 1.
[25] Mehmet Korkmaz (pseudonym), interview by Rita Klages, 25 June 1998, transcript, "Projekt Migrantenbiographien," Heimatmuseum Neukölln, Berlin, p. 6.
[26] Statistisches Landesamt Berlin, *Statistisches Jahrbuch Berlin 1977* (Berlin-Wilmersdorf: Statistisches Landesamt Berlin, 1977), 168.

guest workers reflected this. In the early stages of the *Gastarbeiter* program, foreign labor importation focused on filling mining and manufacturing positions with male guest workers. The mining industry in the
Ruhr region employed large numbers of *Gastarbeiter*, including Turks, to
staff their operations in open-cast and pit-coal mining. These were, in
many ways, the quintessential guest worker jobs: employees worked in
shifts around the clock in high-risk, strenuous, and dirty conditions.
Mining companies began recruiting from Turkey heavily after the guest
worker program extended to that country, and many *Gastarbeiter* saw
mining as a way to get a foot in the door before moving on to better jobs.
While the conditions were difficult, Turkish miners, more than guest
workers in other fields, benefited from continuing education and training
opportunities offered by employers who were interested in producing
and maintaining a qualified workforce.[27]

In addition to working in the coal mines of the Ruhr region, migrant
laborers worked in heavy industry throughout the Federal Republic,
including the manufacture of automobiles. In the BMW factories of
Stuttgart, the Mercedes plants in Regensburg, and the Ford factories in
Cologne, *Gastarbeiter* worked on assembly lines, performing low-skilled
but physically challenging labor in shifts. While the labor-intensive nature
of the work was similar to that in mining, manufacturing companies
generally showed less interest in improving and promoting the skills of
their foreign employees, and relations between the Turkish workforce
and German management were often strained.[28]

West Berlin had its share of heavy industry, including metal production and manufacturing, and also employed large numbers of male guest
workers in light industry and construction.[29] Also in West Berlin, more
so than in the other West German states, women came to constitute a
significant minority of the Turkish *Gastarbeiter* population, making up
well over one-third of all Turkish workers in the city by the early 1970s.
As was the case with their male compatriots, the majority of *Gastarbeiterinnen* were employed in metal production and manufacturing, followed
by consumer goods manufacturing.[30] These jobs in light manufacturing
also entailed assembly line work. Individual guest workers could staff
either a single or various stations in the production process, including the
use of different machines to assist in this work. Women were considered

[27] Hunn, "*Nächstes Jahr kehren wir zurück...*," 218–237.
[28] For a description and analysis of the wildcat strikes at the Ford plant in Cologne, see
Hunn, "*Nächstes Jahr kehren wir zurück...*," 237–260.
[29] Andrea Baumgartner-Karabak and Gisela Landesberger, *Die verkauften Bräute: Türkische
Frauen zwischen Krezberg und Anatolien* (Reinbeck bei Hamburg: Rowohlt, 1983), 82.
[30] Ibid.

desirable workers for light manufacturing positions, which required patience and dexterity, particularly for those involving the assembly of electrical products.

How did Turkish guest workers experience their new workplaces, and how did they begin to use them in ways their employers never intended? For those who came through direct recruitment, the transition into the new job could be a quick and disorienting one. Sevim Özel remembers it being only the second day that she and her new coworkers were in Germany before a translator took them by bus from the company dormitory to the factory. There, they underwent another intensive medical examination and were returned to the dormitory. The next day, the translator picked them up again from the dormitory, this time at five thirty in the morning, to take them to their first day of work.[31] When Siemens hired Azra Demir, she had already been in the country for two months, but the transition to factory work was very difficult. Even though she worked with other Turkish women, she was accustomed to village life, and the atmosphere at the large factory felt strange and overwhelming to her.[32]

Part of the disorienting newness of their workplace stemmed from language barriers. Although many Turkish *Gastarbeiter* worked primarily with other Turkish employees, very often their direct supervisors were Germans, almost none of whom could speak Turkish. In the larger companies, translators were available for assistance with specific situations, but generally not for help with the normal daily routine. Leyla Sezer, who came to West Berlin to work for AEG-Telefunken in the late 1960s, remembers struggling with language barriers, especially in the early days of her employment. She adopted the strategy of just saying "yes" whenever she did not understand what someone asked her. As one can imagine, this strategy led to some awkward situations. During her interview with a German historian, she recounted an incident when her supervisor asked her to leave the machine she was at and work on another. Unsure of what he was saying, Sezer simply replied, "Yes." When he came back to check on her progress later that day, he was surprised to find her still working on the first machine. Later, a German coworker approached her and asked if she would join him for a drink after work. Again, not understanding the question, she answered, "Yes." The next day, the German man confronted her, and angrily asked why

---

[31] Özel interview, 4.
[32] Azra Demir (pseudonym), interview, translation and transcription by Hatice Renç, 9 March 1993, DLSA, MM, 1.

she had not met him the day before. Another coworker, a friend of Sezer's, had to help straighten the matter out.[33]

Turkish guest workers responded to these unfamiliar and overwhelming workplaces in a variety of ways. Many tried to reestablish old social networks as a way to not only cope with their new employment and living situation but also make the most of it. This group used the tools and connections available to them through the workplace and their knowledge of German labor needs and employment practices to bring over adult family members, spouses, and eventually children to live with them in West Berlin. And since company housing allowed little accommodation for families,[34] this reunification inevitably led to Turkish guest workers seeking privately owned apartments and setting up their own households.[35]

While some guest workers sought to reestablish familial connections fractured by migration, others set about building new social networks. Many of the Turkish *Gastarbeiter* were young and unmarried, and instead of delaying marriage until they returned permanently to Turkey, they opted to marry and start families while working in West Germany. Often a family member back in Turkey would arrange their marriage with a suitable partner, but this was not always the case. In some situations, the social networks Turkish guest workers constructed in their workplaces and dormitories served as a critical resource for potential mates. For example, after four years of living and working in West Berlin, Sevim Özel decided that getting married was a good solution to the problem of unwanted attention from Turkish men. Instead of sending word to her parents back in Turkey, in 1969 she turned to a coworker and friend whom she knew had a brother-in-law looking for a wife. The friend introduced the two, and soon after Özel and he married.[36] Özel's marriage illustrates the importance of continuing family relationships, such as between her coworker and brother-in-law, as well as the new networks being formed – both of which were rooted in the workplace.

Özel's marriage also represents one of the many ways in which the composition and meaning of the workplace were shifting from what both

---

[33] Sezer interview, 5.

[34] Marcel Michels, "Ausländische Arbeitnehmer bei Siemens Berlin in den 1960er/70er Jahren" (master's thesis, Ludwig-Maximilian-Universität Munich, 2001), p. 52, SCA.

[35] For a specific example, see Bilge Yılmaz (pseudonym), interview by author, 2 June 2009, transcription by Perrin Saylan, Berlin, Germany. For general discussion of family reunification, see Herbert, *A History of Foreign Labor in Germany*, 217–243.

[36] Özel interview, 7–8.

West German businesses and the state originally intended. The government, in particular, had vested political and economic interests in the temporary nature of the foreign workers' residency and employment. The foreign workers would provide much-needed and inexpensive labor during times of economic growth, paying into a social welfare system that they would not need to use, and then return home if the unemployment rate rose among native Germans. This perception of the guest worker program seemed to be proven true during the 1966–1967 recession when approximately four hundred thousand *Gastarbeiter* left the FRG. In addition, during the 1960s some 30 percent of foreign workers returned to their countries of origin each year, lending credence to the rotation principle and the continued recruitment of *Gastarbeiter*.[37] Yet West German politicians watched the growing numbers of foreign residents who were not a part of the workforce with increasing alarm. In 1961, only 137,200 nonworking foreign residents lived in West Germany, whereas more than half a million were employed. By 1973, the number of unemployed foreign residents in the FRG had grown tenfold.[38] The implications of such statistics were clear: temporary workers were transforming into long-term residents with families, with all the potential consequences that policy makers had hoped to avoid.

The debate about the benefits of employing foreign laborers grew more heated with the 1971 Ordinance on Work Permits, which gave foreigners who had been in the FRG for at least five years the ability to obtain a special work permit independent of the labor market's status. Taking into account that foreign workers from EEC member states were already free of restrictions in obtaining work permits, the new law in effect gave approximately 40 percent of all guest workers a special status that separated their continued stay in the FRG from its economic conditions. By January 1973, Chancellor Willy Brandt was publicly questioning the wisdom of continuing the program, and in July of the same year the government more than tripled the fees for recruiting foreign workers from non-EEC countries.[39] On November 23, 1973, the FRG officially halted the recruitment of those workers, and although the oil embargo was credited by politicians and the media for the *Anwerbestopp* (recruitment halt), as Herbert and Hunn argue, it "had been no more than a supplementary compounding factor" that allowed the government to

---

[37] Ulrich Herbert and Karin Hunn, "Guest Workers and Policy on Guest Workers in the Federal Republic: From the Beginning of Recruitment in 1955 until Its Halt in 1973," in Hanna Schissler, ed., *The Miracle Years: A Cultural History of West Germany, 1949–1968* (Princeton: Princeton University Press, 2001), 207.
[38] Ibid.   [39] Ibid., 208–210.

avoid debates with the labor-exporting countries and "public discussion on the social consequences of the measure."[40]

Yet, what might be good for politics could also be bad for business. Although West German businesses may have acquiesced to the ban in recruiting new guest workers, they were uninterested in letting go of their existing foreign employees. They had not supported proposals in the late 1960s to return to a stricter rotation principle, and, now faced with the prospect of losing their trained foreign workforce, companies actively petitioned to extend their current labor contracts and continued their efforts, which they had begun years before, to educate their "guests" in how to stay and succeed in West Germany.

Preparing Foreigners for Life in West German Society

Although the ban on recruitment initiated a marked shift from the temporary to permanent status of Turkish workers, the transition had been happening gradually over the course of their employment, and West German businesses took an active role in facilitating this development. One way to track this transition is through the in-house newspapers of Siemens and AEG-Telefunken. In 1971, the monthly *AEG-Telefunken Report* began publishing one page with an article translated into the native languages of its guest workers. The purpose of the articles was to educate foreign workers about particular aspects of their rights and duties as employees, safety concerns, company business, and German culture. The earliest articles focus almost exclusively on issues for guest workers as workers. This comes through particularly clearly in the inaugural article, entitled "We, From Our Homeland Germany." It opens by addressing "our esteemed co-worker" and acknowledges that this new workplace can be difficult, particularly as language problems may make one feel isolated "from the community to which one rightfully belongs." This multilingual page promised to keep its foreign coworkers informed of "the most important events in the internal management of the business." And what was the critical issue addressed in this first article? It was a lengthy description of what actions to take and company offices to contact should one fall ill during a vacation from work.[41]

For the rest of 1971 and well into the next year, articles continued to focus mainly on informing foreign employees about the particulars of living and working in Germany as guest workers. These often included

---

[40] Ibid., 201.
[41] "Sizler vatanımızdan Almanya," *AEG-Telefunken Report*, July/August 1971, p. 15, Deutsches Technikmuseum Historisches Archiv (DTHA), Berlin.

topics centered on physical well-being, such as the obligatory nature of health insurance in Germany;[42] the importance of a nutritious diet;[43] identifying public and company warning signs;[44] and automobile safety.[45] Interestingly, only one article throughout the entire run of the multilingual section focused exclusively on German-language acquisition. This article, titled "Guide to Residence Help: Foreign Workers, Learn German!" begins by pointing out, rather unnecessarily, that guest workers' lack of mastery of the German language made contact with their German coworkers and resolution of workplace problems difficult. While "our company" works to ensure that its foreign workers receive translation assistance so as to be aware of their rights, "it will be much better if you understand and speak the same language, the German language." The writer goes on to advise participation in a German-language course or the purchase of "a good grammar manual," and recommends two by name, one for adults and one for children. Although AEG presumably offered its own language courses, the writer does not point the reader in the direction of any specific course.[46] Companies often addressed the problem of language differences by holding their own German-language courses for their foreign employees or by working in tandem with local *Volkshochschule* to develop and offer such courses. In the case of Siemens in West Berlin, the company began collaborating with the *Volkshochschule* in Spandau in the early 1960s to offer weekly, entry-level language classes for Siemens guest workers. These sessions took place at the worksite after hours, were organized into trimesters, and cost three deutsche marks (DMs) for each participant. Those who wanted to pursue higher-level lessons could take such courses free of charge during the workday. Guest workers' limited interest and the lack of well-developed teaching materials and methodologies, however, restricted the success of these measures.[47]

Trade unions also provided language instruction for foreign workers in the Federal Republic. Although not initially supportive of the *Gastarbeiter* program, unions quickly shifted their position in order to influence its implementation. Specifically, unions worked to ensure that migrant

---

[42] "Sizler Almanya'da işçi olarak kanunen bir hastlık sigorta şirketinin azassısınız," *AEG-Telefunken Report*, November 1971, p. 14, DTHA.

[43] "Afiyetler temenni ederiz: Almanya'da yemek söyle yenir," *AEG-Telefunken Report*, January 1972, p. 14, DTHA.

[44] "Isaretler, Levhalar, Renkler," *AEG-Telefunken Report*, April 1972, p. 15, DTHA.

[45] "Her dört Marktan biri vatana: Otomobil sahipleri dikkat!" *AEG-Telefunken Report*, June 1972, p. 14, DTHA.

[46] "Mesken Yardımı kılavuzu: Yabancı işçiler Almanca öğrenin!" *AEG-Telefunken Report*, March 1972, p. 14, DTHA.

[47] Michels, "Ausländische Arbeitnehmer bei Siemens Berlin," 57–58.

laborers received the same pay and protections as their German counter-parts in an effort to make certain that working and social standards did not deteriorate as a result of their employment. Despite these efforts, unions were not particularly successful at involving *Gastarbeiter* in their activities early on because everyone – both trade unionists and the guest workers themselves – considered the situation temporary.[48] In addition, the unions' practice of charging fees, inability to prevent deportation for nonwork related reasons, and restrictions on the ways guest workers could participate made them wary of union involvement.[49] Unions were most successful with *Gastarbeiter* incorporation in places where foreign workers had already joined and facilitated outreach to their compatriots. With *Gastarbeiter* involved, unions began publishing foreign language informational sheets, holding instructional sessions on their goals and activities, and organizing language courses. In 1964, the *Deutscher Gewerk-schaftsbund* (Confederation of German Trade Unions, DGB) sponsored sixty language courses in North Rhine-Westphalia alone. Although the unions tried to foster solidarity between German and foreign workers, they continually had to deal with tensions between the two groups. These tensions were particularly evident after the 1966 and 1973 economic down-turns gave rise to animosity against guest workers, who were depicted as stealing jobs from German workers.[50]

From the late 1960s to the late 1970s, the articles in Siemens' in-house newspaper, the *Siemens Mitteilungen*, illustrate a similar sense of separ-ation between Germans and foreigners by focusing on *Gastarbeiter* as workers and as different from their German counterparts. In early art-icles, this difference is articulated by describing activities among Turkish guest workers. A 1971 article entitled "Foreign Folklore in a Cultural Group at Siemens Berlin" briefly states that, during the previous two years, two new groups were added to Siemens' cultural group (*Kultur-kreis*) in West Berlin: a Yugoslavian folklore club and a Turkish dance and theater troupe. The Turkish group, according to the article, would be hosting a *Heimatabend* for "our Turkish co-workers."[51] Another short article, published two years later, describes an outing for a group of *Gastarbeiter* from a factory in Regensburg. Turks, Yugoslavs, and Tunis-ians enjoyed a day on the Chiemsee in a field trip organized by Siemens

---

[48] Hunn, *"Nächstes Jahr kehren wir zurück..."*, 120–122.
[49] Ray C. Rist, *Guestworkers in Germany: The Prospects for Pluralism* (New York: Praeger Publishers, 1978), 126–129.
[50] Hunn, *"Nächstes Jahr kehren wir zurück..."*, 124–136.
[51] "Ausländische Folklore im Kulturkreis in Siemens Berlin," *Siemens Mitteilungen*, January 1971, p. 18, SCA.

and designed to give these workers the opportunity to get to know their "guest-home from another perspective than the daily working world." The accompanying picture shows a diverse group of men and women, dressed in casual weekend clothes and standing in rows for the photograph.[52] The articles were intended to highlight the leisure activities of Siemens' *Gastarbeiter*, but they also reveal the separateness of the foreign workers from their native German counterparts almost twenty years after the first guest workers came to West Germany and more than ten years after Turks were included in that group.

In December 1973, less than one month after the *Anwerbestopp* officially halted recruitment of workers from non-EEC member states, we see the first article about interaction between German and Turkish coworkers, or rather, one German coworker.[53] The first third of the article, "It's Not Quite Like Home," focuses mainly on two Turkish employees at the home appliance factory in West Berlin. These two men, because of their German-language skills, hold office hours in their factory's *Betriebsbüro* (operation's office), where they are met by their compatriots who seek advice on everything from rental contracts to doctor visits. The article, published in German and Turkish, then shifts its focus to a German superintendent at the plant who took an active interest in helping his Turkish employees get acclimated. Called "Türkenvater" by Turkish journalists, Kurt Emberger realized from the beginning that language and cultural issues would make things more difficult for his Turkish employees. He started a tradition of visiting the dormitories in the evening with a case of beer to get to know his employees better "and make them feel more relaxed."[54] Emberger, the article continues, worked hard to see that Turkish workers had trusted associates on the necessary committees and kept his door open for those who wanted to discuss matters with him personally. The factory also made accommodations for their Turkish guest workers' religious needs, including dietary restrictions and providing a prayer room on the premises. Counseled by company doctors that inadequate nutrition contributed to the poor health of their Turkish *Gastarbeiter*, Siemens also sent out a flyer with Turkish workers' paychecks that encouraged them to join their "fellow countrymen" in the company cafeteria for inexpensive, pork-free meals.[55]

---

[52] "Gastland – einmal anders erlebt," *Siemens Mitteilungen*, October 1973, p. 12, SCA.
[53] "Ganz wie Zuhause ist es nicht," *Siemens Mitteilungen*, December 1973, pp. 5–7, SCA.
[54] Ibid., 6.
[55] "Mittagsessen für türkische Mitarbeiter," Rundschreiben zur Beschäftigung von Ausländischen Arbeitnehmer, Sig. 10585–1, Schlüssel 04610585, SCA.

Despite these efforts, "it took three to four years," Emberger remarks, "for the German workers, including supervisors, to get past their reservations."[56]

Although affirming the success of such measures, the writer of the article comments that "one hears time and again 'At the factory, we feel equal,'" but at government offices and on public transportation Turks still felt as outsiders. Yet he discounts that this is due to discrimination. Instead, the writer argues that these rude interactions are a normal part of daily life that Germans are accustomed to, and that Turks' lack of German language skills lead to many misunderstandings. "One needs to think about both sides," he concludes, and not assume that others see things in the same way we do.[57]

This article demonstrates distinct but interrelated aspects of Siemens' perception of its foreign workers. First, even after more than a decade of their employment, the West German company still viewed its Turkish workers as different and separate from its native German workers. In this case, the writer discusses differences in language, religion, and socio-economic background (there is brief mention that many of the Turkish workers are from rural areas) and concludes an otherwise fairly upbeat piece by mentioning the misunderstandings that those differences can occasion. Yet, even as Turkish workers were still perceived as different, the article evinces a new focus on those workers as multidimensional people, giving space to their perspectives, experiences, and challenges. In discussing their experiences, the workplace comes to the fore as a space of intercultural cooperation and successful integration. The Turkish workers have advocates in the company, and, while acknowledging that the process took several years, the article speaks of the "integration" of Turkish workers in the past tense. In other words, difference, the company contends, does not preclude satisfaction on the job or in society. The transition may be difficult, the writer concedes, but the example of Siemens shows that it is possible.

West German businesses' growing awareness of and concern with their foreign employees' personal lives outside the workplace soon started showing up in articles dealing with family life, social customs, and integration into broader society. An article on AEG-Telefunken's foreign language page concerning school attendance, which came out in January 1973, was aimed at the parents among its foreign workforce. It explains that school attendance was obligatory for all children up to the age of fifteen (specifying both sons and daughters), regardless of whether they

---

[56] "Ganz wie Zuhause ist es nicht," p. 6.   [57] Ibid., 6.

had already completed their required schooling in their country of origin. It also assures parents that "appropriate schools" are available for children with mental or physical disabilities, and that German school authorities want to work with parents concerning their children's education.[58] This was the first time the multilingual section directly acknowledged guest workers' roles as parents of school-age children in West Germany.

The *AEG-Telefunken Report*'s focus on the family continued in the summer of 1974. The Federal Republic, having recently shut down the *Gastarbeiter* program, allowed family members of foreign workers to reunite in West Germany, provided that they adhered to certain stipulations. Although the number of guest workers declined by about half a million in the two years following the *Anwerbestopp*, some proved reluctant to fall in line with the change in policy. Indeed, the total population of foreign residents continued to grow in the wake of the recruitment halt, with nonemployed spouses and children constituting an ever-larger percentage.[59] Some West German companies, including AEG-Telefunken, responded to the shifting political context and demographic changes with efforts intended to facilitate the transition for their foreign workforce, aiming for their continued employment. The *AEG-Telefunken Report*'s article "How Are You Able to Bring Your Family?" spells out point by point what conditions employees needed to meet before they could bring their family to live with them. The requirements included a minimum three-year legal residency in West Germany, proof of adequate housing and means of support for one's dependents, and a close relationship, either as spouses or minor children, with those seeking to come to Germany. The article goes on to detail the necessary paperwork and the government offices responsible for processing the applications. With the exception of the familiar opening refrain of how life in a foreign country can be difficult and lonely and the admission that "it is therefore understandable" that one would want to be with one's family, the tone of the article is relatively dry, in keeping with the pattern of policy-related announcements.[60]

While similar articles continued throughout the 1970s, many of the issues discussed on the multilingual page during this time also reflected an increasing company interest in the private lives and activities of its foreign workforce. In a 1975 article entitled "Leisure Pursuit: Sports,"

---

[58] "Okula gitmek bir Yükümlülüktür," *AEG-Telefunken Report*, January 1973, p. 14, DTHA.

[59] Herbert and Hunn, "Guest Workers and Policy on Guest Workers in the Federal Republic," 211.

[60] "Ailenizi nasıl getirebilirsiniz?" *AEG-Telefunken Report*, July/August 1974, p. 14, DTHA.

the writer tries to impress upon his readers the importance of healthy free-time activities. Working a second job, watching television, or sitting in a bar, he lectures, are not healthy activities, nor are they the best forms of relaxing. We understand, the writer continues, that it will be difficult for you to choose "one of the typical manners of how some Germans pass their free time. But why not try it?" The article then names the company offices that could guide the readers to the appropriate leisure time activities. If the readers wanted to start their own sports clubs, the writer informs them that competing against other teams required both insurance coverage and "official recognition as an organization." The article closes with a caution against allowing "national pride" to add antagonism to sporting events, as sports should be relaxing and serve to establish new personal contacts.[61] Perhaps more than any other to this point, this article demonstrates not just a desire to inform and educate the foreign workers in their employ but also to mold them to fit into German society. It neither refers to how guest workers used free time before coming to West Germany nor acknowledges with more than a passing reference the financial situation that prompted many *Gastarbeiter* to work long hours or more than one job. Instead, the writer enumerates and encourages typical "German" leisure pursuits.

This well-meaning if paternalistic attitude surfaces again in a 1977 article entitled "Life in Society," in which the company attempts to extend its reach into the communities and homes of its foreign employees. The writer begins by explaining that life in a major city "requires of all of us a better understanding and consideration" of one's fellow residents, "especially on the part of families that come from countries with different customs of living" as they seek "to adapt themselves to the new community." These "foreigners" may not understand the reactions of their German neighbors if they continue to live their lives as if they were still in "their fatherland, where in accordance with their southern temperaments" they are accustomed to celebrating holidays more often and more noisily. Their German neighbors, the writer points out, prefer peace and tranquility, and will call the police. It would be much better to have a "friendly dialogue" with one's German neighbors beforehand, explain one's own customs, and reach a compromise that will promote community harmony.

The second half of the article focuses on the use of communal spaces, such as stairways and courtyards, the appropriate use of which, according to the writer, was also important for good relations between neighbors.

[61] "Serbest zaman meşguliyeti: Spor," *AEG-Telefunken Report*, February 1975, p. 14, DTHA.

First, children needed to show respect for others when they were playing in these communal spaces. Second, residents should keep the common spaces clean for the sake of their and their neighbors' good health. In addition, the writer warns, trash that spills out of the receptacles in the courtyard can attract germ-bearing rats. To solve this problem, the article details how foreign workers should break down their garbage into smaller pieces before disposing of it.[62] Although the overarching goal of the article is to promote good community relationships, the writer puts the responsibility for this at the door of the foreigners, assuming that their dirty, disrespectful habits are the cause of discord. The solution? Foreign residents needed to set aside the customs of their "southern temperaments," and adopt the social and hygienic habits of their German neighbors.

This trend of companies acknowledging the settlement of their foreign employees in West Germany and making efforts to provide information relevant to their familial and social, as well as working, lives continued through the second half of the 1970s as family reunification became more visible and commonplace. By 1978, *AEG-Telefunken Report* had published an article on how to deal with a death in the family and, a year later, another on preparation for retirement.[63] The latter article describes how retirement benefits are calculated from income and, as with other policy- and benefits-related bulletins, lists the necessary documentation and government and company offices involved in its distribution. In acknowledging that a generation of foreign residents had reached old age and required attention and information specific to that stage in life, the article recognizes that many were in West Germany to stay. Overall, the trend in the foreign-language articles demonstrates not only West German businesses' growing recognition of the changing status of their "guest workers" from workers to parents to members of society but also shows how the workplace itself was shifting from a space of production to a space of education and partial Germanization.

The *Siemens Mitteilungen* articles during the same years also began to take up the theme of integration, highlighting the diversity of the workforce and stressing the company's efforts at encouraging cross-cultural relationships and cooperation. In late 1980, a writer from the company newspaper gathered together a group of *ausländische Mitarbeiter* (foreign coworkers) in Munich, three women and seven men, to discuss their lives in West Germany and experiences with xenophobia. In "Their Homeland

---

[62] "Toplumda yasantı," *AEG-Telefunken Report*, October 1977, p. 14, DTHA.
[63] "Ailede ölüm halinde nasıl hareket etmeli?" *AEG-Telefunken Report*, June 1978, p. 14, DTHA; "Emekliliğe hazılık," *AEG-Telefunken Report*, November 1979, p. 14, DTHA.

Does Not Let Them Go," the writer opens by musing that Germans and foreigners live and work together, but "do they also belong to us?"[64] Their answers were recorded in their native languages and, interestingly, not translated into German. Instead, the writer summarizes the "surprising" results for the "natives" to read: the vast majority intend to return to their countries of origin soon, two of the three women have children that do not live with them in West Germany, and many feel like they are sitting "between two chairs."[65] The *ausländische Mitarbeiter* reserve criticism for anonymous Germans who blame the "foreigners" for taking jobs from Germans and collecting social welfare benefits. The writer concludes by providing contact information for employees who would like to obtain copies of the foreign-language edition of the *Siemens Mitteilungen*, a resource that most of his interview subjects were unaware existed.

Two years later, against the backdrop of continuing slow economic growth and little change in the unemployment rate, the same reporter attempted a similar project, but with a different tenor that suggested foreign workers were grappling with – and making progress in – becoming a part of German society. This article, entitled "Conforming without Losing Your Identity: Discussions with Foreign Co-workers," focuses on Siemens employees at a factory in West Berlin who had been in Germany for years, spoke German well, and liked their jobs. When asked about problems with integration, the group points fingers in both directions. Some, echoing a previously discussed *AEG-Telefunken Report* article, respond that the foreigners themselves are to blame: they are accustomed to living in a certain way and do not want to change their traditions. Another disagrees. He spent two years working in Brazil, where he encountered groups of third-generation German immigrants who "drink their beer and don't speak a word of Portuguese." "Is someone in Brazil more tolerant than here?" he asks.[66] Despite the disagreement over where to lay blame, all agreed that language was vital to successful integration.

The next day, the writer interviewed a group of young people involved in Siemens' apprenticeship program, asking them similar questions regarding integration. The interns are slightly more circumspect than their adult counterparts, stressing the importance of open discussion and polite perseverance in the face of misunderstanding and discrimination. One young man recognizes the resentment against foreigners but claims nice clothes and a good appearance can go a long way in mitigating such

[64] "Die Heimat lässt sich nicht los," *Siemens Mitteilungen*, December 1980, p. 13, SCA.
[65] Ibid., 16.
[66] "Anpassen, ohne die Identität zu verlieren: Gespräche mit ausländischen Mitarbeitern," *Siemens Mitteilungen*, December 1982, p. 5, SCA.

feelings. There are places that often refuse to admit foreigners, he concedes, but "with my friends, freshly shaven and wearing a tie, I don't have any problems."[67]

The increasingly positive articles continued two years later in "So Wonderful to Be at Home Again: From Foreign Co-workers Who Feel Comfortable Here." This article, supplemented with multiple photographs of smiling, hardworking *ausländische Mitarbeiter*, focuses on three employees who were among the first group of Spanish *Gastarbeiter* to come to West Germany, why they stayed, and their satisfaction with the lives they had built. The reporter, who had also written the previous two articles, also interviewed a Yugoslav woman, a Greek man, and a Spanish couple, and the general tone of the story was one of satisfaction and success. These foreign workers had been at Siemens for decades, were married with children, felt happy with their lot, got along well with Germans, and had no intention of returning "home."[68]

An article in December 1988, at a point when the West German economy seemed to have regained its footing and the unemployment rate had decreased, suggests that, at least for one Turkish employee in a West Berlin factory, the integration process was successful and complete. The sense of his successful assimilation begins with the title "Ein Türke in Berlin: 'Wat ick mache, erleichtert das Leben'" (A Turk in Berlin: What I Make, Makes Life Easier), identifying the Turkish employee as a Berliner down to the diction. Seyfettin Göndöven first came to West Berlin in 1965, arriving on a plane full of Turks with contracts to work for Siemens. A few days after he arrived, Göndöven met a German woman in the *Kneipe* around the corner from his *Wohnheim* (dormitory), whom he married three years later. Their son, the writer affirms, is a "dyed-in-the-wool Berliner."[69] The focus on Göndöven's personal life, though, is brief. The majority of the attention is given to his activities at Siemens. Göndöven had worked in the manufacture of home appliances since first coming to Siemens in the 1960s and was very proud of the product and his work. Multiple photographs of Göndöven and the product – on the assembly line, showing the product to a consumer, using a Siemens coffee maker with his wife – fill the two-page spread, liberally peppered with descriptions of the appliances and their use, even "way out in

---

[67] Ibid., 6.
[68] "'Schön, dass wir wieder Zuhause sind': Von ausländischen Mitarbeitern die sich hier wohl fühlen," *Siemens Mitteilungen*, December 1984, pp. 6–7, SCA.
[69] "Ein Türke in Berlin: 'Wat ick mache erleichtert das Leben,'" December 1988, p. 24, *Siemens Mitteilungen*, SCA. The subtitle of this article is written in a Berliner dialect, suggesting that the "Turk" mentioned in the title has acclimated to the point where he speaks like a local.

Turkey."[70] The pictures and the text taken together not only identify Göndöven as a fully integrated Berliner and valuable Siemens employee but also link the man and the product to each other in a way that seems to make their stories of success inseparable.

These articles on integration in the 1980s suggest a progression that, much like the condition of the West German economy during that time, may be slow and not without stumbling blocks but that could be – and in some cases was – ultimately successful. The titles of the articles trace this development as the emphasis shifts from the connection between foreign workers and their *Heimat* (homeland) to functioning within the host society to feeling "at home" to being identified by a concrete place. What is more, the workplace itself is shown as a site that fosters and promotes integration. Foreign employees, the articles seek to demonstrate, receive support from compatriots and interested German coworkers, learn German, develop important skills, and become a part of a society – all through their achievements in the workplace.

Despite the shift in focus to the factors influencing integration, the newspaper does not, with few exceptions, change the way it refers to Turkish workers and their children as "foreigners" and "guests." Throughout the articles already discussed, writers shift from using *Ausländer* to *ausländische Mitarbeiter* or *ausländische Mitbürger* (foreign fellow citizen) in referring to those employees who came to the company through the *Gastarbeiter* program or from immigrant communities in West Germany. This discursive othering continues and becomes even more noticeable in articles addressing the children of these *ausländische Mitarbeiter*. In 1979, as part of the international "Year of the Child," the *Siemens Mitteilungen* featured a story on a traffic safety clinic held by the day-care center at Berlin Siemensstadt. The cover photograph of that month's issue shows a little boy, about six years old and with a dark complexion, standing on the curb and peering cautiously for oncoming traffic around a Volkswagen Bug parked on the street. The corresponding article also features bright photographs of a multiethnic group of children playing and practicing traffic safety with their parents, care providers, and a police officer.[71] In a letter to the editor two months later, a man from Munich applauded the newspaper for its choice of the little boy for the cover page. He looks cautious but not afraid, the letter writer notes. "How good also," he continues, "that you chose a little foreign guest (*einen kleinen ausländischen Gast*) as the representative. That underlined the international

---

[70] Ibid., 24–25.
[71] "Verkehrserziehung für die ganz Kleinen: Statt Sandkastenspiel auf die Strasse," *Siemens Mitteilungen*, June 1979, cover page, pp. 22–23, SCA.

meaning of the theme 'Year of the Child.'"[72] The use of the word "guest" not only illustrates the reader's distinction between the German children and the children of "foreign coworkers," it also emphasizes the assumed transient nature of their stay in West Germany. The boy, a "little foreign guest," can only temporarily inhabit that space; he does not belong to it.

Although the theme of the traffic safety clinic was not integration, the company day-care facilities at Siemens' Berlin factories did host events aimed specifically at bringing together German and foreign children. In October 1981, the *Siemens Mitteilungen* featured a story on such an event: two day-care centers hosted a play day with the intention of furthering the language development of the foreign children. There are no misunderstandings in the games, the article says, for the children understand each other and get along well. "Together with their German friends, the little foreigners – the majority of whom were born in Berlin – learn 'easy' German." The article adds that parental interest helps their children's progress, and that, through participating in Parents' Evenings, the adults also get the chance to know each other better.[73]

The role of company day care in the integration of the children and their parents shows up again more than a decade later in reunified Germany in an article entitled "Living with Each Other – Learning from Each Other."[74] The cover shot features a colorful picture of a group of kindergarteners (the equivalent of preschoolers in the United States) messily brushing their teeth; the child in the front of the group has darker skin, and the title underneath reads, "Integration Begins in Kindergarten." The goal of the article, the writer informs his readers, is to learn "how Germans and foreigners meet with each other in their free time." At the time, about 60 percent of the children at the Johanna-von-Siemens day-care center were "children of foreign ancestry." The center, according to the article, had become a site of intercultural meeting and friendships, where parents, as well as their children, enjoy the center's activities, "bring specialty foods from their countries of origin, and use the opportunity to get to know each other and break down prejudices."[75] One of the events hosted by the day-care center was a St. Martin's Day celebration.[76] After participating in the parade with their children, the parents

---

[72] "Herzerfrischend," *Siemens Mitteilungen*, August 1979, p. 22, SCA.

[73] "Wenn kleine Ausländer berlinern," *Siemens Mitteilungen*, October 1981, p. 9, SCA.

[74] "Miteinander leben – voneinander lernen," *Siemens Mitteilungen*, December 1991, pp. 4–5, SCA.

[75] Ibid., 4.

[76] St. Martin's Day is a popular saint's day in Germany in honor of Martin of Tours, a former Roman soldier turned monk. Children celebrate by carrying lanterns and singing songs in a procession after nightfall, for which they are given small treats.

gathered in the garden of the Siemens clubhouse and socialized over *Glühwein* and *Bratwürste*. The second half of the article contains interviews with some of the parents, who testify to the value of the day-care center not only for their children's well-being but also for their own relationships with coworkers and their comfort in German society.

The company day-care center, then, in addition to being a physical sign that foreign workers were having families, comes to the fore as a new site to encourage and advance foreign coworkers' and their children's integration into German society. An extension of the workplace, the day-care center provided a space for foreigners and Germans, parents and children, to meet and get to know each other. At the same time, as depicted in the articles, it became a space for foreigners to learn how to be German: how to speak the language, play the games, and celebrate the holidays. Even as the *Siemens Mitteilungen* and the center's coordinators laud the center's positive benefits on integration, they continue to use the German/foreigner dichotomy in their language, even for those children born and raised in West Germany. The continuity of such language throughout the newspaper from the 1970s to the early 1990s reveals the entrenched mind-set that employees and their children "with foreign backgrounds," however valuable as employees and "integrated" into German society, would continue to be regarded as some manner of *Ausländer*.

This situation is perhaps best illustrated in two final examples from the *Siemens Mitteilungen*. The earliest article concerning guest workers appeared in November 1969 and was entitled "New Guest Worker High" (Figure 1). The article explained that the numbers of guest workers in the Federal Republic had reached unprecedented levels, with Turks quickly moving into first place. The accompanying illustration is of a man with dark hair and mustache, holding a large suitcase upon which a chart reflecting the growing numbers of *Gastarbeiter* is drawn.[77] This same character shows up eighteen years later in an article entitled "Guests and Permanent Residents" (Figure 2). On one side of the article, which explains that for many "foreigners" Germany has become a second home, the stereotypical guest worker wears traveling clothes and sits on his suitcase. On the other side, the same character relaxes in an easy chair, wearing house slippers.[78] The two illustrations show the shift from guest workers being defined as transitory – complete with suitcase – to the realization that these guests had made themselves at home. Yet, at the same time, the consistent depiction of "the guest worker's" physical appearance demonstrates a lasting perception of difference.

---

[77] "Neues Gastarbeiter-Hoch," *Siemens Mitteilungen*, November 1969, p. 23, SCA.
[78] "Gäste und Dauergäste," *Siemens Mitteilungen*, November 1987, p. 12, SCA.

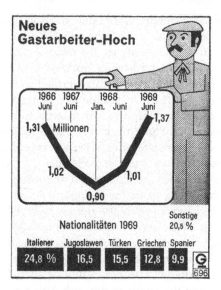

Figure 1. "New Guest Worker High"

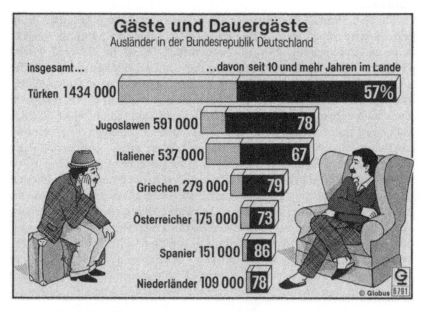

Figure 2. "Guests and Permanent Residents"

Unsettled in German Workplaces, Settling into
German Neighborhoods

Even as Siemens and other West German businesses sought to facilitate
(and be seen as facilitating) their foreign coworkers' transition into and
success in their companies, the workplace remained for many *Gastarbeiter* a space of instability. Whether due to illness, injury, pregnancy, lay-
offs, or being fired, many Turkish workers found that having a job in
West Germany did not mean having job security. In 1970, only 871 Turks
living in West Germany were unemployed. Just five years later, that
number would increase more than fiftyfold, with 46,794 Turks being
reported as out of work. That number decreased to just over 37,000 by
1980,[79] but then shot up again in the early 1980s to more than 90,000 in
1985.[80] By 1971, Turkish workers outnumbered all other *Gastarbeiter* in
the ranks of the unemployed, with the disparity continuing to widen.

The unemployment statistics for *Gastarbeiter* in West Berlin tell a
similar story of workplace instability. According to information compiled by the *Bundesagentur für Arbeit,* just over 1,000[81] of West Berlin's
136,922 foreign residents were unemployed when the government froze
the *Gastarbeiter* program in 1973.[82] Two years later, over 7,000 of the
Ausländer living there were without work.[83] Although that number had
receded to 5,650 by 1980, in the following years it rose again, reaching
more than 14,000 by 1990.[84] These statistics do not speak directly to the
unemployment rates of specific national groups, but between 1973 and
1990 Turkish residents composed between 40 and 50 percent of the
foreign population in West Berlin and most likely experienced levels
of unemployment at least commensurate to their proportion of that
population.[85]

[79] "Arbeitslose Ausländer im Bundesgebiet nach ausgewählten Staatsangehörigkeiten,"
Jahreszahlen 1980, Bundesagentur für Arbeit, p. 71.
[80] "Arbeitslose Ausländer im Bundesgebiet nach ausgewählten Staatsangehörigkeiten,"
Jahreszahlen 1990, Bundesagentur für Arbeit, p. 69.
[81] "Arbeitslose Ausländer nach Landesarbeitsamtbezirken," Jahreszahlen 1985, Bundesagentur für Arbeit, p. 59.
[82] Statistisches Landesamt Berlin, *Statistisches Jahrbuch Berlin 1973* (Berlin-Wilmersdorf:
Statistisches Landesamt Berlin, 1974), 41.
[83] "Arbeitslose Ausländer nach Landesarbeitsamtbezirken," Jahreszahlen 1985, Bundesagentur für Arbeit, p. 59.
[84] "Arbeitslose Ausländer nach Landesarbeitsamtbezirken," Jahreszahlen 1990, Bundesagentur für Arbeit, p. 65.
[85] See Statistisches Landesamt Berlin, *Statistisches Jahrbuch Berlin 1973* (Berlin-Wilmersdorf:
Statistisches Landesamt Berlin, 1974), 41; Statistisches Landesamt Berlin, *Statistisches
Jahrbuch Berlin 1981* (Berlin-Wilmersdorf: Statistisches Landesamt Berlin, 1981), 40;
and Statistisches Landesamt Berlin, *Statistisches Jahrbuch Berlin 1991* (Berlin-
Wilmersdorf: Statistisches Landesamt Berlin, 1991), 52.

As the statistics show the increasingly precarious nature of guest work-ers' employment, the workers' stories reveal the multiple factors at play that made the workplace a volatile, insecure space for the *ausländische Mitarbeiter*. For some, disagreements with their coworkers and super-visors led to a quick dismissal. Before Soner Polat opened his own café in Sprengelkiez, he worked as a translator at a bread factory in West Berlin. In his role as translator, he mediated between Turkish employees and management, a position he held for four years until a dispute with his German boss ended in a fistfight and he was fired.[86] In another case, a Turkish man working for a cleaning firm was fired after he reacted angrily to seeing a coworker (a Turkish woman) behaving in a way he considered inappropriate.[87] For others, it was not a disagreement with supervisors that led to leaving the workplace but rather an inability to understand them. When Beyhan Kaya came to West Berlin in 1973, she went to work at a candy-making factory. Although she worked very hard at her job, after six months at the factory she left to take a position with a cleaning company, pointing to her poor German-language skills as the reason for her change in career.[88] Azra Demir and many of her Turkish coworkers lost their places at Siemens not because of their inability to speak German (which she could) but rather due to their illiteracy.[89]

For women like Kaya and Demir, pressures outside the workplace often exerted their influence on that space, making their continued emp-loyment difficult if not impossible. Sevim Özel succinctly summed up her situation: "Two shifts, three children, housework, visits, family."[90] As the West German business officials had feared, when Turkish workers became wives and mothers, their family responsibilities made their work-ing lives increasingly complicated. Whereas some women were able to arrange childcare through family or neighborhood connections, or with company childcare services, for many others the responsibility of caring for their children made their continued presence in the workplace unten-able. This was the situation for Leyla Sezer. After six and a half years of working for AEG-Telefunken, she had to leave her job after the birth of her second child (having left her first child in the care of family back in Turkey). "There was no one there," she stated simply, "to care for [the baby]."[91] Kaya, who had left her position at a factory and taken a job with a cleaning company, had to leave that job after having her daughter.[92]

---

[86] Soner Polat (pseudonym), interview by Ursula Trüper and Kemal Kurt, 18 June 1993, transcription, p. 15, MMA.
[87] Beyhan Kaya (pseudonym), interview by Hatıce Renç, 9 March 1993, transcription, p. 6, MMA.
[88] Kaya interview, 5–6.   [89] Demir interview, 1.   [90] Özel interview, 16.
[91] Sezer interview, 2.   [92] Kaya interview, 5–6.

Yet this exit from the workplace was not always a permanent one, as in the cases of both Demir and Kaya, who would eventually return to work outside the home. Thus, even though West German companies' fears of losing their female workforce to familial responsibilities were realized, not even their absence from the workplace was a permanent development.

West German businesses' long battle against illness and injury reveals another factor in workplace instability. Despite medical examinations both before and after immigration, safety education, and company doctors, Turkish *Gastarbeiter* were human beings performing arduous and often dangerous tasks, susceptible to sickness and workplace injuries. Hüseyin, in an interview about his work experiences in West Berlin, recalled how the dust at the plastics factory, which he had heard caused cancer, would get into the workers' eyes and noses. They had masks, he explained, but it was too hot to wear them. At a later job for a textile factory, Hüseyin had to take care not to lose a finger to the machines he worked with the whole day.[93] For others, it was not a sudden accident but rather the long process of illness that forced them to leave the workplace. Demir eventually had to leave her job at Sarotti's after fourteen years because her health deteriorated.[94] Kaya's return to the workplace was made necessary when her husband had to leave his job due to hearing loss.[95]

While these factors were largely based on workers themselves, market forces also played an important role in the instability of the workplace. In some cases, this was reflected in increasing mechanization of the production process. Toward the end of her tenure at Sarotti's, Demir watched as one coworker after another was fired. It used to take two or three women to operate one machine, she noted, but now the machine did everything. "We, we are used up. Germany, how could Germany be used up? The whole companies are still running. But with fewer people. But it runs as it did earlier, better!"[96]

As the Economic Miracle that spurred West German officials to bring in guest workers sputtered out, West Berlin in particular felt its loss.

---

[93] Kemal Kurt and Erika Meyer, eds, ...*weil wir Türken sind/ ...Türk oldugumuz için: Bilder und Texte von Türken/ Türklerin resim ve öyküleri* (Berlin: express-Edition, 1981), 40.
[94] Demir interview, 8.   [95] Kaya interview, 6.
[96] Demir interview, 8. Structural changes in the economy beyond increased mechanization of production also played a role. As Joyce Mushaben points out, coal mining operations dramatically decreased in the late 1960s and early 1970s, leaving its foreign miners, 85 percent of whom were Turks by 1975, in an especially unstable position. See Joyce Marie Mushaben, *The Changing Faces of Citizenship: Integration and Mobilization Among Ethnic Minorities in Germany* (New York: Berghahn Books, 2008), 72.

"By the 1970s," Alexandra Richie writes, "the once great economic powerhouse had been reduced to dependency on West German payments to meet its crippling budget deficit."[97] The city had not, since the construction of the Wall, been an easy or attractive location for production. All materials, for example, had to be imported, an expensive and unreliable fact of economic life in the walled city. Some companies, suffering under the oil shock recessions of the 1970s, either closed down entirely or moved their operations to a less expensive location. The workplace itself could disappear out from under the feet of its workforce, as was the case with Sezer's job at a bicycle manufacturing company[98] and Hüseyin's position at the textile factory.[99] Indeed, employment in the clothing industry overall fell 80 percent from 1970 to 1984.[100] Turkish workers at larger firms were not safe from such developments, either. In 1984, after almost a century, AEG-Telefunken shut down the factories at its Brunnenstrasse location in Berlin-Wedding, which had employed significant numbers of *Gastarbeiter* since the 1960s. After reunification, Siemens followed federal subsidies out of Berlin into the *Speckgürtel* (affluent suburbs) region outside the city, leaving behind hundreds of *ausländische Mitarbeiter* to find new positions elsewhere. Thus while some Turkish workers, such as Seyfettin Göndöven at Siemens, found themselves as permanent a part of their workplace as the large machinery they operated, others found that being uprooted and unsettled was as much a fact of life in their workplaces as it was in broader German society.

Faced with continued workplace insecurity, many of those who had come to the FRG as part of the guest worker program decided that it was time to leave and use the skills and savings they had gained to build a more stable life for themselves back in their countries of origin. They found support from the West German government under the leadership of Helmut Kohl. Although initially successful in dealing with the FRG's economic challenges, by the beginning of the 1980s, Helmut Schmidt's coalition government was faced with poor economic growth, rising inflation, and continued unemployment. Its inability to steer the country back on a more economically stable and prosperous course and the defection of the Free Democratic Party (FDP) to the Christian Democratic Union/ Christian Social Union (CDU/CSU) resulted in the collapse of the Schmidt government and the rise of the CDU/CSU led by Helmut Kohl in 1982. Under Chancellor Kohl, the FRG offered lump-sum payments

---

[97] Alexandra Richie, *Faust's Metropolis: A History of Berlin* (New York: Carroll & Graf Publishers, Inc., 1998), 777.
[98] Sezer interview, 2.   [99] Kurt and Meyer, eds, ...*weil wir Türken sind*, 40.
[100] Richie, *Faust's Metropolis*, 777.

to guest workers for their own and their children's repatriation. If they emigrated by September 1984, each worker was eligible for DM 10,500, and the government would pay out an additional DM 1,500 per child. Some 171,000 foreign residents took advantage of the financial incentive and returned to their countries of origin.[101]

Yet not all who had immigrated to the Federal Republic for work or to be with their families wanted or were ready to leave in the late 1970s and early 1980s, and a variety of factors played into their decision to stay. Although many former guest workers found themselves unemployed or precariously employed, others still held what they considered good jobs that they were unwilling to leave and start over back in their home country. In addition, the West German government had, since the *Anwerbestopp*, been sending immigrant communities conflicting messages about their continued residency. For example, although the state had put an official halt to the program in 1973 and, a decade later, offered cash for emigration, in 1975 the Schmidt government rescinded the subsidies paid to guest workers to support their children in their countries of origin, decreeing that only those minors who resided in the FRG would be eligible for the monthly support. Many foreign residents responded to the change in policy by bringing children they had left behind to live with them in West Germany.[102] Family reunification resulted in a much more established immigrant community whose members were now invested not only in their jobs but also their children's education in West Germany. This development, largely a product of the 1970s and 1980s, constituted a strong incentive for the former guest workers to stay in the FRG and is explored in-depth in the following chapters.

Finally, it is critical to take into account what awaited those foreign residents should they return to their countries of origin. For Turkish immigrants and their children, returning to Turkey from the early 1970s to mid-1980s meant returning to a country marked by political, economic, and military conflict. Political instability prompted a military coup in 1971, and, after thousands of civilians were killed in politically motivated violence in Turkish cities in the late 1970s, the military again overthrew the elected government, keeping a tight rein on political activities even after it relinquished control to a civilian government in 1982. In 1974, under the administration of Prime Minister Bülent Ecevit, Turkey invaded Cyprus after a decades-long political conflict and intercommunal violence in the country. Less than a decade later, Turkey

---

[101] Mushaben, *The Changing Faces of Citizenship*, 52.   [102] Ibid., 48.

was dealing with interethnic violence on its own soil as the Kurdistan Workers' Party, partially in response to the crackdown following the 1980 coup, launched an insurgency against the Turkish state in an effort to create an independent Kurdish state. Finally, as a backdrop to and aggravating factor of these political conflicts, the Turkish state experienced significant economic challenges. A combination of broader structural issues, the oil crisis of the early 1970s, and the consequential drop in remittances from workers abroad resulted in rising inflation and unemployment rates that continued to plague the country into the mid-1980s.[103] While life in West Germany presented its own challenges for Turkish immigrants and the second generation, for some those challenges were preferable to those potentially awaiting them back home.

A small but growing number of Turkish residents chose to deal with the instability of the workplace by creating their own work. Already by the 1970s and increasingly in the 1980s, Turkish immigrants were opening up a variety of businesses, from grocery stores, cafés, and restaurants to tailoring shops, video rental stores, and travel agencies. While relatively little has been written regarding the early development of West Germany's Turkish-owned businesses, a 1987 study carried out by social scientists Jochen Blaschke and Ahmet Ersöz sheds light on the backgrounds, motivations, and experiences of small business owners in West Berlin's Turkish community.[104] Their study focused on thirty-four Turkish entrepreneurs (thirty-two men and two women) with businesses on a popular street in the West Berlin district of Kreuzberg.[105] Blaschke and Ersöz concluded that the immigrants' socioeconomic and ethnic backgrounds largely determined the means by which they came to own and operate a business and the extent to which their endeavor was successful. Those coming from a rural area or a provincial town in Turkey, a group that represented the vast majority of Turkish small business owners, were especially likely to view having one's own business as a way to achieve financial security. Indeed, many decided to open up their own store after losing their job in a German company.[106] Having experienced the volatility of the workplace, some Turkish immigrants saw self-employment

---

[103] For an overview of Turkey from the 1950s through the 1970s, see William Cleveland and Martin Bunton, *A History of the Modern Middle East*, 5th ed. (Boulder: Westview Press, 2015), 255–279.

[104] Jochen Blaschke and Ahmet Ersöz, *Herkunft und Geschäftsaufnahme türkischer Kleingewerbetreibender in Berlin* (Berlin: Berlin Express Edition, 1987).

[105] At the time of their research, 8,133 Turkish men and 6,671 Turkish women aged twenty years or older lived in that district, which reveals the small percentage of those embarking on business ownership. See *Berliner Statistik: Melderechtlich registierte Ausländer in Berlin (West) 31. Dezember 1986* (Berlin: Statistisches Landesamt Berlin, 1987), 8.

[106] Blaschke and Ersöz, *Herkunft und Geschäftsaufnahme*, 25–30, 39–40, 67.

as an opportunity to create and inhabit a stable workplace, where one did not have to follow others' orders.[107]

Not only did a growing number of West Berlin's Turkish immigrants consider business ownership a solution to the uncertainty of employment in the German workplace, some also saw it as an opportunity to establish more secure financial and working futures for their children.[108] One of the men Blaschke and Ersöz interviewed left his job of ten years at a textile factory to open his own shop with the goal of creating secure employment for his sons. After two years, he had bought out his partner's share in the bakery and had six employees working for him, including his two sons.[109] This outlook suggests that the process of conscious, permanent settlement was, for at least some of West Berlin's Turkish community, already under way as enterprising immigrants sought to gain a stable foothold not only for themselves but also for their children.

This example of the bakery owner also reveals another important aspect of the Turkish-owned workplace – it was a space of family, not individual, endeavor. Blaschke and Ersöz found that the vast majority of the business owners they interviewed and observed relied on family connections for the initiation and operation of their enterprises. Family often provided both the motivation for opening a business as well as the initial capital through either personal savings or by serving as an intermediary with the bank. Indeed, none of the business owners in Blaschke and Ersöz's study financed their start-up without some form of assistance from family members.[110] In many cases, a spouse or another close family member would arrange for a loan from the bank, as many of the aspiring business owners were unemployed. Family contribution to the operation of the business, however, did not stop at financing. In the majority of cases, family members either worked at the store or held jobs outside of the business in order to provide financial support to the family independent of the store's income. In approximately 18 percent of the businesses in the study, the owners' children also participated in the daily responsibilities of operating the family store.[111] Turkish immigrant–owned businesses, therefore, were often a familial space initiated with the idea of providing a secure workplace for the owner and his or her children, and financed, operated, and supported through the efforts of family members.

At the same time that operating a business tied the owner closely with his or her family, it also forged important and indispensable bonds with

---

[107] Kurt and Meyer, eds., ...weil wir Türken sind, 42.
[108] Blaschke and Ersöz, Herkunft und Geschäftsaufnahme, 67.   [109] Ibid., 41.
[110] Ibid., 61–62.   [111] Ibid., 63–64.

the local and transnational Turkish community. In the early development of Turkish-owned businesses in West Germany, entrepreneurs
would most often open up businesses they believed would fill a need
within the Turkish immigrant community, such as grocery stores and
restaurants where one could buy foods not available in German shops.
One's customers and one's suppliers, then, would often also be one's
compatriots. Such enterprises contributed to what Blaschke and Ersöz,
among others, call "ethnic colonies."[112] In both public and academic
forums, many argued that, by operating in such ethnic niche markets,
Turkish businesses owners were contributing to the production of a
"parallel society" (*Parallelgesellschaft*) apart from broader German society, which hindered both their and their customers' integration.

   Indeed, Turkish businesses did serve as intermediary spaces where
Turkish immigrants could bring the familiarities of home, whether
regarding diet, language, or social engagement, into the host society.[113]
At the same time, however, operating a business dependent on local
customers tied Turkish owners to the daily life of the neighborhoods
in which they lived and worked. During an interview with a freelance
German historian in the early 1990s, a Turkish-German café owner
focused not only on the challenges he faced as a business owner but also
on how these related to the troubles of the neighborhood in general,
including drug use and unemployment in the wake of reunification.[114]
Thus, beginning in the 1970s and increasingly in the 1980s, first- and
second-generation-owned businesses, situated in West Berlin neighborhoods and serving both Turkish and German customers, created spaces
that mediated and encouraged settlement into West German neighborhoods by connecting the business owners to neighborhood interests even
as they facilitated the formation of ethnic communities.

   Although Turkish entrepreneurs hoped to create successful, independent businesses that would give them and their families secure financial
footing in their new home, they often found these workplaces as unstable
and difficult as their German workplaces had been. A variety of factors
influenced the challenges Turkish small business owners faced, particularly those of the first generation. Blaschke and Ersöz stress the importance of the immigrants' social, economic, and work backgrounds both

[112] See Blaschke and Ersöz, *Herkunft und Geschäftsaufnahme;* Rauf Ceylan, *Ethnische Kolonien: Entstehung, Funktion und Wandel am Beispiel türkischer Moscheen und Cafes* (Wiesbaden: VS Verlag für Sozialwissenschaften, 2008).
[113] See Eren Keskin (pseudonym), "Wirt einer Kneipe am Sparrplatz", interview by Ursula Trüper, 1993, audiocassette, DLSA, MMA; Kurt and Meyer, eds, ...*weil wir Türken sind*, 41–42.
[114] Keskin interview.

in Turkey and West Germany prior to business ownership. The majority of small business owners involved in their 1987 study had grown up in the countryside or small towns, although many had lived on the outskirts of larger cities prior to coming to West Germany.[115] Only a minority of first-generation immigrant entrepreneurs had had business experience before emigrating, and the vast majority had only an elementary school education.[116] Perhaps most important to Blaschke and Ersöz is the fact that very few had received any kind of vocational training, either in operating a business or in performing the particular type of work their companies offered.[117] Many of the first-generation immigrants were, in other words, ill-prepared for the demands of owning and operating their own businesses.

In addition to the challenge of lack of training, immigrants had to contend with the barriers to entrepreneurship inherent in their legal status in West Germany. Often, residency permits did not allow Turkish residents to own a business, which led many earlier business owners to pay a German "straw man" to serve as the fictitious head of the company.[118] Problems of the status of residency, mistakes on official documentation, and confusion about city regulations could result in the loss of the privilege of owning a business, and even the loss of residency entirely.[119] In addition to bureaucratic challenges, Turkish businesses, like their West German counterparts, were vulnerable to market forces. An owner of a Turkish restaurant ran his first business, a vegetable shop, with the help of a Turkish friend and a German front man for five years before a financial crisis in the early 1970s forced him to close the shop and return to factory work. Three years later, he obtained the necessary permits from the city and financing from friends and family to open up his own restaurant. The work itself, the man emphasized during his interview five years later, was grueling and the hours long, but much better than having to "dance to the pipes of the *Meister*."[120]

Ownership over the workplace, then, did not always bring about the stability and success that first-generation Turkish immigrants found wanting in the West German workplaces. Lack of experience, bureaucratic hurdles, market forces, and demanding work responsibilities loaded this new space with difficulties that challenged the successful settlement of Turkish immigrants into their new neighborhoods and West German

---

[115] Blaschke and Ersöz, *Herkunft und Geschäftsaufnahme*, 52.   [116] Ibid., 58.
[117] Ibid., 59–60.
[118] Blaschke and Ersöz, *Herkunft und Geschäftsaufnahme*, 41; Kurt and Meyer, eds., . . .*weil wir Türken sind*, 41.
[119] Polat interview, 16.   [120] Kurt and Meyer, eds, . . .*weil wir Türken sind*, 41–43.

society. However, the creation of these new spaces clearly reflects the active attempts of the former *Gastarbeiter* to establish more permanent places for themselves in their new home. The existence of these businesses wove Turkish immigrants – starting with family networks and branching out into suppliers, other business owners, and customers – more tightly together even as it rooted them firmly in the physical and social spaces they had now come to inhabit. This new workplace, although perhaps no more stable than the old one, served a similar function: it provided space for the formation of new relationships and the strengthening of existing ones that allowed Turkish immigrants to gain a more steady – if not entirely secure – foothold in their new home.

Conclusion

Having examined Siemens' and AEG's intentions, Turkish guest workers' experiences, and the changes that occurred when those two forces collided, we return to the question of how the reciprocal influences of the Turkish guest workers and their workplaces shaped the immigrants' permanent settlement in West Germany. The workplace became, through the actions of the Turkish guest workers and the reactions of their West German employers, a space that gave them the purpose to migrate, the financial means of supporting their settlement, and the social networks to rebuild old and create new family relationships that soon led to a new generation being born and raised in West Germany. The daily interaction in the workplace of these factors created a space in which guests could turn into residents.

Companies facilitated this settlement administratively: encouraging *Gastarbeiter* to renew their work and residency permits, using the social networks of their foreign workers to recruit their friends and family members, and assisting their employees (to varying degrees) to navigate the bureaucratic maze of life in West Germany. These efforts initially were in line with political goals for the *Gastarbeiter* program, but as policy makers moved to limit and eventually quash the program in 1973 in the hopes that the "guests" would return home and open up positions for native Germans, their employers instead made efforts to ensure their foreign workers' ability not only to stay in the FRG but also to bring their families and accommodate themselves to the expectations of West German society. Not only did West German companies acknowledge this transition from temporary to permanent both in the workplace and in society more broadly, but they increasingly positioned and promoted themselves as multicultural spaces. Beginning in the early 1970s and more so after the *Anwerbestopp* and throughout the 1980s, in-house newspapers lauded examples of cross-cultural cooperation, highlighted

Gastarbeiter clubs that gave traditional dance and song performances, and interviewed successful foreign workers who told of their satisfaction with their jobs. Such coverage did not deny that *Gastarbeiter* faced difficulties but rather suggested that the workplace was a space where those were being overcome.

Yet settling into German society was not the same thing as being considered a part of it, and companies encouraged their foreign employees to fit themselves into German society and conform to social norms. This was much less of a focus before 1973, but once the West German government effectively forced guest workers with the *Anwerbestopp* to make the choice to remain or return, businesses such as Siemens and AEG-Telefunken adopted a longer-term approach to their workers' settlement and success in West German society. Use of free time, relations with neighbors, personal health and hygiene – German businesses perceived points of differences and encouraged immigrant workers to set aside their own habits and adopt the customs and values identified as more German. The tension between the employers' efforts to smooth their "foreign coworkers'" settlement into German society, as well as in the workplace, and the companies' consistent focus on and articulation of differences helped to set the tone for an ambiguous status of Turkish residents in West Germany as simultaneously foreign and permanent.

Men and women experienced this ambiguity in the course of daily life on the job. On one hand, the connections foreign workers made at work helped them rebuild their families and social networks that made life in West Germany more familiar, settled, and enjoyable. On the other hand, the workplace was not a stable or dependable site. For women, including Sevim Özel, the worsening of the German economy in the 1970s and 1980s as well as the complications of family life kept them moving in and out of the workplace throughout their working lives. Pregnancy, raising children, and caring for ailing or injured relatives divided women's time and energy, rendering their connection to the workplace inconsistent and therefore less secure. For men, the jobs that initially brought them to West Germany began to disappear in the 1980s, leaving them either unemployed and dependent on their wives' incomes or searching for alternate ways to support themselves and their families. Some chose to go into business for themselves, a risky situation that often did not bring the hoped-for stability but did allow a sense of independence and power not present in German companies. That struggle for independence, as well as the placing of Turkish residents on the periphery of German society, would become more pronounced as Turkish guest workers sought to create homes for themselves, first within company dormitories and then, as their families joined them, in apartments in West Berlin neighborhoods.

2   At Home in Almanya

In the 1986 film *40m² Deutschland*, director Tevfik Başer tells the story of a young Turkish woman, Turna, brought from her home in rural Anatolia to West Germany by her new and older husband, Dursun.[1] It quickly becomes apparent to Turna and the viewer that Dursun's gilded promises of a better life were meaningless. When he leaves for work in the morning, Dursun locks the door behind him to protect his wife, he explains, from the dangers and immorality of life in the West German city. When he returns in the evenings, he expects Turna's compliance with his every need. The young bride's home proves no more welcoming than her husband, oppressing her spirit with its dim, cramped rooms and limiting her connection to the outside world to one small window. To the viewer, her home seems a prison, and her husband, a jailer. Freedom and hope appear to present themselves only at the end of the film, as Turna pushes aside Dursun's corpse, opens the front door, and steps, pregnant and alone, out of the building and into the blinding sunlight.

40m² Deutschland debuted, garnering attention and accolades, in a particular political context in the Federal Republic that directly influenced perceptions of Turkish cultural difference and, thus, interpretations of Başer's film. As discussed in Chapter 1, the Schmidt government's failure to restore West Germany to its earlier prosperous economic footing helped open the door for the ascension of the CDU/CSU and the chancellorship of Helmut Kohl. Part of the CDU/CSU's platform included a significant shift in *Ausländerpolitik* (foreigner policy) away from the SPD's more reciprocal view on integration. Reflecting a broader public discussion of the need for a strong and inspiring national identity, the CDU's position stressed integration as the sole work of migrants, the necessity of conforming themselves to German values and culture.[2]

[1] Tevfik Başer dir. and prod, *40 m² Deutschland*, Tevfik Başer Filmproduktion (Hamburg), 1986, videocassette.

[2] For a discussion of the CDU's *Ausländerpolitik* and its broader political and intellectual context, see Chin, *The Guest Worker Question in Postwar Germany* (Cambridge, UK: Cambridge University Press, 2007), 144–158.

Increasingly, attention focused on the perceived plight of migrant women as "a central problem for the work of integration."[3] Whereas initial studies focused on structural factors and the influence of the migration process, Chin writes, "In the first half of the 1980s ... the attention to migrant women shifted from highly nuanced efforts at cultural understanding to a recurring trope of the imprisoned, imperiled Turkish woman."[4]

As a filmmaker, Başer attempted to intervene in this discourse and was quoted in one review as saying that through the film he "would like for the Germans to get to know us [Turkish immigrants], because misunderstanding leads to fear and produces hate."[5] As Chin has demonstrated, however, West German audiences and critics overlooked the long, thoughtful scenes that sought to expand the migration narrative through introducing the importance of social networks and how migration disrupts them.[6] Instead, they saw in the film what they already "knew" about Turkish immigrants, and reduced it to the narrative of oppression and emancipation introduced in the opening of this chapter.[7] The examples of Başer's intentions and reception present a compelling picture of the state of integration discourse in West Germany in the 1980s, yet they neither reveal how Turkish women understood their own positions within their families and broader society nor how they experienced, subverted, and challenged expectations from both spheres. Placing the home at the center reveals the concrete and complex role that site played in the lives of first-generation women and men, as well as their children.

Başer's intense concentration on the home presents the two separate yet critically connected themes that run throughout scholarly work on the subject: (1) housing conditions and (2) gender relations. Earlier studies focused largely on the effects of housing conditions on the ability of first- and second-generation Turkish immigrants to successfully integrate into broader German society. In comparison to West Germans' living conditions, sociologist Ray Rist found that guest workers consistently occupied

---

[3] Ibid., 161.   [4] Ibid., 162.

[5] Heike Mundzech, review of *40 m² Deutschland* by Tevfik Başer. *Frankfurter Rundschau*, 18 January 1986.

[6] Chin, *The Guest Worker Question*, 171–190.

[7] For more on the unintended consequences of *40 m² Deutschland*, see Deniz Göktürk, "Beyond Paternalism: Turkish German Traffic in Cinema," Tim Bergfelder, Eric Carter, and Deniz Göktürk, eds., in *The German Cinema Book*, (London: British Film Institute, 2002), 250–251.

older apartment buildings with fewer amenities in less desirable neighborhoods yet paid more in rent. These conditions reflected the social status given to guest workers and segregated the immigrants from West German society, even as many cited a desire to live among Germans as one of their reasons for moving out of company housing.[8] Paradoxically, the difficulty guest workers faced in finding quality housing and their resultant concentration in particular neighborhoods fueled German residents' fears of ethnic enclaves turning into segregated ghettos.[9] Yet more recently, historian Sarah Hackett has argued that housing patterns among Muslim immigrants in Bremen, the overwhelming majority of whom were Turkish, reflected their own agency rather than the constraints imposed by economic considerations or the host society's discrimination.[10]

Those studies not specifically looking at housing conditions focused instead on family dynamics within the home, especially gender expectations and conflict that rose from familial relations. Scholars who focused on gender initially examined how women's and girls' experiences in Germany affected their positions within the family, beginning with Nermin Abadan-Unat's early study on how working outside the home expanded women's power within it.[11] With studies of the second generation, this understanding of emancipation became more complex and included exploration of the ways the West German society limited women's development and opportunities.[12] More recently researchers have begun to directly examine the effects of migration and life in the Federal Republic on Turkish men and masculinity, including Margaret Spohn's typologies of men's roles within the family and Katherine Pratt Ewing's examination

---

[8] Ray C. Rist, *Guestworkers in Germany: The Prospects for Pluralism* (New York: Praeger Publishers, 1978), 149–175.

[9] Ulrich Herbert, *A History of Foreign Labor in Germany, 1880–1980: Seasonal Workers, Forced Laborers, Guest Workers* (Ann Arbor: University of Michigan Press, 1990), 193–254.

[10] Sarah Hackett, *Foreigners, Minorities and Integration: The Muslim Immigrant Experience in Britain and Germany* (Manchester, UK: Manchester University Press, 2016), 95–97.

[11] Nermin Abadan-Unat, "Implications of Migration on Emancipation and Pseudo-Emancipation of Turkish Women," *International Migration Review* 11, no. 1 (Spring 1977): 31–57.

[12] Umut Erel, "Gendered and Racialized Experiences of Citizenship in the Life Stories of Women of Turkish Background in Germany," in Jacqueline Andall, ed., *Gender and Ethnicity in Contemporary Europe* (Oxford: Berg Publishers, 2003), 155–176. This is also a growing subject for popular (and controversial) studies and memoir literature. See, for example, Necla Kelek, *Die fremde Braut: ein Bericht aus dem Inneren des türkischen Lebens in Deutschland* (Cologne: Kiepenheuer & Witsch, 2005); Seyran Ateş, *Grosse Reise ins Feuer: Die Geschichte einer deutschen Türkin* (Berlin: Rowohlt Taschenbuch Verlag, 2003).

of the construction of the identity of Muslim men in contrast to the modern German national self.[13] Finally, Esin Bozkurt looked at home as a concept rather than a location as a way to understand immigrants' sense of belonging, and how that is influenced both by gender and generation.[14]

The common focus of these approaches is the effects of living conditions and family relationships on immigrants' interactions with German society. What is missing here and what this chapter seeks to add is an examination of the historical development of the home: its role in the relationships between the first and second generations, the changing meaning of home for Turkish parents and their Turkish-German children, and how it reflected both generations' place in West German society. Moving past its representations by political and cultural elites, focusing on the home reveals the more mundane but also ultimately more influential ways ordinary people negotiated the challenges of migration and settlement within a specific historical (and local) context. Although fictional representations such as the account of Turna and Dursun have resonance in the history of the Turkish-German community and give us insight into how public discourses shaped German perceptions of their Turkish neighbors, they tell only a part of a much more complex and diverse story. The spaces of belonging Turkish immigrants and their children forged within the context of the home further anchored their lives in its West German setting, fostering the growth of a diverse immigrant community. It hosted the efforts of both generations not only to ameliorate the struggles they faced in their daily lives outside its walls but also to incorporate the external influences they found appealing. As a result, the home became a space crowded with keen and sometimes competing expectations, often influenced by gender and generational conflicts. In other words, rather than being a space apart, the home was a nexus point between first-generation Turkish immigrants, their children, and West German society. This process began in the earliest homes many of the guest workers experienced, the company dormitories.

[13] Margret Spohn, *Türkische Männer in Deutschland: Familie und Identität. Migranten der ersten Generation erzählen ihre Geschichte* (Bielefeld: Transcript, 2002); Katherine Pratt Ewing, *Stolen Honor: Stigmatizing Muslim Men in Berlin* (Stanford: Stanford University Press, 2008).
[14] Esin Bozkurt, *Conceptualising "Home": The Question of Belonging Among Turkish Families in Germany* (Frankfurt: Campus Verlag, 2009).

The Company *Wohnheim* as a Transitional Space

The formation of new social and familial networks, as well as the continuation of established social relationships, found a nourishing environment in the workplace's domestic extension – the *Wohnheim,* or
dormitory. As mentioned previously, many *Gastarbeiter* were housed by
their employers in company-owned dormitories. These *Wohnheime* came
in many forms, including military barrack–style housing, existing apartment buildings, school-style dormitories, and newly constructed buildings. Although a dormitory might have housed *Gastarbeiter* from more
than one country, they were single-sex residences with strict rules regu-
lating the times and manners in which men and women could interact.
As with the workplace itself, companies wanted the dormitories to be free
of those difficult social problems that sexual and intergenerational relationships prompted.[15] At the same time, company dormitories offered
foreign workers a cheap and easily available housing option that allowed
them to save their wages to send back home at a time when all parties –
the West German and Turkish governments, West German businesses,
and the workers themselves – considered their stay temporary.

Just as West German businesses' expectations for the workplace and
Wohnheim were similar, so too were the ways companies attempted to
build and propagate an idealized version of worker housing. During the
1960s and early 1970s, companies featured these "cozy and beautiful
rooms" that would "lighten the living and working stresses of our foreign co-workers" in the same brochures they developed to woo foreign
workers to employment in West Germany.[16] In one brochure designed
to recruit Turkish and Greek women, Siemens featured a newly built
dormitory that had housed women guest workers from southern Europe
since 1963, all of whom, the company assured the readers, "are happy in
Berlin and feel comfortable in the bright and friendly spaces."[17] The
brochure included pictures of a common room, a bedroom, a kitchen,
and a laundry room. The picture of the common room shows a clean,
well-furnished space with high ceilings framed by drapes. Four young

---

[15] "Beschäftigung von Gastarbeitern: Bisherige Ergebnisse des Arbeitskreises Ausländerfragen im Berliner-Siemens-Bereich," p. 7, 2 October 1970, Sig. 10585–1, Schlüssel
04610585, SCA.
[16] "Das Haus Siemens" p. 2, Sig. 10585–1, Schlüssel 04610585, SCA.
[17] "Bildunterschriften – Siemens Aufnahmen," Rundschreiben zur Beschäftigung von
Ausländischen Arbeitnehmer, Sig. 10585–1, Schlüssel 04610585, SCA. While the
document is not dated, the content, language, and placement in the file suggest
publication in the mid-1960s.

Figure 3. Women's dormitory room in Siemens' brochure

women inhabit the scene: one stands near the record player, deliberating between two albums; another sits at a table and sorts through a box of index cards; and the final two chat at a nearby table. Each woman is dressed in a smart blouse and skirt, with her hair fashionably styled. The scene in the bedroom is similarly set, with two women well dressed and peacefully engaged (Figure 3). One plumps the pillow on her bed, while the other writes a letter at a table.[18] Both pictures promise the viewer access to these clean, airy, well-furnished spaces as well as the chance to achieve the cosmopolitan status of their inhabitants.

These pictures and their message were supplemented by those of the kitchen and laundry room. The picture of the spotless white and stainless steel kitchen features gleaming countertops and appliances, and the corresponding description offers "whoever would like to prepare meals after their own taste can use the communal kitchen. Electric hotplates, pots and pans are there for your use."[19] The kitchen scene features only one woman – dressed more for an evening out than for staying in and cooking – who is preparing a meal in a single blue pot. No ingredients, dishes, or utensils clutter the sanitary countertops. The image of the laundry room is even more bare. A window lets natural light into a room furnished with electric washing machines, a row of basins and water faucets, and what appears to be a water heater. Although the caption

[18] Ibid.   [19] Ibid.

64   Turkish Germans in the Federal Republic of Germany

explains, "In a laundry room with electric washing machines and dryers, the female residents can wash their laundry," no one is present in the room.[20] Unlike the depictions of the common room and bedroom, which present the residents as much as the rooms, the kitchen and laundry room photographs foreground modernity and the bright and shining appliances that the residents may not have access to in their home countries. Even as they highlight the technology, the almost complete absence of women using the appliances reinforces Siemens' depiction of the women as *Bewohnerinnen* (residents) rather than workers in the context of the *Wohnheim*. Yet, it is clear that none of these "bright and friendly spaces" would be available to these women without employment in West German companies such as Siemens or AEG-Telefunken.

The personal photographs of former AEG-Telefunken guest worker Fulya Yüksel reveal similarities in subject matter and themes, and also introduce a more realistic depiction of life in a *Wohnheim*.[21] Yüksel came to West Berlin from Istanbul in 1964 to work for AEG-Telefunken and moved into the company's *Wohnheim* at Stresemannstrasse 30 in Kreuzberg.[22] For the next eleven years, Yüksel worked and boarded with other Turkish guest workers, occasionally capturing her daily life on film. Her subjects in the first few years in West Berlin roughly mirror those from the Siemens brochure but provide a personal perspective. One of her earliest staged pictures echoes the common room photograph of the Siemens brochure. In the photograph labeled "Televizyonlu Salon" (television lounge), Yüksel, dressed in a knee-length skirt with her hair swept up in typical 1960s fashion, stands in front of a large television.[23] Here, the television takes the place of the record player and the subject looks directly into the camera, suggesting to the viewer that she recognizes the significance of the television. Another picture that foregrounds technology is a shot of the kitchen, entitled "Im Wohnheim: Beim Kochen" (In the dormitory: while cooking).[24] As in the Siemens' model kitchen, the focus in Yüksel's picture is the room itself, the long waist-high countertops and the boxy refrigerator. Her choice of subject matter

[20] Ibid.   [21] Fulya Yüksel is a pseudonym.
[22] Eberhard Seidel-Pielen, *Unsere Türken: Annäherung an ein gespaltenes Verhältnis* (Berlin: Espresso/Elef. Press, 1995), 87.
[23] "20.11.1964 Televizyonlu Salon," in Bestand: Fulya Yüksel (pseudonym), BT 163, 6a, Sig. A000202, DOMiD, Cologne.
[24] Im Wohnheim: Beim Kochen, "1965 Berlin, Stresemannstr. 30, Fraun Wohnheim Telefunke" [sic], in Bestand: Fulya Yüksel (pseudonym), BT 150, 1, Sig. B000008, DOMiD.

in these photographs shows that the availability of new technologies was an important part of her experience of these new spaces, which she wanted to document and share.

In the depiction of personal spaces, however, Yüksel's and Siemens' portrayals differed significantly in both the physical makeup of the bedroom and its uses. Unlike the Siemens brochure, whose picture of the bedroom suggests a relatively generous space for two occupants, Yüksel's photographs show the multiple bunk beds that are more in line with other former residents' accounts of their sleeping quarters in the dormitories. Instead of the brochure's single beds with plump pillows, Yüksel and her roommates occupied white metal bunk beds with matching blankets. While the room is less luxurious than its idealized version, Yüksel's pictures display a space both more personal and more social in nature. In one photograph, presumably taken by one of her roommates, Yüksel sits on her bottom bunk, quietly reading a letter.[25] One year later, a roommate snapped another picture of Yüksel in a much different mood. She stands in the middle of the floor, with her arms held out and smiling, as if caught in the middle of dancing.[26] Although the room is tidy, it appears more lived-in than the earlier photograph, with shoes tucked away under the bed and postcards arranged on the walls. This was a space that, by bringing together connections from home and souvenirs from new experiences, guest workers made personal.

At the same time the *Wohnheim* bedrooms served as a personal refuge, they also functioned as social spaces, places where residents formed new friendships and networks. Yüksel demonstrates this visually in a photograph taken of her on a top bunk with four of her friends and fellow residents (including noted writer, Emine Sevgi Özdamar).[27] These are not the sedate ladies of the Siemens brochure, despite similarities in hairstyle and dress. The young women in this picture are smiling and laughing as they lounge with each other on the crowded bed, which bows slightly under their combined weight. Yüksel's photograph hints at the role of the *Wohnheim* as a place to forge new connections, to make new friends of similar age and background with whom one could have adventures that resulted in new postcards being displayed on one's bedroom wall.

[25] "1964 Mektuplar," in Bestand 163, 7a, Sig. A000204, Sig. B000008, DOMiD.
[26] Berlin 1965, Frau in Wohnheim, in Bestand 163, 2, Sig. A000190, Sig. B000008, DOMiD.
[27] Frauen im Wohnheim, Berlin 1964, "Sevgi, Sevim, Filiz, Nuran, Aysel," in Bestand 163, 1, Sig. A000189, Sig. B000008, DOMiD.

Yüksel's depictions of life in an AEG-Telefunken *Wohnheim* reflect the experiences of other guest workers in the dormitories of companies such as Siemens and the chocolate manufacturer Sarotti. Although women's dormitories were generally considered nicer than the men's, most former residents recall sharing their bedrooms with three to five others. Surprisingly, relatively few recount episodes of conflict with roommates.[28] Roommates as well as coworkers, the guest workers who lived together in the dormitories also socialized together, whether that meant staying in and chatting in one's bedroom or going out grocery shopping, dancing, or on weekend excursions. This sort of socialization may well have been an intention of businesses that housed their foreign employees together, and, as in the workplace itself, company officials set out to control the activities of their *Gastarbeiter*.

Yüksel's documentation of life in her West Berlin *Wohnheim* finds resonance in other guest workers' experiences, but her accommodations should not be seen as typical of the living situations of *Gastarbeiter* throughout the Federal Republic. In the 1960s, housing shortages existed across the country, exacerbating the challenge of companies to provide adequate accommodation for their migrant laborers. In addition to constructing new housing, businesses also used existing structures, including old apartment buildings, student dormitories, and military and prisoner-of-war barracks. As Karin Hunn has documented, the living conditions of some of these older structures were lacking, to say the least. In early 1970, the restructuring of the industry with the founding of Ruhrkohle AG necessitated a large influx of labor, and 3,000 workers were requested from Turkey. By August of the same year, 1,295 had arrived, causing severe problems for the company regarding their accommodation.[29]

When Turkish representative Sirri Mete Atsu from the Industrial Mining and Energy Union (Industriegewerkschaft Bergbau und Energie, IGBE) went out to observe the living conditions of Turkish miners, he was shocked by what he saw. "Prisoner-of-war camps would have certainly looked better," Atsu remarked. At one *Wohnheim* for Eschweiler Bergwerksverein, there was one shower for 150 people, and the kitchen and bathroom were in two different barracks. The beds were old, the

---

[28] Sevim Özel (pseudonym), interview by author, 30 June 2009, transcription by Perrin Saylan, Berlin, Germany, 5–6; Alev Yıldırım, interview by Murat Güngör, 27 July 2004, digital recording, "A, Aziza-Interview – 20040272.mp3," DOMiD.

[29] Karin Hunn, *"Nächstes Jahr kehren wir zurück..."*: *Die Geschichte der türkischen "Gastarbeiter" in der Bundesrepublik* (Göttingen: Wallstein Verlag, 2005), 222–223.

rooms were too small to hold the requisite table and chairs, and the building was infested with cockroaches. At another, Atsu discovered that the night watchman unleashed a dog at night to patrol the grounds. When men returned from working the night shift, they routinely had to wait twenty to thirty minutes for the watchman to restrain the dog, so they could enter their "home."[30] These conditions may not reflect the more active hostility toward foreigners (*Ausländerfeindlichkeit*) that guest workers and their families would experience in the 1980s, but the substandard conditions in which some were housed and the lack of consideration for their well-being reflected at least apathy and disinterest. This calls into question the conclusion that discrimination and ill treatment were consequences of the breakdown of the political conception of the guest worker program and the problems that arose from the government's lack of long-term planning.[31]

Even when the conditions were adequate, the dormitories could still be isolated from nearby towns, limiting guest workers' contact to life outside of the workplace. Hayrullah Şenay, who worked as a welder outside of Hamburg, recalled that his employer's *Wohnheim* reminded him of his days in the military. "You couldn't really describe it as bad," he conceded, "but a barrack is ultimately a barrack." He continued, "I lived in that dorm for ... nine years – it was a house of loneliness."[32]

Although living conditions could vary widely, narratives about life in the dormitories, whether from the guest workers themselves, their children, or journalistic accounts, nearly all discuss the company rules that regulated life there. Sometimes the *Gastarbeiter* learned about the dormitories' rules before they even saw the buildings themselves. When Fulya Yüksel landed in West Berlin, a Turkish translator from AEG-Telefunken met her and her new coworkers at Tempelhof Airport, where she explained their dormitory's rules.[33] Among those regulations most

---

[30] Ibid., 222–223.

[31] Herbert, *A History of Foreign Labor in Germany, 1880–1980*, 246–247. While I agree with Herbert that the failure of the guest worker program as a temporary measure without long-term social effects was a primary cause of "the mounting problems between Germans and foreigners" in the 1970s and 1980s (246), prior assumptions and articulations of guest workers' difference and inferiority also played a significant role in their treatment as workers at first and as neighbors later on.

[32] "Wir sind hier, um zu bleiben – Der Moscheegründer Hayrullah Şenay," in Michael Richter, ed., (*Gekommen und Geblieben: Deutsch-türkische Lebensgeschichten*, Hamburg: Edition Körber Stiftung, 2003), 206.

[33] Fulya Yüksel (pseudonym), interview for "Wir waren die erste...," audiocassette MD 0009, Bezirksmuseum Friedsrichshain-Kreuzberg Museum Archiv (BFKA), Berlin.

often mentioned by former residents were the curfew on weekday and weekend evenings and the prohibition on visitors of the opposite sex. These restrictions can be seen as part of West German businesses' efforts to ensure that their *Gastarbeiter* remained a focused, productive workforce, not distracted by social relationships or familial responsibilities.

Many guest workers, however, found ways around the companies' attempts to limit their social lives in this way. The house director and front desk clerk may have been able to restrict who entered the dormitory, but they generally could not keep residents from leaving that regulated space, nor could they control the actions of their employees once they left. Sevim Özel recounts how some of her housemates would avoid the difficulty of the curfew by simply leaving the *Wohnheim* for the entire weekend, returning on Sunday evening before the curfew. Özel also remembers how groups of Turkish men, also guest workers, would wait outside her dormitory, hoping to meet up with the *Gastarbeiterinnen* who were heading out for the weekend.[34] Even though she felt too nervous to meet new people in this way, Özel had the impression that most of the women in her *Wohnheim* had fewer qualms about enjoying an evening at the disco, or perhaps a weekend in the city, with new acquaintances. Yet one did not have to leave the *Wohnheim* to subvert their employers' purposes. Relationships made and maintained in the dormitory could result in new social networks that were at odds with the company's interests. Özel's own marriage, facilitated through a connection with a friend and coworker, shows such circumvention could be subtler and more significant than simply leaving for the weekend.[35]

Working to Make a Home

When Turkish guest workers married, as Özel did, or brought their families to live with them in West Germany, as thousands of others did in the wake of the *Anwerbestopp*, they had to leave company housing and find a new place for themselves and their families to call home. For many first-generation Turkish immigrants, the process of setting up a home began with a long and difficult search for housing. Although the West German government had been eager to bring them in as workers, many landlords were not nearly as receptive to having them as tenants. Indeed, classified advertisements for rental properties would sometimes specify

---

[34] Özel interview, 5–8.
[35] Although company documentation and guest workers' narratives often discuss the controls on heterosexual relationships, there is a uniform silence on the existence of same-sex relationships.

"no foreigners."[36] When interviewed in 1980, one man described his difficulty finding appropriate housing for his family, linking it directly to his ability to integrate into West German society. Despite checking the classifieds in the *Berliner Zeitung* each morning, having a German-speaking friend make phone inquiries, and visiting the *Wohnungsamt* (housing office), he, his wife, and their four children, who had joined him in 1974, were still living in a single-room apartment without a rental contract. He expressed his frustration, asking:

How can you integrate into a society that refuses you a home? The politicians can talk about integration until they drop dead. Now I am very determined, and I can't get on with them anymore (*mit ihnen nicht mehr anfangen*). I find comfort only with my fellow countrymen. We're good enough for work, but not as neighbors (*zum Zusammenleben aber nicht*). And then I'm supposed to integrate with my exploiter![37]

Others, such as Beyhan Kaya, had to move several times in their first years on the rental market, not due to discrimination but rather for financial reasons or because a growing family required more space.[38] Often, connections with family, friends, or neighbors played a key role in finding adequate housing. Leyla Sezer and her husband, who moved to Sprengelkiez in 1969, lived in a one-room apartment that the birth of their first baby made too small. The caretaker of their building, a German woman, had heard of a one-and-a-half-room apartment opening up and told Sezer about it. This connection enabled Sezer and her growing family to move into more suitable housing.[39] Ultimately, most guest workers moved into the districts of Tiergarten, Kreuzberg, and Wedding – areas of the city rendered particularly unattractive to West German residents by their locations along the Berlin Wall and the poor housing conditions due to war damage and subsequent neglect.[40]

---

[36] Kemal Kurt and Erika Meyer, eds., *...weil wir Türken sind/ ...Türk oldugumuz için: Bilder und Texte von Türken/ Türklerin resim ve öyküleri* (Berlin: express-Edition, 1981), 23–29.
[37] Ibid., 23.
[38] Beyhan Kaya (pseudonym), interview by Hatıce Renç, 9 March 1993, transcription, p. 15, DLSA, MMA.
[39] Leyla Sezer (pseudonym), interview by Hatıce Renç and Ursula Trüper, 28 January 1993, transcription, p. 4, DLSA, MMA.
[40] Although Hackett advocates a fuller consideration of immigrants' agency in their housing choices (and I agree), she, too, demonstrates how financial constraints and limited housing availability affected the scope of their choices in Bremen, particularly in the 1970s. See Hackett, Foreigners, Minorities and Integration, 126–127.
    In Chapter 3, I discuss in more detail the poor housing conditions, the growth of immigrant communities, and the effects of city renovation efforts on the residents in the border districts generally and Wedding in particular.

The work did not end when the new home was secured. Rather, for first-generation Turkish immigrants, the home constituted a site of continual labor. Material improvement of the home was one way Turkish immigrants worked to create a space for themselves and their families in their new surroundings. As Turkish families became more settled into their new neighborhoods, they became increasingly interested in improving their direct living conditions. Engin Günükutlu, the representative of Wedding's Büro für stadtteilnahe Sozialplannung (Office for District-Level Social Planning), remembers that, although Turkish residents of Sprengelkiez were uninterested in supporting the city's plans for renovation at first, by the late 1980s they were fully on board. When he visited their apartments to inform them of the city's plans, he noted that they had outfitted their homes well, with nice curtains and furnishings.[41]

The majority of the labor that took place in the home, however, focused less on its material improvement than on the day-to-day efforts of house cleaning and childcare. Most often these tasks fell to the women in the family, many of whom also worked outside the home. Asked if she had good memories of her past twenty-four years in Berlin, Sezer answered, "We didn't have enough time for good memories. You go to work, leave work, pick up the children from kindergarten, go home, as a woman you cook, I don't know ... in the evenings you go to bed and in the morning, always the same."[42] For Kaya, the home was also defined primarily by labor, particularly in regard to the care of her children. In response to a question about her use of free time, Kaya replied that she only got two days off every two weeks, and those were filled with housework. Her son, apparently, preferred her homemade bread to store-bought. "Ugh," she would answer to his request, "do you think your mom's a robot?" Then she would make him the bread.[43] Especially for first-generation women, and not wholly unlike their West German counterparts, the home became almost an extension of the workplace, in that it was a site of constant demands and labor.[44]

---

[41] Engin Günükutlu, interview by author, 9 May 2009, digital recording, Berlin.
[42] Leyla Sezer interview, 10.   [43] Kaya interview, 12.
[44] It is important here to note that this "second shift" for Turkish women in the 1970s and 1980s was not a unique situation for women generally in West Germany, nor was the social attribution of primary childcare responsibilities to mothers. One must remember that the West German state turned toward recruitment of female guest workers in part to maintain the traditional male breadwinner model, which positioned women as homemakers and mothers. See Monika Mattes, *"Gastarbeiterinnen" in der Bundesrepublik: Anwerbepolitik, Migration und Geschlecht in den 50er bis 70er Jahren* (Frankfurt am Main: Campus Verlag, 2005). West German women into the early 1980s still shouldered the majority of the childcare and housekeeping responsibilities, even as the number of part-time working mothers rose sharply. See Eva Kolinsky, *Women*

The reality that women were responsible for the major share of labor in the home reveals another aspect of this site's role in the construction of a sense of belonging: the home as a space of contradiction. This contradiction can be further defined as the almost simultaneous presence of spaces of empowerment and subjugation within the home, and it was heavily influenced by gender relations within the context of the family. For women, as the previous examples illustrated, the home was often a site of subjugation to the family's needs, interests, and, at times, demands. This could be particularly severe for Turkish women who moved to West Germany specifically to marry. Often, these women worked only in the home, and had little contact to life outside that sphere, save for within the Turkish immigrant community. Even more so than with Turkish women who worked outside the home, it was especially challenging for these women to forge independent networks, learn how to access social and financial assistance, or gain the language proficiency necessary to operate successfully outside of their immediate Turkish community. The home was their main site of activity and interaction, within which they were expected to serve the needs of the family.[45]

Although such cases of Turkish women who migrated to West Germany for marriage are often overrepresented in the media for their apparent illustration of extreme cultural difference, *Gastarbeiterinnen* experienced the home as a site of gendered conflict and subjugation. As discussed earlier, Turkish women were often expected to take on the majority of the housework and child-rearing responsibilities, not wholly unlike their German counterparts. Indeed, in some cases, this imbalance in the household division of labor continued even when the wife held more than one job and the husband was out of work.[46] In interviews, some women framed their position in the home, and in relation to their

---

in *Contemporary Germany: Life, Work, and Politics* (Oxford, UK: Berg, 1993), 75–99 and 151–191; Christina von Oertzen, *Teilzeitarbeit und die Lust am Zuverdienen: Geschlechter-politik und gesellschaftlicher Wandel in Westdeutschland 1948–1969* (Göttingen, Germany: Vandenhoeck & Ruprecht, 1999). Participants of the feminist movements of the late 1960s and early 1970s brought the struggles of working German mothers into the political discourse, prompting a fierce debate about the employment of mothers and the proper response of the government to their particular issues. See Sarah Summers, "Finding Feminism: Rethinking Activism in the West German Women's Movement" in Karen Hagemann, Donna Harsch, and Friederike Bruenhoefer, eds., *Gendering Post-1945 German History: Entanglements* (forthcoming).

[45] The stories of these women have been particularly prevalent in a growing body of memoir literature and popular studies, including Ayşe and Renate Eder, *Mich hat keiner gefragt: Zur Ehe gezwungen – eine Türkin in Deutschland erzählt* (Munich: Blanvalet, 2005) and Necla Kelek, *Die fremde Braut: ein Bericht aus dem Inneren des türkischen Lebens in Deutschland* (Cologne: Kiepenheuer & Witsch, 2005).

[46] Kaya interview, 13–15.

husbands, as one of oppression. Nimet Erdem described her husband as jealous and controlling, always asking her where she had been, ordering her not to wear makeup, and telling her what clothes she could wear. "He behaved like women didn't have any right to their own say in the matter," she explained. "Sometimes I thought that I was damned to living like that, to being oppressed. At least, that's how I felt sometimes."[47] For Erdem, the situation was further exacerbated by the fact that her husband had a second wife, with whom he also had children. When they fought, he would leave the apartment they shared and move in with his other wife. Their home was peaceful, Erdem confessed to the interviewer, only when her husband left.[48] Kaya, who married while on vacation in Turkey, complained that after years of marriage her husband still did not listen to or try to understand her.[49] After long days in the workplace, these women and many others came home to a place where they were expected to continue taking orders and working for others' welfare.

Yet women were not the only ones who found the home to be a site of conflict and struggle. Men, in their roles as husbands and fathers, could also feel restricted, limited, or disrespected within the home. For Hamburg resident Demir Gökgöl, his responsibility for the well-being of his family kept him in a marriage that neither spouse wanted and at a job he did not enjoy. Once their son reached a certain age, the couple divorced and his wife returned to Istanbul. Gökgöl eventually left his job, pursuing a career as a musician and an actor.[50] Although Kazım Arslan's family joined him in West Germany for the purpose of rebuilding the household, tensions between Arslan and his wife, as well as between Arslan and his eldest son, also resulted in a family split. He recalled his son's direct disrespect and disobedience, along with disagreement between him and his wife over how to raise the children, as significant sources of conflict within the home. Arslan explained his lack of authority over his son, saying, "I noticed that I didn't have a deep connection with my children, who I only knew from summer vacations when I would visit my family for a couple of weeks."[51] Thus, some men would return home after a long

[47] Nimet Erdem (pseudonym), interview by Fatos Topac and Ursula Trüper, 8 January 1993, translation and transcription by Fatos Topac, p. 6, DLSA, MMA.
[48] Erdem interview, 5.   [49] Kaya interview, 6.
[50] "Ohne Jazz kann ich nicht leben – Der Künstler Demir Gökgöl," in Michael Richter, ed., *Gekommen und Geblieben: Deutsch-türkische Lebensgeschichten* (Hamburg: Edition Körber Stiftung, 2003), 139–158.
[51] "Die Geschichte über Deutschland gefielen mir – Der Bauarbeiter Kazım Arslan," in Michael Richter, ed., *Gekommen und Geblieben: Deutsch-türkische Lebensgeschichten* (Hamburg: Edition Körber Stiftung, 2003), 90–93.

day of taking orders at work to have their authority within the home directly challenged.

Fathers and husbands who tried to exert their authority within the home could also find their wishes and intentions indirectly circumvented by their wives and children. In Erdem's case, she tired of her husband's jealousy and domineering attitude, and, after a while, started ignoring his orders. She and her children also took advantage of his absences to countermand his expressed wishes. When one of their daughters ran away to marry a Yugoslavian man, her father was so angry he forbade his wife from allowing their daughter back into the house. During a time when he was away and the daughter needed a place to stay, however, Erdem received her daughter and son-in-law into the house, although she herself did not approve of the marriage.[52] As in the workplace, those who experienced oppression in the home found ways to subvert the authority and pursue their own agenda.

Decision making, as reflected in the preceding example, constituted a forum within the home in which gender as well as generational power structures came into play. In the late 1980s, as the intertwined issues of the "German" identity of West Berlin and the integration of its Turkish residents came to the fore in political and public debates,[53] psychologists Ute Schönpflug, Rainer K. Silbereisen, and Jörg Schulz conducted a study of decision-making practices in Turkish immigrant as well as German households in that city.[54] The researchers originally set out to explore the influence of social networks on internal family decision making, but their findings suggest the ways working-class Turkish and German families approached certain types of issues. To an extent, the behavior of both groups of families reflected adherence to traditional gender roles. In the case of Turkish immigrant households, the psychologists found that fathers had authority in family and financial issues but had joint influence with mothers in matters concerning the children. Fathers also had less influence in financial decisions than in family matters. In the West German households of similar family makeup and socioeconomic circumstances, each parent exerted equal influence in family and financial decisions, and mothers held authority in regard to the children. Finally, Turkish mothers attributed less influence to their

[52] Erdem interview, 2–3.
[53] This development is examined in Chapter 3 in connection to Turkish-German spaces of belonging in the neighborhood setting.
[54] Ute Schönpflug, Rainer K. Silbereisen, and Jörg Schulz, "Perceived Decision-Making Influence in Turkish Migrant Workers' and German Workers' Families: The Impact of Social Support," *Journal of Cross-Cultural Psychology*, vol. 21, no. 3 (September 1990): 261–282.

children in family decision making than the Turkish fathers did. Ultimately, Schönpflug, Silbereisen, and Schulz conclude that it was cultural factors rather than socioeconomic status that determined the decision-making practices in the families that participated in their study.[55]

The study, despite some problematic elements, provides a thought-provoking perspective on family dynamics in Turkish immigrant households in the late 1980s.[56] Although the authors caution against drawing broad conclusions from the results of the study given the relatively small survey pool (forty Turkish and seventy-two German families participated), their interpretations shed light on the shifting nature of power within the home. For example, the discrepancy in the mothers' perceptions of their children's influence in decisions that concern them suggested to the researchers that Turkish mothers' "own status of low influence in the family leads them to attribute even less power to the child." Fathers' attribution of influence to the children, on the other hand, might have reflected a "partial adaptation to the values of the host society" or "reflect the father's evaluation of the given children's resources," such as those gained through school.[57]

Yet here we see how the migration process, perhaps one of the "cultural factors" to which the authors attribute the difference between Turkish and West German households, influenced family dynamics within the home. Children's importance as translators of the host society for their parents shows up in personal narratives as well as scholarly research and reveals how traditional power relationships became blurred or even inverted within the home. In addition, while fathers retained some authority in financial matters, their influence in this area was not absolute. Mothers, by virtue of their own outside employment and in their role of managers of the household, were important participants in this area. Thus, while the findings of the study suggest that fathers were considered the head of the household and perceived as the ultimate authority figure, that position could be fixed, negotiable, or illusionary depending on the type of decision being made or the fathers' level of knowledge concerning that decision.

The home, however, was not only a forum of competing interests and conflict. It could also be a site of partnership and pride, a space in which

---

[55] Ibid., 280.

[56] It would have been helpful to know, for example, how long the Turkish participants had lived in West Berlin and whether that time was the same for both the wife and the husband. In addition, the authors note the use of "native Turkish interviewers" for those Turkish participants but do not investigate how the background of the interviewers could influence the participants' answers.

[57] Schönpflug, Silbereisen, and Schulz, "Perceived Decision-Making Influence," 279.

married couples worked together to improve their and their children's living situation and general well-being. Azra Demir joined her husband in West Berlin three years after he first moved there, and, in recalling their life together since the couple's reunification, she said, "My husband and I worked together hand in hand, head to head, life to life."[58] For Demir, this sense of teamwork stemmed from her and her husband's continued hard work outside of the home to contribute to the well-being of the whole family. The theme of partnership shows up in other life histories as well, particularly in regard to supporting the development of children.[59]

In addition to being a space of cooperation for the family's welfare, the home also constituted a site in which the first generation could demonstrate improvements in financial security and success. In her memoir, Gülen Yeğenoğlu, a single mother living with her son in Frankfurt, repeatedly references the physical changes and additions she made to her home to make it more livable and enjoyable for her son and herself, from the early days without a refrigerator to when she was able to purchase a new record player.[60] For Erdem Dilşen of Hamburg, living in a home of his own took on the particular significance of success and of rootedness. "Once he [my son] was born," he recounts, "I began to dream of our own house. Sometimes I think the Turk is like a Swabian, he lives by the motto: 'Strive, strive, build a house.'"[61] The home was clearly a site of gendered expectations, power struggles, and disappointment, yet it also provided the first generation with a space through which they could work together to improve their household, both the physical place and the family members who occupied it.

Comfortable and Cramped

The second generation also found the home to be a site of contradiction, although this contradiction could manifest itself in different ways. On the one hand, the home constituted a space of comfort, support, and refuge.

---

[58] Azra Demir (pseudonym), interview, translation, and transcription by Hatice Renç, 9 March 1993, transcription, p. 10, DLSA, MMA.

[59] See, for example, Özel interview.

[60] Gülen Yeğenoğlu, *Almanya'daki Yirmi Yılım* (Istanbul: Milliyet Yayınları, 1988), 42, 51.

[61] "In Uhlenhorst kennt mich jeder: Der Kaufmann Erdem Dilşen," in Michael Richter, ed., *Gekommen und Geblieben: Deutsch-türkische Lebensgeschichten* (Hamburg: Edition Körber Stiftung, 2003), 108. The German text for this expression reads, "Schaffe, schaffe, Häusle baue."

Filiz Güler, daughter of Sevim Özel, grew up with her parents and two siblings in a small apartment in Sprengelkiez in the 1980s. It was a tight space for three children, Güler recalled, "but I naturally never really noticed that, it was a very wonderful childhood."[62] In comparison with other families she knew, her parents gave young Filiz more freedom, they had more of a sense of humor, and "one could also talk with them."[63] The home as a supportive environment also shows up in the memoir of Green Party member Cem Özdemir, whose narrative focuses on his path toward becoming active in German politics. Growing up in small Bad Urach in Baden-Württemberg, Özdemir recounts mainly pleasant and domestic scenes of playing with the neighborhood children, being cared for by his German *Oma* and *Opa* (grandma and grandpa) while his parents were at work, and enjoying evenings when his parents' friends would come over to play cards and drink tea until late in the evening.[64] For Özdemir, home meant a connection to both his familial Turkish and his local Swabian roots through the people associated with that space.

On the other hand, many members of the second generation recalled the home to be a site of conflict, predominantly with parents. Although assertions that their parents' expectations and rules were restrictive and unfair are present in interviews with both sexes, it is more often at the center of young women's narratives.[65] Indeed, some young women made a direct comparison to the treatment of their brothers versus their own when discussing their frustration with parental control. In some families, Filiz Güler remembered, sons were treated like "pashas, who are spoiled and allowed to do everything."[66] Leyla Sezer's daughter, Sanem, told her interviewer that when her brother wanted to leave the house, he simply would say he was going out. When she wanted to leave, however, she had to answer questions about where she was going, who she was going to be with, and so forth, and at the end of all the questions, her parents gave her orders on how to behave. Also, she was expected to do the housekeeping, since her mother worked outside the home. Echoing the sentiments of many first-generation women, the teenager complained, "Go to school, come back from school, end the day with housework and then

---

[62] Filiz Güler (pseudonym), interview by author, 27 May 2009, transcription by Perrin Saylan, Berlin, 2–3.

[63] Ibid., 4.

[64] Cem Özdemir and Hans Engels, *Ich bin Inländer: ein anatolischer Schwabe im Bundestag* (Munich: DTV, 1997), 16–18, 26–27.

[65] For two examples of young men's frustrations with parental control, see Kurt and Meyer, eds., ... *weil wir Türken sind*, 64–67.

[66] Güler interview, 4.

cooking and such, finished. And then the next day go to school again, come home again, and don't experience anything new, what kind of life do I have?"[67]

While many teenagers undoubtedly expressed frustration at their parents' seemingly stifling expectations, Sanem credited the difference in treatment to being Turkish, making direct connections to her parents' mind-set as Turks who left the country in the late 1960s. Her parents' "old-fashioned" attitudes prompted Sanem to hide the fact she had a boyfriend, although she eventually told her mother. Despite her frustration with her parents' treatment, she empathized with their motivations. Her mother, she explained, was afraid that Sanem would drop out of school if she had a boyfriend and was concerned that her daughter's honor would suffer if people learned she was dating. But unlike her friend's mother, who dragged her daughter to a gynecologist to check if she was still a virgin after learning she had spent the morning alone with a young man, Sanem's mom trusted her, something Sanem valued. Her father, although he may not have trusted her, cared for her very much and wanted the best for her, Sanem felt, and this made his controlling attitude understandable to her, if not appreciated.[68]

During her 1993 interview, Sanem did perceive a direct link between being Turkish and her parents' restrictive behavior, but others challenged the cultural connection as a factor in their upbringing. In a 2004 interview, Turkish-German rap artist and Berliner Aziza A. related there was never any sense of growing up "in two cultures" in her family, and that she did not have to confront this topic until journalists began asking her questions about it. During her interview with Murat Güngör, she put the parent-child relationship in a more universal context, explaining that, whereas an eighteen-year-old wants to discover what life is all about, it's the parents who try to decide how much of it their child should experience. For her family, the artist stated, it was not a question of culture but rather of her father worrying about his children being outside late at night because of what could happen. "Child, I trust you," he would say to her, "but I don't trust those other people." Aziza found his argument logical, but still sneaked out of her window and went to Berlin's discos.[69]

For some young women, however, the extreme nature of their parents', and especially their fathers', control precluded any empathy

[67] Sanem Sezer (pseudonym), interview and transcription by Ursula Trüper, 4 March 1993, DLSA, MMA, 9.
[68] Ibid., 14–15.
[69] Alev Yıldırım, interview by Murat Güngör, 27 July 2004, digital recording, "A, Aziza-Interview – 20040272.mp3," DOMiD, Cologne.

or understanding. The growing body of memoir literature from Turkish-German women in the Federal Republic provides numerous examples of such situations. For Seyran Ateş, a well-known lawyer and women's rights activist, the move from Istanbul to Berlin resulted in an immediate restriction of her freedom of movement. In a memoir that focuses on the challenges of gender inequality, Ateş unfolds a narrative of overcoming the obstacles of a harsh family life and religiously restrictive community, which at times threatened both her liberty and her life. As a youth, whereas her brothers were allowed a considerable amount of liberty, Ateş's boundaries were "to the corner on the left and the shoe store on the right."[70] Growing older, she increasingly resented her parents' restrictions: when she was not at school, Ateş was required to be at home, where her parents and older brother treated her like a servant and beat her when she did not please them. As a teenager, she ran away from home twice, returning after the first time when her father promised to reform. Years later, Ateş reflected on the meaning of her parents' apartment door. It was, she writes, "a symbol that I was not allowed to freely make decisions that affected my own life. Physically I broke through that door, but it stayed in my mind for a long time."[71]

As it was for the first generation, home for the second generation constituted a site of contradiction that contained spaces of comfort and conflict, encouragement and repression. These spaces could also be highly gendered, making the home a more restrictive (and sometimes even abusive) place for daughters than it was for sons. The father-daughter relationship was particularly charged, and young women – like their mothers before them – often dealt with their parents' expectations and rules by hiding those aspects of their lives they felt would prompt direct conflict. Yet members of the second generation did not uniformly attribute the challenges they faced in the home to the same source. For some, their parents' Turkish background explained the restrictions they experienced at home, whether the ultimate source was cultural or just parents being old-fashioned. Others, though, saw power struggles with parents as a normal and universal part of growing up. In any case, all struggled with the responsibilities of children with working-class parents, the boundaries set by those parents, and the desire to forge their own independent identities that might or might not have conformed to the expectations of their parents and broader society.

[70] Seyran Ateş, *Große Reise ins Feuer: Die Geschichte einer deutschen Türkin* (Berlin: Rowohlt Taschenbuch Verlag, 2003), 51.
[71] Ibid., 128.

Finally, although somewhat outside the time frame of this study, it is useful to reflect for a moment on the relation of the second generation to their childhood home once they had grown. Some of the second generation found strength and support in the relationships forged and acted out within the home, even if they did not realize it at the time. Although journalist and memoirist Hatıce Akyün recounts little about tension between herself and her parents while growing up in Duisburg, references to her thrill at learning what the word *volljährig* (of age) meant and the self-described wild life she led after moving out strongly suggest her experience of home as a place of at least some restrictions and frustration.[72] Yet in describing her experiences as an adult going back to the home of her parents, her tone is full of affection and humor. Whether drinking tea in her parents' living room among the forest of couches and cushions or sitting around the dining room table with her parents and siblings first enjoying, then suffering through, the enormous and enticing meals her mother prepared, Akyün makes clear that her relationship to that place and its people has shifted from aggravation to appreciation and respect.[73] Akyün's narrative reflects not only the contradictory nature of the home but also how her parents' generation employed the home as a social space, utilizing it for entertainment and to maintain family relationships.[74]

A Center for Social Life

The home is often framed in the context of relationships within the nuclear family, yet one aspect that researchers pay less attention to is how social spaces within that site expanded to include extended family as well as friends. Homes became a primary site of socializing within the growing Turkish community, as family members, friends, and acquaintances dropped in to catch up on the latest news, often without prior notice. Sevim Özel did not always particularly welcome these visits. She and her husband worked different shifts throughout the week and were home and awake at the same time only on the weekends. But then, unfailingly, friends would start showing up on Saturday. There was not

---

[72] Hatıce Akyün, *Einmal Hans mit scharfer Soße: Leben zwischen zwei Welten* (Munich: Goldmann, 2005), 71–72.

[73] Ibid., 24–33.

[74] Interestingly, second-generation narratives do not often describe the home as a place of retreat from an ambivalent, if not openly hostile, outside world. This sort of sanctuary function is seen more in the framework of more independent social spaces in the neighborhood, discussed in Chapter 3.

even time to clean, Özel remembered, as one visitor followed another.[75] Special events, as well as these everyday visits, also took place within the home. When her daughter decided to marry the young man she had run away with, Nimet Erdem insisted, despite the difficulty of the situation and against the wishes of her husband, that her daughter's marriage should be celebrated. Finances made renting a hall untenable, so Erdem hosted the wedding reception in her own home.[76] For the first generation, the home opened up social spaces that enabled them to build and maintain relationships with their extended family, friends, and other members of the Turkish community as well as to demonstrate their hospitality and the material evidence (the new refrigerators, furniture, and curtains) of their hard work outside the home.

The second generation also experienced the home as a site of social interaction and socialization. Unlike the first and second generations' mixed feelings about the home in connection to the nuclear family, however, the latter's narratives of the home as a social space are generally quite positive. Filiz Güler situates her memories of family visits directly within her discussion about her happy childhood. "We had extended family here, uncles and aunts, and we always met every weekend, celebrated birthdays," she recounted. Mostly these visits took place within the home, but occasionally the family would also meet for picnics in nearby Schiller Park.[77] Bilge Yılmaz remembers her relatives and family friends getting together every day after work, either in her parents' home or a relative's apartment. Yılmaz recalled that on those evenings, three or four families would get together, and, after they sent the children off to play quietly:

the women were there and the men were there, you know. The men talked about politics and work situations, the women then naturally about the children, also about work. They of course also worked, and more about cooking and food and talked about raising the children and so on.[78]

The children played either in the apartment or outside in the courtyard.[79] On the weekends, sometimes the family would watch television together: Russian fairy tales on the East German channel or *Sesame Street* for the children, news programs for her father, and the one-hour Turkish-language program for everyone. These visits provided the second generation with the opportunity to interact with other children their own age as

[75] Özel interview, 10.   [76] Erdem interview, 9.   [77] Güler interview, 3, 5.
[78] Bilge Yılmaz (pseudonym), interview by author, 2 June 2009, transcription by Perrin Saylan, Berlin, 8.
[79] Kemal Kurt, "Türkische Familie am Sparrplatz (1993), Neg. 603/24A," DLSA, MMA.

Figure 4. A Turkish-German family in their Sprengelkiez
apartment, 1993.
Photograph by Kemal Kurt.

well as adults, creating a unique intergenerational space important in
their socialization (Figure 4).

Another part of the second generation's socialization within the home
was language learning. For many – if not most – families with two
Turkish parents in the 1970s and 1980s, the primary language spoken
in the home was Turkish. Members of the Özel household communicated solely in Turkish at home, which Filiz Güler now considers to have
been a great benefit to her, as it gave her good facility with her parents'
native language and the skills she needed to learn other languages later in
school.[80] For others, the transition from a Turkish-speaking household
to a German-speaking school system proved a particular challenge and
made some feel dissatisfied with their abilities in both languages.[81]

Even though the primary language in most households was Turkish,
the social spaces within the home could still provide opportunities to
learn German. As we saw in the example of Bilge Yılmaz's family get-
togethers, the television brought German into the home through a variety

---

[80] Güler interview, 1, 10. While in retrospect, Güler appreciates having used Turkish in the
home, as a *Gymnasium* student, she felt frustrated that she worked just as hard as her
German classmates but struggled more because of her own language background. See
Chapter 4.
[81] Kurt and Meyer, eds., ... *weil wir Türken sind*, 45–49; Lale (pseudonym), interview by
Ursula Trüper, 28 May 1992 and 4 June 1992, transcription, DLSA, MMA, 4. The issue
of language in the school will be addressed in Chapter 4.

of types of programming, particularly before the appearance of Turkish-only channels in the late 1980s and 1990s. Occasionally, Turkish parents employed a German *Tagesmütter* (nanny) to care for their children during the workday. Timur, ten years old at the time of his interview in 1993, was partially raised by his German *Tagesmütter* in the Bavarian town of Erding. After his parents moved to West Berlin, his mother stayed home with him, but Timur had very fond memories of his *Tagesmutter*. "She was really nice," he told his interviewer earnestly. "I can never forget."[82] Although these domestic spaces largely socialized the second generation to participate – at least linguistically – with the Turkish community, the home was not wholly separate from the environment in which it was situated. To a lesser extent, intercultural spaces also existed within the home that facilitated the second generation's transition to other social contexts outside of that site.

Conclusion

Turna of Tevfik Başer's *40m² Deutschland* experienced her Hamburg apartment as an empty, alienating place, cut off from the social networks of her old home and the external environment of her new one. In intense scenes throughout the film, she attempts to challenge her husband's restrictions, make connections with the outside world, and understand herself in the context of her newly circumscribed world. Through these powerful scenes, Başer confronts the viewer with the idea of migration as a process of rupture and the consequences of that rupture. Yet neither Turna nor the viewer get a sense of the rebuilding that would follow, because her husband froze Turna's own migration process when he prevented her from making those new connections.

Yet, for the first and second generations, we see the home as con-nected in multiple ways with its surroundings. It was a site crowded with overlapping and conflicting expectations, activities, and occupants. From the first days in the company *Wohnheim* to the later multigenerational apartments, Turkish immigrants created spaces to help them mitigate the stresses of a new environment, build new homes in the familial and physical senses, and define themselves in relation to their families, their local communities, and German society as they understood it. For the occupants of the dormitories, those sites – although their reality did not quite match the glossy brochures – introduced them to challenges and possibilities of life in West Germany, from contending with the West German staff's oversight to familiarizing themselves with a new material

---

[82] Timur (pseudonym), interview by Ursula Trüper, 22 June 1993, audiocassette, DLSA, MMA.

culture. The company dormitories also provided a forum in which they forged new social networks that further facilitated their transition to more permanent residency.

One outcome of that transition was the formation or restoration of families and family life, which necessitated a move from the dormitories to independent apartments. In many ways, the home constituted yet another worksite, as the first generation labored both to improve their physical living situations and to re-create family life in this new environment. For spouses, that second aspect of homemaking entailed special challenges, as both men and women negotiated their relationships with each other and issues of authority. Bringing home a paycheck may have given women more decision-making power in the home, but it did not free them up from bearing primary responsibility for the upkeep of the home and care of the children – a situation hardly unique to immigrant households.

Whereas the first generation could exert more control over the home than their workplaces, the second generation grappled even more with parental expectations and personal desires. For some, this conflict could be intense, even violent, as family members proscribed their activities based on conservative and limiting gender expectations. The memories of girls and young women, even those who considered their parents sympathetic, reflect the effects of, as Doreen Massey wrote, "the attempted consignment/confinement to particular places on the one hand, and the limitation on identity on the other."[83] This situation, however, should not define our understanding of Turkish immigrants' family life. In other cases, parents worked to create supportive environments for their children, and the second generation appreciated the motives, if not always the practical consequences, of that support.

Finally, Turkish immigrants and their children used the home as a social space through which they could build, maintain, and enjoy relationships with extended family and friends. Particularly in the earlier years of settlement, the home was a critical site for socializing and socialization, as Turkish-owned restaurants and cafés were relatively few. Casual entertainment and more formal events gave parents and their children chances to forge and enact a sense of belonging that connected them to a broader community of people with similar backgrounds and experiences. In addition, it provided the opportunity to both demonstrate material successes and gain practical skills and information that helped mitigate family members' interactions with life outside the home.

[83] Doreen Massey, *Space, Place, and Gender* (Minneapolis: University of Minnesota Press, 1994), 179.

The home, ultimately, was a site crowded with contradictions. The spaces family members constructed and attempted to control overlapped, complemented, and clashed with each other. As a result, the platform through which Turkish immigrant families mitigated their connections to the "outside" was constantly evolving, responsive to its inhabitants and the tensions brought in from external sites. These tensions – between genders, between generations, between migrant communities and West German society – continued beyond the walls of the home and found resonance and new expressions in the neighborhood.

3   Around the Neighborhood

Like most Berlin neighborhoods, Sprengelkiez is at its best in the summer. Bordered by a canal, the commercial Müllerstrasse (Müller Street), and a technical college, this thickly populated neighborhood in the Wedding district of Berlin-Mitte can feel a bit grim in the winter, when the gray of the streets and apartment buildings blends with the overcast sky. Warm summer days, on the other hand, bring residents into the Kiez's (neighborhood) public spaces, now shaded by leaf-laden trees and brightened by the occasional flowering window box or bush. On a sunny July day in 2009 when I visited the neighborhood, people were crowding the shop-lined Müllerstrasse, buying groceries, leaving school, or grabbing a quick meal at a convenient *Stehcafe* (stand-up café). They disappeared and reappeared from the subway station, racing across the street to avoid the throng of vehicular traffic. City buses lumbered past, collecting passengers and depositing more into the orderly melee.

A few blocks away from the bustle of Müllerstrasse, I entered a quieter corner of the neighborhood: Sparrplatz (Figure 5).[1] Surrounded by apartment buildings, an elementary school, and a student dormitory, this residential square seems to offer something for every resident. Children would run, climb, and swing until their parents, watching from nearby benches, dragged them away from the playground. Youth challenged each other to games of table tennis, played basketball, or simply loitered underneath the shade of the trees. On the outskirts of the square, a man sat quietly on a bench with a bottle of beer and a dirty rucksack. The sidewalks surrounding the square were filled with residents on their way to and from the day's events, while others sat at tables outside a café, drinking tea and playing backgammon. The pleasant, neighborly environment that the residents and I enjoyed that July day belied the Kiez's troubled reputation, even as it reflected one of the developments often blamed for the neighborhood's problems: a large proportion of "foreign" residents.

---

[1] On Sparrplatz, 2009, photograph by author, Berlin.

Figure 5. On Sparrplatz, 2009

In the late 1960s and early 1970s, guest worker families moved out of company housing and into residential areas, reestablishing their households in whatever apartments were affordable and available to them. Particularly in West Berlin, this often meant small one- or two-room apartments in turn-of-the-century *Altbauten* (old buildings) in various stages of neglect and decay. Life in Sprengelkiez of forty years ago was no exception. Its apartment buildings, sometimes with two *Hinterhäuser* (rear buildings) and a *Quergebäude* (side building), were generally in poor condition, and Sparrplatz itself was a barren field, with sections occasionally used to grow produce. Located in a traditionally working-class district, the neighborhood was one of the most densely populated in the city until the end of the Second World War. In the decades following the war, many families moved out of the area, and the remaining community was largely made up of the elderly, singles, and *soziale Behinderten*.[2] In the 1970s, Turkish guest workers and their families began moving into the shrinking neighborhood, gradually filling up its empty apartments and inhabiting its public spaces.

The movement of Turkish guest workers and their families into the neighborhood initiated two key developments in the settlement of Turkish immigrants into West German society: close proximity to and interaction with German residents on a local level, and the formation of a multigenerational Turkish community. As such, the neighborhood, both as a site and as a trope, has been a topic of academic investigation from scholars of various disciplines. While earlier studies focused on housing conditions and location (as discussed in Chapter 2), more recently scholars have shifted their attention to examining the use of immigrant

---

[2] A term used in the 1960s and 1970s for "socially disadvantaged."

neighborhoods to forge the exclusion and inclusion of its residents. Anthropologist Ayşe S. Çağlar investigates the use of the ghetto trope in German political culture as a way of discursively separating Turkish residents from broader German society. Categorizing Turkish Germans through an ethnically separate urban space, Çağlar argues, blinds the German public to the ways that Turkish-German residents construct their belonging in Berlin in ways that move past ethnicity.[3] Regarding inclusion, cultural geographer Patricia Ehrkamp explores how Turkish residents of Duisburg-Marxloh formed spaces of belonging within the context of their homes and neighborhoods. For Ehrkamp, consumption, both of goods in local stores as well as of media within the home, constitutes a significant tool employed by first- and second-generation Turkish residents to make their surroundings their own.[4] Although these studies are critical to understanding the role of discourse and transnational connections in forging (and denying) belonging, it is also important to take into account the historical context in which Turkish immigrant communities developed, including how the Cold War shaped both their physical settlement and their more abstract relationship to West German society. Examining the neighborhood in its historical context also allows us to see how the development of immigrant neighborhoods was not necessarily a defensive posture but rather a process of building new spaces that met the needs of both the first- and second-generations.[5] Finally, focusing on the neighborhood brings to light the local and place-specific ways that the Turkish immigrants and their children oriented themselves to German society and invested themselves within it.

In this chapter, I explore how Turkish immigrants and their children experienced daily life within their neighborhood, accommodated themselves to these new places, and, through their presence and actions,

---

[3] Ayşe S. Çağlar, "Constraining Metaphors and the Transnationalisation of Spaces in Berlin," *Journal of Ethnic and Migration Studies* 27, no. 4 (October 2001): 601–613.

[4] Patricia Ehrkamp, "Placing Identities: Transnational Practices and Local Attachments of Turkish Immigrants in Germany," *Journal of Ethnic and Migration Studies* 31, no. 5 (March 2005): 345–364.

[5] Joyce Marie Mushaben, *The Changing Faces of Citizenship: Integration and Mobilization Among Ethnic Minorities in Germany* (New York: Berghahn Books, 2008), 79. Here, Mushaben writes, "Marginalized in every sense, imported laborers responded by forming enclaves that sustained Turkish identity, necessary in case of an eventual return." Ethnic enclaves did serve to maintain immigrants' sense of Turkishness and to provide a feeling of home, but the contention that ethnic enclaves formed wholly as a defensive or protective measure is overstated. They also were spaces in which the first and second generations actively sought to make sense of and, to varying degrees, join the community around them, something that Mushaben herself demonstrates later when she writes about Turkish businesses (176–185).

changed them. The broader context of the Cold War, and more specifically the ways in which West Berlin was identified with and responded
to it, played a key role in both the physical development of the neighborhoods and the meanings and significance attached to those spaces.
In academic and public discourse, as well as in the memories of local
residents, neighborhood sites were seen as spaces of conflict and separation. Although this was certainly the case, the neighborhood also provided the setting for intercultural and intergenerational conversation and
collaboration that forged new spaces of belonging for the first and second
generations.

A Brief History of Wedding and Sprengelkiez

An examination of the development of spaces of belonging within the
neighborhood requires a thorough look at the daily experiences of Turkish immigrants and their children at the local level. To this end, I have
selected the neighborhood of Sprengelkiez as a lens through which to
explore those experiences in-depth while simultaneously drawing on previously conducted interviews and secondary literature that address these
themes in other locations. The district of Wedding, similar to Kreuzberg
and Neukölln, has a large and diverse population of *Mitbürger mit Migra-
tionshintergrund* (fellow residents with a migration background) who
came to settle there during the years of the *Gastarbeiter* program and
after. Yet Wedding has generally been overlooked by scholars and media
in favor of the more well-known "Little Istanbul" or the increasingly
popular (or notorious) Neukölln. With its underresearched, well-
established, and diverse population of Turkish and Turkish-German residents, Wedding serves as fertile ground on which to explore the experiences of Turkish immigrants.

Originally more of a village with gardens and stables on the outskirts of
Berlin, Wedding had by the mid-nineteenth century become a district
within the city, its garden houses replaced by five-story apartment buildings with one or two side buildings. The trade and industry centered
in Wedding brought in a working-class population, which in turn contributed to an increasingly left-leaning political milieu. By the 1920s, Wedding
had become a stronghold for the Social Democratic Party (SPD) as for the
newly formed Communist Party (KPD). Residents of "Red Wedding"
were thus generally not receptive to the rise of the National Socialists, who
rioted through the district after the Reichstag fire on February 27, 1933.

Wedding, and with it Sprengelkiez, experienced significant destruction
during the Second World War. The district saw heavy fighting in the last
days of the war, with Schulstrasse, a street just outside of Sprengelkiez,

serving as a front line for three days. By the end of the war, more than one-third of all apartments in the district were destroyed, approximately three and a half million cubic meters of rubble lay in the streets, and the population had shrunk to less than three-quarters of its prewar size.[6] Among the buildings destroyed by bombing were many of those surrounding Sparrplatz. Frau B., a longtime resident of the neighborhood, remembered the last bomb that fell in the neighborhood. She, her children, and other residents of her building had sought shelter in the basement during the raid. Thinking all was clear, a neighbor decided that she and her two children would return to their apartment. Frau B. had just left the basement with her own children to follow the neighbor when she heard a noise overhead, and raced back down into the shelter. The bomb crashed into the hall, taking out the entire staircase above the second stair. Those who had left the basement were stuck in their apartments until the fire department came by with a ladder to let them down.[7]

Although some aspects of neighborhood and district life resumed quickly after the end of the war, adequate living space remained an urgent need throughout the forties and fifties. In 1961, the East German government constructed the Berlin Wall along Wedding's eastern and southeastern borders with Prenzlauer Berg and Mitte, prompting many Germans to move out of the district. They left behind neighborhoods worn by time, war, and neglect, but their departure also opened up opportunities for guest workers and their families for affordable, if not desirable, housing. By the early 1960s, the city government had decided that, for districts such as Wedding and Kreuzberg, large-scale *Sanierung* (demolition and reconstruction) would address the need for adequate housing, change the districts' working-class image (and perhaps even composition), and, in the context of the growing Cold War, and turn the district into a "shop-window" of the West.[8] Those buildings included in the *Sanierung* plans were purchased by a few large companies who would work with the city to carry out the demolition and reconstruction. Many of the long-term residents moved to other parts of the city, allowing the corporations to rent out the vacated apartments in the interim before the *Sanierung* would take place. These apartments, which were available only temporarily, in poor condition, without their own toilets, and sometimes

---

[6] Bezirksamt Wedding von Berlin, eds., *Der Wedding im Wandel der Zeit* (Berlin: Bezirksamt Wedding, 1985), 17–35.

[7] Ursula Trüper, "6. Der Krieg," in "Die Leute vom Sparrplatz: Eine Ausstellung im Heimatmuseum Wedding, März 1995" (Unpublished manuscript, Mitte Museum, 1995), DLSA, MMA.

[8] Ursula Trüper, "7. Sanierung," in "Die Leute vom Sparrplatz: Eine Ausstellung im Heimatmuseum Wedding, März 1995," DLSA, MMA.

without hot water, were considered undesirable, and their rents were correspondingly low. The city's guest worker population, facing both financial restraints and discrimination in the housing market, therefore found these apartments accessible and affordable, and began to move into their neighborhoods, including Wedding's Sprengelkiez.[9]

A look at population statistics regarding Turkish residents in Wedding reveals how that community grew and changed in the years following the *Anwerbestopp* in 1974. The first three graphs demonstrate the change in composition of Wedding's Turkish population by gender and age. Figure 6A depicts those between birth and twenty, the majority of whom were born in West Germany or were brought there by their parents. The next graph, Figure 6B, charts the population change among twenty- to fifty-year-olds, the group most likely to have come to the FRG to work or to rejoin their spouses abroad. Figure 6C focuses on the population over fifty years of age. Members of this group generally migrated to West Germany as workers or spouses of workers, and, of the three, this one shows the most consistent growth over time. For those under the age of fifty, the graphs reveal a decrease in population in four years after the *Anwerbestopp*, ostensibly as some *Gastarbeiter* took advantage of financial incentives for return migration offered by the German government. The population continued to grow in the years after 1978, with a temporary dip around 1984. Although men generally outnumbered women, the male/female population gap narrowed over time, with the exception of those over fifty.

The final graph, Figure 6D, brings the three age groups together to display overall population changes from the *Anwerbestopp* to reunification. This figure highlights two realities that, together, both counter and explain local perceptions about the district's Turkish population. First, among some West German residents, there was a sense that in the 1980s there were suddenly large numbers of Turkish immigrants in their neighborhoods; however, although the overall numbers do reveal a growing population, that growth was gradual. Yet the compositional change may explain this view, as youth and those over fifty, whose numbers grew the most, were more likely to be visible in public spaces than their working relatives.

The Opportunities and Boundaries of Social Spaces

In many ways, the neighborhood served as an extension of the home for both the first and second generation. The early Turkish residents of

---

[9] Engin Günükutlu, interview by author, 9 May 2009, digital recording, Berlin.

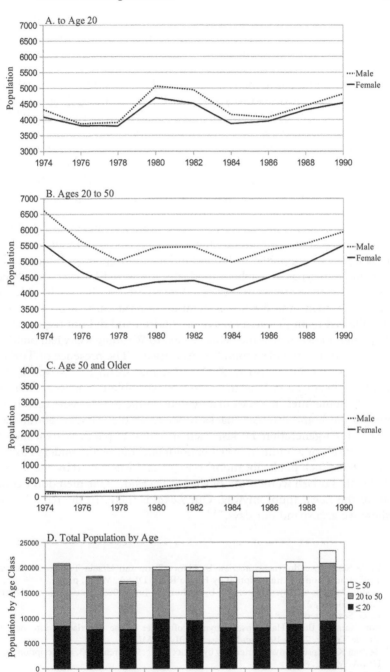

Figure 6. Turkish population in Berlin-Wedding, 1974–1990
Source: Statistical Reports compiled by the Statistisches Landesamt Berlin
from 1975 to 1991. (See Bibliography for full bibliographic references.)

Sprengelkiez may not have known many other people when they first moved to the neighborhood, but they soon settled into their new surroundings and made connections with their neighbors. Leyla Sezer's description of neighborhood life – that "everyone knew everyone" – echoes the sentiment of many longtime residents, and those who felt less well-acquainted with their neighbors at the time of their interview consistently referenced the closer ties they had held in years past.[10] For Sevim Özel, even now a trip to the store always includes seeing acquaintances, as "every few steps I meet someone, hello, hello."[11] Although the transition to life in West Germany (and specifically on Sparrplatz) was difficult for Sezer, "bit by bit we got used to it," she related. "So, if I'm away, everything's strange to me. Now if I come back again, this Sparrplatz, like my home..."[12]

Turkish residents turned their neighborhood into an extension of their homes through the formation of new social spaces, both in the neighborhood's preexisting public realm and in local, immigrant-run businesses. The different types of neighborhood sites employed for everyday socializing reflected a distinctly gendered form of socializing. In general, Turkish women from the first generation utilized outdoor public spaces that allowed them to watch over their children and did not require them to spend money, such as the benches next to Wedding's city hall building or those around the playground on Sparrplatz. The presence of Turkish women socializing on Sparrplatz led German residents as well as the media to begin describing the scene as resembling "an Anatolian village."[13] Sometimes, those women who had time to meet with each other outside the home brought snacks to share as they chatted about their days.[14] First-generation Turkish men also utilized public spaces, such as train stations or a fountain near Leopoldplatz, but by the mid-1970s and mid-1980s, such public locations were generally occupied by and associated with Turkish women. As Beyhan Kaya said, "Our men don't come out of the *Lokal* [pub] anyway. Our *Lokal* is there. In the park. That's where we also spend our days."[15]

[10] Leyla Sezer (pseudonym), interview by Hatice Renç and Ursula Trüper, 28 January 1993, translation and transcription by Hatice Renç, DLSA, MMA, p. 3.
[11] Sevim Özel (pseudonym), interview by author, 30 June 2009, transcription by Perrin Saylan, Berlin, 27.
[12] Leyla Sezer interview, 8.
[13] For example, Beate Hahn (pseudonym), cofounder of the Sparrladen, interview by Ursula Trüper, 7 July 1993, audiocassette, DLSA, MMA.
[14] Beyhan Kaya (pseudonym), interview by Hatice Renç, 9 March 1993, transcription, p. 6, DLSA, MMA., 8.
[15] Ibid., 8.

When Turkish entrepreneurs began opening businesses in the 1970s and 1980s, their cafés, bars, and restaurants not only provided the first generation with spaces of consumption where they could feel more confident that the food preparation adhered to certain dietary restrictions, they also presented a setting for the construction of new social spaces outside the home. In general, these new sites were utilized foremost by first-generation Turkish men. Whether having breakfast before their shift started at work or enjoying a leisurely glass of tea in the afternoon, Turkish men inhabited these places and used them to create primarily single-sex spaces for socializing.[16] In *Ethnische Kolonien: Entstehung, Funktion und Wandel am Beispiel türkischer Moscheen und Cafés*, sociologist Rauf Ceylan examines the ways these Turkish-owned cafés affected their patrons' perception of and integration into the host society. Using the Duisburg district of Hochfeld as a case study, Ceylan charts the development of the Turkish café scene from the opening of the first teahouse in 1975 through the following three decades. The study reveals not only the diversity and divisions within the Turkish community but also the ways that the cafés themselves furthered the isolation of that community within the host society.[17]

When the first Turkish-owned café opened in Duisburg-Hochfeld in 1975, it served as a space where Turkish men could use their free time to pursue their own interests and traditions apart from broader German society, which many found unwelcoming and discriminatory. The first café, Adem's Café, served as a local meeting point where Turks from a spectrum of political, ethnic, and religious affiliations socialized, but as the Turkish population grew, such cafés proliferated and began to reflect the internal divisions within that community.[18] Not only were Turkish men being further isolated from German society, Ceylan argued, but they were also self-segregating from others in the broader Turkish community.[19] This effect was particularly detrimental for unemployed customers, for whom the local café became a place of refuge or "flight" where they went to pass time and escape the four walls and responsibilities of the home and the judgment of the community.[20] The proliferation of Turkish-owned cafés narrowed these men's connections further, making it that much more difficult to find work if they were looking.

---

[16] Kemal Kurt and Erika Meyer, eds, ...*weil wir Türken sind/* ...*Türk oldugumuz için: Bilder und Texte von Türken/ Türklerin resim ve öyküleri* (Berlin: express-Edition, 1981), 41–42.
[17] Rauf Ceylan, *Ethnische Kolonien: Entstehung, Funktion und Wandel am Beispiel türkischer Moscheen und Cafes* (Wiesbaden: VS Verlag für Sozialwissenschaften, 2006).
[18] Ibid.,185–193.   [19] Ibid., 215–216.   [20] Ibid., 207–210.

In Sprengelkiez, the growth of the local Turkish population also gave rise to immigrant-run businesses designed to meet the social needs of the neighborhood's newer residents. Longtime German residents watched as some of the older, traditional *Kneipen* (pubs) gave way to establishments such as Gordon's,[21] the bar run by Eren Keskin, and Şafak, a café operated by Soner Polat.[22] These cafés served the Turkish and Turkish-German men in the neighborhood, although the relatively small size of Sprengelkiez meant cafés were fewer in number than in Duisburg-Hochfeld and appeared to have less of a homogenizing effect on their clientele. Although not as numerous, these teahouses were highly recognizable and well known. In good weather, Şafak's patrons moved their conversations and backgammon games to the sidewalks in front of the café located across from Sparrplatz, making them even more visible to their neighbors. In this way, as with the Turkish women sitting around the playground at Sparrplatz, first-generation men and the places they inhabited in the neighborhood began to categorize and define one another. Although local cafés served as separate social spaces, their location served to make Turkish men a more visible part of their local environment.

Like their parents, the second generation also used the neighborhood as a forum to create independent social spaces that pushed the boundaries set for them within the context of the home. For the second generation in particular, the neighborhood was a site of identity construction and of finding out how they understood themselves in the context of the sometimes conflicting expectations of home and society. Much socializing with friends took place at each other's apartments, but young Turkish Germans also met up in various places throughout the neighborhood, including in local parks, in front of their schools, on Sparrplatz, or simply on street corners.[23] Like many teenagers, they went to the movies, played sports, and talked about school, family, romantic relationships, and the future. Yet, as in the home, gendered expectations of acceptable behavior

---

[21] The name of the *Kneipe* "Gordon's" was later changed to "Pamukkale."

[22] See, for example, Christine Lange, Viola Werner, and Thomas Hofmann (pseudonyms), interview by Ursula Trüper, 27 July 1994, audiocassette, DLSA, MMA; Eren Keskin (pseudonym), "Wirt einer Kneipe am Sparrplatz", interview with Ursula Trüper, audiocassette, side A, DLSA, MMA, Berlin, 1993; and Soner Polat (pseudonym), interview by Ursula Trüper and Kemal Kurt, 18 June 1993, transcription, DLSA, MMA.

[23] Filiz Güler, email to author, 4 June 2009; Emre and Erkan (pseudonyms), interview by Ursula Trüper, 7 December 1993, audiocassette, DLSA, MMA; Timur (pseudonym), interview by Ursula Trüper, 22 June 1993, audiocassette, DLSA, MMA; Filiz Güler (pseudonym), interview by author, 27 May 2009, transcription by Perrin Saylan, Berlin, 3.

exerted strong influence over how second-generation youth experienced and operated within these different spaces.

Girls and young women felt the effects of this social control most acutely, blaming the large Turkish community in their neighborhood for their lack of freedom. "If we're out till 6:00pm," Lale, the teenage daughter of Turkish immigrants, complained, the neighbors "say 'why are you out, go home', and such things. I think that's way more strict [than the Germans]!"[24] Her neighbor Aylin agreed. People in her neighborhood, she explained, were very concerned about appearances, and it was important to them that a young woman be a virgin. Although she was angry about the ways Turks ran each other down, Aylin qualified her explanation of the reasons for this kind of social surveillance. "How should I say this: the people here are actually quite old-fashioned," Aylin explained. "Of course, there are also people who are very modern now, and such, but many people here are totally old-fashioned. They think old-fashioned and, yeah, because of that they worsen all relationships." For Aylin, then, the social surveillance and control she experienced was not the manifestation of culture or tradition but rather outdated values and thinking. Her mother trusted her, she related, and did not mind if Aylin chatted on the street with a "guy," but when the reports of her daughter's behavior got back to her parents, it hurt their pride.[25]

Whatever prompted their Turkish neighbors, the result of the social policing was clear: the spaces young women created and inhabited in the neighborhood became increasingly constricted as they transitioned from childhood to adulthood. Afraid of drawing the attention of their neighbors, young women regulated their behavior in public, taking care to not be seen in situations that could be perceived as inappropriate. Even girls with relatively lenient parents were affected by these social restrictions. Filiz Güler, after talking about the ways religious observance showed up in her primary school, explained, "One is raised with it, I mean, I always paid attention to it, too, that I wasn't seen on the street if I was talking with a guy and like I already said, my parents probably wouldn't have had anything against that."[26] Other young women spoke repeatedly of wanting to feel free; to be able to take part in activities that German girls their age did, such as dancing or swimming; or to simply "go out" without being watched, questioned, and reported on.[27] The social restriction

---

[24] Lale (pseudonym), interview by Ursula Trüper, transcription, 28 May and 4 June 199, DLSA, MMA, 5.

[25] Aylin (pseudonym), interview and transcription by Ursula Trüper, 22 December 1992, DLSA, MMA, 2–3.

[26] Güler interview, 17.

[27] For example, Lale interview, 6; Kurt and Meyer, eds., ... weil wir Türken sind, 68–69.

of these spaces constantly reminded young Turkish-German women that they were held to a different standard than their German classmates and friends. At the same time, it made belonging to the neighborhood's Turkish community seem to come at the price of personal freedom.[28] For young Turkish-German women, the social spaces they created in the neighborhood allowed them a measured amount of autonomy from the home, but it came with strict boundaries whose trespass came with distinct costs.

While young Turkish-German men often inhabited the same neighborhood sites and participated in similar activities as young women, the network of social control was not as concerned with their activities and therefore exerted less power on their social spaces. This did not mean, however, that young men were free from the influence of negative gender expectations and stereotypes. Family as well as Turkish neighbors pressured these youth to keep their behavior within acceptable bounds and to stay out of "trouble," and some of the more hostile German neighbors cast them in the role of troublemaker regardless of their conduct.[29] In addition, such negative gender stereotypes limited young men's access to structured social spaces. Organizers of neighborhood activities curtailed these youths' participation out of concern over violence, a phenomenon that will be discussed later in this chapter. For some young men, struggling in school and with little interest in what they saw in their future for work, membership in their neighborhood's or district's gang meant belonging to a group of people and a place in which they could gain and exercise power. Turkish street gangs served as a significant space of belonging for many young men in West Berlin, forging a connection between national (Turkish) and locally based identities. These gangs began to emerge in West Berlin in the late 1970s, but it was not until

---

[28] In the context of reunified Germany, Katherine Ewing has argued that cinematic and social work discourses have produced a stereotype of Turkish rural culture that, rooted in Islam, dictates the subjugation of women by repressive men. These discourses, she contends, have to an extent been internalized by Turkish Germans and influenced their understanding of their own identities and life trajectories. See Katherine Pratt Ewing, *Stolen Honor: Stigmatizing Muslim Men in Berlin* (Stanford: Stanford University Press, 2008), 85–93. Although compelling for the postreunification case, it fits less well in the FRG in the 1970s, when the social work discourse focused more on social and economic factors for women's emancipation, or better, perhaps in the 1980s, when the focus shifted to oversimplified conceptions of "cultural difference." See Rita Chin, *The Guest Worker Question in Postwar Germany* (Cambridge, UK: Cambridge University Press, 2007), 160–165.

[29] Margaret Fischer (pseudonym), interview by author, 20 May 2009, transcription by Perrin Saylan, Berlin.

the late 1980s and early 1990s that they became more widely prevalent.[30] Their development and role as a space of belonging will be explored more thoroughly in the Chapter 6, which deals with Turkish-German spaces in postreunification Berlin.

A Changing Neighborhood

Although it is clear that the home and neighborhood played a significant role in the formation of an interconnected Turkish community and spaces of belonging (and exclusion) within that community, the extent to which these settings and spaces both enabled and were used to promote inter-cultural relationships is more ambiguous. Living in close proximity gave German and Turkish residents regular opportunities to interact, and some used these circumstances to get to know their new neighbors. When Sezer declared that around Sparrplatz, "everyone knows everyone," she did not exclude her German neighbors from that relationship. Instead, she specifically referenced those connections: "Turks, Germans, they know us all, we know them, too. If we come out, we know everybody. The Germans know Turks, Turks know Germans."[31] Kaya, who changed apartments multiple times before she and her family settled into Spren-gelkiez, recalled having very positive interactions with her German neigh-bors over the years. She had particularly fond memories of one of her landlords, whom she called "Dad." During her pregnancy, he would always ask after her health and give her fresh fruit from his garden, including, she fondly remembered, ten wonderful smelling quinces.[32]

Yet such positive interactions seem not to have led to close interper-sonal relationships among German residents and the first generation. As Sezer's words illustrate, there was still in the early 1990s a distinct sense of "us" and "them," which, as we will see later in this chapter, was present among German residents as well. Some Turkish residents attrib-uted this sense of separation from Germans and West German society as evidence of *Ausländerfeindlichkeit* (xenophobia). Although the Turkish residents of Sprengelkiez who gave interviews did not point to specific examples of their German neighbors' *Ausländerfeindlichkeit*, most shared stories of experiencing discrimination, and a few expressed concern about their own safety and the safety of their children. In her 1993 inter-view, Demir blamed the conflict between Germans and Turks, which she saw as intensifying in recent years, wholly on the Germans. She went so

---

[30] Joachim Gästel, "Black Panthers, Fighters und Türkiye Boys," "Jugendcliquen im Wed-ding: Von den Wilden Cliquen zu Banden und Fighters" Ausstellung (JWA), MMA.
[31] Leyla Sezer interview, 8   [32] Kaya interview, 13–14.

far to declare that "every day we're near death," perhaps reflecting on the neo-Nazi arson attack only a few months prior on two houses in Mölln that resulted in the death of two Turkish girls and a fifty-one-year-old woman.[33] Other first-generation Turkish immigrants have been more circumspect, conceding that the fault for any *Gegeneinander* (conflict) could be found on both sides.[34] Regardless of to whom blame was assigned, the experience of discrimination and fear of violence served as a wedge between German and Turkish residents, fostering a sense of separateness even as they carried out their daily lives side by side.

The reactions of German residents to the settlement of Turkish immigrants and their children also reflect an acknowledgment of separateness. This distinction between the German and Turkish residents began with the first Turkish families who moved into the neighborhood, but it grew markedly more pronounced as the number of Turkish residents increased over the years. Interestingly, while Turkish residents have lived in Sprengelkiez since the mid- to late 1960s, many German residents date their presence in the neighborhood to the early 1980s. "We say in the neighborhood that it happened pretty abruptly over three years ... over three, four years," related Klaus Wolfermann, resident of Sprengelkiez since the late 1960s. Wolfermann recalled one of his neighbors remarking at the time that "one day I looked out the window, everything is Turkish."[35]

Often, the growing presence of Turkish neighbors was connected directly to those social spaces they constructed within the landscape of the neighborhood, such as the cafés discussed earlier. Some met this development with at least tacit acceptance. When asked in an interview about *Zusammenleben* (living together) in the Kiez, Peter Krause, who moved to an apartment on Sparrplatz in 1981, first described how he helped a Turkish family in his building when their son was having trouble in school. After this, he mentioned the local Turkish bar and the presence of Turks in public places.[36] Krause did not seem particularly concerned about the appearance of these "Turkish" spaces or residents. Similarly, Anja Vogel referenced direct interaction she had with her

---

[33] Azra Demir (pseudonym), interview by Hatıce Renç, 9 March 1993, translation and transcription by Hatıce Renç, DLSA, MMA, Berlin, 4.

[34] For example, "In Uhlenhorst kennt mich jeder: Der Kaufmann Erdem Dilşen," in Michael Richter, ed., *Gekommen und Geblieben: Deutsch-türkische Lebensgeschichten* (Hamburg: Edition Körber Stiftung, 2003), 115.

[35] Klaus Wolfermann, interview by author, 10 June 2009, transcription by Perrin Saylan, Berlin, 11.

[36] Peter Krause (pseudonym), interview by Ursula Trüper, 21 July 1993, audiocassette, DLSA, MMA.

Turkish neighbors, specifically how Turkish mothers brought their babies to her for advice once they learned she was a nurse. Vogel, however, went a step further than Krause and sought to distinguish and defend "our Turks" from the troubles other Germans in the neighborhood had with Turks. The Turks who cause trouble, she maintained, are not "our Turks"; they come in from outside. She continued by explaining that the Turks who grew up on Sparrplatz and went to school with her daughter were, at the time of the interview, in their twenties and thirties and still friends with each other. They are not foreigners, she insisted, they have lived in the neighborhood their whole lives.[37]

Not all German residents, however, greeted their new neighbors or the changes they made in the neighborhood with such acceptance or even ambivalence. Some longtime German residents used the language of nostalgia to express their unhappiness, decrying the loss of "German" spaces and the proliferation of "Turkish" or "foreign" spaces in the neighborhood. Such was the case during a 1994 joint interview with a woman who had lived on Sparrplatz since before the Second World War and a man who had grown up there since his birth in 1965. The two discussed the various small businesses – *Kneipen*, a drug store, a soap shop – that had disappeared from the neighborhood and the Turkish cafés and *Kneipen* that took their place, making it clear that they considered the developments unsatisfactory.[38] In addition, the interviewees framed the transition in terms of cause and effect, without taking into account the impact that larger chain stores moving into the neighborhood had on these small German-run businesses, as other residents had done.[39]

In other cases, German residents were more blatant in laying blame at the feet of their *ausländische Mitbürger* (foreign fellow citizen) for the decline of the quality of neighborhood life. Margaret Fischer first moved to Sprengelkiez in the mid-1970s, drawn by the opportunity to have a larger apartment for herself, her husband, and their four children. There was a strong sense of community in the neighborhood when she first moved in, she recalled. Neighbors knew, socialized with, and cared for each other; the public spaces were clean and safe. "Yeah, and here on Sparrstrasse then, more and more *ausländische Mitbürger* moved in. I don't want to say anything else, you know?" Fischer concluded with a short laugh.[40] She attributed each negative development in the

---

[37] Anja Vogel (pseudonym), interview by Ursula Trüper, 29 June 1993, audiocassette, DLSA, MMA.

[38] Lange, Werner, and Hofmann interview.

[39] For example, see Wolfermann interview, 26–27.   [40] Fischer interview, 1.

neighborhood – fighting on the playground, the closure of German-owned businesses, litter in common spaces – to its growing foreign population.[41] Although Turkish families were already living in Sprengelkiez when Fischer and her family first moved there, in her memory there was a clear transition from the nearly idyllic German community to the apathetic, unfriendly foreigner-majority neighborhood. Her personal interactions with her Turkish neighbors were characterized mainly by their indifference and animosity, with the notable exception of a young school friend of her son who would visit their house and enjoy meals containing pork with them.[42] For Fischer, the creation of Turkish spaces constituted a process of alienation from the neighborhood she had valued and enjoyed, and signaled the Turkish residents' unwillingness to integrate into their immediate environment and German society more broadly.

Media coverage of West Berlin's growing immigrant population reflected German residents' concerns about the ability and willingness of their Turkish neighbors to integrate into West German society. Newspapers across the country were particularly interested in the situation in West Berlin and, starting in the early 1970s, published numerous articles concerning the size of the Turkish population, the reactions of German residents, and the efforts of the Berliner Senate to deal with the "problem" of foreigners. It is important to bear in mind the economic problems facing the Federal Republic at the time, as well as how West Berlin's particular geography exacerbated these conditions. The "economic miracle" that had fueled West Germany's recovery and brought guest workers in by the thousands in the 1950s and 1960s was, by the early 1970s, a thing of the past. As discussed in Chapter 1, West German officials had already been concerned with the weakening economy and rising unemployment by the time the oil crisis provided a useful cover for halting the guest worker program. The economic downturn became particularly sharp in West Berlin, which, given its geographic and political challenges, had never been an especially attractive location for businesses, many of which had to be wooed into settling in the city with government subsidies. West Berlin, then, reflected the broader country's concerns about their own economic and social conditions.

The focus on West Berlin also brings to our attention the importance of the city's position in the broader Cold War. When the division of Berlin prompted the Western Allies to invest in and promote West Berlin as an exemplar of Western democracy, progress, and capitalism, the

---

[41] Ibid., 1, 7, 5.   [42] Ibid., 5.

city's identity became defined in large part by the Cold War context and its own symbolic significance. As "a capital city of the free Western world," West Berlin was not only a German city but also an international one.[43] President John F. Kennedy's identification with Berliners in his famous speech during his visit to the city in 1963 exemplifies the significance of Cold War Berlin; symbolically, the fate of its citizens and the fate of the West were linked. For West Germans and the rest of the Western world, West Berlin was important because of where it was and what it stood for. And for West Berliners, that internationally recognized symbolic identity informed how they saw their own city and themselves.[44]

During the 1970s, and then especially in the 1980s, fissures and conflicts within West Berlin began to challenge its image as a city defined by its international symbolism and relationships. For many in West Germany, the influx and settlement of thousands of guest workers and their families, particularly those from Turkey, constituted a direct threat to the city's identity. Districts bordering the Wall, and particularly Kreuzberg, drew the sharp and increasing attention of West German politicians, the public, and the media. In a 1973 article in *Spiegel* entitled "The Turks Are Coming – Save Yourself, if You Can," the author emphasizes the shift in identity from "true Kreuzberg" to a place where "highly visible customers from the Orient"[45] frequent the Turkish-operated businesses that make up the landscape. Statistics call attention to the large numbers of Turkish in relation to German residents, and the writer compares the previous year's increase of the "Turkish colony" to the size of a brigade.[46] This "colony," the reporter contends, has developed into a "ghetto" not unlike New York's Harlem.

Concerns about the impact of immigrants on the city, however, continued to make headlines throughout the 1970s and into the 1980s as city officials sought to stem the tide and influence of what some termed the "torrent of foreigners" (*Ausländerstrom*). In 1975, the city government implemented a ban (*Zuzugssperre*) that restricted foreigners from moving into certain parts of the city considered to have reached their capacity

[43] "In Berlin bummeln" in "Deutscher Text für Broschüre zum Anwerben von Arbeitskräften aus Griechenland und der Türkei," p. 2, Rundschreiben zur Beschäftigung von Ausländischen Arbeitnehmern, Sig. 10585–1, Schlüssel 04610585, SCA. Although the document is not dated, the content, language, and placement in the file suggest publication in the mid-1960s.
[44] See Emily Pugh, *Architecture, Politics, and Identity in Divided Berlin* (Pittsburgh: University of Pittsburgh Press, 2014), 62–105.
[45] In German, "unübersehbar Kundschaft aus dem Morgenland."
[46] "Die Türken kommen – rette sich, wer kann," *Der Spiegel*, Nr. 31/1973, p. 24.

for absorbing immigrants. In November 1981, Senator of the Interior Heinrich Lummer (CDU) issued an order restricting teenaged Turks from joining their families already living in West Berlin. A reporter from *Die Welt* who covered the decision cited worrying statistics related to immigration and births as well as fears of criminality and left extremism among the city's Turkish population. Both the CDU and the SPD, the reporter affirmed, agreed that stopping the growth of Turkish ghettos in the German city was a priority.[47] An article published a week later in the *Rheinischer Merkur* also identified areas of West Berlin densely populated by Turkish immigrants as slums, ghettos, and colonies. "Integration is not occurring," the reporter asserted. With Turkish families overrunning German neighborhoods and Turkish children flooding German schools, was Berlin even "still a German city?"[48]

A 1981 piece in the *Frankfurter Allgemeine Zeitung* with the headline "The Borders of Berlin's Integrative Ability" posed a similar question.[49] The article opens by using statistics to detail the significant demographic shifts experienced by West Berlin since the mid-1960s; nearly 400,000 Germans had left the city and more than 240,000 "foreigners" had moved in, making up 12 percent of the city's population. Turkish immigrants – numbered at 120,000 – represented a "disproportionate" number of that group.[50] The writer then proceeds to discuss the political debates about how to deal with this growing foreign population, including efforts to change regulations in a way that would prevent the immigration and residency of unemployed foreigners. The city itself, the writer contends, was becoming "overly full" of foreigners in general, and Turks more specifically. To illustrate this point, the reporter singles out Kreuzberg, saying that two-thirds of that district's residents were Turks. In addition, foreign children were taking up more and more space in Kreuzberg's primary schools. The writer concludes his article by pointing out that of those foreigners eligible to apply for citizenship, very few showed interest in this opportunity.[51] The "foreigner problem," politicians and the media agreed, was in no small part to blame for

---

[47] Hans R. Karutz, "Ausländerstrom schwillt immer bedrohlicher an," *Die Welt*, 28 November 1981, 5.

[48] Jürgen Engert, "Ist Berlin noch eine deutsche Stadt?" *Rheinischer Merkur*, 4 December 1981, 3.

[49] Hans Haibach, "Die Grenzen der Integrationskraft Berlins," *Frankfurter Allgemeine Zeitung*, 27 November 1981, Bundespresseamt Archive (BPA), Berlin, accessed 7 April 2009.

[50] Ibid.

[51] Ibid. The writer does not detail the long, difficult process of naturalization, however.

"the threatening collapse of the city culture" and damaged the identity of West Berlin.[52]

The use of the ghetto metaphor and the fears expressed about the potential (or impending) loss of Berlin's German identity reflect two concurrent situations: (1) West Germany's struggle to come to terms with the long-term consequences of the guest worker program and imagine the shape of a new multicultural society and (2) West Berlin's Cold War identity. As Çağlar has argued for reunified Germany, use of the ghetto metaphor stigmatized Turks and Turkish Germans based on ethnicity and confined them to particular areas of the city. Constraining immigrants and their activities within the discourse in the 1970s and early 1980s to limited areas thus oversimplified the ways the first and second generations had already become an established and interwoven part of the city's dynamics. Yet, although in reunified Berlin the ghetto discourse was part of a broader effort to create "a controlled and domesticated type of cultural diversity," two decades earlier West German politicians were more concerned about maintaining West Berlin's German identity – one directly connected to its relationship to the Cold War – than crafting a new, multicultural society.[53]

As we have already seen, the West German state had been concerned about leftist extremism among guest workers and had published a newspaper specifically for the *Gastarbeiter* in large part to "immunize" them against the threat of communism.[54] The media in the 1970s and 1980s focused more often on the "over-foreignization" of districts than communist infiltration among Turkish immigrants,[55] yet behind the constant references to the aging German Berliner population, the high birth rates in immigrant communities, and the rising unemployment rates and supposed criminality of Turkish youth was an underlying message of instability and uncertainty. If West Berlin were not a stable, Western

---

[52] Friedhelm Kemna, "Das neue Berlin-Gefühl: Chancen für den Aufstieg mit Weizäcker," *Die Welt*, 27 May 1982, 9. See also Annegret Schröder, "Ausländerproblem: Berlin ist viertgrösste Türkenstadt der Welt," *Handelsblatt*, 30 November 1981, BPA, accessed 7 April 2009; Heinz Kühn, "Wenn wir erst einmal die Türken los sind...," *Vorwärts*, 1 April 1982, BPA, accessed 7 April 2009; and Liselotte Müller, "Türken von Berlin wollen keine Deutschen werden," *Hannoverische Allgemeine*, 10 July 1982, BPA, accessed 7 April 2009.

[53] Çağlar, "Constraining Metaphors and the Transnationalisation of Spaces in Berlin," 605.

[54] See Chapter 1. See also Brian J. K. Miller, "Reshaping the Turkish Nation-State: The Turkish-German Guest Working Program and Planned Development, 1961–1985," (PhD dissertation, University of Iowa, Iowa City, 2015), 147–152.

[55] For an article that expresses both fears, see Hans R. Karutz, "Ausländerstrom schwillt immer bedrohlicher an," *Die Welt*, 28 November 1981, 5.

democracy with the functional attendant institutions (effective government and schools, for example), what would it be?[56] In order for West Berlin to maintain its postwar identity, "Berlin," Interior Minister Heinrich Lummer stated bluntly in a 1982 *Rheinische Post* article, "must stay German."[57] Yet population trends suggested the once-capital city was becoming less and less German. The growth of immigrant communities had no corresponding development among native Germans. Starting in 1970, fewer young West Germans moved to West Berlin than moved from it. By the mid-1970s, nearly a quarter of its population was over sixty-five years old, and it had twice the pensioners of any other West German city. Even into the late 1980s, fifteen thousand more people left West Berlin than were enticed to settle in it.[58]

For West Berlin to stay German, it was essential that immigrants become German. This emerged in the media as the second goal of governmental actions concerning the city's foreign population. If too many foreigners concentrated in a particular district, it was argued, it would become increasingly difficult for them to "integrate" into German society. It would create a "cultural distance" between German "natives" and the new arrivals, as well as facilitate the growth of ethnic enclaves in German cities.[59] Although references to emerging ethnic "ghettos" suggest a dark connection to the Jewish ghettos of the Nazi past, politicians, journalists, and scholars seemed more concerned about the potential for the development of US-style poverty-stricken ethnic neighborhoods in German cities. At this point, two separate conversations in West German political discourse merged in the press: (1) challenges to the successful integration (still relatively undefined) of foreign residents and (2) the persistently poor living conditions of lower-class populations in cities. While *Sanierung* programs had already highlighted that foreign families often lived in substandard conditions,[60] now the national press

---

[56] One newspaper article answered the question with its headline: "Foreign Problem: Berlin Is the Fourth Largest Turkish City in the World," Annegret Schröder, "Ausländerproblem: Berlin ist viertgrösste Türkenstadt der Welt," *Handelsblatt*, 30 November 1981, BPA, accessed 7 April 2009.

[57] Stadach, "Berlin muß deutsch bleiben."

[58] Alexandra Richie, *Faust's Metropolis: A History of Berlin* (New York: Carroll & Graf Publishers, Inc., 1998), 776–777.

[59] "Viele Berliner Türken haben Heimweh," *Süddeutsche Zeitung*, 18 May 1983, BPA, accessed 7 April 2009.

[60] See "Sanierungsskandal im Wedding: Sparstrasse [sic] 24 droht Zwangsräumung," *die tageszeitung*, 9 February 1983, Presse Inhalte: Sozial – Spi W, MMA; "Sparrstrasse 24: Mietern drohnt Zwangsräumung," *Berliner Morgenpost*, 10 February 1982, Presse Inhalte: Sozial – Spi W, MMA.

connected those living conditions with foreign residents' ability to integrate into both their immediate surroundings and German society.[61] The importance of immigrants' everyday experiences in the home and neighborhood assumed a central role in the debate over integration.

In Sprengelkiez, however, the experience of the *Sanierung* opened up an intercultural space for German and Turkish residents to work together toward a common goal. Housing in working-class neighborhoods throughout the city – especially in the districts of Wedding and Kreuzberg – had become run-down through a combination of war damage, neglect, and general wear and tear. The city began to address the situation through large- and small-scale *Sanierung* programs beginning in the 1950s and 1960s. Two distinct motivations drove the citywide project. The first stemmed from a belief held since the early nineteenth century in the political use of urban planning to shape a more socially balanced, healthy populace. For postwar West Berlin, city planners considered *Sanierung* as part of a larger project of "rehabilitating the moral character of West German society within the family/domestic sphere."[62] The second motivation drew from the city's immediate political and geographic context: if West Berlin was to be "capital city of the free Western world," it would have to do something about the crumbling tenement buildings that could not bear up this image. In the 1960s and early 1970s, city planners focused their efforts on outlying districts, and pursued large-scale projects such as Gropiusstadt in Neukölln and Märkisches Viertel in Reineckendorf.[63] As city planners turned their attention to the inner districts, particularly Kreuzberg and Wedding, they met with significant resistance from district residents, who protested vehemently (and sometimes violently) against the city's plans and methods. In the late 1970s and early 1980s, neighborhood activism in Kreuzberg especially took on a political bent that used the issue of housing to criticize not only the city government but also the West German state for its alliance with the United States and what protestors considered the FRG's capitalist and militarist character.[64]

---

[61] "Viele Berliner Türken haben Heimweh"; "Beteiligungsmodelle können den Ausweg weisen," *Frankfurter Rundschau*, 17 July 1985, BPA, accessed 7 April 2009.

[62] Carla Elizabeth MacDougall, "Cold War Capital: Contested Urbanity in West Berlin, 1963–1989," (PhD dissertation, Rutgers, The State University of New Jersey, New Brunswick, 2011), 66. See also Stephan Lanz, "Inclusion and Segregation in Berlin, the 'Social City,'" in Jeffry M. Diefendorf and Janet Ward, eds., *Transnationalism and the German City* (New York: Palgrave MacMillan, 2014), 55–71.

[63] Märkisches Viertel was built from 1964 to 1974 in Wittenau, but in 1999 Wittenau became part of the district of Reineckendorf.

[64] For a fascinating discussion of the connections between West Berlin urban planning, local activism, and the Cold War context, see MacDougall, "Cold War Capital."

By the late 1970s and early 1980s, the city's attention also had reached Wedding's Sprengelkiez, and, although the trend of *Kahlschlagsanierung* (complete demolition and reconstruction) had given way to smaller-scale projects, the initial plans called for the complete demolition of multiple tenanted apartment buildings, including several around Sparrplatz. Klaus Wolfermann, who had at this point been living on Sparrplatz for more than a decade, found out through a friend at the *Bausenat* about the city's plans for the demolition of his apartment building. Wolfermann's mother, who owned the building, had applied for funds to upgrade the windows. When the application reached the friend's desk, his supervisors approved the renovation for the front building but not for the *Hinterhaus*, which was "not to be maintained in the long run." The friend passed this information on to Wolfermann, who wrote a letter to the city requesting further information but received no answer. And then suddenly, Wolfermann remembers, there was preparation for the *Sanierung*.[65] Wolfermann, on staff at a local university and active in the antinuclear power movement, was highly dissatisfied with both the city's intentions for his neighborhood and their handling of the matter, and began to meet with tenants of his building, who decided collectively to challenge the city's plans. The population in Sprengelkiez, and particularly around Sparrplatz, had been undergoing significant structural changes in terms of age and ethnic makeup. Younger German families had been moving out of the neighborhood for years. In their place, German university students and Turkish *Gastarbeiter* had moved in, attracted by the low rents and neighborhood amenities. A number of the German students living in Sparrstrasse 21 formed a *Wohnhausgemeinschaft* (tenants' cooperative), working together to improve the condition of their common home. When the city's *Sanierung* plans threatened to displace them, they joined Wolfermann's effort.

While the campaign against *Sanierung* in Kreuzberg was characterized by public demonstrations and house occupation, the residents of Sprengelkiez opted for a less dramatic approach. The group of resident activists, called the Mieter-Initiative-Sparrplatz (Tenants' Initiative), wrote letters to city officials, politicians, and local media. They held information sessions for their neighbors and met with representatives from the various offices involved in the *Sanierung*. Their agitation and refusal to quietly accept the city's plans prompted the creation of a new office to act as liaison between the residents and the city in matters regarding the social implications of local infrastructure: the Büro für stadtteilnahe

---

[65] Wolfermann interview, 18.

Sozialplannung (The Office for District-Level Social Planning, BfsS). Although the BfsS was a branch of the city government, its workers saw themselves as advocates for the neighborhood's residents, and they met with the local activists to find a solution that would address the neighborhood's needs and concerns.

The inclusion and participation of Sprengelkiez's Turkish residents was a critical aspect of activities of the both the Mieter-Initiative and the BfsS. "We were always open to the Turks ... Germans, Turks, we only spoke of residents," said Wolfermann. "Yes, we wanted to achieve a better situation for the residents ..., we couldn't care less, which nationality they were."[66] While Wolfermann remembers little friction or suspicion between the two groups, Zafer Turan, then the BfsS representative, saw the need to establish trust with the Turkish residents. When he showed up as a Turkish-speaking representative of the BfsS to talk with them about an alternate plan for the *Sanierung*, Turan recalled, it took time for the Turkish residents to move past their skepticism.[67] Flyers announcing community meetings and containing updates related to the *Sanierung* were published in German and Turkish, including one that invited all those interested to attend the monthly meetings held at Wolfermann's apartment.[68]

The importance of Turkish residents' participation was not merely symbolic. By the early 1980s, first-generation Turkish immigrants and their children made up a significant segment of Sprengelkiez's population. As residents of apartment buildings around Sparrplatz, Turks were disproportionately affected by the city's plans for renovation. Part of these plans included eviction from those buildings slated for demolition, a situation highlighted in local press coverage regarding the *Sanierung*.[69] Indeed, some saw the city's plans for districtwide *Sanierung* as part of an effort by politicians to diminish the number of foreigners living in Wedding, whom they assumed would be easy to evict from their apartments in neighborhoods planned for demolition and reconstruction.[70] The BfsS, however, saw resident-supported renovation and modernization as a way to promote the breakdown of segregation in the neighborhood,

---

[66] Ibid., 18.

[67] Zafer Turan (pseudonym), interview by Ursula Trüper, 11 October 1993, audiocassette, DLSA, MMA.

[68] Mieter-Initiative-Sparrplatz, "Stadterneuerung: Untersuchungsbereich Sparrplatz," Der Senator für Bau- und Wohnungswesen, April 1981, Presse Inhalte: Sozial – Spi W, MMA.

[69] See "Sanierungsskandal im Wedding," *taz*, 9 February 1983; "Sparrstrasse 24," *Berliner Morgenpost*, 10 February 1982.

[70] Turan interview, 11 October 1993.

specifically separation based on age and nationality.[71] Eventually, the city, the BfsS, and the residents of Sparrplatz came to a satisfactory compromise: in general, the *Vorderhäuser* (front buildings) and *Seitenflügel* (side wings) would be renovated, including the modernization of plumbing, whereas the second *Hinterhäuser*, which were in poor condition and received little natural light, would be demolished.[72] In addition, the community organization and the BfsS continued to work on developing the neighborhood to meet the needs of its residents, such as improving the playground and social spaces on Sparrplatz itself.

The first generation's participation in the neighborhood activism that convinced the city to alter its renovation plans demonstrates the active process of space-making Turkish immigrants undertook to make a home for themselves and, consequently, the reciprocal nature of integration at the local level. Turkish residents had become a part of the neighborhood, and the German instigators of the Mieter-Initiative, by including them in the community effort, acknowledged both their right and responsibility as neighbors to take action and ensure the best possible solution for their common home. Confronted with this united and persistent front, city officials changed their plans, and Sprengelkiez itself was physically affected as a result.

The Turkish residents of Sprengelkiez were not lone examples of immigrant activism in West Berlin during the 1970s and 1980s. Many Turkish immigrants – guest workers, students, and refugees – had been active in ethnic organizations that ran the ideological and cultural spectrum from left-wing internationalists to the extreme-right Gray Wolves to hometown-based sports clubs.[73] Scholarship on immigrant organizations during the 1980s has pointed to the fact that foreigners had higher rates of participation in associational life than Germans,[74] arguing that such participation helped immigrants as collectives make connections that promoted their knowledge of German institutions and wield a certain

---

[71] *Büro für stadtteilnahe Sozialplanung, Vorbereitende Untersuchungen Berlin-Wedding: Untersuchungsabschnitt C, Neue Hochstraße – Sparrplatz* (West Berlin: Der Senator für Bau- und Wohnungswesen, 1983), 71.

[72] Günükutlu interview.

[73] Alexander Clarkson discusses several of these types of organizations within the context of West Berlin in "Circling the Wagons: Immigration and the Battle for Space in Berlin," in Leila Simona Talani, Alexander Clarkson, and Ramon Pacheco Pardo, eds., *Dirty Cities: Towards a Political Economy of the Underground in Global Cities* (New York: Palgrave Macmillan, 2013), 110–134.

[74] Ertekin Özcan, *Türkische Immigrantenorganisationen in der Bundesrepublik Deutschland: Die Entwicklung politischer Organisationen unter türkischen Arbeitsimmigranten in der Bundesrepublik Deutschland und Berlin West* (West Berlin: Hitit Verlag, 1989), 325–326; see also Mushaben, *The Changing Faces of Citizenship*, 53.

amount of power with those institutions. Alexander Clarkson argued that immigrant activists made such an impact at the highest levels of government and has demonstrated how homeland-oriented activism among immigrants in the FRG shaped the state's own political development and foreign policy.[75] Yet, whereas Clarkson identifies homeland-oriented activism as the paradoxical vehicle through which some immigrants became more incorporated into West Germany,[76] by the 1970s and 1980s many immigrants considered the FRG home, at least for the foreseeable future, and the example of Sprengelkiez suggests that some of the first generation had local roots and interests that motivated their activism and spurred change.

Although the community's response to the *Sanierung* opened up an intercultural space and brought the neighborhood together with a common purpose, did it have lasting effects? When asked this question, Wolfermann first answered in the affirmative. "In the beginning, yes. And it exists still. I'm still greeted by a few." Of course, he added, some have moved away and back to Turkey, but he had visited an old neighbor there when taking trips down south. Later in the interview, Wolfermann amended that their collective action did not result in strong individual relationships between German and Turkish residents but instead set the stage for other neighborhood-wide efforts, such as women's breakfasts in the community center.[77] Zafer Turan and Engin Günükutlu each supported this assessment, citing the community festivals as evidence of the results of the campaign against *Sanierung*.[78] Outside of the circle of community leadership, however, memory of the *Sanierung* and the neighborhood's collective action against it faded. First-generation Turkish residents interviewed a decade later who were not directly involved did not mention those events, and the second generation exhibited no memory of them. Rather, the intercultural space opened by the *Sanierung* seemed to have lasting effect in setting the stage for community-based activism that promoted the formation of new public spaces of interaction, not in directly fostering cross-cultural friendships.

Intercultural Spaces and the Second Generation

Although the second generation had little involvement in or memory of the *Sanierung*, the neighborhood provided the setting for a host of

[75] Alexander Clarkson, *Fragmented Fatherland: Immigration and Cold War Conflict in the Federal Republic of Germany, 1945–1980* (New York: Berghahn Books, 2013), 2–7.
[76] Ibid., 186.   [77] Wolfermann interview, 21, 23.
[78] Turan interview; Günükutlu interview.

other spaces that allowed Turkish-German children and youth to forge intercultural relationships. These spaces, both informal and structured, brought local children from a range of nationalities into social interaction with each other and enabled Turkish-German children to gain skills and support that promoted their settlement into the neighborhood. Spaces for play were among the first informal intercultural spaces to open up for the second generation. Initially, children often created spaces for play in the *Hinterhöfe* (courtyards) of their apartment buildings, as their parents wanted them to stay close to home.[79] In the common space of the *Hinterhöfe*, as well as other neighborhood locations, the second generation came into contact with other children in their building, sometimes forging friendships that eased their transitions to school.[80]

For those who lived near or on Sparrplatz, the square also provided for the formation of friendships through informal play. The playground, which evolved and grew over the years thanks to residents' advocacy and activities, now boasts a full complement of swings, slides, teeter-totters, and monkey bars. Much of the square is shaded by trees in the summer, and benches around the playground and throughout give parents a place to rest while keeping an eye on their children. Some of the later renovations to the park added features aimed at serving the neighborhood's middle and high school–aged youth, including ping-pong tables and a fenced area for soccer. Younger children, though, seem to have benefited most from the social spaces that the Sparrplatz park hosted.[81]

Turkish children were not only able to meet their neighbors and have the opportunity to make new friends, they also learned and practiced their German-language skills. In some cases, informal social spaces in the neighborhood, such as the park at Sparrplatz, provided the second generation with a better setting to learn German than their schools did. Elif, who was in all-Turkish classes for her six years in primary school, saw the multicultural spaces of play on Sparrplatz as an opportunity to improve her German-language skills in a way she felt she could not at school. On Sparrplatz, she recounted, she had Spanish, Greek, Yugoslavian, and German friends, and she made a deliberate effort to spend time with them, rather than other Turks, so she would be forced to speak in German.[82]

---

[79] Bilge Yılmaz (pseudonym), interview by author, 2 June 2009, transcription by Perrin Saylan, Berlin, Germany, 3.
[80] Timur interview.   [81] Emre and Erkan interview.
[82] Elif (pseudonym), interview and transcription by Ursula Trüper, 11 December 1992, DLSA, MMA, 1.

These informal neighborhood spaces also nourished friendships that started in the context of the school and exposed Turkish-German children to new experiences, lifestyles, and expectations. When Lale spent time with her German friends outside of school, they would wander around the neighborhood, chat with each other, and perhaps enjoy some ice cream. Socializing with her German friends in the informal atmosphere of the neighborhood gave Lale a sense of how different parental and community expectations influenced these girls' daily lives. She felt that her German friends were "more free" than she was, based on how they could use the unstructured neighborhood spaces and the relationships they were allowed to pursue within them.[83] Although there is little evidence of the second generation visiting their German friends at home, when such visits did occur, Turkish-German children and youth could learn more about the daily lives of their German friends, including new types of foods, family dynamics, and holiday celebrations.[84]

In addition to the various informal spaces the second generation created within the neighborhood, they also utilized more structured forums that German community organizers instituted with the specific goal of providing social, educational, and intercultural spaces for local children and youth. These formal spaces developed in Sprengelkiez in the 1980s with the opening of two sites: (1) the Sparrladen community center and (2) the Ostergemeinde (Oster Church) youth group. The story of the Sparrladen begins with Katrin Mayer, a German social worker and the eventual founder of the community center. In the mid-1970s, Mayer worked for a government agency that focused on providing assistance to immigrant women and children in abusive situations. She became increasingly dissatisfied with the short-term nature of the solutions her agency implemented; at the same time she was shocked by the statistic that half of all children in the city's *Sonderschule* were Turkish.[85] Mayer could not believe that all those children were cognitively/developmentally disabled and wanted to understand why they were sent to such schools in the first place. As she explored the matter further, she discovered that many Turkish families did not send their children to kindergarten, which could cost DM 50 per child, and that they generally lived in areas of the city populated predominantly by other Turks. In addition, there were only two bilingual classes in West Berlin by 1982, one in Schöneberg and another in Kreuzberg. Turkish children, she found, were unable to understand their lessons when they entered the first grade, so they would

---

[83] Lale interview, 3–4.   [84] Fischer interview, 5.
[85] *Sonderschule* are schools for cognitively/developmentally and physically disabled children.

fail and be sent to the *Sonderschule*. The problem, Mayer concluded, "lay in the German language."[86]

The more Mayer learned, the angrier she became that no one was trying to solve this growing challenge. She resolved to act. Having located the source of the problem in language difficulties, Mayer decided the best course of action was to teach Turkish children (as they were from the largest immigrant group) the German language through play, which would give them a better chance to succeed once they entered school. Through a connection with the BfsS, she found a Turkish woman who was studying to be an *Erzieherin* (teacher or school aide) and was interested in partnering with Mayer.[87] With the help of the tenants' cooperative in Sparrstrasse 21, they began reaching out to Turkish parents in the neighborhood. First, they stuffed mailboxes with bilingual flyers explaining their project, and next, they went from apartment to apartment so the Turkish families could ask them questions about themselves, their plans, and their funding sources. By 1982, Mayer and her (now) two Turkish partners were playing with and teaching thirty to forty children on Sparrplatz and looking for a place to use during the winter months.[88]

During the next three years, the "Sparrladen," as they came to call their community center, went through several changes in staff and location. With the exception of Mayer, the staff of the center turned over several times, and the center moved from a shared space with another community organization to their own location in a former apartment on Sparrplatz. Funding from the city enabled them to secure this site and hire a full-time *Erzieherin* and a social worker, as well as three to five assistants.[89] By February 1985, Mayer, her cofounder Beate Hahn, and their coworkers were ready to declare the Sparrladen's official opening, which they and the children celebrated with a large party.

Mayer and Hahn's plan for the Sparrladen was to create a culturally mixed environment in which children with immigrant backgrounds would gain the language and social skills they needed to succeed both in school and in German society. To this end, the center's workers put together set groups from waiting lists, including a group for young children just entering the first grade, another for children in primary school, and a *Mädchengruppe* (girls' club) for young women in secondary school. In addition, they started two groups for local women: one for young German mothers to help them obtain their diplomas, and another

[86] Katrin Mayer (pseudonym), cofounder of the Sparrladen, interview by Ursula Trüper, 6 July 1992, audiocassette, DLSA, MMA.
[87] Mayer did not mention the name of her first partner during her interview.
[88] Mayer interview.   [89] Hahn interview.

for Turkish women, aimed at bringing them out of the isolation of
the home and into contact with other women. The center also hosted a
local *Volkshochschule* class for illiterate women. Mayer made an effort to
have an equal number of Turkish and German assistants, but at the
Sparrladen all were expected to speak German. If someone spoke Turkish (and was caught), he or she had to pay for the mistake by putting
a penny in a jar. Finally, Mayer and her coworkers strove to achieve a
balance between parental trust, which included both walking the girls
home if activities ended after dark and not allowing men into Sparrladen,
and transparency to the community, symbolized by the center's large
windows.[90]

The success of Sparrladen, based on Mayer's original goals, was mixed.
At first, children with both German and immigrant backgrounds took
advantage of the programs and activities offered at the Sparrladen. However, the Turkish parents, Hahn explained, began to consider Sparrladen
"their center," and although the workers tried to counter this mind-set,[91]
according to Mayer, the Turkish children pushed out the German children who were coming to the center.[92] After a while, the German children stopped coming to the community center, and it became, as Hahn
phrased it, a "rein-türkisch" (purely Turkish) establishment. Attempts to
bring together the two women's groups proved unsuccessful,[93] and Turkish began to mingle with the German being spoken during the center's
daily activities.[94]

Despite these deviations from the original plan, Mayer felt fairly satisfied with the work being accomplished at the Sparrladen, pointing to
positive feedback during Parents' Evenings as evidence of the center's
role in helping immigrant children learn German.[95] The workers succeeded in gaining the trust of many Turkish parents in the neighborhood
who sent their children to Sparrladen, and they would occasionally
volunteer to assist the center's workers with particular activities. For
young people from the neighborhood, including Timur, Sanem, and
Lale, Sparrladen constituted an easily accessible place in their everyday
landscape where they could meet with friends, improve their German,
and participate in fun activities – all of which deepened their sense of
belonging to the neighborhood in which the center was located. In addition, for young women, the community center was a structured social
space free of the negative connotations of the more informal spaces they
inhabited in the neighborhood that might draw the unwanted attention of

[90] Ibid.   [91] Ibid.   [92] Mayer interview.   [93] Hahn interview.
[94] Former Sparrladen assistant, conversation with author, 10 July 2009, Berlin.
[95] Mayer interview.

the Turkish community's social control. One of the things Sparrladen failed to provide, however, was a structured space for young men to socialize and participate in organized activities. Mayer regretted this lack, and although she considered opening a music center for young men, she ultimately did not out of concern over the possibility of violence.[96]

While Turkish boys past primary school did not have structured spaces available to them at the Sparrladen, another local site – the Ostergemeinde – began in the mid- and late 1980s to make efforts to include the neighborhood's Turkish youth, boys and girls, in their activities. When Hans-Peter Meyendorf was hired by the Protestant church in 1985 to take over direction of youth activities, he and a core group of church youth decided that their recreational activities should be open to the entire community, including Turkish youth. "We couldn't do integration," Meyendorf explained; that was not his job or his goal. Instead, he and the youth group wanted to bring people in the neighborhood together for fun and community, and they started by inviting their Turkish friends and acquaintances, some of whom they had known since kindergarten, to a variety of small activities and larger events.[97]

One of the exciting, if short-lived, events planned by Meyendorf and the youth group was a series of open parties that took place in the church's basement. Supported by Meyendorf and a few older teenagers from the church, the youth group planned the evening, picked out the music, decided on snacks and drinks, and invited their friends from the neighborhood. In the beginning, the open parties were a success; a mix of local youth showed up, danced, socialized, snacked, and were sent off shortly before ten o'clock by the same *Rausgeschmissen* (throwing-out) song. Unfortunately, after a few weeks "tourists" – Meyendorf's word for Turkish-German youth from outside the neighborhood – arrived and began causing trouble. Meyendorf and the older youth volunteers had to start collecting weapons at the door and having conversations with the troublemakers about appropriate behavior. Then, one week, someone threw a tear gas canister through the basement window into the room where the party was being held. When someone throws tear gas at a demonstration, Meyendorf pointed out, at least people are in the open air and the gas can dissipate quickly. But their parties were in a basement, a small, confined space. Another time, someone else used a fire extinguisher to the same effect. The "party tourism" was becoming dangerous, and Meyendorf and the youth group discontinued the open parties.

---

[96] Mayer interview.
[97] Hans-Peter Meyendorf, interview by author, 20 July 2009, digital recording, Berlin.

The Ostergemeinde's parties may not have enjoyed a long run, but they did provide a structured space in which the neighborhood's Turkish youth could socialize informally with members of the youth group. They were also able to learn about the youth group's smaller-scale activities, and several Turkish-German youth became regular participants. It is important to note that the small group's activities were not religiously based. "Simply a group of friends," Meyendorf clarified. "It's not always about the big book." This group met regularly for a variety of free-time activities, including playing soccer in nearby Rehberge Park, listening to music, playing cards, making videos, and taking weekend trips. After the Wall fell, the weekend trips included tours throughout Berlin and into the surrounding countryside, including a house the pastor owned on the former border with East Germany. Occasionally, the youth group took trips out of the country, although they stayed within Europe to avoid trouble with visas. The makeup of the group was consistent, with older members rotating out and younger people coming in over the years, and Meyendorf felt they got to know each other fairly well in the course of their time and activities together.[98]

Despite the core group of participants getting along well together, the same could not always be said of the rest of those who took advantage of the space and activities the church offered in the afternoons. In the early 1990s, as a part of a citywide study of how young Berliners dealt with cultural differences, journalist Eberhard Seidel-Pielen interviewed three Germans who regularly met in the Ostergemeinde's Jugendkeller (basement) with other neighborhood youth.[99] Although Seidel-Pielen describes the church's Jugendkeller as "a place where exclusion will not be allowed," the youths' answers reveal an internal self-segregation of German and Turkish participants. When he arrived for the interview, Seidel-Pielen found the Turkish youth occupying the main front room and his German interview subjects in a small office in the back.

In response to his question about whether all the different groups of people who use the Jugendkeller got along well together, the girl and two boys (ages twelve, fourteen, and fifteen respectively) were unanimous in their negation. Sandra explained that they occupied different rooms because "they [the Turkish youth] come here, act all cool and think everything belongs to them." She continued, "The Turkish youth are older, they talk mostly about us, but always only in Turkish, hardly ever

---

[98] Meyendorf interview.
[99] Eberhard Seidel-Pielen and Klaus Farin, *Der Gewalt die Stirn bieten: Berliner Jugendliche auf der Suche nach neuen Normen und Umgangsformen im kulturübergreifenden Milieu. Miteinander Leben in Berlin* (Berlin: Ausländerbeauftragte des Senats, 1992).

in German." She knew the Turkish youth talked about them, she said, because a Yugoslavian friend of hers who understood Turkish would tell her what they were saying.[100] Oliver and Peter were more concerned with being beaten up, mentioning repeatedly that the Turkish youth (whom Meyendorf clarified later in the interview were chiefly young men) responded to situations that annoyed them with threats of violence.[101] To avoid confrontation, they would leave the front room when the older Turkish youth showed up. Yet even as they occupied separate social spaces within a common youth center, the interviewees were not ready to say the Turkish youth did not belong in the site itself. If Turks were excluded, Sandra reasoned, they would just sit outside on the street, and if Germans were excluded they would do the same. The Jugendkeller "should be for everyone," she concluded.[102]

When Meyendorf entered the discussion toward the end of the interview, he complicated the "us" versus "them" dichotomy the youth had set up. Meyendorf pointed out that they had forgotten about a couple of youth whom they likely did not think of as foreigners anymore and who interacted with them as a matter of course and participated in common activities. "The closer the contact one has," Meyendorf explained, "the less one sees another person as a foreigner" and the more he or she becomes like a friend. At the same time, he added that the interviewees had also left out the fact that there were a couple of German youth who socialized with the Turks in the front room.[103] Perhaps the two examples Meyendorf highlighted were the beginnings of a common, intercultural social space being created in the Jugendkeller. Just a year later, when Seidel-Pielen returned to conduct a follow-up interview with the same three German youth, they reported that the situation had markedly improved even from the previous year.[104]

The second generation's use of and experiences in structured intercultural spaces reveals several aspects of their settlement into the neighborhood. First, as within the home and informal social spaces, gender played an important role in the extent to which Turkish Germans could participate in and belong to intercultural spaces. For young women, the Sparrladen, whose workers made direct efforts to connect with their parents and which provided an all-female space, constituted a place where they were able to socialize with friends, as well as benefit from and enjoy the center's activities, without feeling anxious about how their participation would be perceived. Despite their realization that such

[100] Ibid., 29.   [101] Ibid., 29–30.   [102] Ibid., 30.   [103] Ibid., 32.
[104] Eberhard Seidel-Pielen, *Unsere Türken: Annäherung an ein gespaltenes Verhältnis* (Berlin: Espress/Elef. Press, 1995), 127.

spaces were sorely needed, however, community workers at the Sparrladen did not offer activities for young men, based on their reputation for violence. The Jugendkeller deliberately opened its doors to young Turkish-German men, choosing to engage with them and deal with whatever issues arose.

Second, Turkish-German participation in both informal and structured intercultural spaces illustrates their willingness, and sometimes eagerness, to take part in activities outside of the Turkish community, or the so-called *Parallelgesellschaft*. Whether motivated by a desire to improve their German-language skills, to enjoy new experiences, or just to have fun, the second generation took advantage of those opportunities to an extent that sometimes overwhelmed the German organizers and participants. Finally, in forging spaces of belonging within those sites, Turkish Germans sometimes made themselves so "at home" that they alienated other German participants. Particularly in the more structured sites, such as the Sparrladen and Jugendkeller, some of the German children felt that the Turks were taking over and changing the site into a "Turkish" space. This sentiment echoes that of their parents in regard to the proliferation of Turkish social spaces in the neighborhood and contributed to further antipathy among neighborhood residents, despite the bridges being formed and the blurring of lines between the two communities.

Conclusion

Despite their reputation as central to Germany's Turkish *Parallelgesellschaft*, the neighborhood had a more nuanced effect on the settlement and sense of belonging of Turkish immigrants and their children in German neighborhoods and society. Although their initial housing choices were constrained by West Berlin's housing shortage and their own financial situations, Turkish immigrants, and, later, the second generation, actively embedded themselves in their local neighborhood and worked to shape the environment in ways that both addressed their social needs and aspirations as well as reflected the influences of their other everyday spaces. As Sarah Hackett argues, this should not be immediately read as an unwillingness or inability to integrate.[105] Through the new spaces of

---

[105] Hackett's sources about Turkish-Muslim housing decisions and patterns, however, constrain her to concluding that the desire to live in ethnic neighborhoods is evidence that Turkish immigrants were "content to coexist alongside their host populations." Sarah Hackett, *Foreigners, Minorities and Integration: The Muslim Immigrant Experience in Britain and Germany* (Manchester, UK: Manchester University Press, 2016), 95.

belonging forged by the first and second generations and their German neighbors, the neighborhood became a primary site of integration, both spatial and reciprocal. This process, however, neither ran smoothly within the Turkish-German community nor between that community and its German neighbors.

Perhaps one of its most overarching characteristics in the lives of the Turkish-German community is the neighborhood as a space of contradiction. On one hand, the first and second generations created and experienced the neighborhood as a space of comfort and community. As first-generation immigrants moved into Sprengelkiez and other West Berlin neighborhoods and formed multigenerational communities throughout the 1970s and 1980s, the neighborhood provided social and intercultural spaces that brought residents together and helped Turkish immigrants and their children forge a stronger sense of community. For the first generation, social spaces in the neighborhood gave them the opportunity to relax and enjoy themselves in a place unconnected to the responsibilities of the home (Figure 7).[106] The second generation constructed similar spaces of belonging, but, more so than their parents, they used these spaces to forge relationships with residents of other ethnic and national backgrounds, making connections and gaining skills that would help them succeed later on.

On the other hand, both the first and second generations experienced the neighborhood as a site of conflict and struggle. This conflict was generally the result of two distinct, yet sometimes intertwined sources: (1)gendered expectations of behavior and (2) intercultural struggle over shared spaces. Women and girls, especially, experienced restrictions on their personal freedom and social opportunities based on what their families and the neighborhood's Turkish community considered appropriate behavior for their gender. Young women in particular were subjected to social control that limited their social spaces in the neighborhood. Yet gendered expectations did not affect only women; the same social control network that monitored young women's activities also judged their families' reputations based on those activities. In addition, as one sees in the example of the Sparrladen, German preconceptions about young Turkish-German men excluded them from spaces and opportunities available to young women and children in the neighborhood.

This last point illustrates the other main source of conflict in the neighborhood: friction between German and Turkish or Turkish-German residents. From broader fears about the perceived threat to West Berlin's

---

[106] Teahouse on Sparrplatz, photography by author, Spring 2009, Berlin.

Figure 7. Teahouse on Sparrplatz

identity to more localized concerns about park benches and pubs, the
spaces of belonging that the growing Turkish-German community constructed in the neighborhood met with resistance. Not only did Turkish
neighbors sometimes encroach on the social spaces young Turkish-
German women were trying to build, but some German residents also
felt that these *ausländische Mitbürger* were "taking over" common spaces
and pushing out familiar landmarks of the German neighborhood. For
some, although not all, of the spaces constructed by the Turkish-German
community, it was more a connection to a physical place rather than an
abstract society that helped them feel a sense of belonging – a situation
that frustrated the second generation just as it did German neighbors.

We should not forget, however, that in forging spaces of belonging that
linked them to specific places, the first and second generations invested
and interested themselves in neighborhood life. When an external threat
to their neighborhood and homes presented itself, such as in the case of

the city's original *Sanierung* plans for Sparrplatz, Turkish immigrants joined their German neighbors in protest. Their local focus and activism prompted the city to change its plans to accommodate the concerns of residents, which resulted both in the neighborhood's physical alteration and laying the groundwork for further neighborhood-based activities and projects. Even as national newspapers decried the "foreigner problem" and West Berlin's Turkish ghettos, first-generation immigrants and their German neighbors worked together to improve their common, local community.

Despite the common ground and interests some Turkish and German neighbors discovered and acted on in Sprengelkiez in the 1980s, as the number of immigrants in the neighborhood increased, so did the feeling among some German residents that the root of the neighborhood's problems was its foreign population. The discourse of immigrants as a problem extended from the neighborhood into local schools, where the second generation came into contact with new opportunities for, and challenges to, their sense of belonging.

4   Learning to Belong

Perhaps even more than the workplace and neighborhood, the school has been a site charged with expectations, symbolic importance, and practical challenges in connection to the growth and belonging of the Turkish community in German society. When Turkish families reunited with their relatives working in the Federal Republic and settled into residential neighborhoods, their children began attending West German primary and secondary schools. This development presented both political and pedagogical issues for West German governmental and educational authorities as they grappled with the question of whether to prepare these children for a life in West Germany or a return to their *Heimatland* (homeland). The answers to this question ranged across the spectrum according to the political makeup of the individual states. Yet the federal government, the media, the West German public, and Turkish immigrants themselves largely agreed that the school constituted the most important site for promoting the successful integration of foreign children into West German society.

Widespread agreement on the significance of the school for guest worker children (*Gastarbeiterkinder*), however, did not preclude controversy. To many German parents and teachers, the presence of foreign children in their local schools seemed sudden, overwhelming, and unwelcome. The same newspaper articles that reported on the growing numbers of foreign residents in West German cities often highlighted extreme examples of schools with high percentages of foreign students (*Ausländerschüler*), using words such as *Hochburg and Überflutung* to describe the situation.[1] This transformation of German classrooms,

---

[1] *Hochburg* means stronghold, and *Überflutung* refers to a flood, inundation, or overflow. For examples, see Hans Haibach, "Die Grenzen der Integrationskraft Berlins," *Frankfurter Allgemeine Zeitung*, 27 November 1981, BPA, Berlin, accessed 7 April 2009; Annegret Schröder, "Ausländerproblem: Berlin ist viertgrösste Türkenstadt der Welt," *Handelsblatt*, 30 November 1981, BPA, accessed 7 April 2009; Heinz Kühn, "Wenn wir erst einmal die Türken los sind ...", *Vorwärts*, 1 April 1982, BPA, accessed 7 April 2009;

parents feared, would diminish the quality of their own children's education, as teachers' attention would be taken up by students unable to understand the lessons.[2] Such concerns and reports merged to form the dominant narrative in the discourse about the education of "foreign" children.[3]

Much of the academic scholarship regarding the second generation and school has examined similar themes to those at play within the dominant narrative, and these have generally coalesced around the central issue of education for "successful" integration. Whereas Herbert Koch's early study presented a relatively positive tone about the potential of the school as a site of integration for *Gastarbeiterkinder*,[4] scholars in the late 1970s and 1980s focused on the lasting challenges of and for children of migration background in German schools. The school may have assisted in partial economic integration, scholars argued, but it was also a key element in social isolation.[5] The decrease in funding for their specific educational needs as well as the sustained focus on these children as "special problems" for the school system exacerbated that isolation.[6] Comparisons of the educational achievements of German and non-German students generally concluded that students with migrant backgrounds were underperforming relative to their German peers.[7] Their

Liselotte Müller, "Türken von Berlin wollen keine Deutschen werden," *Hannoverische Allgemeine*, 10 July 1982, BPA, accessed 7 April 2009.

[2] Such feelings came up in my own interviews as well. See Margaret Fischer (pseudonym), interview by author, 20 May 2009, transcription by Perrin Saylan, Berlin, Germany; Andreas and Christine Zimmermann, interview by author, 18 May 2009, transcription by Perrin Saylan, Berlin.

[3] This narrative continued to thrive in political debates and public discussions in reunified Germany, evidenced by the growing tendency of some German parents to send their children to schools in districts with smaller populations of "foreign" residents. See, for example, "Oma mit guter Adresse," *Der Spiegel*, 26 October 1998, pp. 94–97.

[4] Herbert R. Koch, *Gastarbeiterkinder in deutschen Schulen* (Königswinter am Rhein: Verlag für Sprachmethodik, 1970). Koch was drawing on his experiences and the data he collected as a school inspector in Düsseldorf.

[5] For example, Ray C. Rist, *Guestworkers in Germany: The Prospects for Pluralism* (New York: Praeger Publishers, 1978); Joyce Marie Mushaben, "A Crisis of Culture: Isolation and Integration among Turkish Guestworkers in the German Federal Republic," in İlhan Basgöz and Norman Furniss, eds., *Turkish Workers in Europe: An Interdisciplinary Study* (Bloomington: Indiana University Turkish Studies, 1985), 125–150.

[6] Ursula Boos-Nünning and Manfred Hohmann, "The Educational Situation of Migrant Workers' Children in the Federal Republic of Germany," in Lotty van den Berg-Eldering and Jo Kloprogge, eds., *Different Cultures, Same School: Ethnic Minority Children in Europe* (Berwyn: Swets North America, 1989), 55.

[7] M. Alamdar-Niemann, D. Bergs-Winkels, and H. Merkens, "Educational Conditions of Turkish Migrant Children in German Schools," *Anthropology and Education Quarterly* 22, no. 2 (June 1991): 154–161; Susanne Worbs, "The Second Generation in Germany: Between School and Labor Market," *International Migration Review* 37, no. 4 (Winter 2003): 1011–1038.

consistently poor performance in school, researchers more recently argued, whether due to language difficulties, educational policies, or discrimination, put their integration into German society at risk.

Despite growing consensus around the importance of education for the successful integration of the second generation, schools in the 1970s and 1980s received little guidance on how they were to accomplish this vaguely defined goal. The federal nature of the West German education system, shifting political winds, and the continued insistence that the FRG was "not a country of immigration" created an environment in which schools and families at the local level had to grapple with the question: How were the children of Turkish immigrants to learn to belong in West German society?

At the same time, the second generation began to come of age at a period when the economic conditions and political will that had made their parents' immigration and ready employment possible had all but disappeared. Although the first generation had certainly experienced their own challenges, the strength of the West German economy in the 1960s provided a context in which West German businesses, politicians, and the public welcomed their presumed temporary presence among the workforce. Yet the second generation began to approach working age when the West German economy, and particularly the West Berlin economy, faltered and fell. Unemployment rates grew, and West German politicians and the public were suddenly surprised by the fact that their temporary guests did not "return home" but rather sunk their roots deeper into West German soil. In West Berlin, jobs and German residents left the city at an alarming rate, leaving the local government to grapple with a dearth of employment opportunities and a growing population of second-generation youth who would need to be prepared for and find a place in the labor market.

Thus, as the second generation entered West German schools in increasing numbers throughout the 1970s and 1980s, they encountered a site imbued with a host of shifting motivations, expectations, methods, and goals. In this unsettled environment, Turkish-German students came into contact with West German institutions, their German peers, and other students with immigrant backgrounds and began to learn what it meant to be "German." How did students, teachers, and parents negotiate the conflicting and shifting spaces of the school? And how did this site, considered so central to the "successful integration" of its immigrant students evolve to define that goal and prepare their students for it? Finally, how did the spaces within the school that Turkish-German students confronted, created, and experienced prepare them for life beyond its doors?

To answer these questions, I examine the variety of spaces the second generation created and experienced within the levels of compulsory schooling, before turning my attention to the role of the *Volkshochschule*[8] in their construction of belonging, taking into account both formal instruction and informal socialization.[9] Even as their students absorbed both the deliberate and unconscious lessons of what it meant to belong in West Germany, so, too, did the schools have to learn new ways to accomplish their traditional mandate of preparing the youth to succeed in and contribute to German society. In the broader context of the contradictory mandate of promoting integration in a nonimmigration country, local schools, then, became the prime mediators of a conflicted sense of belonging that was profoundly shaped by individual initiatives and experiences of teachers, parents, and students alike.

Conflict in Compulsory Education

The debate over the role and responsibilities of school in the lives of children with migrant backgrounds began years before Turkish students started filling the seats in West German classrooms. In the early to mid-1960s, the rapid growth in the numbers of guest worker children in schools across the country, combined with debates about the developing European Community and reform movements regarding the West German educational system, prompted politicians at the federal level to take an active interest in education policy. Initially, the majority of politicians, as well as the Standing Conference of the Ministers for Education and Cultural Affairs,[10] held to the idea of the rotation principle and concluded that if guest worker children were to be educated in German schools, they should be prepared to reintegrate into their country of origin. This perspective shifted in the late 1960s and early 1970s with the recognition that many guest workers were extending their stay and bringing their families to live with them in West Germany. Under the Social Democratic- Free German Party coalition, the federal government adopted a dual and contradictory strategy of encouraging the return of

---

[8] The *Volkshochschule* is similar to the U.S. community college in that it is not obligatory and offers a variety of classes to the community.

[9] The distinction between formal instruction and informal socialization is not always a neat one. As later examples will show, informal socialization occurred in formal classroom settings, whereas formal instruction took place in social groups and theater clubs. As such, this chapter discusses the two forms of education but is not organized along those – at times – blurry lines.

[10] The Standing Conference of the Ministers of Education and Cultural Affairs is a federal body that issues policies to the *Länder* (states) regarding education but does not have the power to enforce its suggestions.

migrant workers to their countries of origin while promoting the integration of *Gastarbeiterkinder* into German society through education in the West German school system.

In the years following the *Anwerbestopp* (recruitment halt), the significant growth and diversification of the immigrant population forced politicians to view guest workers and their families not simply from a perspective of labor policy but also to begin to consider long-term social and economic effects of their settlement. Yet, at that point, little was known about the lives of the guest workers apart from their employment, and government authorities at all levels sponsored sociological studies to fill the significant gaps in their knowledge about this segment of the population. Sociologists, particularly those drawing on systems theory in their conception of the relationship between modernization and migration, focused on the "plight" of second-generation migrants and emphasized the role of schools in countering tendencies toward social conflict and in facilitating their integration into German society.[11]

Recognition of the establishment of significant immigrant communities coupled with the findings of researchers about those communities led politicians to increase their reliance on the West German school system as a tool to combat ghettoization of ethnic minorities and improve their position in the labor market – and ultimately to promote the integration of *Gastarbeiterkinder*. In 1975, the Social Democratic Party – the dominant partner in the SPD-FDP coalition that governed West Germany from 1969 to 1982 – articulated a platform that framed integration as a reciprocal process between foreigners and Germans, and "viewed interaction and exchange between these cultures as a prerequisite for successful integration."[12] Chancellor Helmut Schmidt reinforced his party's commitment to taking a more active role in immigrant integration through his appointment in 1978 of Heinz Kühn as the first *Ausländerbeauftragter* (Commissioner for Foreigners' Affairs), a position that would serve as an advocate for foreigner residents at the national level. In a memorandum released in the following year, Kühn baldly stated that many of the former guest workers were now "immigrants" and needed to be fully integrated into German society. Kühn dedicated a significant portion of the memorandum articulating and advocating the connection between intercultural understanding, education, and the integration of immigrant youth, a position the SPD later adopted as part of its platform.[13] For the SPD, the school served as a critical site of the

---

[11] Rita Chin, *The Guest Worker Question in Postwar Germany* (Cambridge, UK: Cambridge University Press, 2007), 95–97.
[12] Ibid., 99. [13] Ibid., 104–105.

cultural learning and exchange that would facilitate the integration of second-generation youth into German society.

Economic downturn and increasing political conservatism, however, shifted the discussion from the integration of children with a migrant background to questioning the ability and desire of immigrants in general to integrate into German society. When the CDU articulated its own integration policy in 1977, it promoted "peaceful coexistence" between Germans and foreigners and sought to ameliorate the most significant disadvantages the latter experienced. Yet, the CDU maintained the idea of cultural difference and argued for the preservation of that difference in order that foreigners and their families would return to their homelands.[14] Such positions continued to be popular within the CDU/CSU when it came to power in the Bundestag (federal parliament) in 1982 with Helmut Kohl as chancellor. Although the government continued to view the school as an important weapon to combat ghettoization and the growing unemployment levels of foreigners, the tenor of the debate – at least at the federal level – had grown more critical.[15] The CDU repudiated the SPD's more reciprocal understanding of integration and argued that it was the work of foreigners to accommodate themselves to German society. Turkish immigrants were singled out as the most culturally and possibly irreconcilably foreign, placing schools in the even more difficult position of facilitating the integration of a group increasingly deemed as incapable of the deed.

A basic description of the German educational system is helpful when considering these political and policy debates and their implications. In general, children are required to attend primary school (*Grundschule*) for four to six years, depending on the state, after which time they continue on to one of four different types of secondary schools (*Oberschulen*) based on their academic ability and their parents' wishes. The *Gymnasium* is the highest level of secondary schooling and prepares students to proceed on to university, commencing with a diploma called the *Abitur*. The intermediate-level secondary school is the *Realschule*, which educates students for lower- and mid-level white-collar and vocational occupations. The *Hauptschule*, the lowest level of secondary education, teaches the same subjects as the *Realschule* but at a slower place, offers vocational training, and ends with the *Hauptschulabschluss* (certificate of secondary

[14] Ibid., 97–99.
[15] For an in-depth study of the influence of political developments on the development of educational policy regarding *Gastarbeiterkinder*, see Brittany Lehman, "Teaching Migrant Children: Debates, Policies, and Practices in West Germany and Europe, 1949–1992" (PhD dissertation, The University of North Carolina at Chapel Hill, 2015).

education). Finally, the *Gesamtschule*, a product of reform movements of the late 1960s and early 1970s, combines the other three schools into one and thus offers a number of possible certificates of completion. Students coming from *Haupt-*, *Real-*, and *Gesamtschulen* who take part in an apprenticeship (*Lehre* or *Ausbildung*) must also be enrolled in a *Berufsschule*, where they learn skills for their occupation not taught on the job. Each level of German secondary schooling has its own duration, certificate(s) of completion, and track to a particular type of occupation, with its corresponding place in the social strata. Thus, debates about the role of the school in the integration of *Gastarbeiterkinder* implied not only their participation in German society but also what their place in that society would be.

While these debates were taking place at the federal level, the states were designing and implementing their own educational policies, resulting in a wide variety of approaches to the education of guest worker children. As Hackett has shown for the city-state of Bremen, city officials there endeavored as soon as the early 1960s "to integrate guest-worker children as quickly as possible," and, although their approaches to that end developed over the course of the following decades, the intent remained the same.[16] On the other end of the spectrum was the state of Bavaria, which continued to use the rotational labor policy as its basis for guest worker children education throughout the 1970s, seeing its responsibility as preparing immigrant students to return to their parents' homeland. On a practical level, for many students this meant classes conducted in the children's parents' native language, with lesson materials provided by their home countries. Rist concluded in his 1978 study that this approach neither prepared students effectively for their assumed "return," nor did it adequately educate them for a successful life in West Germany.[17] As early as 1971, West Berlin's strategy for foreign student education had come to reflect Bremen's approach and was based on the premise that the second generation needed to be equipped to lead successful lives in the Federal Republic.[18] Citing evidence that showed guest workers were staying, bringing in their families, and having children in growing numbers, school officials' goal for the program was the quickest possible integration of foreign children into the West German school system. Foreign students were placed in classes with German students and had additional German- and Turkish-language instruction

[16] Sarah Hackett, *Foreigners, Minorities and Integration: The Muslim Immigrant Experience in Britain and Germany* (Manchester: Manchester University Press, 2016), 190.
[17] Rist, *Guestworkers in Germany*, 206–222.   [18] Ibid., 227.

in smaller, separate classes.[19] The program in West Berlin also adhered to (or at least attempted to adhere to) a 20 percent cap of foreign students in each German classroom and, until the 1980s, left teaching of the children's native languages to the consulates and embassies of the sending countries, supplying those classes with facilities and maintenance.[20] West Berlin officials felt that integration of foreign children into the school system was a necessary step toward their success in German society at large.

Despite the good intentions of Berlin school officials, leftist critics charged the program with seeking the "Germanization" of foreign children. The lack of incorporation of their foreign students' languages and cultures ignored "an important pedagogical tool" and broke the connection between home and school. Also, the practical implementation of the 20 percent cap meant that those foreign students who exceeded the quota were educated in separate classes, entirely composed of other foreign students. During the 1976–1977 school year, half of all guest worker children in secondary vocational school were educated in foreigner-only class. West Berlin schools further experienced high dropout rates among their foreign students.[21]

Nationwide statistics concerning foreign students showed consistent overall growth in the school system, yet uneven representation in the different levels of education. Between 1970 and 1980, the number of foreign students in *Grund-* and *Hauptschule* increased fivefold. Although this figure may reflect success at the lower levels of education, a look at the rates of increase in the *Realschule* and *Gymnasium* are less encouraging. During the same ten years, the percent of foreign students in *Gymnasium* grew from 1 to 2 percent, and in the *Realschule* it rose from less than 1 percent to just over 2 percent.[22] In 1979, 22 percent of all West German children were students at a *Gymnasium*, compared to 0.0046 percent of all guest worker children.[23] On the other end of the spectrum, the number of foreign students in the *Sonderschule* grew more

---

[19] Children in Turkish language class, Berlin 1972, from Martin Greve and Tülay Çınar, *Das Türkische Berlin*. Miteinander Leben in Berlin (Berlin: Die Ausländerbeauftragte des Senats, 1998), 44.

[20] Rist, *Guestworkers in Germany*, 226–228.

[21] Ibid., 228–232. In 1976, the chief administrative official of education estimated that 60 percent of foreign students left before finishing their studies.

[22] Sekretariat der Kultusministerkonferenz, *Statistische Veröffentlichungen der Kultusminister-konferenz: Ausländische Schüler in der Bundesrepublik Deutschland, 1970 bis 1983* (Bonn: KMK, 1984), 43–83.

[23] Nermin Abadan-Unat, "Identity Crisis of Turkish Migrants: First and Second Generation," in İlhan Basgöz and Norman Furniss, eds., *Turkish Workers in Europe: An Interdisciplinary Study* (Bloomington: Indiana University Turkish Studies, 1985), 9.

than six times as large during the 1970s.[24] Critics charged that foreign students with language difficulties were often sent to the *Sonderschule* despite having no physical or learning disabilities. The dual strategy of integration and preparation for return also did not serve the foreign children well in regards to education in the 1970s – nor was it very successful in readying them for the job market once they left school. A 1979 questionnaire completed by *Gastarbeiter* parents revealed that 46 percent of young adults ages sixteen to twenty did not have a job or an apprenticeship position and were not attending school.[25] Even Bremen, which Hackett argues had taken a relatively pro-integration stance as early as the 1960s and been responsive to the needs of its immigrant students, faced significant challenges in their successful education of and preparation for the job market.[26]

Whereas such statistics depict generally poor performance of foreign students in West German schools, the personal narratives of Turkish Germans reveal multiple and interrelated challenges that made the school a site of struggle. One of the first struggles the second generation faced was overcoming the language barrier. Although some had the opportunity to learn German as children on the playground or from childcare providers, many others entered school with little to no know-ledge of the language. And for those who had attended school in Turkey, they also had to adjust to a different educational system. Such was the case for Hanife Kurtal: half of the school year passed before she began to understand what was going on around her. With the help of a parent volunteer, she improved her German well enough to take part more actively in classroom activities, noticing as she did that the lessons were very different from those she had had in Turkey.[27] Not being able to fully participate in class negatively affected the second generation's ability to learn their lessons, often working to isolate them from their fellow classmates.

Being in one of the many foreigner classes (*Ausländerklassen*) mitigated the social isolation the second generation felt from their peers, but it also hindered students' ability to learn German, despite the additional German-language classes given there. Deniz, a young woman born in

[24] Sekretariat der Kultusministerkonferenz, *Ausländische Schüler in der Bundesrepublik Deutschland*, 96.
[25] Ulrich Herbert, *A History of Foreign Labor in Germany, 1880–1980: Seasonal Workers, Forced Laborers, Guest Workers*, translated by William Templar (Ann Arbor: University of Michigan Press, 1990), 242.
[26] Hackett, *Foreigners, Minorities and Integration*, 199–201.
[27] Kemal Kurt and Erika Meyer, eds., *. . . weil wir Türken sind/ . . . Türk oldugumuz için: Bilder und Texte von Türken/ Türklerin resim ve öyküleri* (Berlin: Express-Edition, 1981), 46.

West Berlin to Turkish guest workers, recounted being in "Turkish classes" all the way through *Grundschule* and into *Oberschule*. She and her classmates spoke in Turkish with each other, although their teacher was German.[28] Some officials, including West Berlin's Schulsenatorin (Senator for Education) Hanna-Renate Laurien (CDU), insisted that "pure foreigner classes" (*reine Ausländerklassen*) did not lead to isolation from German society, but few of those interviewed mentioned having close friendships with Germans in their schools.[29]

Even after second-generation students knew German well enough to participate more fully in classroom activities and lessons, German as a subject often proved a persistent challenge. An examination of the diplomas (*Abgangszeugnisse*) from a Wedding secondary school in the mid- to late 1980s reveals a Turkish-German student body with diverse academic strengths and weaknesses. Yet a significant minority – averaging about one-third over the course of six years – earned a "4" or worse in their German courses.[30] For those students who immigrated to the FRG as young adults, the difficulty in achieving language proficiency quickly enough to do well in school could be insurmountable. This struggle with language could also affect otherwise high-achieving students in the more advanced levels of the German school system. Filiz Güler, armed with ambition and a stack of report cards littered with 1s, proceeded on to *Gymnasium* with the official recommendation of her primary school. Once there, however, the academic challenge set her back on her heels. The subject matter was harder, the expectations higher, and in addition Güler felt that language made the *Gymnasium* a greater challenge to her than her German classmates.[31]

Güler felt motivated to do well in school and had parents who supported her education, but this was not the case for all young women. Others struggled more with conflicting expectations, lack of interest, or lack of support. Families, and sometimes also the young women themselves, considered school to be unnecessary or a distraction from their

[28] Deniz (pseudonym), interview by Ursula Trüper, 12 December 1992, transcription, p. 1, DLSA, MMA.

[29] "Senatorin Laurien für reine Ausländerklassen: Deutsche Kinder dürfen nicht zur Minderheit werden," *Berliner Morgenpost*, 13 August 1982, BPA, accessed 7 April 2009. Deniz K. mentioned making friends with a German girl who was in the classroom next to hers during her first year in *Oberschule*.

[30] Abgangszeugnisse – Theodor Plievier Oberschule, academic years 1985/86 through 1990/91, accessed 23 April 2009, Theodor Plievier Oberschule (Hauptschule), Berlin. Grading in the German school system is done on a numbered scale, with "1" being the highest grade one can receive and "6" the lowest.

[31] Filiz Güler (pseudonym), interview by author, 27 May 2009, transcription by Perrin Saylan, Berlin, 9.

duties to the family or their futures as housewives and mothers.[32] Lack
of motivation could lead to young women leaving school before they
received the training necessary to prepare them for the German job
market. Although this perspective was considered more common in the
early 1970s when Turkish parents viewed their settlement in West Berlin
through a shorter-term lens, it continued into the 1980s when the Turkish community was well established in the city. In the late 1980s, for
example, Deniz left school after the ninth grade at age fourteen without
doing an *Ausbildung* so she could run away and marry her boyfriend.[33]
And whereas some young women voluntarily left school early, others,
including Azra Demir's eldest daughter, were kept home by their parents
to take care of the household. Demir expressed regret over the decision but explained that it was a common practice in the neighborhood,
and no one had told them school attendance was mandatory. The local
Grundschule did, however, send a letter to their home, saying they must
send their second daughter to school.[34]

Difficulties with language or parental expectation were not the only
sources of conflict at school, however. Güler's transition from *Grundschule*
to *Gymnasium* reveals another challenge encountered by the second generation at school: conflict with their teachers and fellow classmates. Sometimes this conflict was spurred by teachers' different (and discriminatory)
expectations of their foreign students relative to their German ones. One
of Cem Özdemir's first memories of school is of a day in kindergarten
when another child's water pistol went missing. Özdemir was accused of
stealing the toy, and the teacher, who "had probably developed her pedagogical approach between 1933 and 1945," Özdemir writes, was not going
to allow him to go home until it was "found." When the toy was found, no
one bothered to apologize to Özdemir for the false accusation.[35] More than
a decade later, although Güler had received the official recommendation
of her school to proceed to the *Gymnasium*, a few teachers cautioned her
against it, saying that it could be too difficult for her. She recounted,
"[I have] also heard that from others, that it's said to so-called children
with a migration background, 'hmmm, careful, I wouldn't recommend the
Gymnasium to you.'"[36]

Although none of the Sprengelkiez second-generation interviewees felt
that hostility toward foreigners (*Ausländerfeindlichkeit*) was a daily event

[32] Ibid., 8.   [33] Deniz interview, 1.
[34] Azra Demir (pseudonym), interview, translation and transcription by Hatıce Renç,
9 March 1993, p. 10, DLSA, MMA.
[35] Cem Özdemir and Hans Engels, *Ich bin Inländer: ein anatolischer Schwabe im Bundestag*
(Munich: DTV, 1997), 24–25.
[36] Güler interview, 2.

during the school day, many could still give specific examples of their fellow students displaying blatant aggression and xenophobia. Deniz described an incident in the sixth grade when some of the German students in the class next to hers told the Turkish students that they all needed to "go away."[37] Others endured name-calling such as "Scheiss-Ausländer" and "Scheiss-Türke."[38] When Emre and a group of friends stirred up trouble at their *Oberschule*, it was the sole German participant – the young man was careful to point out – who turned them in, resulting in Emre being expelled from school.[39] Such events, even when not clearly motivated by xenophobia, led many Turkish-German students to feel cut off from their teachers and classmates more generally, and set the groundwork for further misunderstandings, conflict, and distrust.

Struggle, exclusion, and discrimination continued at the *Berufsschule*, both on an individual and an institutional level. Many who completed their studies at *Haupt-*, *Real-*, or *Gesamtschule* and wanted to continue on to do an apprenticeship found positions difficult, if not impossible, to come by. For some, the problem was a legal one. In 1974, the federal government passed a law prohibiting foreign youth who had immigrated that year and after from receiving a work permit. The immigrant youth would have to wait five years before they could apply for the permit, which was required not only for employment but also for apprenticeship positions.[40] Thus, despite legal immigration, one part of the migrant population, sometimes referred to as the one-and-a-half generation, was barred from obtaining legal job-training and employment. In other cases, it was not official barriers that kept them from apprenticeships but rather employer prejudice. A young Spanish student, the only one of her female classmates to not secure an apprenticeship, described her search to a *Spiegel* journalist: she went to a dozen different doctors' and dentists' offices to apply for a position as an assistant but found at each practice that their apprenticeship was "already filled." "Maybe it's natural, that they want to take Germans first," said the Spanish woman resignedly, but she finds it "just so stupid," that the doctors "always want to know the same thing, where I come from and what my parents do. We're not lepers."[41]

---

[37] Deniz interview, 1.
[38] Lale (pseudonym), interview by Ursula Trüper, 28 May 1992 and 4 June 1992, transcription, pp. 7–9, DLSA, MMA.
[39] Emre and Erkan (pseudonyms), interview by Ursula Trüper, December 1993, audiocassette, DLSA, MMA.
[40] Wolfgang Gehrmann, "Keine Chance für Nesibe Alatas: Im Kampf um Lehrstellen und Arbeitsplätze bleiben die Gastarbeiterkinder auf der Strecke," *Die Zeit*, 21 March 1980, accessed online.
[41] "Gemeine Lumpen, Saulgeis – rauswerfen," *Der Spiegel*, 26 December 1977, p. 46.

In a 1981 report, the Federal Ministry of Education and Science concluded that only one-quarter of all foreign youth of the age of compulsory vocational training (between fifteen and eighteen) were continuing their education or had obtained an apprenticeship. For those who immigrated to West Germany as teenagers, this statistic rose to 50 percent.[42] As the population of Turkish and Turkish-German residents in West Berlin in the 1980s climbed and their levels of unemployment remained higher than those of their West German neighbors, politicians, social scientists, and the media began increasingly to link the difficulty of foreign youth, particularly those who had immigrated more recently, to secure apprenticeships to failed integration and a perceived growth in youth violence. Journalists used phrases such as "social time bomb"[43] and "social explosive," noting that Turkish youth experienced the highest levels of unemployment and inability to secure an apprenticeship.[44] Throughout the 1980s, West German schools and businesses sought to address the challenges of preparing immigrant youth for the job market through a variety of programs,[45] and to some extent they succeeded, as a 1990 report from the Federal Ministry of Education and Science recognized in its emphasis on the positive trend of increasing numbers of foreign youth enrolled in vocational training.[46] Yet the press continued to stress the relationship between lack of opportunity for foreign youth and participation in organized violence. One *Spiegel* article published in 1990 frames the connection explicitly, labeling its young interviewees either by their gang affiliation or their level of education.[47] Discrimination and conflict in the school system, illustrated through lack of opportunity for apprenticeships, the media concluded, led *ausländische Jugendliche* (foreign youth) into a life of crime.

Although second-generation students were often on the receiving end of hostility in school, some Turkish-German students instigated conflict. Teachers documented these classroom conflicts in students' files, report cards, and letters home to parents. Most cases were relatively minor – being distracted during lessons, not turning in their homework, or

[42] Der Bundesministerium für Bildung und Wissenschaft, *Arbeiterkinder im Bildungssystem* (Bad Honnef: Bock, 1981), 41, 46.
[43] Ruth Hermann, "Die soziale Zeitbombe tickt: Immer mehr junge Ausländer werden in die Kriminalität gedrängt," *Die Zeit*, 3 November 1978, accessed online.
[44] "Ausländer: Schmerzhafte Grenze gezogen," *Der Spiegel*, 7 December 1981, www.spiegel.de/spiegel/print/d-14351381.html (accessed 9 July 2011).
[45] Specific examples are discussed later in this chapter.
[46] Der Bundesminister für Bildung und Wissenschaft, *Grundlagen, Perspektiven, Bildung, Wissenschaft: Berufsbildungbericht 1990* (Bad Honnef: Bock, 1990), 120–124.
[47] "Jeder Deutsche ein Nazi," *Der Spiegel*, 19 November 1990, www.spiegel.de/spiegel/print/d-13502026.html (accessed 9 July 2011).

smoking on school grounds – and merited reprimands or letters home.[48] Others, however, more actively challenged authority. Despite receiving positive evaluations throughout *Grundschule*, one young woman's behavior took a different turn once she reached the seventh grade. At first her rebellion was relatively minor and passive, but her challenges to teachers' authority grew more apparent and included directly insulting her teacher.[49] The space of conflict and hostility within the school, then, was something the second generation contributed to, even when they did not create it.

Parents, too, found the school to be a site of struggle and, at times, hostility. In some cases, these struggles stemmed from Turkish parents' limited schooling background or lack of understanding of the German school system. Prior to 1972, the Turkish educational system consisted of primary and secondary schools, with only five years of primary school education being compulsory. A diploma was awarded with the successful completion of each level. The German system, however, required longer attendance, and had a more complicated series of tracks and diplomas. One *Realschule* principal explained such conflicts with the following example: a Turkish-German student's parents were upset with the school because they wanted their son to be a doctor and, apparently, did not realize that the type of secondary school their son attended did not allow for that possibility.[50] For someone not familiar with or raised in the West German system, understanding its various tracks and their implications could be a considerable challenge.

In other cases, parents entered into an ongoing conflict between their children and the school's teachers or administrators. When Elif's teacher sent her to the principal's office for refusing to stop eating during class – but not the two German girls who were also snacking, the young woman told her interviewer – the principal sent her home for three weeks. When she returned, the principal informed Elif that she faced further penalties for missing so much school. Elif's stepmother demanded that she be transferred to another school, threatening him with a formal accusation to the education supervisory council. Elif transferred to a new school and

[48] Female student's personal file in Schülerbogen, Kl. 10a, Fr. Shambyaks, Abschluss 1989, and female student's personal file in Schülbogen, Kl. 10, Fr. Siebold, A-Ko, Abgang 1990, Herbert-Hoover-Schule (Realschule) (HHS), accessed 27 May 2009, Berlin, Male student's personal file, Schülerbögen, Kl. 10b, Fr. Rosenow, H-Z, Abgang 1992, HHS, accessed 27 May 2009, Berlin, Germany.
[49] Female student's personal file in Schülerbogen, Kl. 10a, H. Schriefer, A-J and K-Z, Abgangs 1990, HHS, accessed 27 May 2009, Berlin.
[50] Erik Weber (pseudonym), interview by author, 25 May 2009, Berlin.

received her *Hauptschulabschluss*.[51] Other parents also countered school officials' expectations and decisions in order to advocate for their children's improved educational opportunities. When his son's teacher wanted to move him from a Hamburg *Gymnasium* to a *Hauptschule*, Behçet Algan went to school to discuss the proposed change with the teacher and refused, politely, to have his son moved. His son finished his schooling with high marks and went on to study law.[52]

Whether it was parents arguing with school administrators over their children's educational options, teachers trying to exert their authority over students with unruly behavior, or students encountering hostility from their fellow classmates, the school was a site of constant conflict and struggle. Certainly much of this conflict was common to schools; German teachers, for example, had dealt with similar disciplinary issues among their students long before the children of Turkish guest workers entered their classrooms. Yet the second generation's experiences of conflict, and in particular those that included prejudice, in this site worked to separate them from the other students and their German teachers. Rather than having the integrating effect that many West German politicians, school administrators, Turkish parents, and the general public had hoped for, the spaces of conflict within the school often made it difficult for many members of the second generation to feel as though they belonged either to their school or to broader society.

A Land of Opportunity

Part of the reason the school could be so full of conflict was precisely because the participants involved realized the potential advantages this site could offer the growing number of children with a migrant background. The earlier examples of parents' advocacy, even as they reveal the difficulties foreign children and their parents faced in school, illustrate the perception of the school as a highly significant place for the well-being of their children. Many parents, originally intending to spend a limited amount of time in West Germany, lengthened their stay out of consideration for their children's futures. According to a 1973 survey in the Ruhr region, 31 percent of parents considered their children's education a motivating factor in their decision to lengthen their stay, and

---

[51] Elif (pseudonym), interview and transcription by Ursula Trüper, 11 December 1992, transcription, p. 3, DLSA, MMA.

[52] "Altona ist mein Dorf: Der Friseur Behçet Algan," in Michael Richter, ed., *Gekommen und Geblieben: Deutsch-türkische Lebensgeschichten* (Hamburg: Edition Körber Stiftung, 2003), 70.

55 percent said their children's occupational interests influenced their decision. Sixty-one percent wanted their children to continue schooling, and 24 percent preferred their children be involved in an apprenticeship. In 1974, a more extensive survey in Cologne found that 32 percent of parents saw the *Abitur* as the educational goal for their children, 31 percent wanted an apprenticeship or certification from occupational schools, and 12 percent would be satisfied with the *Hauptschulabschluss*.[53] A similar survey a year later among Turkish immigrants also indicated that a significant number of parents were staying longer than intended out of concern for their children's education; women in particular placed weight on vocational and professional training for their children.[54]

The narratives of the first-generation parents bear out the statistical evidence that their children's education was a major motivating factor in lengthening their stay in the Federal Republic.[55] In an example from a family in Hamburg, Hadiye Akın articulated the situation of many parents in the first generation. Recalling her husband's plan of leaving Germany after three years, she remarked, "But then the children came. And, ... if the children are in school, you can forget about going back."[56] Not only did some first-generation Turkish immigrants see German schools as advantageous for their children, but their own participation in that space opened up new opportunities for themselves as well. More so at the primary school level, teachers invited their students' parents into the classroom to contribute to and join in special festivities, which allowed Turkish parents to become more familiar with their children's teachers and the school itself and brought them into contact with other parents.[57]

For the second generation, the spaces of opportunity they encountered and created within the context of their primary and secondary schools enabled them to form and maintain friendships and other social relationships similar to those they experienced in their neighborhoods. Some

[53] Czarina Wilpert, "Children of Foreign Workers in the Federal Republic of Germany," *International Migration Review* 11, no. 4 (Winter 1977): 481–482.

[54] Ayse Kudat, "Personal, Familial, and Societal Impacts of Turkish Women's Migration to Europe," in UNESCO, ed., *Living in Two Cultures: The Socio-Cultural Situation of Migrant Workers and Their Families* (Paris: The UNESCO Press, 1982), 299.

[55] For examples, see Kudat, "Personal, Familial and Societal Impacts of Turkish Women's Migration to Europe," 299; Wilpert, "Children of Foreign Workers in the Federal Republic of Germany": 481–482.

[56] "Ich bin, wie ich bin: Die Lehrerin Hadiye Akın," *Gekommen und Geblieben: Deutsch-türkische Lebensgeschichten*, (Hamburg: Edition Körber Stiftung, 2003), 52.

[57] Ute Schmidt (pseudonym), interview by author, 29 June 2009, transcription by Perrin Saylan, Berlin, Germany, 4. I discuss the parents' role in cultural exchange at school later in this chapter.

made friends quickly, easing the transition into this new site and setting a positive tone for the rest of their career at school.[58] For others, the transition was decidedly rockier but ultimately successful. Fellow students, however, were not the only ones that helped the second generation forge a sense of settlement and belonging in this space. In some cases, a kind and patient teacher or principal helped students feel more comfortable, eased the difficulties of schoolwork, and created a positive impression of Germans in general.[59] This type of space could also be very significant for youth, and especially young women, for whom the home was a stifling or even abusive place. As a young child, Seyran Ateş preferred her school to home because at school her teachers respected and praised her for her achievements.[60] The support Ateş and others like her received at school made them want to invest themselves and their energy in that relatively safe and welcoming space.

Positive relationships with teachers and fellow students often had more tangible benefits than an abstract sense of comfort and belonging. Friendships with fellow classmates made one feel more a part of the school as a whole but could also mean assistance with schoolwork, protection from bullies, and help learning German. In the fourth grade, Lale went from nearly drowning during swimming lessons to being the second best in her class by the end of the year because of the help of a friend.[61] One of Elif's teachers, on learning that her student wrote poetry, put her into contact with a women's center (*Frauenladen*) where Elif gave a reading that brought her an invitation to share her poetry on a television show.[62] Elif also received timely support from a colleague at her *Berufsschule*, who would drive her home after class so she could avoid being hassled by a rejected suitor.[63] Thus, some of the connections the second generation forged at school offered them skills and support that helped them develop personally and operate more successfully in that space.

Just as the school fostered relationships that helped Turkish-German students succeed academically, it also offered more formal avenues for the second generation to consider and prepare for their adult lives. For

[58] Bilge Yılmaz (pseudonym), interview by author, 2 June 2009, transcription by Perrin Saylan, Berlin, 2.

[59] Kurt and Meyer, eds., . . . *weil wir Türken sind*, 53–55; Emre and Erkan interview.

[60] Seyran Ateş, *Grosse Reise ins Feuer: Die Geschichte einer deutschen Türkin* (Berlin: Rowohlt Taschenbuch Verlag, 2003). 67.

[61] Lale interview, 18.

[62] Elif interview, 5. Elif ultimately declined the invitation to be on the television program, as some of her poetry concerned her relationship with her father, and she did not want those sentiments to get back to him.

[63] Ibid., 7.

students who attended a *Haupt-*, *Gesamt-* or *Realschule*, an internship (*Betriebspraktikum*) was a part of their formal instruction. Students were given a variety of professions to choose from, some of the more popular being in the fields of health care, customer service, industry, and manufacturing.[64] Such courses exposed student participants to possible future occupations, taught them some of the skills they would need to succeed in those positions, and sometimes also helped them to make contacts in that particular industry. Other students participated in *Lehre* and *Ausbildung* (school-facilitated apprenticeships) that served a similar function. Those involved in apprenticeships also had to attend courses at a *Berufsschule*, where they would learn those skills that were not part of on-the-job training. Bülent Kaplan began his *Lehre* at age fifteen, one of two Turks among the forty apprentices. Between his responsibilities at the company and the *Berufsschule*, he did not have much free time, but he still enjoyed going to a *Kneipe* with his Turkish and German colleagues and occasionally playing soccer.[65]

Large businesses, such as Siemens and AEG-Telefunken, also coordinated with *Berufsschulen* and brought "foreign students" into their apprenticeship programs, often highlighting this fact in their company newspapers. In a 1982 *Siemens Mitteilungen* article, two of the young Turkish-German "Azubis"[66] interviewed described the types of jobs they were training for and what positions they hoped to hold in the future.[67] In the early 1980s, Siemens also instituted a "Benachteiligten-Programm" (program for the disadvantaged) at its Frankfurt branch that focused on bringing young Germans without their *Hauptschulabschluss* and "foreigners" (which included those born in Germany and recent immigrants) with language difficulties into an apprenticeship program. Through this training program, apprentices learned either telecommunications or electrical systems installation.[68] Such formal training, conducted in tandem by *Berufsschulen* and West German companies, was essential for youth in the Federal Republic in order for them to succeed on the job market once they left school, and students were aware of its significance.

[64] Günter Linkiewicz, ed., "Ernst-Schering-Oberschule, Gesamtschule, 12. März 1986" (Berlin: Ernst-Schuling-Oberschule, 1986), 92.
[65] Bülent Kaplan (pseudonym), interview by Ursula Trüper, 14 June 1993, audiocassette, DLSA, MMA.
[66] "Azubis" is slang for "Auszubildende," or apprentices.
[67] "Anpassen, ohne die Identität zu verlieren: Gespräche mit ausländischen Mitarbeitern," *Siemens Mitteilungen*, December 1982, p. 6, SCA.
[68] "Trotzdem sind wir Fremde hier," *Siemens Mitteilungen*, December 1986, 3-page article, page numbers unknown, SCA.

Many of the more future-oriented members of the second generation saw these courses as opportunities to improve their own situations and make their futures more secure. After Aylin completed her *Realabschluss*, she continued on to do an apprenticeship as a foreign-languages secretary. It would be a good career, she thought, and allow her to be independent of her family and the need for a husband.[69] Sanem, who was sixteen years old and dating a man seven years her senior at the time of her interview, was adamant about finishing her *Ausbildung* and starting a career before getting married. Her reasons for wanting a career were both practical and personal. What if her husband got sick? Then they would need her income. But she also wanted to put her training into action and have an interesting life. "The main thing is," Sanem explained, "if someone asks me, 'what are you,' I say 'yeah, I'm a trained retail saleswoman,' I've got something [to fall back on]. And I don't say, 'yeah, I finished 10th grade, and now I sit at home.' Then why did I go to school for ten years? For nothing. For nothing at all!"[70] Many young Turkish-German women like Sanem seized the opportunity to attain financial security and a measure of independence.

A Space of (Cross-)Cultural Education and Socialization

One of the opportunities the school presented for both its students and teachers was to create a space of cross-cultural education. The student body and, in later years, the teaching staff constituted an increasingly ethnically diverse population, one that rubbed shoulders on a daily basis and spent a significant chunk of their waking hours together. This continually close proximity, along with the school's mandate to equip its foreign students for a successful transition into West German society, provided the conditions for the development of spaces within the school in which students and teachers, whether purposefully or by accident, could learn about each other's languages, customs, and traditions. Sometimes, these interactions led only to shallow exchanges or the perpetuation of stereotypes. Interviews with some German administrators and teachers, for example, revealed very generalized knowledge based on perceived religious differences: "Turks" celebrate Ramadan, do not eat pork, and women sometimes wear headscarves.[71] Despite this, encounters between

---

[69] Aylin (pseudonym), interview and transcription by Ursula Trüper, 22 December 1992, transcription, p. 2, DLSA, MMA, 2.

[70] Sanem Sezer (pseudonym), interview and transcription by Ursula Trüper, 4 March 1993, transcription, pp. 8–9, DLSA, MMA.

[71] For example, Paul Hoch (pseudonym), principal of a *Grundschule*, interview by Ursula Trüper, 29 October 1993, audiocassette, DLSA, MMA.

Turkish-German students, their classmates, and their teachers through formal instruction and informal social activities did result in spaces of cross-cultural education, however limited they may have been.

Most of the structured cross-cultural education occurred within the context of the classroom, as teachers worked to fulfill their role as imparters of German language and culture to their foreign students. In the classroom, those from the second generation who had attended school in Turkey encountered a new educational system with different lessons, expectations, and ways of interacting than they had previously experienced. Language learning became one of the first spaces of cultural education the second generation encountered. In many cases, *Gastarbeiterkinder* received special German-language instruction in addition to those given in the course of daily classroom lessons. At a primary school in Sprengelkiez, these additional classes consisted of four to five students who would be taken out of their regular class for a few hours each week for German lessons.[72] Early language instruction was fairly piecemeal, stitched together by teachers in response to an immediate need rather than as a result of training and preparation. By the mid-1980s, however, teachers and some school administrators began to address the situation more systematically, developing strategies for teaching their foreign students German language and culture more efficiently and effectively.[73]

Schools concerned themselves with more than preparing their foreign students to enter German society, however. Particularly in the 1970s and stretching into the 1980s, West German schools were also expected to equip the *Gastarbeiterkinder* for the increasingly unlikely *Rückkehr*, their family's return to their country of origin. For the children of Turkish immigrants, this task was to be carried out by teachers from Turkey who were selected by the Turkish government and held special classes in German schools.[74] Their classes were conducted solely in Turkish and consisted of Turkish-language instruction, geography, history, and other subjects, opening up another space of cultural education for the second generation, particularly those who had been born in West Germany or immigrated at a very young age.[75] Although embedded in its local environment, these Turkish language and culture courses, more than the other spaces created in the context of the school, reflected the

---

[72] Maja Herbert (pseudonym), interview by Ursula Trüper, 16 June 1993, audiocassette, DLSA, MMA.

[73] This process is discussed more at a later point in this chapter.

[74] Ruth Mandel, "A Place of Their Own: Contesting Spaces and Defining Places in Berlin's Migrant Community," in Barbara Daly Metcalf, ed., *Making Muslim Space in North America and Europe* (Berkeley: University of California Press, 1996), 155.

[75] Güler interview, 13–14.

continuing and developing transnational ties between the Turkish government and its citizens abroad. A significant motivation for the Turkish government to participate in the guest worker program had been the perceived economic benefit of remittances in the short term and the return of skilled workers able to play an important role in the economy's modernization in the longer term. Maintaining the emigrant community's sense of Turkish identity, then, was of vital interest to the Republic.[76] The Turkish courses constituted a direct connection between the Turkish government and the second generation, reinforcing an Ankara-approved type of Turkish identity in West Germany.

While many considered these classes to be educating the children about their *Heimatland*, it is important to remember that many if not most of the second generation knew Turkey only from childhood memories, their parents' stories, or vacations to visit family. For those born in West Germany, the connection to Turkey was even more tenuous. In addition, few had received formal education in the Turkish language or in the history, politics, and culture of their parents' country of origin. This was particularly true at the primary school level, and over time it became increasingly the case in secondary school as the Turkish community grew more established and immigration laws more stringent regarding family reunification. Thus, these Turkish classes constituted a space of cross-cultural education, teaching the growing numbers of Turkish-German children for whom Turkey was simultaneously the *Heimatland* but not their home.

Students were not the only ones who encountered and were affected by these new cross-cultural spaces. Although likely not a majority, some German teachers found themselves learning Turkish in their efforts to successfully communicate with and teach their foreign students. For some, this occurred primarily if not entirely in the context of their own classrooms during the course of their lessons. Ute Schmidt, a preschool teacher, described her shock at the number of *Ausländer* in her class when she first started at a primary school in Sprengelkiez. "But it was exciting and interesting," she said, recounting her experiences. She began by learning how to pronounce all of her students' names correctly,

---

[76] The importance of maintaining "Turkishness" in West Germany is discussed further in Chapter 5 in connection with the link between religious, cultural, and national identity. For a fascinating look at the education of returned migrants in Turkey, see Brian J. K. Miller's fourth chapter, "The First Lesson Was the Independence March: Return Migration, Re-adaption Programs & National Identity in 1980s Turkey," in "Reshaping the Turkish Nation-State: The Turkish-German Guest Worker Program and Planned Development, 1961–1985" (PhD dissertation, The University of Iowa, Iowa City, 2015), 165–203.

and soon she was learning Turkish words. "I have to say ... I can't say a whole sentence correctly," she confessed, "but I can understand a lot of words. I had to, because I, when I tested the kids, whether they named colors or numbers or their body parts, I had to learn all of that."[77] Schmidt grew close to many of her students, enjoyed warm support from their parents, and remained in touch with a number of them even after her retirement.

Other teachers enrolled directly in Turkish-language classes as a way to equip themselves for the challenge of a multicultural classroom. When Sabine Müller started teaching in West Berlin in the mid-1970s, a quarter of the students in her first class were the children of immigrants. Müller decided soon thereafter to take a Turkish course and learn the differences between the German and Turkish languages, as most of her foreign students were Turkish. She also drew on her Turkish colleagues, first those employed by the Turkish government and later independent teachers, for help with the new language and in communicating with her students.[78] For Müller, understanding her students' language was part of being a good teacher, and her efforts contributed to a space of cross-cultural education that would gradually extend beyond her own language learning to incorporate all of her students and the classroom itself.

Particularly in the earlier years of immigrant settlement and until the mid- to late 1980s, few teachers received education or training specific to the instruction of *Ausländerkinder* (foreign children). Many in West Berlin and throughout West Germany struggled to effectively teach increasingly diverse student populations, but some took it upon themselves to develop strategies and programs to meet these new challenges. In West Berlin, a movement to incorporate both German and Turkish languages into classroom instruction began in the early 1980s with two teachers at a primary school in the district of Kreuzberg.[79] Teachers in other districts with high foreigner populations, such as Wedding and Tiergarten, looked on their efforts with interest. Especially in the beginning, the bilingual education approach was very much a grassroots effort, as interested teachers met with each other, discussed the pedagogy, and developed their own instructional materials. Soon, however, teachers took the idea in a different direction. Instead of using *zwei-sprachige Erziehung* (bilingual education) in foreigner-only classes, they integrated the concept into mixed classrooms of German and migrant students.

---

[77] Schmidt interview, 3.
[78] Sabine Müller (pseudonym), interview by author, 14 May 2009, transcription by Perrin Saylan, Berlin, 1.
[79] Müller interview, 4.

By the mid- to late 1980s, similar programs were springing up all over the city, aided by funding from the sympathetic Red-Green (SPD-Grünen) coalition government in the Berliner Senate.[80] At its high point, approximately sixty schools throughout the city offered bilingual classes to their students.[81]

Bilingual education came to Wedding primary schools in the late 1980s and early 1990s, due in part to the efforts of Sabine Müller. Eager to be an effective teacher and willing to try new things, Müller began incorporating the approach into her own classroom and soon became a passionate advocate and developer of the program. "I observed how wonderful it is for the children and also for the parents," she explained. As part of the program, the classroom furniture and tools are labeled with tags bearing both their German and Turkish names. The students and parents come into the classroom "and discover: Aha! There's something Turkish, there's something Turkish, there's something Turkish. My language is accepted, and I'll be accepted, too."[82] For Erol Kayman, another primary school teacher who has worked in Tiergarten and Wedding, one of the strongest pedagogical features of the bilingual approach has been building on students' previous knowledge, which makes them feel more confident in the classroom and encourages their learning process.[83]

The implementation and practice of bilingual education created a space that allowed for all participants to be involved in daily classroom activities on a relatively even level. At the same time, the bilingual educational program did not limit itself to bridging language differences; teachers incorporated other exchanges, such as celebrating holidays from different cultures in the classroom, and often emphasized commonalities in particular religious or cultural traditions. Müller illustrated this aspect of the program with the example of Abraham, a central figure in the Muslim holiday of the *Opferfest* (Festival of the Sacrifice) as well as in the Christian Bible.[84]

Such holiday celebrations did not occur solely in bilingual classrooms. Turkish-German students learned about and experienced German holidays and traditions in classrooms and schoolwide celebrations throughout the year, and provided parents with the opportunity to experience and contribute to the classroom as a cross-cultural space. When Schmidt's

---

[80] Ibid., 2.
[81] Erol Kayman (pseudonym), interview by author, 29 May 2009, digital recording, Berlin.
[82] Müller interview, 4.   [83] Kayman interview.   [84] Müller interview, 4.

preschool class celebrated St. Martin's Day, parents brought homemade baked goods and joined in the class party, part of which took place in a nearby Catholic church. "They thought it was fantastic," Schmidt remembered, that they could take part in the festivities and the singing. Schmidt credited parental participation in this and other class celebrations with helping parents feel more comfortable in the classroom and with the school in general.[85]

Thus, primary and secondary schools played multiple and at times conflicting roles in the lives of Turkish-German students, their parents, and their teachers. As with their parents in the workplace, Turkish-German students in primary and secondary schools came into direct contact with Germans, institutions, and expectations that alternately served to embed them in the host society even as they continued to define the second generation as "foreign." Some Turkish-German students were able to achieve personal and academic success with a combination of their own initiative, assistance from friends, parental encouragement, and teacher support. For many others, the challenges of conflicting expectations, language difficulties, and lack of informed parental and institutional support proved a significant stumbling block, leading to weak performance in school and poor preparation for the job market. West Berlin's relatively early focus on preparing foreign students for life in the Federal Republic may have set the perimeters for the discourse about school as the central site of *Gastarbeiterkinder* integration, but lack of teacher training and institutional reform hindered its practical implementation.

Yet the city's ad hoc approach to integration also gave rise to grassroots efforts among teachers and parents to develop events and methods that directly addressed the challenges faced by their schools. In the 1980s and early 1990s, the experiment of bilingual classes began to open up spaces that recognized the potential contribution of a multicultural approach to the education and success of all students.[86] Such spaces reflected the growing influence of the second generation on the school and addressed, to an extent, the mandate of equipping these students for life in West Germany. At the same time, they represented early efforts, also present at the Wedding Volkshochschule, at promoting not just immigrant integration but also a more multicultural society.

---

[85] Schmidt interview, 4.
[86] Despite this success, administrative support and funding for *zwei-sprachige Erziehung* programs began to wane in the mid-1990s as more well-to-do German families moved out of the central districts of the city and into more suburban areas. By 2009, only five of the original sixty schools still offered bilingual classes. See Kayman interview.

The *Volkshochschule* as Community Mediator

While primary and secondary schools educated their foreign students for success within the German school system and eventually society, Wedding's *Volkshochschule* (VHS) had the related objective to facilitate the successful adjustment of West Berlin's foreign residents to the city. Reaching out to the city's immigrant (especially Turkish) population and German residents, beginning in the mid-1970s the VHS used language courses, career preparation, social events, and cultural offerings to promote cross-cultural understanding and mutual accommodation. These efforts opened up spaces related to, and yet distinct from, those present in required schooling. There were purposefully intermediary spaces designed to equip immigrants to lead productive lives in West Germany and relate with Germans as well as to help Germans understand their new neighbors, and creative spaces that promoted collaboration between Germans and immigrants on cultural projects. As in primary and secondary schools, students struggled with coursework, peers, and teachers; found opportunities to learn skills that would improve their chances for financial success; and learned about West German society and culture. Yet the approach adopted by the VHS and the voluntary participation of the first and second generation in its programs combined to create unique spaces of belonging that worked to further weave them into the fabric of the city.

Housed in a building on Müllerstrasse and then later in a Wedding *Oberschule* not far from the Sprengelkiez neighborhood, the *Volkshochschule* was well-situated to observe and react to the changing demographics of that district. By the mid-1970s, the school already had what was then called the "Türkenprogramm," headed by Sever Sarioğlu. Director Sarioğlu, according to his successor Dr. Eduard Ditschek, "set the tone" early on by making the personal decision that the VHS needed to offer something that would engage and assist the growing Turkish community in the surrounding neighborhoods.[87] The early efforts of the Wedding Volkshochschule reflected the findings of early sociological work on guest worker communities and the arguments of the first *Ausländerbeauftragter*, Heinz Kühn, among others, that emphasized the importance of education providing practical assistance in overcoming everyday challenges to immigrants' lives and work. The initial offerings consisted mainly of language courses in both German and Turkish at a variety of levels. The German-language courses took place in schools around the

---

[87] Dr. Eduard Ditschek, interview by author, 11 May 2009, transcription by Perrin Saylan, Berlin, 16.

Figure 8. German course for immigrants at Wedding's
Volkshochschule, 1970

district and were offered both in the afternoons and evenings so as to
accommodate both Turkish-German youth and their working parents
(Figure 8).[88] Early Turkish courses were geared at promoting literacy in
one's native language, stressing the development of reading and writing
skills.[89]

The VHS's efforts at offering practical assistance extended beyond
language instruction to also include career training and preparation. As
with language classes, the VHS saw courses designed to teach marketable
skills to immigrant students as an important way to facilitate their integration into the city and began offering such courses in the mid- to late
1970s. From the start, the VHS had specific target groups in mind, based
primarily on gender and age. In a 1981 report to a working group on
Ausländerforschung (foreigner research), then director Sarioğlu wrote
that courses in sewing, cooking, hair styling, and cosmetics were "especially interesting for female participants," while teenage boys and men
were "naturally more interested in technical fields," such as "practical
photography, car repair, technical drafting, and electronics."[90] Articles

---

[88] German Course for Immigrants at Wedding's Volkshochschule, 1970, from Martin
Greve and Tülay Çınar, *Das Türkische Berlin*. Miteinander Leben in Berlin (Berlin:
Die Ausländerbeauftragte des Senats, 1998), 16.
[89] "Wedding Halk Yüksekokulu: Türkler için Almanca Kursları," promotional literature,
Wedding Volkshochschule, personal files of Dr. Eduard Ditschek (EDF), accessed on
26 May 2009, Berlin, 0–5.
[90] "Betr.: Ausländerforschung in der Bundesrepublik und West-Berlin," report by Sever
Sarioğlu to Prof. Dr. Detlef Bischoff, Wedding Volkshochschule, EDF, accessed 26 May
2009, 2.

in Turkish-language newspapers concerning the VHS's course offerings occasionally, although not always, reflected the gendered and generational targeting. A 1986 article in *Hürriyet* highlighted the woodworking and truck mechanics courses offered for young men and the tailoring and hair-styling courses for girls and women.[91] A year later, however, another article in *Hürriyet* simply listed some of the available courses, such as computer and typing courses, labeling the textile and beauty classes for girls and women.[92]

As we have seen, in the late 1970s and early 1980s the growing body of sociological research on the guest worker community in the Federal Republic stressed the social and economic instability of immigrant youth as a source of potential conflict and violence, advocating education to promote their successful integration.[93] And, although some secondary schools and West German businesses sought to address this situation among school-aged youth, politicians and the media throughout the 1980s stressed a link between unemployed immigrant youth, social unrest, and crime. Beginning in the early 1980s, the VHS increasingly turned its attention to youth ages sixteen to twenty-five whose chances for successful integration were seen as particularly threatened due to either their recent arrival (which meant they had not been through the German school system), their lack of a secondary school diploma, their unemployment, or a combination of these factors. In cooperation with the Wedding *Arbeitsamt* (Employment Office), the VHS began in 1982 to offer a thirteen-month career preparation course for "*Sonderschule* graduates, foreigners with language difficulties, and youth who only went to *Hauptschule* through the eighth grade."[94] The program, called Hauptschulabscluss für Arbeitslose (Secondary School Certificate for the Unemployed) or HASA, was geared as much toward developing self-confidence and overcoming learning difficulties as toward learning marketable skills. Classes met five days a week, climbing to an eventual forty-hour week by 1985. From 1983 to 1992, 321 students had participated in the program, including 252 "Inländer" and 69 "Ausländer."[95] Of those participants, 5.1 percent remained unemployed after

[91] "Wedding VHS yabancılar için kurslar düzenliyor," *Hürriyet*, 4 September 1986, EDF, accessed 26 May 2009.
[92] "Wedding VHS'de ögrenciler için çok kurs var," *Hürriyet*, 15 January 1987, EDF, accessed 26 May 2009.
[93] Chin, *The Guest Worker Question in Postwar Germany*, 95–97.
[94] "10 Jahre Berufsvorbereitende Vollzeitlehrgänge: mit internem Abscluss des einfachen und erweiterten Hauptschulabschluss, 1982–1992, Wedding," Wedding Volkshochschule, EDF, accessed 26 May 2009, 2.
[95] "Inländer" is a term meaning "native" or "local" that was developed ostensibly as a way to connect foreigners and natives linguistically while still distinguishing between them.

completion of the program, and 10.3 percent worked as unskilled labor. The remainder (and vast majority) worked in a range of careers, from childcare and medical professions to technical careers and industry.[96] Through the HASA program, the VHS created a space that recognized and addressed the reality that secondary schools, for a variety of reasons, were unable to prepare certain local youth – both German and foreign – for the challenge of the city's difficult job market.

In 1985, the *Volkshochschule* hired Dr. Eduard Ditschek with the mandate to bring together the *Türkenprogramm* and the *Deutsch als Fremdsprache* program under a single department, originally called the *Ausländerprogramm*. Eventually renamed the *Interkulturelles Bildungsprogramm* (Program for Intercultural Education), this newly formed department brought together under one roof the language, job training, and cultural offerings directed toward the district's immigrant population – offerings that grew and changed in response to the dynamic neighborhoods around them.[97] Beginning in the fall of 1985, the VHS, in cooperation with *Familienfürsorge* (family welfare services), held a Turkish language and literacy course for women in a building on Sparrplatz, "in a space that is, for other reasons, trusted by [the women] and nearby their apartments." The following semester, the two institutions planned a similar German-language and literacy course in the same location for those participants.[98] The number and types of language courses continued to expand, so that in the first two semesters of 1987 the Wedding Volkshochschule provided 74 German courses with a total of almost 5,000 classroom hours and 15 literacy courses with more than 1,500 hours of instruction.[99]

The VHS also continued to create spaces to mediate between second-generation youth and the difficult job market in the city. Although the statistics suggest HASA proved successful for the majority of its participants, by 1987 the VHS had decided a separate preparatory course was needed for the *Späteinsteiger* – foreign youth who came to Germany at an age where they were no longer required to attend school. "For these participants," a HASA report reads, "the training course offers practically the only chance to be able to learn a professional career in Germany."[100] The course, entitled V-HASA or Vor-HASA (*Vorkurs zum*

---

[96] "Ibid.," 20–21.   [97] Ditschek interview, 1.

[98] "Kooperation mit Selbsthilfegruppe, freien Trägern und andere in der Ausländerarbeit engagierte Institutionen," Vb IV 101, Betr.: Vb-A-Bericht, Wedding Volkshochschule, EDF, accessed 26 May 2009, 1.

[99] "Interkulturelles Bildungsprogramm: Bestandsaufnahme und Perspektive (1987)," Wedding Volkshochschule, EDF, accessed 26 May 2009, 1.

[100] Ibid., 18.

Hauptschulabschlusslehrgang, Preparatory Course for Secondary School Certificate Training), combined intensive German-language lessons with career training and sociopedagogical work in its effort to point immigrant youth "to the possibilities and routes to integration in education and career."[101]

A report on the class of 1990–1991 gives us an overview of that year's participants and provides insight into the diversity of the population known as the second generation. Twenty-five of the twenty-seven students who started the course completed it; nineteen were women and six were men. Only five of the students had been born in West Germany. The rest had been born in Turkey, and, of those, most had only lived in the FRG for a couple of years. Much of this chapter has focused on members of the second generation who had either been born in West Germany or immigrated as young children. Yet, as the participants of the 1990–1991 V-HASA program demonstrate, Turkish youth continued to immigrate to West Germany well into the late 1980s. These young immigrants, based on their age and because they joined parents already living in the FRG, became part of the second generation, despite having little if any access to the advantages of the West German education system. The VHS's unique position as a center for adult education and a community mediator meant it was well placed to address the needs of this segment of the second generation.

All the students in the 1990–1991 V-HASA program identified as Muslims and lived at home with their parents, who, with only two exceptions, had unlimited employment permits. Two-thirds "felt comfortable" (*wohlfühlen*) living in Berlin, and none planned to return to Turkey in the near future. At the beginning of the course, 80 percent of the program's participants wanted to pursue further education and training after completion rather than go directly into the workforce.[102] One month after completion of the course, nine had begun a course for qualification in sewing, four were waiting to start the HASA program, one had an apprenticeship at an upscale department store, two more had applied for apprenticeships in technical drafting, and another was receiving training at a foundation for disadvantaged youth. The numbers, the report insists, do not tell the whole story: the participants "improved their language abilities, greatly increased their school and general knowledge,

---

[101] "Vollzeitlehrgang für ausländische Jugendliche: zum Abbau schulischer Defizierte und zur Vorgereitung auf einen Beruf im Bereich Textil/Bekleindung, V-HASA 1990/91," Bezirksamt Wedding von Berlin Abteilung Volksbildung and Volkshochschule Wedding, EDF, accessed 26 May 2009, 4.
[102] Ibid., 5–8.

gained a clear picture of the field of textiles and clothing, and acquired a basic facility with data processing and typing."[103]

Each of these VHS course offerings, from the cosmetics classes to the V-HASA program, aimed to provide its participants – primarily members of the growing and diversifying Turkish-German community – with practical skills that would better facilitate their settlement into life in Berlin and German society more generally. Although the school's available courses and the marketing of those courses often reinforced a gendered understanding of which professions were appropriate for whom, it is unclear whether VHS officials and instructors were driven by their own preconceptions of men's and women's work or by what they thought would draw Turkish students. What is clear, both in the language and job training courses, is an increasing focus on women and young adults, two groups the VHS saw as particularly in need of intermediary spaces that would enable them to gain valuable skills for their personal and financial well-being. And the continuation and proliferation of such courses strongly suggests that their target audiences considered them a worthwhile opportunity and utilized these spaces for their own advancement.

In addition to formal instruction, the VHS also hosted clubs and events aimed at facilitating social interaction both within particular immigrant communities and between immigrants and Germans. In the mid-1980s, the VHS began to hold a biweekly *Frauenkreis* (women's group) for Turkish women, almost all of whom had moved to West Germany to join family there. "Fixated on their traditional, gender-specific role," facilitator Serpil Dalaman wrote for the VHS catalog of cultural offerings, the participants "have almost no contact with the outside world." The goal of the *Frauenkreis* was to introduce these women to each other and to their new surroundings, expanding both the physical and social environments in which they moved.[104] At their biweekly meetings, the participants heard informational presentations by guest speakers on subjects such as "the role of women, child-rearing, health, and legal issues," which the women followed up with lively discussion. The women also went on sightseeing trips and excursions designed to introduce them to the larger city outside of their neighborhood. Finally, the *Frauenkreis* hosted events open to German participants,

[103] Ibid., 27.
[104] Serpil Dalaman, "Türkischer Frauenkreis," in Ursula Diehl, Gisela Weimann, and Eduard Ditschek, eds., *Kunstvoller Alltag: Kommunale Kulturarbeit der Volkshochschule Berlin-Wedding* (Berlin: FAB-Verlag, 1990), 122.

creating a space where they could share aspects of Turkish culture (particularly food culture).

Like the V-HASA program, the *Frauenkreis* brought together instruction with social support, albeit in a less formal setting. Although not attempting to train the women in a particular career, the VHS and Dalaman clearly wanted to equip the participants with tools to develop their own self-confidence and an understanding of life in their new home. The meetings allowed women to learn about aspects of the host society in a safe, middle space between their homes and the society itself. One of the women's excursions took them to a media network's Turkish editorial department, where a female moderator interviewed the participants. In response to a question about the usefulness of the *Frauenkreis*, one woman answered, "I was freed from my loneliness. Now I have built a network of social connections and a group of friends." She concluded by wishing that as many women as possible would participate in their meetings.[105]

Yet the VHS was not only interested in facilitating the social and economic progress of the local immigrant population. In keeping with the definition of "integration" as a process of cultural understanding and exchange earlier articulated by the SPD, the VHS under both Sarioğlu and Ditschek also organized special, one-time events specifically geared toward bringing foreign residents and Germans into contact with each other. Sometimes these events were purely social in nature. In January 1974, the VHS organized a "German-Turkish" evening at Wedding's city hall, complete with food, drink, music, and dancing. Although the atmosphere at the beginning was strained, soon, the newspaper account assured its readers, "through drinks, cookies, and a thick haze of cigarette smoke, Germans and foreigners came quickly together."[106] Around one hundred Germans and immigrants, mostly Turks, participated in the event, chatting and dancing in the front hall of the city hall for three hours. Coordinators at the VHS considered the evening such a success that they talked about making it a regular event and discussed finding a bigger space to accommodate the crowds.[107]

At other times, the VHS organized events that presented their audiences with performances by the different cultural groups that operated under its auspices. In the early 1980s, one such event, entitled "'Orient-Rock' and Turkish Folklore," brought together traditional Turkish

---

[105] Ibid., 123.
[106] "Bei Getränken und Keksen kamen sich Ausländer und Berliner näher," *Berliner Morgenpost*, 13 January 1974, EDF, accessed 26 May 2009.
[107] Ibid.

folklore, dance, and music with a modern rock band that fused American rock music with "oriental elements" to produce a sound that the program writer described as "navigating an integration course."[108] With this particular event, the VHS aimed to form a bridge not only between Germans and foreigners but also between generations. The cost for attending was kept relatively low (three marks for adults, one and a half for students and the unemployed), and the snack time, complete with Turkish food and a variety of drinks, would "hopefully offer enough opportunity for friendly exchange."[109] With these types of events, the VHS hoped to combine education and socializing to introduce different elements of the surrounding community to one another.

Despite the popularity of some of its events, the Wedding VHS was not always successful in its efforts to bring together different members of the community, at times due to lack of interest of the targeted, potential German participants. In 1988, Michael Weiß and Ataman Dalaman organized a weekend getaway for participants in the HASA program with the intention of bringing together German and Turkish youth to get to know each other better, learn about one another's culture, and, in particular, for German students to hear about the experiences of their Turkish peers. Only one German student, a young woman, ended up participating in the weekend trip, however.[110] Even though the weekend proved a good opportunity for Turkish-German students to discuss the challenges they faced and draw support from one another, the intended middle ground for cross-cultural engagement and understanding largely failed to materialize. At the same time, however, it illustrates, together with the earlier examples of social and cultural events, that the VHS worked not only to facilitate immigrants' introduction to and successful settlement in West Berlin but also to create intermediary spaces through which German residents would come to better know and understand their "new neighbors."

A Collaborative and Creative Space

These seminars, events, and concerts were all a part of the Wedding Volkshochschule's efforts to be, in the words of director of the *Interkulturelles*

---

[108] "'Orient-Rock' und türkischer Folkloretanz: Eine Veranstaltung der Volkshochschule Wedding," program notes, Wedding Volkshochschule, EDF, accessed 26 May 2009, 2. No date other than "Freitag, 31 Mai" is on the document; however, the address of the VHS and that it fell under the auspices of the "Ausländerprogramm" suggest the event took place in the early 1980s.
[109] Ibid., 2.
[110] Christian Blees, "Am Frühstücktisch fehlten die Oliven," *Der Tagesspiegel*, 26 June 1988, EDF.

Bildungsprogramm Dr. Eduard Ditschek, "a site of meeting and exchange
[that] brings people from different cultures together."[111] In addition to
one-time events, the VHS instituted and hosted projects that stressed
the "exchange" aspect of Ditschek's words. For these projects, the
VHS intended that Germans and their "ausländische Mitbürger" would
come to better know and understand each other through the process
of collaboration in artistic production. The VHS's efforts to promote
cross-cultural understanding and integration through artistic production
reflect the convergence of three trends present in 1980s West Berlin.
We have already seen two of these trends play a significant role in the
education of second-generation Turkish Germans during this time. First,
the VHS's artistic programs reflected the continuing influence of the idea
of cross-cultural understanding as a key part of the process of integration.
Second, the government's relative lack of a clear articulation and direction on how to accomplish "integration" left its practical implementation
to interested parties at the local level, including the Wedding VHS.

The third trend to take into account in order to understand how the
VHS's activities fit within the broader historical context is West Berlin's
struggle in the 1970s and 1980s with its own identity, and the image it
projected to the rest of the world. As we have seen in earlier chapters,
its waning importance in the Cold War, the demographic shifts that
made the city's population more ethnically diverse and therefore less
"German," and highly visible and sometimes violent protests against
the government, prompted within the city if not an outright crisis of
identity, then at the very least a deep concern with the city's image
internationally.[112] Yet West Berlin's struggle with its own identity can
be traced back to the first days following the construction of the Wall,
which forced the city to take strong (and expensive) steps to construct
and sustain its image as a "world city." In its efforts to make West Berlin
look the part of a *Weltstadt*(cosmopolitan city), urban planners designed
and constructed numerous buildings for the arts.[113] In addition to physical manifestations of culture, the government tried to encourage a
flourishing arts scene, opening new institutes and schools dedicated to
visual and performance art. Even as it provided tax breaks and subsidies

---

[111] "Mit Ausländern ins Gespräch kommen," *Lokal-Anzeiger*, 6 February 1991, *Jugend-theater Presse* Binder, EDF
[112] See Emily Pugh, *Architecture, Politics, and Identity in Divided Berlin* (Pittsburgh: University of Pittsburgh Press, 2014), 62–105; Carla Elizabeth MacDougall, "Cold War Capital: Contested Urbanity in West Berlin, 1963–1989," (PhD dissertation, Rutgers, The State University of New Jersey, New Brunswick, 2011), 231–278.
[113] Alexandra Richie, *Faust's Metropolis: A History of Berlin* (New York: Carroll & Graf Publishers, Inc., 1998), 798–803.

to businesses to keep their West Berlin branches or open new ones, the government likewise throughout the 1960s and into the 1970s poured money and resources into encouraging and supporting artists, playwrights, writers, and musicians to live and produce in the city.[114] As Chancellor Kohl emphasized in the context of West Berlin's celebration of the city's 750th anniversary in 1987, Berlin was "a world city," "a place of exchange for new ideas, a an important center of creativity."[115] The Wedding VHS's approach to communal experiences and integration through the arts was embedded in the broader context of West Berlin's focus on fostering a vibrant arts scene, but it reflects more its decentralized, local-level manifestations such as Wedding's Fabrik Osloerstrasse and Kreuzberg's professional Turkish theater, Tiyatrom (My Theater).

Whereas film series, art exhibitions, and multicultural clubs played a role in producing this collaborative, creative space, perhaps the most public example of cross-cultural artistic production during the 1980s and early 1990s was a German-Turkish theater workshop that came to be named Kulis. The story of Kulis highlights the importance of individuals in the creation of a particular space, even as it reflects the influence of the community and common experiences. In addition, by comparing the Wedding VHS's theater workshop to Rita Chin's examination of the University of Munich's Institut für Deutsch als Fremdsprache (DaF), we can see how the process of cultural production and the balance of power among participants in those spaces affected the ways in which they understood and addressed the concept of integration.

When Dr. Eduard Ditschek became the director of the then *Ausländerprogramm* in 1985, the department's largest cultural program was a combination of Turkish folklore courses, which included traditional Turkish music and folk dance. Ditschek continued to support this program when he assumed directorship, but he and others at the Wedding VHS also wanted a cultural program in which "an intellectual discussion concerning life as migrant and immigrant" could take place. As a university student, Ditschek had studied general and comparative literature, and his own gravitation toward theater as the *Ausländerprogramm*'s next cultural program was met and sharpened by the application of Yekta Arman for the position of theater director.[116] The thirty-two-year-old Arman had been working as an actor and director since completing his formal training as an actor in Istanbul fourteen years earlier. Beginning in

[114] Ibid., 790–798.
[115] From *Berliner Morgenpost*, 6 January 1987, as quoted in Richie, *Faust's Metropolis*, 808.
[116] Ditschek interview, 2.

1984, he was a member of Kreuzberg's Tiyatrom,[117] and he came to the VHS with the notion that he should not just be working with professional Turkish actors. Arman was looking for a place where he could do theater work with young people from immigrant backgrounds. "And so we came together, Yekta and I," recalled Ditschek, "and that was 1986."[118]

Although both Arman and Ditschek originally hoped for a balance of students with German and immigrant backgrounds, from the beginning the majority of the young actors came from Turkish families.[119] Participants were generally working-class youth in their late teens to early twenties and lived in districts throughout the city – although mostly in Wedding, Kreuzberg, or Neukölln.[120] During the ten years that it operated, the German-Turkish Youth Theater (Deutsch-Türkisches Jugendtheater), later renamed Kulis, was made up of around twenty-five participants, a third of whom formed a core that stayed with the group between six and seven years.[121] As the significant majority of the participants came from Turkish backgrounds, much of the conversation during practices took place in Turkish. This could be difficult for Ditschek and the German youths, who understood little or no Turkish. At the same time, the language and cultural differences spurred the "intellectual discussion" that Ditschek and the VHS had hoped for, and proved to be one of the elements of group participation that young people found most appealing. "It's really a lot of fun and really interesting to do theater with Turkish friends," twenty-six- year-old electrician Markus Eitel told the *Nord-Berliner* newspaper. "You also get a look into Turkish mentality that otherwise you only perceive superficially." His nineteen-year-old fellow actor Aylin Uyunc added, "The idea, that Germans and Turks do theater together, I think it's great. And after [my first] play, I'm definitely going to keep participating."[122]

The participation of all the young actors in the development and preparation of each play reveals the extent to which the VHS served as host to collaborative, creative spaces in the lives of older second-generation youth in particular. Whereas the first production, *Yaşasın şiir/ Hoch lebe die Poesie* (see Figure 9), brought together poetry from German

---

[117] "Auch Deutsche können den Sketch auf türkisch verstehen," *Der Tagesspiegel*, 8 November 1986, *Jugendtheater Presse* Binder, EDF.

[118] Ditschek interview, 2.

[119] The program from the group's first production lists twenty-two actors with Turkish names and seven with German names. "Yaşasın şiir/ Hoch lebe die Poesie," Deutsch-Türkisches Jugendtheater/ Türk-Alman Gençlik Tiyatrosu, Volkshochschule Berlin-Wedding, 29 May 1986, EDF, 3.

[120] Ditschek interview, 4.   [121] Ibid., 13.

[122] "Die Inszenierung ist wieder konfliktträchtig aufgebaut," *Der Nord-Berliner*, 29 March 1990, *Jugendtheater Presse* Binder, EDF.

Figure 9. The German-Turkish Youth Theater, 1987.
Photograph by Nada Fink.

and Turkish literary traditions, subsequent productions were original plays or series of sketches developed by Arman, Ditschek, and the actors themselves. First they decided on a topic, then the actors wrote scenes or ideas around that theme. Arman collected the students' thoughts and compiled them into a rough draft, which he gave to Ditschek for revision. Once the revision was ready, the whole team set to work bringing the play to the stage. The intentions of the group's founders, the makeup of the participants, and the collaborative way in which both parties worked created a space that coalesced into a series of productions dealing directly with the challenges of cross-cultural communication and multicultural life in Berlin. After the first production, all projects were original plays or sketches developed by Arman, Ditschek, and the student actors. They examined the relations between German and Turkish coworkers,[123] explored the dynamics of interaction and conflict within a classroom,[124] and depicted the second generation's struggles with daily life and violence.[125] Through this space, the actors – both Turkish and German – were able to create representations of their own experiences and ideas, to exercise and hone

[123] Eddi Ditschek, "Das Deutsch-Türkische Jugendtheater der Volkshochschule Wedding," in Ursula Diehl, Gisela Weimann, and Dr. Eduard Ditschek, eds., *Kunstvoller Alltag: Kommunale Kulturarbeit der Volkshochschule Berlin-Wedding* (Berlin, 1990), 101.
[124] Eddi Ditschek, "So eine Klasse: Eine neue Produktion des Deutsch-Türkischen Jugendtheaters der Volkshochschule Wedding," *Vis-à-Vis*, December 1988/January 1989, Binder: Altbestand Wedding 11.1987–04.1990, MMA.
[125] "Die Band und die Bande: Eine neue Produktion des Deutsch-Türkischen Jugendtheaters der Volkshochschule Wedding," *Vis-à-Vis*, May 1991, Binder: Altbestand Wedding 11.1987–04.1990, MMA.

their skills in acting and the theater, and to collaborate with and learn from other youth they may not have otherwise befriended.[126]

The influence of this collaborative, creative space started in the Wedding *Oberschule* where the group practiced and expanded to include sites throughout Wedding and other districts in Berlin. Ditschek smiled as he recalled how the theater group "practically occupied" the basement of the *Oberschule* where the VHS was based, practicing late into the evenings and putting up posters to personalize the space.[127] Their first performance took place in the auditorium of the VHS, with subsequent performances throughout the city. From their debut, the German-Turkish Youth Theater attracted a diverse audience, ranging from local German and Turkish residents to more prominent guests such as Commissioner for Foreigners Barbara John and Turkish consul Mehmet Gücük.[128] The group played for receptive and responsive audiences in other cities as well where they traveled for competitions, fulfilling Ditschek and Arman's second goal: educating the community about both the work of the youth theater and the VHS more generally.[129]

Audience members were not the only ones to learn about the efforts of this multicultural Jugendtheater, however. The group's composition and the subject matter of their plays attracted the attention of the newsprint media, from district-level monthlies such as *Vis-à-Vis* to widely circulating dailies including *Der Tagesspiegel*, *Hürriyet*, and *Tercüman*. In stark contrast to the more common media representations of Turkish-German youth as failing to integrate or potentially violent, coverage of the *Jugendtheater* performances was consistently positive in tone, with both German- and Turkish-language newspapers applauding the youth for taking on the difficult topic of daily *Nebeneinander* (coexistence).[130] The group's engagement with the contemporary problems of immigrant youth and the challenges of integration were a constant focus of the news coverage. In the words of one *Milliyet* article, the strength of the

---

[126] This last aspect was of central importance to the *Interkulturelle Bildungsprogramm*, which, Ditschek stressed time and again in VHS literature and newspaper articles, was about learning from one another more than integration. For example, see Ditschek, "Das Deutsch-Türkische Jugendtheater der Volkshochschule Wedding," 100–102; Ditschek, "So eine Klasse; and Eddi Ditschek, "Volkshochschule als Ort Interkultureller Bildung," *Vis-à-Vis*, September 1990, Binder: Altbestand Wedding 11.1987–04.1990, MMA.

[127] Ditschek interview, 11.

[128] "'Yaşasın şiir' yeniden sahneleniyor," *Hürriyet*, 29 May 1986, *Jugendtheater Presse* Binder, EDF.

[129] Ditschek interview, 4.

[130] It is interesting to note that, despite the similar tone in press coverage, the Turkish-language papers often used the possessive "our youth" when discussing the actors of Turkish background in Kulis.

production, in this case *Sketch-Topf* in 1987, was that it "depicts the problems of Turks or Germans on one hand, and on the other compels thought through laughter."[131] Kulis's productions and the coverage they received attracted the attention of the Turkish Parents Association of Berlin-Brandenburg and resulted in a high point in the life of the group: the reception of the Mete Ekşi Prize in 1992.[132] It was a proud moment for all the participants. "I can still well remember the presentation ceremony," Ditschek recounted with quiet pride. "I still have the certificate that we received, and I think we received twenty-five hundred marks." He laughed. "Naturally we put the money right into the next production."[133]

During the ten years it had been in existence, Kulis performed 10 premieres and gave over two hundred performances, with around 150 youth participants.[134] Under the auspices of the Wedding Volkshochschule, the staff and students formed a collaborative, creative space in which they pursued their common interest in theater and could address, on their own terms, the challenges and conflicts they saw in the community around them. Through the performances of these collaborations and their news coverage, this creative, cross-cultural space extended beyond its origins at the VHS through the local community and, albeit to a limited extent, broader German society.

The similarities shared between the Wedding VHS's *Ausländerprogramm* and the University of Munich's DaF are significant and perhaps most revealing when we narrow our focus to the VHS's youth theater program and the DaF's writing contests. Both were begun (the first writing contest in 1979 and the youth theater program in 1986) with the specific intention of bringing nonnative German speakers into cultural production through the use of the German language.[135] In addition, the participants' personal experiences were assumed and encouraged to inform the subject matter of their artistic product. For the DaF, although

[131] "Gururlandık ...", *Milliyet*, 13 March 1987, *Jugendtheater Presse* Binder, EDF.
[132] Mete Ekşi, born and raised in Kreuzberg, was the son of Turkish immigrants. In 1991, Ekşi was attacked with a baseball bat and killed by a young man from Marzahn when he tried to mediate a fight between three German brothers from Marzahn and a group of Turkish youth from Kreuzberg. The prize, given by the Turkish Parents Association of Berlin-Brandenburg, was set up a year later to advance initiatives that worked toward peaceful relations between Germans and foreigners. "Durchs Theater Zugang zu Ausländern gefunden," *Der Tagesspiegel*, 22 November 1992, *Jugendtheater Presse* Binder, EDF.
[133] Ditschek interview, 9.
[134] Yekta Arman, "1985–1995 10 Jahre KULIS: Deutsch-Türkisches Theater an der Volkshochschule Wedding," *Jugendtheater Presse* Binder, EDF.
[135] Chin, *The Guest Worker Question in Postwar Germany*, 106–107.

directors Harald Weinrich and Irmgard Ackermann kept the subjects of the contests broad, they reflected the theme of being or feeling foreign in West Germany.[136] Regardless of whether they immigrated through the guest worker program or moved to the FRG to attend university, nonnative writers could, as Director Weinrich stated, give Germans "the chance through this literature to perceive ourselves as foreigners and Germany as a foreign country."[137] The productions of Kulis operated in a similar way, as youth with Turkish and German backgrounds presented plays based on what they experienced and understood as the reality of their and their neighbors' everyday lives. Audiences and the media received their productions as authentic depictions of, in the words of the *Milliyet* article, "the problems of Turks or Germans" that prompted playgoers to better understand and sympathize with one another, and thus an important part of the integration process.[138]

Yet despite these similarities in intention and reception, key differences existed between the approaches of the DaF and the Wedding VHS that reflect the influence of the latter's more communal and local character. First, the Kulis theater group was an intentionally collaborative space. Although still hierarchical, each production involved the input and participation of every person involved. As a result, the *process* of production – from conceiving the idea to brainstorming the script to putting on the play – constituted the practice of cultural exchange and understanding that proponents of reciprocal integration in the 1970s and 1980s articulated. Second, Kulis productions, although reflecting on broader social developments, were intensely local. The DaF's writing competitions drew on writers from across the country, compiled their contributions in edited volumes for a broad German audience, and promoted the winners of its Chamisso Prize as partners for a national dialogue on immigrant experiences and integration. The Wedding VHS's youth theater program comprised local students who mounted productions for mostly local audiences. Whereas the DaF's anthologies were intended to help Germans "perceive themselves as foreigners" and thus have a better understanding of the "other," Kulis productions were, in part, designed also to hold a mirror up to their audience, who could recognize themselves, their coworkers, their classmates, or their neighbors in the unfolding story. The actors were not being put forth as partners in

---

[136] For example, the subject for the inaugural competition in 1979 was "Germany – A Foreign Country," and the following year it was "As a Foreigner in Germany," Chin, *The Guest Worker Question in Postwar Germany*, 107.

[137] As quoted in Chin, *The Guest Worker Question in Postwar Germany*, 129.

[138] "Gururlandık...."

dialogue but rather to put forward a dialogue they had among themselves and inviting the audience to participate.

Finally, the comparison between the DaF and the Wedding VHS raises interesting questions about the agency of minority participants in these German-led institutions. Chin examines this tension in the case of the DaF, demonstrating that, although the DaF directors set the terms of participation and selected both who would be published in their antho- logies and who would be awarded the distinguished Chamisso Prize, minority writers could and did pursue other publishing options and promoted *Ausländerliteratur* through separate organizations with different ideological orientations.[139] Yet the leadership and orientation of the DaF itself was not fundamentally altered. With the Wedding youth theater group, the intentions of its founders were subverted almost from the beginning. Rather than a relatively balanced ratio of West German and immigrant students, the majority of the youth who participated came from Turkish backgrounds, as did one of the directors. This affected the language used during rehearsals as well as the development of the differ- ent productions. And, although Arman and finally Ditschek would be the last to revise a script, neither director had the final say in the fate of Kulis.

After ten years of collaboration, Kulis began to change shape. Some of the students were ready to move on; they had jobs and families that made participation in late-night rehearsals and productions difficult. Another faction took the opposite route. The "theater-obsessed," as Ditschek referred to them, wanted to form the group into a professional theater troupe, which, for them, meant finding a new director and cutting ties with the VHS. "We [Arman and Ditschek] felt like the youths' behavior was like a little mutiny or a little revolution," Ditschek recalled, "but in reality it was a quite normal emancipation process." Ditschek and Arman stepped aside, and the remaining participants continued on with a new director.[140]

Conclusion

The hopes, expectations, and responsibilities invested in the school by teachers and students, politicians and parents, administrators and advo- cates created a space rife with contradiction. Charged, beginning in the mid 1970s, with the responsibility of facilitating the successful integra- tion of guest worker children, but given little more to go on than a

---

[139] Chin, *The Guest Worker Question in Postwar Germany*, 105–137.
[140] Ditschek interview, 14. Unfortunately, the new incarnation of Kulis did not meet with much success, and disbanded not long after the director left the group.

definition of integration that changed with the political and economic winds, schools sought to provide entry into West German society for immigrants in a nonimmigration country. The schools endeavored to give Turkish-German students the tools for success, but the second generation's experiences in that site taught them more than language skills and cultural literacy. As their parents had in the workplace, the second generation learned that their belonging was in large measure defined by their Turkish background. Turkish-German youth dealt with this exclusion in a variety of ways. Some, with the benefit of support-ive parents or an encouraging teacher, challenged others' perceptions, achieved a measure of academic and personal success, and proved that they "belonged." Others responded to the difficulty of the lessons and the apathy or hostility of classmates and even teachers by constructing a sense of belonging separate from the school. Particularly for those who immigrated as older youth, the school presented a formidable challenge of the need to quickly learn not just a new language but also a new system of education.

Yet even as Turkish-German students struggled with the academic and social difficulties of school, they also found and created within it spaces of opportunity that enabled them to pursue their own interests and goals. Young women, perhaps even more so than their male peers, saw in school the chance to equip themselves with the tools necessary for future independence, for a career that would keep them from having to rely on, and thus be subject to, their families for financial support. It is important to note that many of these experiences were not unique to Turkish Germans, or even to children with migrant backgrounds. All students created and experienced these spaces of opportunity within the context of the school, and the Turkish-German students' use of them reflects the ways in which they were settling in and adapting to school life and expectations.

The Turkish-German youth were not the only ones adapting, how-ever. School administrators, teachers, and even the physical classrooms themselves were changing in response to these new students. Although Turkish-German students were the intended target of cross-cultural edu-cation, some West German teachers found themselves learning Turkish, becoming familiar with Turkish traditions and customs, and adapting their lessons and teaching styles to more effectively educate their increas-ingly diverse classes. This last effort found an organized outlet in the development of bilingual education. Beginning at the grassroots level, teachers developed a bilingual approach to the education first of *Gastar-beiterkinder* and then of mixed classrooms, where the incorporation of German and Turkish promoted the participation of all the students in this space of cross-cultural education. In an economic environment where students could not rely on stable employment in the sectors that had brought their parents to the FRG, both secondary schools and the Wedding Volkshochschule responded to the particular need of older youth to prepare for their entry into West Berlin's workforce by developing programs specifically designed for the challenges of language proficiency and obtaining the necessary apprentice and intern positions. The advancement of bilingual education methods and programs such as the HASA and V-HASA reflect the broader development of grassroots, decentralized efforts to promote integration in the face of continued insistence that Germany was not an immigration country and the lack of comprehensive governmental policy regarding integration that official position enabled.

Although it took years for this position to be officially defined and promoted, the Wedding Volkshochschule played an important role as an intermediary and a *Begegnungsort* (place of encounter) for members of the community around it. Both at the individual and institutional level, the VHS responded proactively to the changing composition and needs of its local community. Along with more traditional language and job skills courses, the administrators and instructors at the VHS created deliberate spaces of cross-cultural understanding that they hoped would serve to bring the community together rather than simply prepare one segment to fit into the larger whole. What began in the 1970s with language and Turkish folklore courses, over time developed into efforts designed to both address the economic challenges facing immigrant communities as well as creative programs that emphasized engagement with contemporary issues rather than celebrations of cultural traditions and arts. In doing so, they reflected a definition of "integration" that posited the importance of exchange and understanding, designing both one-time events and longer-term projects to foster such a climate. While they often met with limited success, the collaborative nature of such spaces highlighted the importance placed on communication rather than assimilation, giving their participants the opportunity to move past superficial understanding to grapple with the issues and challenges they found most prevalent in their everyday lives. Such spaces began, in small and piecemeal ways, to shift the borders of belonging in West German society.

5   Making Space for Religion

It is not always an easy thing to find a mosque in Berlin. In recent years, purpose-built mosques have become a more visible part of the urban landscape, but the majority of the city's eighty-plus Islamic religious centers are tucked away in *Hinterhöfe*, readily accessible to those who know where to go but invisible or elusive to strangers. Often housed in former factories or warehouses, these mosques have provided spaces for worship, education, and socialization for the city's Muslim community, the bulk of which has its origins in the Turkish guest worker population. And, just as that burgeoning community made space for itself in workplaces, neighborhoods, and schools, so too did its religious places begin to become a part of the urban landscape. Even though these places of worship seemed increasingly a part of daily media reports about Turkish "foreign residents," finding an actual mosque could prove to be a challenge.

My own visit to the Yunus Emre mosque on Reinickendorfer Strasse in early June 2009 is a case in point. I found the building easily enough. It stood on a moderately busy street, the immediate area characterized more by businesses than apartments. The trees, already in full leaf on a late spring morning and scattered among the buildings and along the street, saved the atmosphere from the depressing concrete blandness that less affluent commercial zones in Berlin tend to have. A sign on the front of a long, two-story building heralded my destination. Passing through the hall, I entered a large courtyard, a chain-link fence separating the open space from the neighboring building to the left and a vacant lot just beyond the bushes across the concrete yard ahead.

I tried the nearest door first and went up a flight of stairs, finding at the top a small room littered with shoes, some pairs lining the wall in an orderly fashion and other, smaller ones scattered impetuously across the floor. The entry led to a larger room that appeared to run the length of the building. It was a Saturday morning, and an elderly man was holding a class in Turkish for a group of young boys at a long table. A woman, perhaps in her mid-thirties with blue eyes and a fair complexion, greeted me and introduced herself as Melek. My interview partner had not yet arrived, so Melek hospitably gave me a brief tour of the mosque, describing some of the events that took place there and explaining the religious function of the furnishings. A deep crimson carpet, patterned to orient supplicants toward Mecca, covered the floor, its expanse interrupted only by two support pillars in the middle of the room and a small pulpit to the right of the *mihrab*[1] on the far wall. On that morning it was empty, but Melek described to me how it fills up on Friday afternoons. Like the previous room, the prayer hall was spotless, orderly, and, in the absence of a table of young boys, serene. This was not a "proper" mosque, Melek explained, one built specifically for its present use, but it served its purpose.[2]

The elderly man speaking Turkish, the young boys studying the Qur'an on a sunny Saturday morning, the young woman in a headscarf, the spacious prayer room: each of these elements has been the subject of political, media, and academic discourse concerning the growth of Islam in Germany. Although not a topic of interest in the earlier years of the guest worker program, scholarship on Islam in Germany, and Europe more generally, has exploded in the past twenty years. Researchers from across the social sciences and humanities have investigated the meanings, practices, and perceptions of Islam as a way to understand its role in the Turkish-German community. More specifically, scholars have sought to understand Islam's influence on the relationship between that community and broader German society. One of the early questions scholars have explored is why religion seemingly became more important to the Turkish-German community over time. Yasemin Karakaşoğlu and Andreas Goldberg, among others, attribute this development to family reunification in the 1970s, but they also viewed it as a defensive posture assumed in the face of perceived hostility by Germans.[3] As Germans witnessed the growth of immigrant communities and the increasing visibility of Islamic observance, many reacted with an anxiety and hostility that worked to isolate immigrants – and their children – from broader German society.

---

[1] A *mihrab* is a small niche in the wall that directs the attention of the worshippers toward Mecca.
[2] Description of author's visit to the Yunus Emre Mosque, 6 June 2009, Berlin, Germany.
[3] See Andreas Goldberg, "Islam in Germany," in Shireen T. Hunter, ed., *Islam, Europe's Second Religion: The New Social, Cultural and Political Landscape* (Westport: Praeger Publishers, 2002), 30–47; Yasemin Karakaşoğlu, "Turkish Cultural Orientations in Germany and the Role of Islam," in David Horrocks and Eva Kolinsky, eds., *Turkish Culture in German Society Today* (Providence: Berghahn Books, 1996), 157–179.

Such feelings of isolation and insecurity within the Turkish immigrant community, scholars have contended, prompted the first generation to emphasize Islamic and traditional cultural values that reinforced a patriarchal power structure.[4] Scholarship focused on gender (which, until recently, was almost entirely about women) has invariably tied the position of women to the practice of Islam. The headscarf as a symbol of patriarchy, oppression, community identity, and individual agency has long been at the center of this debate, both in Germany and other European countries.[5] Studies, both popular and academic, have concentrated especially on second-generation Turkish-German women, examining the role of Islam in young women's emancipation and participation in broader German society.[6] More recently, scholars have reversed the perspective on this question, asking instead how Germans have used perceived religious and cultural differences as a way to exclude members of the Turkish community (all of whom are assumed to be Muslim), and particularly men, from being "German."[7]

The purpose-built mosque, in a sense, is the architectural version of the headscarf. Its appearance and multiplication has been the second highly visible indicator of the Islam's growth in the Federal Republic.

[4] See Shireen Hunter, ed., *Islam, Europe's Second Religion: The New Social, Cultural and Political Landscape* (Westport, CT: Praeger Publishers, 2002); Barbara Freyer Stowasser, "The Turks in Germany: From Sojourners to Citizens," in Yvonne Yazbeck Haddad, ed., *Muslims in the West: From Sojourners to Citizens* (Oxford: Oxford University Press, 2002), 52–71; and Dursun Tan and Hans-Peter Waldhoff, "Turkish Everyday Culture in Germany and Its Prospects," in David Horrocks and Eva Kolinsky, eds., *Turkish Culture in German Society Today* (Providence: Berghahn Books, 1996), 137-156.

[5] For an insightful treatment of this issue in the French context, see Joan Wallach Scott, *The Politics of the Veil* (Princeton, NJ: Princeton University Press, 2010).

[6] See Nermin Abadan-Unat, "Identity Crisis of Turkish Migrants: First and Second Generation," in İlhan Başgöz and Norman Furniss, eds., *Turkish Workers in Europe: An Interdisciplinary Study* (Bloomington: Indiana University Press, 1985), 3–22; Mehmet Yasin, "Gather Up the Bales, We Are Going Back: Lost Generation, Runaway Girls Are Speaking," in İlhan Başgöz and Norman Furniss, eds., *Turkish Workers in Europe: An Interdisciplinary Study* (Bloomington: Indiana University Press, 1985), 175–191; Umut Erel, "Gendered and Racialized Experiences of Citizenship in the Life Stories of Women of Turkish Background in Germany," in Jacqueline Andall, ed., *Gender and Ethnicity in Contemporary Europe* (Oxford: Berg, 2003), 155–176; Seyran Ateş, *Grosse Reise ins Feuer: Die Geschichte einer deutschen Türkin* (Berlin: Rowohlt Taschenbuch Verlag, 2003); Necla Kelek, *Die fremde Braut: ein Bericht aus dem Inneren des türkischen Lebens in Deutschland* (Cologne: Kiepenheuer & Witsch, 2005); and Peter P. Mandaville, "Muslim Youth in Europe," in Shireen Hunter, ed., *Islam, Europe's Second Religion: The New Social, Cultural, and Political Landscape* (Westport: Praeger Publishers, 2002), 219–229.

[7] Katherine Pratt Ewing, *Stolen Honor: Stigmatizing Muslim Men in Berlin* (Stanford: Stanford University Press, 2008), 2–17.

Scholars researching the dynamics of mosque construction have examined the various actors and elements of the controversy that almost invariably ensue, finding this visual marker of Islam to be a persistent wedge between Muslim communities and German society.[8] Yet whereas critics of such construction projects have often pointed to the mosque as evidence of a "parallel society" (*Parallelgesellschaft*) and a hindrance to immigrant integration,[9] other scholars, such as Rauf Ceylan and Thomas Schmitt, have argued that, despite the often intense controversy, a purpose-built mosque can and has served an integrative function for immigrant Muslim communities.[10] The extent to which they have operated in such a manner, however, remains a point of contention among academics, politicians, and the media alike.

In this chapter, I examine the mosque as a religious, cultural, and social space for the Turkish Muslim community in the Federal Republic, focusing in particular on its contested location both apart from and within German society.[11] The relevance of the mosque both as a local site and a symbol changed markedly over the course of the 1970s, 1980s, and into the 1990s as the Turkish population shifted from a temporary workforce to an established, multigenerational community. This chapter identifies the layers of purpose and use that, over time, shaped the mosque as a space, and explores how those, in conjunction with the physicality of mosques, affected the relationships between the Turkish community, West German society, and the environment in which the first and second generations conducted their daily lives. The progression of Muslim religious spaces in the Federal Republic in general and West Berlin specifically – from the early, ad hoc prayer rooms to "courtyard" mosques, and, finally, purpose-built mosques – requires me to stretch the temporal scope of this chapter beyond the main time frame of this book. Yet, by doing so, we can see more clearly how the changing nature of the Turkish community as well as German perceptions of the Muslim

---

[8] Gerdien Jonker, "The Mevlana Mosque in Berlin-Kreuzberg: An Unsolved Conflict," *Journal of Ethnic and Migration Studies* 31, no. 6 (November 2005): 1067–1081.

[9] Christine Brunn, *Moscheebau-Konflikte in Deutschland: Eine räumlich-semantische Analyse auf der Grundlage der Theorie der Produktion des Raumes von Henri Lefebvre* (Berlin: Wissenschaftlicher Verlag, 2006).

[10] Rauf Ceylan, *Ethnische Kolonien: Entstehung, Funktion und Wandel am Beispiel türkischer Moscheen und Cafes* (Wiesbaden: VS Verlag für Sozialwissenschaften, 2006); Thomas Schmitt, *Moscheen in Deutschland: Konflikte um ihre Errichtung und Nutzung* (Flensburg: Deutsches Akademie für Landeskunde, 2003).

[11] It is important to note that I am looking primarily at mosques with predominantly, if not wholly Turkish membership. Turks and Turkish-Germans constitute the overwhelming majority of Muslims in Germany, and most mosques draw from distinct ethnic or national groups for their membership.

population interacted to shape and reshape mosques both practically and symbolically. In this chapter, then, I examine the formation of Turkish Muslim communities in the 1970s and their development into more formal religious organizations with fixed places of worship in the 1980s. Chapter 6, in which I trace the continuities and changes in the Turkish-German community's everyday landscape in the postreunification context, will discuss the connection between purpose-built mosques and belonging in the Turkish Muslim community in the 1990s and early 2000s.

As the growth of Muslim communities and places of worship were a part of national and transnational discourses, I examine media representations throughout the Federal Republic in order to compare discursive constructions of "the mosque" with lived experience. Perhaps more than any other site in the Turkish-German community's everyday landscape, the mosque was a space strongly tied to developments beyond its own environment. National debates and agendas, transnational relationships, and international events impinged on the local context, and these influences were clearly reflected in (and propagated by) both German- and Turkish-language media, which stressed the critical role of the mosque in the lives of Turkish immigrants. For the growing Turkish Muslim community, mosques served simultaneously as a site of religious and cultural preservation, but their potency in political and media discourses often outweighed their importance to the daily lives of the first- and second - generation Turkish-German Muslims.

Religious Spaces and Social Well-Being

Neither government involved, it seems, gave much thought to the religious lives and well-being of the Turkish workers who participated in the bilateral labor contracts that first brought them to the Federal Republic of Germany in the 1960s. The West German government's interest in the guest worker was economic; they constituted a quick and relatively inexpensive way to get the West German economy back on its feet. To restate a now-common refrain, they called for labor, not people.[12] Nor did the government in the Republic of Turkey feel compelled to account for the religious needs of its citizens abroad. The parties in power during

---

[12] This phrase has become ubiquitous in connection with the history of *Gastarbeiter* in West Germany, making the original source difficult to place. However, some locate its origin in Max Frisch's 1967 book, *Überfremdung: Offentlichkeit als Partner* (Frankfurt am Main: Suhrkamp, 1967).

the 1960s and 1970s in Turkey represented that country's strongly secularist political tradition, viewing religion as a private matter that did not
have a place in policy formation.[13] Referring to both West Germany and
Turkey, Ceylan writes, "The public and cultural life moved to the background, because the minimal, material goals had priority."[14] As such,
when the first waves of Turkish guest workers arrived, they found little
space for religious observance.

Guest workers' narratives suggest that the workers themselves gave
little thought, at least at the beginning, to how they would worship in a
foreign country. For the same reasons that they largely tolerated minimal
living conditions and difficult work, Muslim guest workers initially did
not take significant steps to institute places of worship. Communal religious practice, and particularly ritual prayer, however, soon became a
way for these uprooted individuals to experience and express solidarity with their countrymen.[15] When Turkish Muslims began to look for
places where they could gather together for prayer, they found their
options limited. Some companies responded to the requests of their
Muslim employees and provided space within the workplace for common
prayer. As we saw in Chapter 1, on the urging of a German superintendent sympathetic to his Turkish employees' needs, a Siemens factory in
West Berlin offered a room for Muslim workers to use for prayer, in
addition to making efforts to address their dietary restrictions.[16]

Yet this was not always, or even often, the case. Frequently, Muslim
guest workers congregated outside the workplace in order to pray together. They met in the basements and attics of the company dormitories, in
whatever spaces were available and would suit the purpose. One Turkish
man recounted, "I moved to Hochfeld on November 23, 1973. I looked
right and left for a mosque, but didn't find one." Instead, he and some of
his coworkers would drive to a prayer room in another part of the city.[17]
When larger gatherings, such as holiday festivals, required more space
than the informal prayer rooms could offer, the men would have to find
another place to worship. In one such case, a group of guest workers in
Duisburg-Hochfeld, with the help of a Turkish translator, negotiated with
a local church to rent space for Ramadan and *Opferfest*.[18] Yet, even when
these men could find the space to worship, they still lacked a religious
authority figure, an imam, to lead them in prayer. Instead, the men would

[13] Stowasser, "The Turks in Germany," 60.   [14] Ceylan, *Ethnische Kolonien*, 130.
[15] I use the masculine version consciously, as I have yet to find reference to early
Gastarbeiterinnen participating in this type of common prayer.
[16] "Mittagsessen für türkische Mitarbeiter," Rundschreiben zur Beschäftigung von
Ausländischen Arbeitnehmer, Sig. 10585–1, Schlüssel 04610585, SCA.
[17] Ceylan, *Ethnische Kolonien*, 130.   [18] Ibid., 130–131.

choose among themselves someone to perform the duties of the imam. Improvisation, then, was the rule for religious observance in the early years of Turkish immigration to West Germany.

By the 1970s, however, many Turkish Muslims were growing tired of this ad hoc manner of worship. At the same time, family reunification changed the character, and thus the needs, of the Turkish immigrant community. The arrival of families began to formalize religious observance and called for both a change of place for worship and a shift in focus to include social services that would assist spouses and children with the transition to life in a new country. This prompted the first physical relocation of prayer rooms. Men who had moved out of the dormitories could not hold religious services there, and prayer rooms in company factories were not sufficient for larger-scale religious services. The growing community needed fixed sites adequate for their changing religious and social needs. Thus, prayer rooms moved from the attics and basements of the company dormitories to larger spaces off courtyards, in former factories, workshops, and, in one case at least, even an old bar.[19] These new mosques constituted the first formal institutions formed by Turkish *Gastarbeiter* and reflected not only the changing community demographics but also a growing realization that their return to Turkey would be further in the future than they had originally planned. The mosques, then, were some of the first roots the Turkish community put down in German soil.

Ceylan traces the founding of the first mosque in the district of Duisburg-Hochfeld in 1974, showing how the institution developed out of the needs and initiative of a group of Turkish *Gastarbeiter* in that city. After approximately fifteen years of gathering in makeshift prayer rooms and acting as their own imams, the group decided to take the step of establishing their own mosque. Each step proceeded on the initiative, funding, and muscle of the guest workers, without guidance from the Islamic umbrella organizations that would soon work to unite mosques and believers under their direction. Ceylan argues that this mosque and the early ones to follow were not subject to the same regulations as they would have been in Turkey and thus, as with German immigrant churches in eighteenth-century United States, were informed and shaped by the context in which they developed.[20]

In 1974, the Osmanlı Camii opened its doors for service.[21] As the only mosque in Duisburg, Ceylan writes that it "offered a cultural center and an emotional refuge."[22] Muslims living throughout the city went to the

[19] Ibid., 127.   [20] Ibid., 133–138.   [21] *Camii* is Turkish for "mosque."
[22] Ceylan, *Ethnische Kolonien*, 138.

Hochfeld mosque to socialize and pray with each other. In the beginning, users of this new common space came from diverse backgrounds, including different political or religious orientations and even non-Turkish Muslims. Outside of the oversight and control of bosses and dormitory directors, the men met to attend to their spiritual well-being but soon began drawing on the knowledge and experiences of fellow believers to aid them in other aspects of their lives as well. The mosque was becoming a site where Turkish immigrants could both see to their social needs and to their religious obligations.

As the Turkish Muslim community expanded, so, too, did the social spaces within their mosques. The aging of the first generation and the new members of the community added layers of social services to its original intent. For many elderly Muslim men, the religious and social spaces of the mosque assumed an even greater importance in their lives, as they shifted from the working world to the slower, more reflective pace of retirement. Praying, studying the Qur'an, and discussing religious subjects with fellow believers gave them a feeling of "inner peace" that many did not find at home, distracted by the "nonsense" of the television and the banality of daily life.[23] Some mosques included a tearoom (*Teestube*) to encourage such social spaces where members could socialize with old friends and coworkers.[24] The mosque also connected these elderly men with younger members of the religious community from whom they could receive emotional support and practical assistance. By bringing together old friends and linking the older generation with the younger, the mosque therefore not only improved the quality of their lives, it rooted them more firmly in their local community.

For women, and particularly those who moved to West Germany to rejoin their husbands, the mosque could provide space for socializing, participating in community events, and negotiating the social and bureaucratic mazes of the host society. Whereas the home and neighborhood constituted the main social spaces for Turkish immigrant women, some also found the mosque a safe and familiar space to meet with friends. This could take place either in prearranged gatherings, for example during preparations for a communal festival, or more informally, such as pausing for a chat when dropping off the children for *Koranschule* (Qur'an instruction school). In addition, mosques began offering German language and literacy classes for women, and would provide the space for local organizations – such as the Wedding Volkshochschule – to conduct

---

[23] Ibid., 148–151.   [24] Ibid., 151.

language classes.[25] These classes brought women in to participate in the life of the mosque even as they enabled them to engage with West German society on a more confident, or at least more informed, footing. Many mosques, however, did not consider programs for the social well-being of women to be a priority, and it has only been more recently that such spaces have opened up for interested women.[26] The Beyazid Mosque in Berlin-Wedding, for example, began offering German-language classes for women some thirty years after its founding.[27]

Mosques quickly expanded to include the youth of their communities. Some mosques offered recreational activities for local Muslim youth, including sports teams, as a way to engage them in the life of the mosque community and provide them with a safe and healthy environment.[28] Mosques with more financial and personnel resources have also offered homework assistance, computer programs, and other similar support. As with the spaces of social well-being offered to women, these initiatives have been more recent developments. Local Muslim communities have used their mosques as sites to promote the well-being and success of their children in German society through such programs; however, the most dominant space for Muslim youth in the mosque was, and continues to be, religious education in the form of the *Koranschule*.

Learning to Be a Turkish Muslim

If the mosques began as a site for the first generation's religious observance, they found a new and even more pressing need among their founders' children. In culturally Christian West Germany, many Turkish Muslim families faced the challenge of raising children who would be religiously and culturally rooted in Islam and the Turkish state. Muslim parents and the mosques they attended and supported both made the connection between their religious and cultural identities; in other words, being Muslim – to their minds – was part of being Turkish, and the mosque had a vital role to play in cultivating and maintaining those related identities. A January 1978 article in the European edition of the Turkish daily *Hürriyet*, entitled "Politics Has No Place in a Mosque,"

[25] Irina Leffers and Christholde Thielcke, "Zwischen Religion und Jugendarbeit: Angebote und Aktivitäten," in Gerdien Jonker and Andreas Kapphan, eds., *Moscheen und islamisches Leben in Berlin* (Berlin: Ausländerbeauftragte des Senats, 1999), 30–34.
[26] Hamza Chourabi and Riem El-Solami, "Moscheenräume, Räume für Frauen?" in Gerdien Jonker and Andreas Kapphan, eds., *Moscheen und islamisches Leben in Berlin* (Berlin: Ausländerbeauftragte des Senats, 1999), 35–40.
[27] Mehmet Asker (pseudonym), interview by author, 8 June 2009, Berlin. [28] Ibid.

articulated the role of the mosque in meeting this challenge. Next to a picture of the president of Bremen's Turkish Islamic Cultural Association with a group of *Koranschule* students, the caption reads: "Through the major efforts of the Islamic Association in Vegesack, our children who are growing up under a German influence are also having the spirit of religion and loyalty to the homeland through the organized Qur'an courses." Further into the article, the writer reiterates the importance of this project, stating that the efforts of President Hasan Kızılkaya and his organization "have been unified" on the necessity "to educate the youth who have forgotten their Turkishness and their religion."[29]

The perceived need for the second generation to be rooted in Islam and "Turkishness" required that the mosque become a site of religious and cultural education and preservation. *Korankurse* (Qur'an courses), then, became a standard part of religious life in West German mosques from the mid-1970s onward. Such was the case in two Berlin-Wedding mosques visited by residents of Sprengelkiez: the Beyazid mosque and the Yunus Emre mosque.

The Beyazid mosque is a longtime member of the Association of Islamic Cultural Centers (Verband der Islamischen Kulturzentren, VIKZ), the first Islamic umbrella organization in the Federal Republic. Founded in 1973 and headquartered in Cologne, the VIKZ today has more than three hundred member communities across the country and represents a Turkish Sunni-Hanafi branch of Islam, with ties to Süleymancılar organizations in Turkey. Socially and religiously conservative, the VIKZ considers itself politically neutral and has, from early on in its operation, focused its attention on the education of Muslim youth.[30] The Beyazid mosque began its life as a small prayer room on Sparrstrasse, moving to its present location on Lindowerstrasse in 1976. Although the organization that operates the mosque has offered a variety of religious and social services since its founding, in those early years the mosque was open only for prayer times, Friday prayer, and *Koranschule*. At the time, Mehmet Asker, now an official of the mosque, was a student taking the *Korankurse*. There were many more children in the *Korankurse* in those days, Asker remembered, which were held during the weekdays after school.[31]

---

[29] "Camide politikanın işi yoktur," *Hürriyet*, 1 January 1978, p. 6, Staatsbibliothek zu Berlin – Zeitungsabteilung (SBZ), Berlin.

[30] Kerstin Rosenow, *Organizing Muslims and Integrating Islam in Germany: New Developments in the 21st Century* (Boston: Brill, 2013), 168; "Organisation," VIKZ e.V. website, www.vikz.de/index.php/ueber-uns.html, accessed by author, 9 June 2016.

[31] Asker interview.

The Yunus Emre mosque community first started meeting in a small apartment in 1976 before moving to its Reinickendorf location, and later became affiliated with the Turkish-Islamic Union for Religious Affairs (Türkisch-Islamische Union der Anstalt für Religion or Diyanet İşleri Türk-İslam Birliği, DITIB), which was founded in 1984. Unlike the VIKZ, DITIB has direct connections to the Turkish state, specifically the Ministry of Religious Affairs (Diyanet İşleri Başkanlığı), which has had the responsibility of sending Turkish imams to affiliated mosques in the Federal Republic. The Ministry of Religious Affairs' practice of sending imams to Europe began in the late 1970s as a way to provide religious leadership during Ramadan. Yet as leaders of religious organizations outlawed within Turkey fled in the wake of the 1980 military coup, the ministry began to take a more active role in cultivating relationships with European mosques and bringing them under its leadership. Along with then president Kenan Evren, the ministry considered the step a necessary "counteroffensive" to keep expatriate religious leaders from forming strong European branches of their movements and turning Turkish migrants against the Turkish state.[32] Youth education was one focus of the leadership, and the Yunus Emre mosque, like the Beyazid mosque, offered *Korankurse* from the early days of its founding.[33] These *Koranschulen* became a familiar space for numerous Turkish-German children in Sprengelkiez whose parents sent them there for religious instruction throughout the 1980s.

The spaces that developed in response to the second generation consisted of religious education centered on the Qur'an itself, as well as exposure to religious rites and practices. *Korankurse* differed among mosques, but they were generally single-sex classes held by Turkish-speaking instructors. The children learned to read and recite the Suras in Arabic, although most of the students could not translate the text into a language they understood.[34] *Koranschule* was meant to introduce and connect young Muslims to the holy text and focal point of their community's religious belief and, at the same time, expose students to the forms of religious worship and obligation. The location of the classes, within the center of the Muslim community, served to expose and familiarize the youth with Islamic religious life. Those *Koranschule* that held single-sex classes and encouraged (if not required) young girls to wear a

[32] Thijl Sunier and Nico Landman, *Transnational Turkish Islam: Shifting Geographies of Religious Activism and Community Building in Turkey and Europe* (Boston: Palgrave Macmillan, 2015), 49–53.
[33] Onur Korkmaz (pseudonym), interview by author, 6 June 2009, Berlin.
[34] Asker interview.

headscarf, impressed upon the students a visual and social form of religious observance distinctly different from the educational spaces they experienced at school.[35] The location, language, and format of instruction demonstrated to students the mosque's interpretation of the values and practices of Islam, some of which found resonance with their lives outside the mosque and others of which separated them from other everyday spaces. On one hand, *Koranschule* provided its students a shared experience with others of similar background and gave them a way to make sense of their world through a religious lens. On the other hand, the experiences and lessons of *Koranschule* were not likely to find resonance outside the immigrant community, adding to its students' sense of difference from German society.

Photographs of a mosque on Lindowerstrasse in Berlin-Wedding reflect the ways in which Turkish-German children were exposed to and experienced religious instruction and practice. Taken by writer and photographer Kemal Kurt for a museum exhibit in 1993[36], the pictures show young students taking part in *Koranschule* and a prayer meeting. The image of young girls and women in *Koranunterricht* (Qur'an class) shows a spacious room with light filtering through sheer curtains pulled over the windows on one side of the room (Figure 10). Around two dozen girls and young women kneel or sit cross-legged on the carpeted floor in small groups throughout the room. Some are bent studiously over the work in front of them; others look across the room or chat with their neighbors. Their clothing suggests both modesty and chilly weather. Similarly, everyone in the room wears a generous headscarf, although the ages of the youngest girls suggest these were donned for the purposes of the class.[37] Finally, an older woman – presumably the teacher – has stood up in front of her own desk and is talking with the students nearest her.[38]

The photograph of the young boys' *Koranunterricht* (Figure 11) shares several attributes with that of the girls'. About a dozen students kneel in front of small wooden desks, each with its own Qur'an open on top. Their respect for the religious nature of the space is shown by their

---

[35] It is worth noting, however, that the single-sex nature of these classes was not wholly at odds with the social spaces Turkish-German youth encountered and formed within the neighborhood, as seen in Chapter 3.

[36] Although taken in the early 1990s, the images also reflect descriptions of participants in Wedding mosques in the 1980s.

[37] At the time this photograph was taken, it was less common for women and almost unheard of for young girls to wear headscarves in Sprengelkiez.

[38] Kemal Kurt, "Moschee Lindowerstr. (1993), Neg. 26/32A," DLSA, MMA, Berlin, Germany.

Figure 10. Girls' *Koranunterricht*, mosque in Lindowerstrasse, 1993.
Photograph by Kemal Kurt.

Figure 11. Boys' *Koranunterricht*, mosque in Lindowerstrasse, 1993.
Photograph by Kemal Kurt.

shoeless feet and the prayer caps that cover several of their heads. The
teacher, perhaps in his thirties or forties, wears a white collared shirt
with a dark tie and a serious demeanor as he leads the class.[39] Both
photographs certainly depict a classroom scene, but with clear differences from what the children experienced in school. The head coverings,

[39] Kemal Kurt, "Moschee Lindowerstr. (1993), Neg. 621/6A," DLSA, MMA.

Figure 12. Prayer service, mosque in Lindowerstrasse, 1993.
Photograph by Kemal Kurt.

the kneeling desks, and the single-sex environment set the *Koranschule* apart, marking it as a unique and distinctly religious space.

A third photograph shifts its focus in terms of subject, depicting instead a group of men and boys in prayer (Figure 12). The photographer stands to the front and side of the participants, capturing them as they perform communal prayer. The group is a diverse one: a man in work overalls stands near another in slacks and a sports coat; boys pray next to older men. Yet they all face in the same direction, going through the same physical motions of ritual prayer – standing, kneeling, bowing.[40] For the boys in the photograph, the space in which they are participating is one of religious education. Like apprentices, they learn their religious obligations through action, praying alongside their fathers, brothers, and fellow Muslims. At the same time, it constitutes a space of religious preservation. The participation of the second generation in the religious life of the mosque helped ensure the continuation of that community. As such, *Koranschule* and communal prayer were not only about teaching the

[40] Kemal Kurt, "Moschee Lindowerstr. (1993), Neg. 619/25," DLSA, MMA.

second generation to be good Muslims but also about identifying with and taking part in the broader (and local) *ummah*.[41]

The second-generation Muslim youth responded to the efforts of their elders in a variety of ways. For some, their exposure to religious life as a young person led to increased participation as an adult. Mehmet Asker attended *Koranschule* at the Beyazid mosque as a young boy and later came to serve the mosque in an official capacity.[42] Similarly, Onur Korkmaz participated in *Koranschule* and religious celebrations at a mosque in Berlin-Wedding while growing up, ultimately moving into a leadership position in the Yunus Emre mosque as an adult.[43] Ceylan posits that the participation of the second generation, members of which have increasingly pushed for purpose-built mosques, reflects a broader desire to be a part of German society and to make a permanent space for the Muslim community within it.[44] Werner Schiffauer would agree, but in his study on the Islamic organization Millî Görüş, he acknowledges that the second generation's assumption of leadership roles does not necessarily mean the beliefs and practices of those particular organizations and mosques will come to reflect a more liberal "Euro-Islam."[45] In any case, it is clear that at least for some among the second-generation Muslims, the mosque became a central point of both their religious and their working lives.

For many others, however, *Koranschule* was an obligation or rite of passage that, at least initially, did not lead to greater participation in local religious life. Conducted in Sprengelkiez in the early 1990s, a series of

---

[41] The *ummah* encompasses the global Muslim community.   [42] Asker interview.
[43] Korkmaz interview.   [44] Ceylan, *Ethnische Kolonien*, 175.
[45] Werner Schiffauer, *Nach den Islamismus: Eine Ethnographie der Islamischen Gemeinschaft Millî Görüş* (Berlin: Suhrkamp Verlag, 2010), 225–266. The Islamic Community of Millî Görüş (Islamische Gemeinschaft Millî Görüş, IGMG) is one of the major Islamic umbrella organizations in the Federal Republic, and has one of the most troubled histories. Its roots trace back to Turkish politician Necmittin Erbakan, who had earned his engineering PhD in Germany and, back in Turkey, inspired a series of religious and political movements with his vision of a strong Turkey rooted in an Islamic identity. The political parties that formed in response to this vision were periodically outlawed in Turkey, but Europe offered new and relatively open spaces for Turkish immigrants sympathetic to Erbakan's vision and with transnational ties to its adherents back in Turkey. They formed mosque communities and coalesced into umbrella organizations, the West German version of which split from the VIKZ in 1975 and in 1995 adopted its current form and name, Islamische Gemeinschaft Millî Görüş. Due to its ties to political groups in Turkey, the organization has been labeled "Islamist" by the German government, and has been considered by many in Germany as "anti-integration." It has also been under investigation by German authorities for its connections to a charity with ties to Hamas, as well as for its antidemocratic and anti-Semitic statements. For more on Millî Görüş, see Schiffauer, *Nach den Islamismus*; Rosenow, *Organizing Muslims and Integrating Islam in Germany*, 249–303.

interviews with young Turkish-German girls in their early teens reveals an ambivalent attitude toward such religious spaces. For some, *Koranschule* was a normal part of the summer, but attendance would be broken up by family vacations and lessons forgotten with the resumption of school in the fall. Religion was "important" but complicated, and better put off until they were older.[46] One young woman, Lale, attended *Koranschule* early in the mornings and spent her time in class getting into trouble with her friends. Yet Lale contended that it was good for parents to send their children to the mosque to learn about the Qur'an. Although she mused that she would likely do the same with her own children, what they (and she) would actually learn did not seem especially important to her. "They shouldn't learn too much," Lale explained, "but they should go. That'd be good for me, too."[47] For Lale and her peers, participation in the educational spaces of the mosque was a valuable experience (albeit one whose value was perhaps clearer in retrospect) but not one that called them into deeper relationship or identification with the mosque community. Instead, *Koranschule* constituted a rite of passage, "good" and perhaps necessary for its own sake but not a significant factor in their daily lives.

Finally, some among the second generation found *Koranschule* neither personally compelling nor generically good. Rather, their reaction to participation in spaces of religious education took on a decidedly negative tone. Whereas in some cases this was due to general disinterest on the part of the student, in others the conduct of the instructors made the space unwelcoming or even hostile. The Özels are not a particularly religious family. Although the father is a devout Muslim, he "doesn't force us, 'you must do this,'" Sevim Özel explained. When the children came of age, however, Özel and her husband sent them to the local mosque for *Koranschule*. But the teachers, Özel recalled, were "a little strange. They hit hand [*sic*] or did something like that. My husband heard, says, 'No, you [kids] can't go anymore.'" "We were there for maybe two, three weeks at most and that was it," her daughter, Filiz Güler, added.[48] Özel followed the story about her children's *Koranschule* experience with another about a local *Hoca* (teacher) who convinced a member of the mosque to entrust his savings to him and then absconded

[46] Aylin (pseudonym), interview by Ursula Trüper, transcription, 22 December 1992, pp. 11–12, DLSA, MMA.

[47] Lale (pseudonym), interview by Ursula Trüper, transcription, 28 May and 4 June 1992, pp. 14–15, DLSA, MMA.

[48] Sevim Özel (pseudonym), interview by author, 30 June 2009, transcription by Perrin Saylan, Berlin, 22–23.

with the funds – a story she seemed to find more amusing than upset-
ting.[49] The negative experience of the *Koranschule*, coupled with their
parents' leniency in matters of religious observance, distanced the Özel
children from participation in institutional religious life, a separation they
maintained in adulthood. Thus, despite the overarching goal to weave
the second generation into the fabric of the observant Muslim community, Turkish-German children's experiences in the mosque could and
sometimes did alienate them from that site and the type of religious
observance it symbolized.

Preserving and Practicing Turkishness

The mosque, however, was not an exclusively religious space. Tightly
intertwined with religious observance were the practice and preservation
of Turkish identity, an identity the Turkish government took active steps
to cultivate and maintain. Mosques became centers of Turkishness for
both the first and second generations. For the second generation, spaces
of cultural preservation focused on connecting children to their parents'
(and, ostensibly, their) Turkish roots. The European edition of *Hürriyet*,
a nationalist and secularist daily, took an active role in shaping the
symbol of the mosque as a space of religious and cultural preservation –
a physical location of Turkishness "abroad." The 1978 *Hürriyet* article
mentioned earlier in this chapter was not alone in pointing out the
necessity of educating "our Turkish children" "who have forgotten their
Turkishness."[50] Nearly a decade later, *Hürriyet* continued to highlight
the importance of cultural as well as religious education in these spaces.
In an article about the 1986 opening of a mosque in Berlin-Wedding, the
writer quotes an announcement by the Turkish-Islamic Union for Religious Affairs' (DITIB) attaché in Berlin, Hayrettin Şallı, that describes
the goals and activities of the new mosque. "The biggest problem of our
citizens living abroad," Şallı contends, "is the future of their children who
are growing up far away from the national and religious culture and the
air of their homeland."[51] The first remedy for this problem, he argues, is
a religious education intertwined with elements of Turkish culture and
nationalism, such as the singing of the national anthem. DITIB, however, along with other Islamic organizations, did not see religion-focused
education as the single solution to preserving Turkish culture in the
second generation youth. Şallı continues:

---

[49] Ibid., 23.   [50] "Camide politikanın işi yoktur," p. 6.
[51] "Nuruosmaniye Camii ibadete açıldı," *Hürriyet*, 20 November 1986, p. 18, SBZ.

Along with Qur'an and religious information classes, another class on Turkish is given and place is allotted in classes and homework to topics that would familiarize students with Turkish culture and the Turkish homeland. Also, keeping in mind that they are living in a foreign country, students are suggested to be in mutual understanding and good relations with the people of this country. Through this way we are trying to serve the national and religious culture.[52]

Turkish Islamic organizations used mosques not only as centers of religious learning but also as places through which Turkish-German youth could be connected to the "Turkish homeland" and the cultural elements inherent in that connection. Their efforts contributed to the fusion of religious and national identity among the second generation, reflected in Lale's description of Islam as the "Turkish religion."[53]

Turkish-German youth, however, were not the only participants in these spaces of religious and cultural preservation, as Islamic organizations extended the opportunities to practice and perform the "Turkish religion" to their parents' generation as well. In addition to the spaces of religious observance discussed earlier in this chapter, mosques served as a place to gather and celebrate Islamic holidays. These celebrations, such as for Ramadan and the Festival of Sacrifice (Kurban Bayramı), brought the first and second generations together to the mosque, infusing religious holidays with national traditions and culture. As these holidays constituted significant community events, Turkish-language newspapers, such as *Hürriyet*, consistently reported on the activities surrounding Ramadan and Kurban Bayramı in West Germany throughout the late 1970s and 1980s. The composition and number of attendees made up an important aspect of *Hürriyet*'s coverage of religious celebrations. In August of 1977, "just as it happens every year [Turkish] mosques around Europe filled up with the faithful."[54] The following year the writer echoed the earlier story: "Just as it happens every year, this year as well with the start of Ramadan our mosques abroad filled to the brim and spilled over."[55] "The tens of thousands" of "Berlin's Turks passed through the streets of Berlin in droves, running to the mosques from the early hours of the morning" in September 1983. This article continues to describe the scene: "With many of the believers being unable to fit into mosques and *masjids* [smaller prayer rooms] in the city, they prayed in the courtyards and fulfilled their duties towards God."[56] In June 1986, "despite it being a working day, the mosques filled up and overflowed to the gardens and

[52] Ibid.   [53] Lale interview, 14.
[54] "Ramazan'ın ilk cuması gurbette muhteşemdi," *Hürriyet*, 21 August 1977, p. 1, SBZ.
[55] "Gurbette camiiler doldu, tastı ...", *Hürriyet*, 7 August 1978, p. 1, SBZ.
[56] "Berlin, bayramda Türkiye'yi yaşadı," *Hürriyet*, 23 September 1983, p. 17, SBZ.

streets with the faithful on the morning of bayram."[57] Whether the descriptions reflect actual attendance or the reporters' rosier version, the repeated focus on numbers sought to underline the universal and heartfelt religious observance of Turkish Muslims abroad.

In addition to stressing the numbers filling the mosques and spilling out of them, the writers constantly connected these faithful back to their kinspeople in Turkey. Participants were referred to as "our compatriots," "Muslim Turks in Berlin," "Berlin's Turks," and "our citizens," along with other similar identifiers. By focusing on the mass of the gatherings, these labels linked the Turks living in West Germany to those in Turkey through their religious and national identities and emphasized both their devotion to religion and their place within a larger Muslim Turkish community. Articles also highlighted distinguished guests who joined in these religious celebrations.[58] Local religious leaders, representatives from the national Islamic umbrella organizations, important business leaders, visiting officials from Turkey – these participants, singled out among the "droves" of the faithful, strengthened the connections of local worshippers to those across the country and back in Turkey. At the same time, they lent a degree of legitimacy and establishment to the proceedings. Such guests would not have been present at the early celebrations of Ramadan in the back rooms of bars or rented halls of churches. Now, in these official mosques, they stood as the religious and cultural figureheads of an established Turkish Muslim community.

Together with these visiting dignitaries, the men, women, and children of West Germany's Muslim community celebrated the holidays with a mixture of religious and cultural traditions. Prayer was a central feature of these events. Through the practice of ritual prayers and giving thanks, individual participants became part of the larger body of believers. Newspaper articles stressed this fusion through repeated use of phrases such as "unity," "being together," and "hearts became one."[59] In addition to ritual prayers, participants also appealed to Allah regarding developments in Turkey. In the late 1970s, during a period of escalating violence between left- and right-wing forces that resulted in the death of thousands and culminated in Turkey's 1980 military coup d'état, *Hürriyet* recounted the prayers of the faithful in West Germany being "for our country's and our people's peace, for Turkey to come out of the straits it

---

[57] "Bir bayram daha geçti," *Hürriyet*, 21 June 1986, p. 15, SBZ.
[58] For examples, see "Ramazan'ın ilk cuması gurbette muhteşemdi," p. 1; "Gurbette camiiler doldu, tastı …," p. 1; "Ramazan'ın bereketi Berlin'de yaşandı," *Hürriyet*, 29 August 1978, p. 3, SBZ; "Berlin, bayramda Türkiye'yi yaşadı," p. 17; "Aksemsettin Camii ibadete acıldı, *Hürriyet*, 29 May 1986, p. 20, SBZ; "Bir bayram daha geçti," p. 15.
[59] "Berlin, bayramda Türkiye'yi yaşadı," p. 17.

is currently in and for the terror in the country to be finished."[60] The prayers, together with their communal performance, connected participants to each other through their common faith and national identity.

Participants also reinforced their national and cultural identities through a second major attribute of religious festivals: food. Particularly at the iftar dinners during Ramadan, food played a central role in communal religious gatherings; the preparation and consumption of these celebratory meals gave the first generation an opportunity to enact their cultural traditions "even while abroad," and pass them on to their children. Articles about iftar dinners were often accompanied by photographs of men and women sitting around tables of food, celebrating together. In an article about an iftar meal at a mosque near Frankfurt in 1977, the meal itself almost becomes a guest as the writer describes the scene: "Present at the table decorated with many various Turkish foods ranging from baklava to börek were [the visiting dignitaries.]"[61] A year later, a writer goes into greater detail about the composition of the meal. Next to two pictures again displaying the men's and women's iftar tables is a list of the foods present at the "spectacular" iftar: "5 sheep, 800 lahmacun, 100 pide, 300 watermelons, and 50 kilos of yogurt." The participants assured the reporter that they would remember this iftar for many years to come.[62] In the following years, articles focused less on the exact makeup of the meal than on the practice of consuming it communally.

As fervent as the prayers and as present as the tables of food were the emotions that the religious festivals brought out. Sorrow and happiness, joy and disappointment – participants experienced and displayed a range of feelings, but the causes of such emotions seem to be more distinct. On one hand, there was a palpable undercurrent of sadness that permeated the events, a feeling a DITIB attaché labeled in 1985 as "the pain of being abroad."[63] Religious holidays and the festivities they brought reminded Turkish Muslims that they were far from home. Living in a non-Muslim society complicated full and proper participation in religious festivities. Work schedules overlapped with the timing of religious obligations, and animal-cruelty laws made ritual sacrifices difficult. In celebrating together, participants "tried to dissipate the feelings of sadness coming from being far away from their relatives and families."[64]

---

[60] "Gurbette camiiler doldu, tastı . . .," p. 1.
[61] "Gurbet'in Ramazan'ı memleketi aratmıyor," *Hürriyet*, 30 August 1977, p. 13, SBZ.
[62] "Ramazan'ın bereketi Berlin'de yaşandı," p. 3.
[63] "Yoneticiler Bayramımızı kutladı," *Hürriyet*, 27 June 1985, p. 15, SBZ.
[64] "Gurbette camiiler doldu, tastı . . .", p. 1.

The constant reference to distance from loved ones and homeland, of being abroad in a "foreign world," emphasizes the source of the sadness, but being together "alleviated the unhappy feeling" through its creation of a space of cultural preservation and performance.[65] Here again, media coverage focused on the iftar dinners of the Turkish community in West Germany. As the special meal at which Muslims break their daily fast during the month of Ramadan, the iftar reaches the level of national holiday in Muslim-majority countries such as Turkey. Celebrated abroad, this ritual of breaking one's Ramadan fast became a way of connecting to one's memories and traditions of the homeland. A newspaper article from the late 1970s recounts how "the iftar dinner eaten in the men's section passed with jokes and happiness," whereas "the women had the opportunity to sweetly talk with each other."[66] Through communal celebration, participants created a space to experience and celebrate their Turkishness. As the title of a 1983 article states, "Berlin Lived Turkey during Bayram." "Muslim Turks of Berlin," the reporter writes, "lived the joy of being together on such a day despite being so far away from the homeland.... Forgetting all resentments and hugging each other after the prayers, the believers who filled the mosque had the opportunity to live the *bayram* air of Turkey."[67] "Turkey," then, could be re-created within the context of these spaces of religious and cultural preservation.

For the majority of the Muslim Turkish-German community, the mosque constituted the physical and symbolic center of both religious education and celebration. Yet, it is important to bear in mind that for many Turkish Muslims the mosque was more a symbol of their religious identity than it was a fixture in their everyday landscape. The thousands that attended the major religious and cultural celebrations did not respond to regular Friday services with the same level of interest or engagement. Aside from attendance at *Koranschule* and holiday celebrations, the mosque existed only on the periphery of their lives. Also, the level of engagement was often different even within families. The father of the Özel family, for example, was its only member to attend the mosque with any regularity.[68]

Moreover, not all immigrants from Turkey were Sunni. The same relative tolerance of religious spaces that allowed outlawed Sunni movements such as Millî Görüş and the VIKZ to (re)organize in the Federal Republic also gave religious minorities, including the Alevis, the opportunity to

---

[65] "Yoneticiler Bayramımızı kutladı," p. 15.
[66] "Ramazan'ın bereketi Berlin'de yaşandı," p. 3.
[67] "Berlin, bayramda Türkiye'yi yaşadı," p. 17.   [68] Özel interview, 22–23.

more openly form religious communities and develop what Betigül Argun has called "subsidiary public spheres."[69] Repressed by the Turkish state, many Turkish and Kurdish Alevis came to the FRG as guest workers, the majority of whom settled in West Berlin and began, in the 1980s, to more actively participate in cultural and political organizations. Local responses by Alevis to persecution of their fellow believers in Turkey reflected both the strong transnational ties and also the growing public presence of the religious minority in the West German context.[70] Although there were few Alevis living around Sparrplatz in the 1980s and early 1990s, a small community did meet in a room on Lindowerstrasse in the early 1990s. One young man who participated in the community stressed to his German interviewer the relative flexibility of religious practice and gender equality in comparison to his Sunni neighbors – both themes that have become a part of Alevis' public identity and contributed to a general perception of their being more "integrated" than their seemingly more conservative Sunni counterparts.[71] Finally, for a significant minority of Turkish immigrants and their children, the mosque played neither a practical role in their daily lives nor a symbolic role in their identity for the simple, if often overlooked, reason that they were not religious. Although in recent years it has shifted from this course, the modern Turkish state was founded and perpetuated on strong secular principles that enforced the subordination of religion to the state and worked to separate Islam from the Turkish national identity – at least within the borders of the Turkish state. For many of the first and second generation, their Turkishness did not include Islam, despite mosques' and the Turkish state's efforts to make that connection in the West German context.

From the mid-1970s through the 1980s, the *Koranschule* brought the youth into the mosque and informed them of the tenets of the "Turkish religion" of Islam, and prayer services and holiday celebrations taught them how to practice their religion as well as their parents' cultural traditions. Likewise, observing religious holidays created space for the first generation to fulfill religious obligations and participate in Turkish cultural traditions as members of a larger community. Although these spaces clearly promoted a sense of belonging within the Turkish Muslim community through shared religious and cultural beliefs and traditions,

[69] Betigül Ercan Argun, *Turkey in Germany: The Transnational Sphere of Deutschkei* (New York: Routledge, 2003), 6.
[70] Joyce Marie Mushaben, *The Changing Faces of Citizenship: Integration and Mobilization Among Ethnic Minorities in Germany* (New York: Berghahn Books, 2008), 151–153.
[71] Emre and Erkan (pseudonyms), interview by Ursula Trüper, 7 December 1993, audiocassette, DLSA, MMA.

to what degree did they affect the relationship of the first and second generations to broader West German society?

A Space Apart, or a Part of Society?

Perhaps more than any single aspect of Turkish immigration to the Federal Republic, the growing presence of Islam and Muslim believers in that culturally Christian state has been the most controversial. Time and again, that controversy has featured the mosque as its focal point, and the language of difference and distance has figured prominently in public discourse regarding the physical spaces of Islam. The early prayer rooms used by the first generation elicited little response from the West German media and political sphere, but the appearance of the *Koranschule* at the local level increasingly brought the issue from the private rooms off the courtyards to the center of national public consciousness. Although family reunification prompted the opening of *Koranschulen*, it was not until the late 1970s that West German politicians and media began to focus on the mosque as a present and growing threat. This sense of danger was heightened, if not caused by international events, namely the Islamic Revolution in Iran.

Due to a small but active Iranian student and émigré community, the West German public was not wholly unaware of the events unfolding in Iran during the late 1970s.[72] Yet when the widespread protests against Mohammad Reza Shah Pahlavi seemed to coalesce under the leadership of the Muslim cleric Ruhollah Khomeini and the Iranian Revolution transformed into the Islamic Republic in 1979, the FRG, along with the rest of the world, was stunned by the outcome. That a Western-oriented monarchy in a relatively affluent country could be overthrown and replaced by a popularly supported, authoritarian Islamic state was deeply disturbing, not only for international relations with Iran but also for its implications for how non-Muslim states perceived Islam. For many in the West, including the Federal Republic, Islam was no longer simply a religion, but now had the possibility of fostering and becoming a politically radical and powerful movement. The timing of the Iranian Revolution, therefore, had a significant influence on how West Germans perceived and approached internal Muslim communities, the majority of

[72] Alexander Clarkson has written a fascinating account of the anti-shah activism of Iranian students and émigrés in the Federal Republic and their interactions with the West German state during the 1960s. See Alexander Clarkson, *Fragmented Fatherland: Immigration and Cold War Conflict in the Federal Republic of Germany, 1945–1980* (New York: Berghahn Books, 2013), 151–175.

whom were former Turkish guest workers. The specter of an inter-national and violent Islamic political movement combined with the domestic experience of a growing Muslim population operating outside the oversight and understanding of West German society. This collision produced calls to be aware of and address the emerging threat.

The spring of 1979 saw a burgeoning of media attention to the *Koranschulen* in West Germany, with articles focusing on how instructors in those schools were passing on more than religious instruction to their students. In an article entitled "In the Middle of Germany: Turks Drill Hate into Children," a reporter for the conservative *Welt am Sonntag* opens by describing the lessons young Turkish children would learn in their "particular type of Sunday school": warnings that seemingly friendly German teachers were Christian missionaries or Jewish agents in disguise, the forbidding of friendships with Germans, and the sanc-tioning of killing anyone who went against such lessons. The strangeness and threat of these "underground" and "illegal" *Koranschulen* are com-pounded by the reporter's description of the class itself. "The lesson takes place in dank basements or dark courtyards," the reporter writes. "It lasts three to six hours. The teachers are dressed entirely in black" – calling to mind the radical mullahs of revolutionary Iran. The separation of boys and girls, along with the covering of girls' hair, accentuates the foreignness of the situation, and the use of corporal punishment implies a propensity toward violence. The instructors, the reporter informs, belong to the extreme-right Turkish opposition party known as the Gray Wolves. Originally formed in the 1960s as a youth wing of the far-right Nationalist Movement Party, by the late 1970s the Gray Wolves were a paramilitary organization responsible for the murder of hundreds of Alevis in the 1978 Maraş Massacre and hundreds more left-wing activists and university students during the violence leading up to the military coup of 1980. Their history of recruiting youth and fomenting violence struck a chord with the reporter, who contended that, although outlawed in Turkey, the Gray Wolves used *Koranschulen* in West Germany to indoctrinate the youth in Turkish nationalism and a hatred for their host society.[73]

The themes introduced in this article – the foreignness of *Koranschulen* and their dangerous mixture of religion with radical politics – continued in the West German media throughout the late 1970s and into the 1980s. To some, the perceived increasing radicalism and fanaticism of mosques in West Germany could be tied directly to the Ayatollah Ruhollah

---

[73] "Mitten in Deutschland: Türken säen Haß in Kinder," *Welt am Sonntag*, 11 March 1979.

Khomeini's call for international Islamic revolution.[74] The Federation of German Trade Unions (DGB) contributed its voice to the growing hum of concern in April 1979. Warning that *Koranschulen* were "insular" and led "mainly by unauthorized persons" who taught "reactionary fanaticism and hostility to all strangers," the DGB lamented the inability of the federal government to oversee the classes and advocated bringing such religious instruction into public schools.[75] Karl-Heinz Göbel, head of the DGB's department for foreign employees, argued that doing so would ensure instruction by qualified teachers and avoid creating a state within a state.[76]

Some officials from Islamic organizations in West Germany tried to counter the growing concern and suspicion. Necdet Demirgülle from the Islamic Cultural Center in Frankfurt explained to *Die Welt* that *Koranschulen* were the only alternative for Turkish children to learn about Islam, as it was not included in religious instruction in German schools. "In our Koranschulen," Demirgülle told the reporter, "children are advised [that] they must cooperate with the structure of this society and live peacefully with each other."[77] Mohammed El-Sayed, secretary of the Islamic Community of southern Germany, told a reporter from the *Münchener Merkur*, a conservative daily out of Bavaria, that the children in his organization's *Koranschule* learned "prayer, order, cleanliness –and how one behaves toward other people."[78] These public statements were geared toward presenting the *Koranschule* in a light that would make it seem not only nonthreatening but also familiar. Many Germans, however, remained unconvinced by such assurances. Concerns persisted about the alien nature of mosques and Muslims as well as of their connections to political extremists and terrorism. Islamic organizations' secrecy surrounding the sources of their finances – rumored to come from Libya – contributed to public fears about the potential for their local *Koranschulen* to become, in the words of one reporter, a site that acted as an agent "for ideas that could serve as the basis for political terror."[79]

---

[74] Horst Zimmermann, "Wenn Suren-Pauken zum Pflichtfach wird: Gegen Khomeinis Jünger sind die Behörden machtlos," *Saarbrücker Zeitung*, 26 April 1979. See also Frank Lämmel, "Koranschulen in Deutschland: Feindbilder im Namen Allahs? *Münchener Merkur*, 14/16 April 1979.

[75] "DGB gegen Koranschulen – Farthmann: Wir sind machtlos," *Die Welt*, 9 April 1979.

[76] "An Koranschulen nicht nur Religion? DGB wendet sich gegen Indoktrinierung türkischer Gastarbeiterkinder," *Süddeutsche Zeitung*, 9 April 1979.

[77] Martina Kempff, "Mohammeds Wort soll Einzug an den Schulen halten," *Die Welt*, 17 April 1979.

[78] Frank Lämmel, "Koranschulen in Deutschland: Feindbilder im Namen Allahs? *Münchener Merkur*, 14/16 April 1979.

[79] Zimmermann, "Wenn Suren-Pauken zum Pflichtfach wird."

Although the perception of the mosque as a separate and threatening space remained, the early 1980s saw a shift in focus from the menacing specter of politically extremist Islam to the impact on the Turkish children who attended *Koranschule*. To be sure, the West German public and politicians were still concerned about an Islamic fundamentalism at odds with their political and secular values, but by the 1980s the discourse had changed. Now, the consequence to be averted was not simply hostility toward German society but also the hindrance of successful integration of Turkish children into that society. Bundestag representative Thomas Schroer (SPD) articulated this growing consensus in a 1982 article entitled "How Integration Is Hindered: Koranschulen Are Breeding Grounds for Resentment." Schroer states his case bluntly, arguing that "Koranschulen established in all Germany's major cities hinder the opportunity to live together. They are breeding grounds for prejudices," he continues, that teach not only the Qur'an and the Islamic moral code but also spread anti-Semitism, advocate the oppression of women, and practice corporal punishment – all in sympathy, if not cooperation, with the fascist Gray Wolves.[80] Schroer's points about the secrecy of the mosques, the lack of oversight, and the opposition of such organizations to the secular Turkish state draw from the anxieties that arose in the 1970s. Yet in his article, the West German politician gave voice to a new and growing concern – that children who attend *Koranschule* would be intolerant of religious and cultural differences and thus less able to integrate than other migrant children.[81] "Whoever sends his child to Koranschule," Schroer warns, "harms him, because he forces the child to remain foreign."[82]

The solution, as Schroer and many others like him saw it, was taking Islamic religious instruction from the dark and secretive corners of the courtyards and placing it in the public schools, where it would receive necessary oversight. Muslims had a right to religious freedom, and Turkish children, he reasoned, had a right to religious education in the public schools, just as Christian children did.[83] Similar sentiments and criticisms echoed throughout the press in the early 1980s. While the secrecy surrounding the mosque prohibits one from knowing much about what happens within, reporter Liselotte Müller contended, it was clear "that it strengthens the youth's defensive posture against the host society. In recent days, the intolerant direction of Islam has won the upper hand." Bringing Muslim religious instruction into the public

---

[80] Thomas Schroer, "Wie Integration verhindert wird: Koranschulen sind Brutstätten für Ressentiments," *Sozialdemokratischer Pressedienst*, 1 March 1982, p. 4, BPA.
[81] Ibid., 4.   [82] Ibid., 5.   [83] Ibid.

schools, Müller argued, would "give space to an enlightened and tolerant form of Islam."[84]

West German concerns about the lessons taught in courtyard mosques continued throughout the 1980s, as did efforts to move Islamic instruction from the mosque into public schools. Yet this effort ran against significant obstacles, one of which stemmed from the differences in organizational structures of the major religious communities in West Germany. In order to receive support from the state and to have one's religion taught in public schools, members of a particular confession needed a central administrative body that could represent all adherents in the country. Christian and Jewish communities each had their own single organization that fulfilled this requirement; West Germany's Muslims did not. In addition, the lack of a central governing body with the ability to enact countrywide educational reform, in this case for religious instruction, meant that efforts to bring Islamic instruction into the public sphere and under West German oversight had to be on the state level. The struggle over the place of Islamic instruction would continue into the 1990s in reunified Berlin, with its resolution not coming until 2001, as we will see in Chapter 6.

Another significant development of the 1990s and early 2000s I explore in Chapter 6 was the growing number of purpose-built mosque construction projects. As Turkish Muslim communities became more established throughout the 1980s and 1990s, their religious organizations sought to create spaces of worship and community that would serve their needs and reflect their identities. These efforts met with resistance at the local level as well as in the national discourse around the place of Islam in German society, which contained echoes of the earlier debates we have examined here. The 1970s and 1980s, in many ways, set the stage for the increasingly public and passionate debates to come.

Conclusion

More than any of the other sites discussed previously, the mosque demonstrates the changing composition and character of the Turkish-German community over time. From the impromptu and informal spaces of communal prayer created by guest worker men to the multifaceted religious, social, and cultural institutions that would later be run by their children, the importance, purpose, and reach of the mosque has broadened far past

---

[84] Liselotte Müller, "Türken von Berlin wollen keine Deutschen werden: Senat dringt auf Einbürgerung/ ‚Dritter Weg' ist keine Dauerlösung," *Hannoverische Allgemeine*, 10 July 1982, BPA.

its original context. That Turkish Muslims used the mosque as a means to create spaces of belonging within their daily landscape is apparent; the extent to which those spaces have served to facilitate integration into West German society, however, is less clear-cut.

From the beginning, Turkish Muslim immigrants constructed the mosque to address needs unknown, unacknowledged, or overlooked by both the Turkish government that sent them and the West German state that received them. Mosques became a way to fulfill religious obligations as well as preserve and perform a religious and cultural identity that did not have a place in West German society. This was especially true for first-generation men. As guest workers, they founded the first courtyard mosques, assuming a role leadership and authority that they generally did not enjoy in the workplace. The mosque became not only a site of religious observance but also one of social networking and, in Ceylan's words, an "emotional refuge" where they could find serenity amid the banality and stress of daily life.[85] For some first-generation women, the mosque held similar if not equal importance as a social and cultural space, enabling a smoother transition into the host society or allowing them to maintain social lives apart from that society. The mosque, particularly in its earlier years, was, however, a space dominated and primarily utilized by men.

Koranschule taught the second generation the fundamentals of Islam, and at the same time purposefully educated them into a particular definition of what it meant to be Turkish – nurturing an identification with the Turkish homeland through language and lessons. This pairing of Turkish culture and nationalism with religious instruction grew more apparent in the 1980s as the probability of the *Rückkehr* diminished. Youth responded differently to the lessons given at the mosque, running the gamut from becoming involved in the administration of the mosque to avoiding it entirely as adults. *Koranschule* in the 1970s and early 1980s seemed to purposefully take the second generation out of West German society, physically and culturally. Even when West Germany was not held at arm's length as an enemy, that it was foreign in comparison to the homeland was a sentiment expressed both deliberately and unconsciously.

This "pain of being abroad," however, could be soothed by participation in religious and cultural festivals hosted by the mosque. Turkey – as the immigrants remembered it – was re-created in West Germany. These events allowed the first generation to celebrate their religious and cultural

---

[85] Ceylan, *Ethnische Kolonien*, 138.

identity while they introduced the second generation to the cooperative performance of both their identity as Muslims and as Turks. Both the Turkish state and the daily *Hürriyet* reinforced the role of the mosque as a separate space within and through which Turkish Muslims and their children could connect to the traditions and values of their homeland. The Ministry of Religious Affairs, prompted by concerns of the proliferation of activists and organizations in Europe considered hostile to the Turkish state, began sending officially trained imams in the early 1980s to Turkish communities abroad and consolidating many of those under its own umbrella. *Hürriyet* continued this work of discursively connecting the mosque to immigrants' religious and national identities by tying local religious celebrations and participants to their counterparts in Turkey and stressing the aspect of "re-creation" of Turkey in the diasporic context.

The West German media also stressed and perpetuated both this foreignness of the mosque in the West German context as well as the connection between Islam and Turkish identity. The growing recognition of the long-term settlement of Turkish guest workers and their families during the mid-1970s coupled with the dramatic and unsettling events of the Iranian Revolution in 1979, producing an increased anxiety about what transpired in the unmonitored corners of local Muslim communities. The radical political nature of the Iranian Revolution and transnational connections (perceived and actual) between Islamic organizations in West Germany and Turkey produced a new image in the West German press and public of Muslim immigrants as secretive, infiltrated by and subservient to foreign extremists, and unable to integrate into a democratic and modern West German society. The role of the Iranian Revolution was critical in this intense and anxious focus on Turkish immigrants as Muslims. First by forging links between West German mosques and Iranian-style extremist political Islam, and then through their consistent depiction of the *Koranschule* as a threat to integration, public discourse emphasized a foreignness and threat at odds with West German values. Largely ignored before the Iranian Revolution, Muslim spaces in general and mosques more specifically were constructed over the 1980s as distinctly non-German spaces, alien at best and deleterious to state security at worst.

Ultimately, examining the relationship between the mosque and the sense of belonging among the first and second generation reveals how the local level influenced and was influenced by national and transnational contexts. For many, the local prayer room and then mosque enabled them to participate in a religious community almost absent in the host society before their arrival, tied them more tightly to their local environments and neighborhoods even as it connected them to trans-national relationships, and assisted in the transition to life in the FRG. At the institutional level, the mosque began to put Muslims as a community on more equal footing with German society. Yet at the same time, and especially in its earlier years of operation in West Germany, mosques constantly reminded Muslim immigrants and their children that they were living abroad, and, in many cases, actively taught separate national and cultural identities in the second generation.[86] In addition, through-out the 1980s, both West German and Turkish states and media rein-forced the identity of Muslims as foreign, and effectively encouraged the conflation of Turkish and Muslim identities, despite the fact that not all members of the Turkish-German community considered religion an important, or even a relevant, part of their identity. Thus, mosques came to exist both within German society and on its margins, with the tension between the two representing, however inaccurately, perhaps the defining feature of the Turkish-German community.

[86] The extent to which mosques would reinforce a separate national and cultural identity depended (and still depends) on whether the umbrella organization with which they were affiliated encouraged open dialogue and integration or emphasized the maintenance of Turkishness. Today there are still many mosques that conduct their religious education and services in Turkish and Arabic only, although this is certainly not universal.

6   Belonging in Reunified Germany

For Bilge Yılmaz, the fall of the Berlin Wall was nothing short of momentous. A resident of Wedding since her parents brought her to West Germany at the age of eight, the then twenty-four-year-old woman had grown up with the Wall's presence and implications in her daily life, and she felt its destruction keenly. Yılmaz and her family followed the events on the television news, but that was not enough. "At the time, we had visitors from West Germany, from Stuttgart," Yılmaz recalled. "We went with them [to the Wall] and there was a ton of people on the street, on either side.... We tried, too, to break down that battered wall. We still have pictures of it, that was really so wonderful, it was a pure experience."[1]

Yet what started as the "wonderful" event of a divided country becoming whole, Yılmaz related, soon turned sour as first her employer and then her husband's left Berlin for more financially attractive locations elsewhere. As manufacturing jobs emigrated from the area, the neighborhood suffered. "The people suddenly didn't have work," Yılmaz explained, "if no more work, then no more money." Local businesses started to shut down. At this point in her narrative, German reunification becomes European unification, bringing with it the euro and higher prices. The "economic hardship" of reunified Germany became more than many families in the neighborhood could handle.[2] The Wall had fallen, but the financial and social challenges facing residents in Sprengelkiez had only intensified.

The worsening economic situation throughout Germany in the early post-reunification years opened a space for right-wing extremists and neo-Nazis to blame the country's financial woes, and especially its high unemployment rates, on nonethnic Germans. Whether they were recently arrived asylum seekers or second-generation youth who had

---

[1] Bilge Yılmaz (pseudonym), interview by author, 2 June 2009, transcription by Perrin Saylan, Berlin, 20.
[2] Yılmaz interview, 20–21.

lived their whole lives in Germany, so-called foreigners became a target of political rhetoric and, on several tragic occasions, physical violence. In 1991, a mob attacked a hostel in Hoyerswerda that housed Mozambican laborers, part of a larger series of attacks against asylum seekers and former contract workers in the East. In 1992, hundreds of rioters converged on a housing complex for asylum seekers in Rostock-Lichtenhagen, throwing Molotov cocktails and clashing with police. That same year, three Turkish residents of Mölln were killed in a firebombing of their home. The violence continued into the following year: four skinheads set fire to a house in Solingen belonging to a Turkish family. Two women and three young girls died, and fourteen other family members were injured. While the Solingen attack in particular galvanized hundreds of thousands to denounce far-right radicalism and march in support of multiculturalism, it was clear that the struggles of the newly reunified German state were not limited to ethnic Germans.

Although the connection is often lost in discussions of German reunification, the Wall separating the two Germanys played a significant role in the lives of Turkish immigrants and their children. Each major stage of the Wall's existence had ramifications for the Turkish-German community. Its construction prompted the sharpening of the labor crisis that brought Turkish *Gastarbeiter* to the country, and to West Berlin in particular. Its presence defined district boundaries and, at least in part, neighborhood character. Finally, its physical removal changed both the political makeup and economic conditions of the reunified state, weakening the foundation on which the Turkish-German community had begun to construct its belonging.

Recently, scholars have begun to widen their research into the effects of German reunification to include the impact on the country's ethnic minority communities. At the forefront of scholarship into the effects on the Turkish-German population is social scientist Nevim Çil. Focusing on generation, Çil demonstrates the close ties between identity and belonging and brings out new perspectives on the meanings of *Mauerfall* (fall of the Berlin Wall) and reunification.[3] The first generation, she argues, experienced reunification as a disappointment, as their economic contributions to Germany were ignored and their own employment positions were lost. Although the second generation as a body experienced reunification as a social collapse rather than an economic one, their reactions differed depending on their age at the time of *Mauerfall*. The older youth, who had generally worked hard to incorporate themselves

---

[3] Nevim Çil, *Topographie des Außenseiters: Türkische Generationen und der deutsch-deutsche Wiedervereinigungsprozess* (Berlin: Schiler, 2007).

into German society and succeed economically, grew disillusioned as belonging in the unified German state took on an increasingly ethnically based bent. For those in their preteens during reunification, the process constituted a moment of self-awareness in which they came to realize their place at the margins of German society. Thus, for those in the second generation, Çil argues, "Turk" became a synonym for "outsider," an identifier of one's position in a minority group.[4]

If Çil is correct and the fall of the Wall and German reunification left members of the Turkish community feeling pushed farther toward the margins of German society, how did that development unfold in their daily lives? How were the spaces in their everyday landscapes affected by the events of 1989 and 1990? Did all their spaces of belonging deteriorate due to reunification, or were there ways in which the Turkish-German community became more settled in post-1989 Germany?

This chapter provides an overview of those spaces of belonging during the years following reunification, tracing the lines of continuity and highlighting new developments both within Sprengelkiez and in Berlin more broadly. A look at the Turkish-German community throughout the 1990s and beyond reveals a diversification of its experiences, which had significant consequences for members' sense of belonging. As with broader German society, the consequences of reunification accentuated many of the challenges already facing Berlin's Turkish-German community, such as the unstable job market and the continuing pressure on schools. Yet reunified Berlin also witnessed a growing level of interest from many corners in seeking answers to persistent issues through cross-cultural dialogue and action. Despite the very real challenges to Turkish-German belonging posed in the reunification environment and the accompanying disillusionment, the Turkish-German community managed to solidify its foundations within and identification with Berlin and make key entrées into German society.

Working Hard, Hardly Working

As discussed in Chapter 1, an economic downturn in the 1980s followed by the upheaval caused by reunification resulted in a significant destabilization of the workplace for many first-generation Turkish immigrants. Although ethnic Germans also suffered job losses and workplace instability, the situation was especially acute for non-German workers. Turkish workers, in particular, suffered. Throughout the country, the Turkish

---

[4] Nevim Çil, "Türkische Migranten und der Mauerfall," *Aus Politik und Zeitgeschichte*, 21–22 (May 2009): 40–46.

unemployment rate rose from 10 percent in 1990 to 24.8 percent only five years later. In comparison, the general unemployment rate in 1995 was 10.8 percent and 16.6 percent for all *Ausländer*.[5] In Berlin alone, the unemployment rate by the mid-1990s had reached 16.4 percent for native Germans and almost 27 percent for workers with an immigrant background.[6] For some Turkish workers, their move into the ranks of the unemployed was the result of their jobs emigrating out of the city, as was the case with Yılmaz and her husband. Others, however, pointed the finger of blame at the newly arrived former East Germans. One disaffected young man told a reporter, "I've lived here for nineteen years. But when I try to find work, I find nothing. Employers look at [people from the former East] and think, 'I can pay them a little less, and besides that, they're my countrymen. Why should I leave them in a bind?'"[7] Whatever the direct cause, those who had originally come to Germany in order to work found that goal seriously challenged in the years following reunification.

Yet, even as a stable workplace became increasingly elusive, a growing number of immigrants sought stability and independence by opening businesses of their own. In 1981, only 4.7 percent of all *Ausländer* in West Germany owned their own business. By the time the Wall fell, that number had increased to just over 7 percent. By 1995, 8.5 percent of all *Ausländer* in the "old" *Bundesländer* (federal states) were self-employed.[8] In the mid-1990s, Turks represented the second largest group of non-German business owners, coming in behind Italians. The statistics for Berlin are particularly notable and reflect in part the active engagement of Commissioner for Foreigners Barbara John in the decision of the Berliner Senate in the wake of reunification to offer advisory support and start-up capital for aspiring business owners. Between 1991 and 1994, the overall number of self-employed nonethnic Germans rose approximately 53 percent, with very similar gains (in terms of percentage, not real numbers) among men and women.[9]

According to a 1997 study of Turkish-owned businesses in Berlin by Hedwig Rudolph and Felicitas Hillmann, the majority of entrepreneurs

---

[5] Armin Fuhrer, "Türkische Unternehmen boomen," *Die Welt*, 14 July 1997, 15.
[6] Hedwig Rudolph and Felicitas Hillmann, "Döner contra Boulette – Döner und Boulette: Berliner türkischer Herkunft als Arbeitskräfte und Unternehmer im Nahrungsgütersektor," in Hartmut Häußermann and Ingrid Oswald, eds., *Zuwanderung und Stadtentwicklung* Opladen: Leviathan, 1997), 93.
[7] "In Kreuzberg kommandieren wir," *Der Spiegel*, 19 November 1990, 161.
[8] The "old" *Bundesländer* refers to those states that made up the Federal Republic of Germany prior to reunification.
[9] Joyce Marie Mushaben, *The Changing Faces of Citizenship: Integration and Mobilization Among Ethnic Minorities in Germany* (New York: Berghahn Books, 2008), 180.

did not open businesses as a way to escape unemployment. Similar to Blaschke and Ersöz's study ten years prior, Rudolph and Hillmann found that most based their reasoning on either the desire to be their own employer or to create an alternative to factory work. In addition, the vast majority relied on family both for financing of the business and for labor.[10] Initially, most of these new businesses were in the food services industry, as immigrant entrepreneurs flocked to this sector in numbers relatively high compared to their German counterparts. In 1992, one-quarter of all immigrant-owned businesses in the country were in the food services industry, compared to 6 percent of German-owned companies. For Berlin, one-third of all new businesses opened by immigrants were in this sector – and 36 percent of those were Turkish. Of the 1,129 Turkish-owned food service businesses in Berlin in the mid-1990s, the three most common were *Imbisse* (fast-food counters) with 422, grocery stores with 204, and restaurants with 150.[11]

The presence and proliferation of Turkish-owned businesses began to change the way that Berliners, Germans, and foreigners (such as tourists) perceived and experienced the city. Berlin became known for its ubiquitous Turkish *Imbisse*, which served up *Döner* kebabs for the person on the go.[12] By the mid-1990s, the *Stehcafes* that clustered near transportation hubs and around tourist destinations were as likely to offer *Döner* as they were currywurst, and, although tourists continued to flock to sites such as Checkpoint Charlie and the Brandenburger Gate, many now also headed to Kreuzberg – advised by their guidebooks – to see (and consume) "Little Istanbul."[13] In constructing new spaces to address their own financial and personal goals, Turkish and Turkish-German business

[10] Rudolph and Hillmann, "Döner Contra Boulette," 100–101. Interestingly, in her study of Muslim immigrants (the vast majority of whom were Turkish) in Bremen, Hackett cites a 2001 study by the Zentrum für Türkeistudien that found only approximately one-fifth of all Turkish business owners who participated in the survey sought assistance or advice in setting up their own businesses. The majority of those who did so asked for support from family and friends, but the stark difference between Berliner business owners and their Bremen counterparts begs the question of what factors accounted for such a discrepancy. See Sarah Hackett, *Foreigners, Minorities and Integration: The Muslim Immigrant Experience in Britain and Germany* (Manchester, UK: Manchester University Press, 2016), 75–77.

[11] Ibid., 95–98.

[12] Eberhard Seidel-Pielen, Aufgespießt: *Wie der Döner über die Deutschen kam* (Hamburg: Rotbuch, 1996).

[13] Regarding the changing perception of Berlin, guidebooks for Germany and Berlin in 1989 and 1990 often mention the presence of Turkish immigrants, particularly in connection with Kreuzberg. During the next two decades, however, the Turkish community and "ethnic" businesses not only characterize parts of the city, they have become tourist destinations. For a few of examples, see these editions of the popular Lonely Planet guides: David Stanley, *Lonely Planet: Eastern Europe on a Shoestring*

owners had redefined parts of the city not just for the immigrant community or the local neighborhood but also internationally. And, in consequence, they created new spaces of economic opportunity for the city.

At the same time, the mid-1990s saw the beginning of a transition from first- to second-generation business ownership. The second generation, having grown up and been educated in Germany, was better equipped to deal with German bureaucracy as well as with diverse customers and suppliers. "It's not a problem for me to think multiculturally," a twenty-nine-year-old owner of a construction company with twenty employees told a reporter from the *Berliner Morgenpost*. The reporter noted that the naturalization rate among business owners was particularly high, as citizenship could smooth out bureaucratic tangles significantly.[14] Hackett also notes the higher rates of citizenship among Turkish businesspeople in Bremen than the general population, and posits that "founding a business was often the result of both a desire to be economically independent and a feeling of loyalty to Germany."[15] Whereas in the Berlin case I have found little evidence of an abstract devotion to the Federal Republic as a motivating factor in starting a business, it is clear that immigrant-owned businesses reflected "integration and a commitment to their local surroundings."[16] Operating a business created spaces that anchored members of the Turkish-German community and re-created the urban landscape to reflect its changing social makeup.

A 2007 study carried out by researchers at the Fachhochschule für Technik und Wirtschaft Berlin offers a look at developments in immigrant-owned businesses into the decade following Rudolph and Hillmann's study. Locating their study in Berlin-Mitte (comprising Wedding, Mitte, and Kreuzberg), the researchers sought to investigate the growth and composition of the "ethnic economy," and identified three types of enterprises. The first, which constituted 25 percent of the 272 businesses in the study, employed family members and had a single-ethnicity customer base. The second (50 percent) included German customers as well, and the third (25 percent) had both German customers and employees.[17]

(Hawthorn: Lonely Planet, 1991); Steve Fallon, Anthony Haywood, Andrea Schulte-Peevers, and Nick Selby, *Lonely Planet: Germany* (Hawthorn: Lonely Planet, 1998); and Andrea Schulte-Peevers, Kerry Christiani, Marc Di Duca, Anthony Haywood, Catherine Le Nevez, Daniel Robinson, and Caroline Sieg, *Lonely Planet: Germany* (Footscray: Lonely Planet, 2010).

[14] Britta Petersen, "Jenseits von Döner Kebab," *Berliner Morgenpost*, 26 July 1998, p. 39, Presse Inhalte: Sozial-Spi. W, MMA.

[15] Hackett, *Foreigners, Minorities and Immigration*, 73.   [16] Ibid., 86.

[17] P. Kayser, F. Preusse, J. Riedel, and B. Umbreit, *Ethnische Ökonomie als Chance der Standortenentwicklung* (Berlin: Fachhochschule für Technik und Wirtschaft und Institut IKO, 2008), Vorwort.

The average "ethnic" entrepreneur was a man between the ages of thirty-six and forty-five years old, who had earned a *Gesellenbrief* (certificate of apprenticeship). Proprietors of Turkish background constituted the bulk of business owners in the ethnic economy (173 out of 272). Similar to the findings of Rudolph and Hillmann's study, an overwhelming majority were sole proprietors of their business and worked in the retail or food service industry.[18] In addition, the Fachhochschule researchers found that some 30 percent of businesses in the ethnic economy were owned and operated by women.[19] This is a significant difference from Rudolph and Hillmann's study, which, ten years earlier, had located no women proprietors of Turkish-owned businesses in the food services sector.[20] As the later study does not break down business ownership by type and ethnicity, it is not possible to tell the role Turkish-German women played in the ethnic economy. The difference between the two studies is, however, still remarkable and suggests a growing role of second-generation women in the city's business leadership.

The spectrum of Turkish and Turkish-German experiences in the workplace after reunification is striking. At one end, first-generation (and, eventually, second-generation) workers were expelled from the labor market or failed to gain entry. At the other end, however, a stratum of the Turkish-German community created new spaces for themselves, their family members, and their employees to earn a living and participate in the city's economic life. Through the space-making process, they rooted themselves more deeply in their local community, and they changed Berlin's physical landscape and its national and international image. Such a wide range of experiences suggests that, for those who were part of the labor force in postreunification Germany, one's sense of belonging may have become even more tied to one's socioeconomic status than one's ethnic identity or membership in a minority group.

Building Bridges, Guarding the Gates

Just as the post-1989 workplace was marked by bipolar experiences, so, too, were impressions of the home and neighborhood sites. In the years following reunification, Wedding (along with the rest of Berlin) saw the burgeoning of organizations, initiatives, and efforts directed toward improving its residents' situations. Whereas they may have held this very general goal in common, the types of communal spaces that surfaced and their methods of dealing with perceived challenges varied widely and, in

[18] Ibid., 43–49.   [19] Ibid., 44.
[20] Rudolph and Hillmann, "Döner Contra Boulette," 101.

part, reflected the ongoing debates about both the definition and desirability of multiculturalism of the late 1980s and 1990s. Two types of local organizations in Berlin, and Sprengelkiez more specifically, took opposing courses of action to improve the lives of local residents: (1) those that advocated multiculturalism and cooperation to overcome social and economic problems and (2) those that sought protection and belonging through violence and ethnic separatism.

The Kommunales Forum Wedding (Community Forum of Wedding) is an example of a grassroots organization that has worked to improve living conditions in the neighborhood environment through civic engagement and support of local initiatives. Banding together in November 1988, partially as a consequence of local activism during the conflict over the *Sanierung*, the forum's original members reflected the diversity of their neighborhood: university employees and the unemployed, clergy and renters' advocates. The founders were initially motivated by the high levels of unemployment and poverty in their Kiez, and sought to involve local residents in combating such challenges through programs ranging from lunches for senior citizens to neighborhood beautification.[21] As part of a diverse district, the forum also engaged in promoting cross-cultural understanding and cooperation. In this vein, it inaugurated a working group in 1999 called Interkulturelle Kommunikation in der Kommune (Intercultural Communication in the Municipality, IKK). The IKK was coordinated by a representative from the forum as well as one from Volkshochschule Wedding, and brought together interested local participants and various experts in a quarterly public forum where they discussed the challenges of multiculturalism and instituted projects aimed at furthering cross-cultural cooperation.[22]

The forum's activities and orientation reflected a continued role of independent actors in the discussion and work of integration on the local level seen throughout the 1980s. At the same time, it demonstrates how such actors – from the Tenants' Initiative (Chapter 3) and the VHS (Chapter 4) to the forum – considered integration as a part of improving local life that would benefit whole communities, not just foreigners. For the forum, perhaps even more than for the VHS, integration was not an end goal but rather a step along the way toward community well-being. The group's efforts to improve the quality of life in Sprengelkiez earned

[21] "Agentur für gesellschaftlich nützliche Qualifizierung und Beschäftigung im Sprengelkiez – Warum es uns gibt," http://kommunales-forum-wedding.de/cms/index.php?page=warum-es-uns-gibt (accessed 11 August, 2011).
[22] "Projekt: Interkulturelle Kommunikation in der Kommune (IKK)," *Newsletter Zukunftskonferenz Müllerstrasse*, no. 7 (December 1999), Veranstaltungen im Wedding (1992–2004), MMA, 1.

them national recognition when they received the Living Democracy prize from Bundestag president Rita Süssmuth in 1998. In an article covering the event, the reporter noted that the organization continued its efforts to improve life in its Kiez, despite losing its office due to an inability to pay rent.[23]

Shortly after receiving the Living Democracy prize, the Kommunales Forum was formally joined in its efforts for neighborhood renewal by Berlin's city government, as it followed suit with concerted, locally based efforts that identified the connections between economic conditions, neighborhood health, and integration. By the mid-1990s, it had become painfully clear that unemployment, poverty, and deteriorating infrastructure were affecting some neighborhoods at levels far exceeding those of others. In addition, the costs associated with reunification made city officials more amenable to tenement restoration and funding of local initiatives than they had been in previous decades.[24] In response, the city government instituted a new program, called *Quartiersmanagement* (Neighborhood Management, QM), in hopes of finding solutions to these entrenched social and economic problems. The QM's mandate reflected that of the Kommunales Forum: developing and supporting self-help projects through which local residents could improve their own situation.

As a "problem Kiez," Sprengelkiez was one of the first to be "managed," and the Sparrplatz QM and Kommunales Forum wasted little time in cooperating in their like-minded efforts.[25] Residents, however, had mixed reactions to the new organization. Although some saw its opening as positive for the Kiez, others questioned its ability to enact real change.[26] The more cynically minded wondered whether the new

[23] "Preis für Kiez-Engagement," *Berliner Morgenpost*, 25 January 1998, Presse Inhalte: Sozial-Spi. W, MMA.

[24] Alexander Clarkson, "Circling the Wagons: Immigration and the Battle for Space in West Berlin, 1970–1990," in Simona Talani, Alexander Clarkson, and Ramon Pacheco Pardo, eds., *Dirty Cities: Towards a Political Economy of the Underground in Global Cities* (Basingstoke: Palgrave Macmillan, 2013), 130–132.

[25] "Problemkiez wird jetzt gemanagt: Weddinger Sparrplatz soll vor weiterem Niedergang bewahrt werden," *Tagesspiegel*, 27 February 1999, Presse Inhalte: Sozial-Spi. W, MMA.

[26] Dilek Güngör, "'Viel verändern wird sich hier nicht': Am Sparrplatz haben nur wenige einen Job? Quartiersmanager sollen die Lebensqualität verbessern," *Berliner Zeitung*, 8 August 1999, Presse Inhalte: Sozial-Spi. W, MMA. Funding continued to be an issue, and, in 2011, the forum filed for bankruptcy. See "Der Verein Kommunales Forum Wedding e.V. hat Insolvenz angemeldet – Aktivitäten und Projekte im SprengelHaus gehen weiter!" www.sparrplatz-quartier.de/Der-Verein-Kommu nales-Forum-Wedding-e-V-hat-Insolvenz-angemeldet-Aktivitaeten-und-Projekte-im-Spr.2935.0.html?&L=0%25252522%25252520and%25252520, 2 September 2011 (accessed 25 June 2016).

initiative was simply further political window dressing, intended to look as if the government was addressing local problems but more interested in advocating multiculturalism than dealing with economic issues.[27] Whatever the locals' opinions of them, the QM staff hit the ground running. Over the course of their first nine months in operation, they designed and carried out a survey among the residents with the intention of uncovering the neighborhood's positive attributes and areas for improvement. While the majority of respondents replied that they felt at home in their Kiez, both German and non-German residents expressed the desire for more cross-cultural contact with their neighbors, and generally blamed non-Germans for the lack of contact.[28] One concrete way the QM sought to address residents' wish for more interaction with their neighbors was through the opening of a neighborhood center on Sprengelstrasse in 2001. The SprengelHaus, as it later came to be called, began as a 131-square-meter meeting space and event center for Sprengelkiez, but in the intervening years it has grown both in size (now 930 square meters) and scope, hosting a variety of local clubs, classes, events, and forums. This expansion suggests a continued and growing relevance of SprengelHaus's purpose and locals' desire to create spaces of exchange and communal assistance and action.[29]

By the end of the 1990s, many of the initiatives put forth to encourage cross-cultural connections had come to focus on religion. Although contention over religious instruction in the schools, the proliferation of mosques, and the increasing visibility of practicing Muslims made religious differences a flashpoint, advocates of multiculturalism believed they were also an opportunity. Local actors began to create spaces of interreligious dialogue that were designed to foster a multiculturalism that emphasized cross-cultural communication and understanding. Religion, or rather, discussion about religion, became a purposeful multicultural space. Alongside the intercultural communication effort hosted by the Kommunales Forum and the Volkshochschule, the QM in Soldinarstrasse partnered with a Tiergarten association to initiate a similar interreligious dialogue. The meetings, which began in November 1999

---

[27] Margaret Fischer (pseudonym), interview by author, 20 May 2009, transcription by Perrin Saylan, Berlin, 6–7.

[28] "Gutes multikulturelles Miteinander im Kiez," *Berliner Morgenpost*, 27 October 1999, Presse Inhalte: Sozial-Spi. W, MMA.

[29] For more on SprengelHaus, see its website: http://sprengelhaus-wedding.de/geschichte/. I was fortunate enough to be invited by one of my interview partners to one of the then recurring events hosted by the SprengelHaus, a Sunday brunch, in July 2009. There were perhaps a dozen people around the table, most of whom seemed to be regulars who enjoyed the chance to socialize with one another over a well-laid table.

and took place at the Wedding Volkshochschule, brought together participants interested in learning more about the different religions represented in their district. At its second meeting, the group discussed abstract theological issues, as well as what different religions had to say about the problems faced by their neighborhoods. In addition, participants suggested communal religious holiday celebrations as a way to forge interreligious ties. The next meeting was scheduled to take place the following month at the Islamic Cultural Center on Lindowerstrasse, the first step in a plan to visit local places of worship. The meeting closed with a prayer – in German and Turkish – "for unity."[30]

Spaces of interreligious dialogue extended beyond working groups and institutes of higher learning. Local activists initiated less formal programs that reached into the daily lives of residents. Bilge Yılmaz, a community-minded person with children, initiated a project with coworkers at the Ostergemeinde's kindergarten to bring interreligious understanding to some of the youngest members of the Kiez. Beginning in 2003, Yılmaz and her colleagues – another Turkish German and two Germans – introduced an element of religious education into the children's day once each week. They would celebrate various festivals together, talk about how their families observed religious holidays, and tell stories that the different religions held in common.[31] Although Yılmaz felt the children enjoyed and benefited from their efforts, after four years she and her colleagues decided to stop the program. Yılmaz blamed the contemporary political climate for the lack of similar programs in the neighborhood and continued her activism through participation in other local multicultural initiatives.[32] The focus in these interreligious dialogues, whether between local lay and religious officials or amid a kindergarten class, on finding points of commonality and respecting differences demonstrates a continuity from discussions in the 1980s about multiculturalism as a new way to conceive of German identity.[33] Although these discussions may have been muted in the wake of reunification and the consequent "patriotic shift" back toward a homogeneous German identity, some local actors energetically and deliberately carved out spaces of cross-cultural dialogue and cooperation they hoped would nourish a growing multicultural society.

---

[30] "Projekt Interreligiöser Dialog," *Newsletter Zukunftskonferenz Müllerstrasse*, no. 7 (December 1999), Veranstaltungen im Wedding (1992–2004), MMA, 3–4.
[31] Yılmaz interview, 10.   [32] Ibid., 11.
[33] Rita Chin, *The Guest Worker Question in Postwar Germany* (Cambridge, UK: Cambridge University Press, 2007), 242–246.

Efforts to expand spaces of belonging for those with an immigrant background were also under way at the federal level, most visibly present in the heated debate in the late 1990s over reforming Germany's citizenship law. Up to this point, immigrants and their children had found it almost insurmountably difficult to obtain citizenship, which since 1913 had been based on ethnic descent (jus sanguinis). In order to be naturalized, aspiring citizens had to prove a range of economic, political, and cultural qualifications, pay up to DM 5,000 in application fees, and overcome "the ultimate hurdle of bureaucratic discretion" from the civil servant reviewing their case.[34] The SPD-Green coalition government under the leadership of Gerhard Schröder led the push for reform, and, after almost two years of intense debate and political struggle, the new citizenship law was enacted – one which officially extended the definition of German identity by adding the option of citizenship based on birth (jus soli). This expanded definition of political belonging, however, included specific constraints – one parent had to have lived in the Federal Republic for a minimum of eight years and held a certain residency status for at least three years. In addition, children whose parents met those requirements had to also officially choose German citizenship by the time they reached the age of twenty-three or their citizenship would expire.[35]

Reactions from the Turkish-German community reflected its diversity of backgrounds and experiences. Some approached the issue of German citizenship from a practical angle, seeing value in the expanded political rights and responsibilities and the excising of an extra layer of bureaucracy from their lives and businesses. Entrepreneurs, for example, sought naturalization more often than was the case more broadly in the Turkish-German community. For others, though, the symbolism of being a German citizen motivated their decision. As we saw in the Introduction, when a German historian asked Eren Keskin about German citizenship in the early 1990s before the reform made the prospect more feasible, his response did not speak to the difficulties involved in the process but rather to citizenship's value in his everyday life. "We have black heads," he answered, "and everyone knows we are not Germans."[36]

[34] Mushaben, The Changing Faces of Citizenship, 33.
[35] Chin, The Guest Worker Question, 262–263. In 2014, the requirement to officially choose German citizenship by age twenty three (Optionspflicht) was eliminated in response to the recognition of complicated bureaucratic processes it imposed on youth, the consequences of which would primarily be experienced by Turkish Germans. My thanks to Joyce Mushaben for bringing this to my attention and for her incisive comments on the German citizenship law.
[36] Eren Keskin (pseudonym), "Wirt einer Kneipe am Sparrplatz," interview with Ursula Trüper, audiocassette, side A, DLSA, MMA, 1993.

When I asked Engin Günükutlu, the representative of Wedding's Office for District Social Development, whether he had German citizenship, he simply smiled, shook his head, and said he was a Turk. He gave his answer like a simple statement of fact. Although he had lived and worked in Berlin for decades, loved the city, spoke excellent German, and married a German woman, Günükutlu felt that his Turkish identity precluded exchanging his Turkish nationality for a German one.[37] Günükutlu had constructed a belonging for himself that did not require (and even did not have room for) a change in passports.

At the same time that the Kommunales Forum and residents such as Bilge Yılmaz were trying to improve local conditions through intercultural cooperation, and politicians in the Bundestag were pushing for (and against) an expanded political definition of "Germanness," a different group of people pursued the solution to their problems down another track altogether. Angered by experiences of prejudice and alienated by feelings of foreignness, some young men sought to create spaces of belonging and empowerment through participation in street gangs. Turkish street gangs began in the 1970s, developing out of networks and friendships in the neighborhood and at school and prompted in part by the desire of young Turkish men to protect themselves and their communities from skinheads. In addition to this early motivation, the spaces of belonging to Turkish-German youth created within the context of gangs were strongly rooted in local sites, and, before the fall of the Wall, members focused on defining themselves against other immigrant-background street gangs.[38] In the 1980s, fights between gangs from different districts – such as Wedding's Black Panthers and Kreuzberg's 36 Boys – could be frequent and violent.[39] Members also exerted their belonging and authority in their districts by congregating together at neighborhood events or popular local businesses, such as street festivals and movie theaters.[40]

The fall of the Berlin Wall had ramifications that contributed to young men's motives for joining gangs and opened up opportunities for members to expand their activities and influence. The loss of jobs, the difficulties in obtaining apprenticeships, and the high rates of unemployment suffered by the Turkish-German community created a bleak prospect for economic security and success among the second generation

---

[37] Engin Günükutlu, interview by author, 9 May 2009, digital recording, Berlin.
[38] "Bulldogs," interview with Murat Güngör, "Zwei, drei Jahre Almanya ..." Exhibit, digital recordings 20050503.mp3, Dokumentationszentrum und e.V. DOMiD.
[39] Joachim Gästel, "Black Panthers, Fighters und Türkiye Boys," "Jugendcliquen im Wedding: Von den Wilden Cliquen zu Banden und Fighters" Ausstellung (JWA), MMA.
[40] "Bulldogs" interview.

in the 1990s. At the same time, consumption played an increasingly important role in their identity and self-presentation. "We came from a generation that was really influenced by the television," one former member of Moabit's Bulldogs related during a group interview in 2005.[41] Achieving a certain style and "self-presentation," in the words of the former gang members, however, required money, which they pursued through extortion and drug dealing. "It was obviously about the money," another Bulldog remarked.[42] With funds from these illicit activities, gang members could purchase the consumer goods they wanted, and that made them look the part. Unimpressed with the grocery stores and *Döner* stands of their fathers and put off by the social stigma of living off the system, these young men fought for a lifestyle they were either unwilling or unable to achieve otherwise.[43]

In addition, when the Wall disappeared so, too, did the boundary that separated Turkish street gangs in the western districts from skinheads and neo-Nazis in the East. Yet it is important to note that burgeoning white supremacy activities encouraged by the one hundredth birthday of Adolf Hitler and an election that brought the Republikaner party into the Berlin House of Representatives enflamed the situation even before the fall of the Wall.[44] Whereas Wedding itself remained fairly quiet during this time (one researcher credits the approximately five hundred members of the Streetfighter gang with keeping the peace), other parts of the city erupted in violence.[45] At a demonstration held to mourn the death of Ufuk Sahin, a man stabbed to death by a German racist on May 1, 1989, neo-Nazis gave the nearly seven thousand participants the Hitler salute before attacking the demonstrators. A group of Turkish gang members emerged from the crowd, and a violent battle between the two sides ensued as police tried to protect the crowd and stop the fighters. Such incidents shortly before the fall of the Wall, together with the increasing number and violence of racist attacks such as those in Rostock and Mölln (1992) and Solingen (1993), sharpened an atmosphere of fear and anxiety among Turkish-German communities, even when members had not personally experienced hostility.[46]

Turkish-German street gangs in Berlin sought to protect their neighborhoods and exert their dominance by actively seeking out potential

---

[41] Ibid.   [42] The young man's exact words were, "es ging ganz klar um die Cola."
[43] "Bulldogs" interview.
[44] The Republikaner is a right-wing populist party whose main political platform is opposition to immigration.
[45] Gästel, "Jugendgangs der Neunziger Jahren."
[46] Mushaben, *The Changing Faces of Citizenship*, 73–74.

threats. In the group interview with the former Bulldogs members, one man recounted that there were "three hundred youth gangs [in the East] that hated us." The fall of the Wall refocused their purpose (or target); it was not about heading over to Kreuzberg to beat up "some Ahmet," one of the men explained. He and his associates would drive into East Berlin and the surrounding communities, looking for Germans who "hated foreigners."[47] In 1990, one *Spiegel* article reported the police estimated the number of "armed youth" in West Berlin at around four thousand.[48] For the Turkish gangs in these western districts, skinheads and neo-Nazis remained the primary enemy. As time passed, however, territorialism assumed a greater role, and gangs again turned their attention to conflicts between neighborhoods and districts.[49] The city attempted to deal with the increase in gang activity through a combination of law enforcement, social workers, and mediated discussions between different gangs.[50]

Young Turkish and Turkish-German men connected with Berlin gangs saw the several benefits to their involvement. First and foremost, young men felt gangs provided them with a sense of belonging, both to the people in the group and also to a particular place. Within the spaces of belonging created within the context of the gang, participants fulfilled specific roles – drug dealing, theft, break dancing, graffiti, and so forth – that contributed to the group's identity and success. Through the gang's collective identity, individual members crafted their own "self-presentation" and achieved "self-confidence."[51] In addition to belonging to a network, gang members belonged to and exerted authority over a place. Turkish-German gangs were, as already noted, strongly territorial. As one 36-er told a journalist in 1990, "We say it like this: Kreuzberg belongs to us. We are in charge here. What we say, goes."[52]

The second part of the young man's statement illuminates another advantage of gang membership: power. In an environment of high unemployment, visibly escalating hostility to perceived foreigners, and loss of social standing due to reunification, gangs offered spaces through which young men (and some young women) could step out of the role of victim and fight back. And fight they did. "Violence was like breakfast," a former Bulldog explained. Participating in violence proved the young men's masculinity and enhanced their reputation, a connection members made

[47] "Bulldogs" interview.
[48] "So ein Grfühl der Befreiung," *Der Spiegel*, 12 November 1990.
[49] Barbara Supp, "Die Droge heißt Respekt," *Der Spiegel*, 26 May 1997, pp. 110–113.
[50] "So ein Grfühl der Befreiung."   [51] "Bulldogs" interview.
[52] "In Kreuzberg kommandieren wir," *Der Spiegel*, 19 November 1990, p. 160.

bluntly and repeatedly during the interview.[53] It was also an integral part of drug dealing and extortion, activities that brought gang members the money they wanted to craft and maintain their image. Similar to the other community-based organizations discussed earlier, gang members attempted to solve the socioeconomic challenges they were facing, but through the medium of ethnic separatism and violence. They rejected both the calls for intercultural cooperation to build a multicultural society and demands to conform to a homogenizing German identity, choosing to eschew national belonging in favor of a self-awareness built on shared ethnic background and highly localized identity.

Multiculturalism in the Classroom

The two decades following reunification saw the continuation of challenges to education in a multiethnic context that had begun to surface in the 1970s and 1980s. On one hand, school administrators and teachers were still trying to deal with high percentages of students for whom German was not their first language. Particularly in working-class neighborhoods where immigrant communities tended to settle, educators faced the pedagogical challenge of teaching lessons to students with, at times, vastly different German language skills. Maja Herbert, a teacher of forty years, began working at a primary school in Sprengelkiez in 1990. The number of children per teacher at the school, she said, made effective teaching especially challenging. In one class, Herbert told a researcher, there were twenty-four Turkish students and one German teacher. They simply could not understand each other. "It's madness," she said with a laugh. Herbert insisted that the school needed more space for classes, more teachers, and more money. We are a rich country, she explained, but we skimp when it comes to our children.[54]

Ute Schmidt, a preschool teacher at a local primary school in the 1980s and 1990s, saw what she considered a lack of funding for and attention to teacher preparation as well. Schmidt recalled how she and her colleagues received very little, if any, special training regarding teaching in a multiethnic classroom. Sometime after reunification, however, the city senate began to take a more direct leadership role in the educational spaces created to equip teachers for the challenges posed by diverse student

---

[53] "Bulldogs" interview.
[54] Maja Herbert (pseudonym), interview by Ursula Trüper, 16 June 1993, audiocassette, DLSA, MMA.

populations, including providing a German-as-a-second-language course for a number of Berlin teachers at a school of education. "The Senate was pretty clever," Schmidt remarked wryly, "they gave us a certificate, but not so that they would have to pay us any better."[55] Although the city would open more spaces for teacher education in the 1990s, the majority of instructors continued to rely on experience, rather than formal training, to deal with the unique challenges presented by diverse classrooms. In addition, even as these top-down spaces slowly grew, some of the more grassroots programs began to wane. For example, the bilingual education programs that grew out of the less hierarchical collaborative spaces fostered by teachers such as Sabine Müller and Erol Kayman (Chapter 4) continued to shrink throughout the mid-1990s and early 2000s due to lack of administrative support and funding. By 2009, only five of the original sixty schools still offered bilingual classes.[56]

In a reunified Berlin, there were some teachers who did not have the sort of on-the-job training on which many of their colleagues relied: those from former East Berlin. East Berliners generally did not have much contact with foreigners, as the East German government had kept its contract laborers largely separate from the host society. As a result, when teachers from the former East obtained positions in western districts, such as Wedding, Kreuzberg, and Neukölln, they were confronted with new personal experiences and pedagogical challenges. Filiz Güler, who grew up in Wedding and now works there as a primary school teacher, remembers when East German teachers began working in her district. "Naturally, they hadn't had any contact with foreign children," Güler recounted, "and I still always hear, even though ten or more years have passed, that they can't deal with them, or are really different."[57] In addition to the difficulties this could cause in the classroom, at times it also prompted tensions between the teachers themselves. Primary school teacher Sabine Müller noted the strained relations between colleagues at her own institution. "After German reunification many Turkish people experienced that they were again pushed to the back of the line," Müller explained. "That was also for Turkish teachers; people came from Berlin, from [East Germany], that had no university degree, but despite that

[55] Ute Schmidt (pseudonym), interview by author, 29 June 2009, transcription by Perrin Saylan, Berlin, 7.
[56] Erol Kayman (pseudonym), interview by author, 29 May 2009, digital recording, Berlin.
[57] Filiz Güler (pseudonym), interview by author, 27 May 2009, transcription by Perrin Saylan, Berlin, 11.

they took some courses, and immediately became public employees, and made the same money as those that had worked here for thirty years."[58]

It was a combination of factors, then, that led to deteriorating conditions in a number of urban schools in the late 1990s. Even before the Programme for International Student Assessment (PISA) examinations were given and analyzed, many residents of Germany looked on the situation of their local schools and endeavored to send their children to schools outside their neighborhood, to schools with fewer perceived foreigners.[59] Some used relatives' addresses to get their children into more desirable schools; others opted to send their children to private or religious institutions. Whereas the majority of such parents were ethnic Germans, some Turkish parents followed suit and enrolled their children in schools with lower numbers of foreign students in hopes of improving their children's language learning and educational opportunities.[60]

The release of the first PISA report in 2000 revealed a situation in German schools much worse than many had assumed. Almost a quarter of all fifteen-year-old students either could not read or could barely do so. Scores in math and science were similarly shocking. The lowest performing students were young men either from migrant backgrounds or from socially disadvantaged families. In addition, Germany had the largest gap between the highest and lowest levels of achievement of any of the thirty-two participating countries.[61] The results sparked much debate over the ability of the German school system to address the needs of children with migrant backgrounds and concerns that it had failed to fulfill its role as their means of social advancement. Critics pointed out the high percentage of students with Turkish background who failed to graduate from secondary school (approximately half in 2002) or obtain an *Ausbildungsplatz* (apprenticeship training position) if they did graduate (around 40 percent). "Nowhere in Europe," wrote one reporter, "are the abilities of students so far apart from one another, and in almost no country does the background of the children have so great an influence on educational achievement as here. This applies especially to the foreign

---

[58] Sabine Müller (pseudonym), interview by author, 14 May 2009, transcription by Perrin Saylan, Berlin, 11.

[59] The PISA is an analysis conducted by the Organization for Economic Cooperation and Development (OECD) that evaluates the scholastic level of fifteen-year-olds across the world. The first PISA test was conducted in 2000, and has been held every three years since.

[60] "Oma mit guter Adresse," *Der Spiegel*, 26 October 1998, 94–97; and Fischer interview, 13.

[61] "Die Pisa-Analyse: Sind deutsche Schüler doof?" *Spiegel Online*, 13 December 2001, www.spiegel.de/schulspiegel/0,1518,172357,00.html (accessed 27 July 2011).

problem children of the educational system."[62] The scores in the second PISA evaluation in 2003 rose somewhat, but the relative success rates of students with migrant backgrounds continued to concern education officials, teachers, and parents alike. In the years following reunification, the school continued to be imbued not only with the responsibility for equipping children with migrant backgrounds for the practical and cultural skills for success in Germany but also the blame when inconsistent training, funding, and expectations kept the target ill-defined and in motion.

Muslims and Islam in and beyond the Mosque

Religious spaces, in particular, expanded and changed shape after German reunification. As previously discussed, in the first decades of Turkish immigration to and settlement in West Germany, practicing Muslims utilized temporary sites or rented spaces they could use to fulfill their religious obligations. These spaces consisted of almost entirely preexisting sites in the local landscape, and, as the return home remained on the mental horizon of the first generation, they did not set out to construct purpose-built mosques to serve the needs of their religious community. However, by the 1990s, it had become clear that the *Rückkehr* was a receding dream, particularly for the second generation. Islamic organizations and mosque communities began to consider constructing "real" mosques in which they could perform their religious obligations.

This move from the courtyards to the street front has met with varying degrees of both resistance and support from Germans in the neighborhoods of the proposed renovation and construction projects as well as the public more broadly. The balance of opposition and support often determined the measure of success Muslim organizations would have in their construction projects. One of the earliest attempts to construct a purpose-built mosque started with the members of the Mevlana mosque, affiliated with the Islamic Federation of Berlin,[63] and Millî Görüş, who had a history of conflict with secular and leftist Turks in the area that

---

[62] Martin Spiewak, "Weil Deutschland alle Schüler braucht," *Die Zeit*, p. 6 June 2002, www.zeit.de/2002/24/Weil_Deutschland_alle_Schueler_braucht (accessed 28 July 2011).

[63] The Islamic Federation of Berlin (Islamische Föderation Berlin) was founded in 1980 in West Berlin as an umbrella organization with twenty-six member mosques and Islamic organizations. It was the Berlin affiliate of the Islamische Gemeinschaft Millî Görüş, with continued links to that organization, and has likewise been under scrutiny by German authorities for Islamist positions. Yet, in 1998, the Islamic Federation was also the organization awarded the responsibility of facilitating courses in Islam in Berlin's public schools. See below.

212 Turkish Germans in the Federal Republic of Germany

enhanced their sense of being persecuted for their religious beliefs by German society. In the late 1990s, this community began to take measures to construct a purpose-built mosque near their current location on Kottbusser Tor. The Mosque Foundation, a committee set up to facilitate the building of the mosque, met with roadblocks at each step in the process. First, they discovered that the land they purchased as the site for their mosque – a plot they had been attempting to buy for more than fourteen years – had been sold to them at twice its actual value. Rather than trying to hold the seller accountable, the Mosque Foundation sued the municipality, contending that they had changed the plot's official designation in order to hinder the construction of the mosque.[64] This was only the first in a series of missteps by the Mosque Foundation and miscommunications between that body and the municipality.

During the next several years, the Mosque Foundation developed and presented a number of plans for construction to the municipality as well as to its own members. The more modest plans, which called for renovation of the existing building and the addition of an extension, met with the municipality's approval but were unpopular within the mosque community. This constituency wanted a larger building that reflected its use and the money invested. The Mosque Foundation responded with plans to demolish the existing structure and build a much larger mosque in its place, complete with an elaborate facade and minarets. These plans pleased the mosque community but were rejected by the municipality, which contended that they had not agreed on such a structure. Straining relations with the governing board still further was the Mosque Foundation's intention to include a large shopping mall underneath the mosque that would help offset the costs of construction and maintenance. To this, the municipality responded that, whereas a religious and cultural center was appropriate, "a shopping mall belongs in a different department all together. It is against all existing regulations."[65] The Mosque Foundation responded to the city officials by publicly accusing the municipality of discriminating against Muslims. Money and media problems continued to trouble the Mosque Foundation, and the pressure applied to Millî Görüş after the terrorist attacks of September 11, 2001, caused the Islamic Federation of Berlin to break its connection with that organization.[66] The purpose-built mosque for the Mevlana mosque community never made it off the drawing board, and its members continue to worship in their original accommodations.

[64] Gerdien Jonker, "The Mevlana Mosque in Berlin-Kreuzberg: An Unsolved Conflict," *Journal of Ethnic and Migration Studies* 31, no. 6 (November 2005): 1070–1073.
[65] Ibid., 1074.   [66] Ibid., 1076–1079.

Figure 13. Central Mosque, Cologne

A look at a later example of disputed mosque construction throws into starker relief the elements of the debate surrounding the Turkish Muslim community's move from invisibility to a public presence, providing a useful comparison to the earlier and relatively quieter situation in Berlin – the Central Mosque of Cologne (Figure 13).[67] In spring of 2006, after ten years of plans, struggles, and compromise, DITIB received permission to build the first representative mosque in the city of Cologne – the largest in Germany.[68] At more than one hundred thousand, Cologne has one of the largest Muslim populations in the country but had no large, central mosque. Instead, in the tradition of Muslim communities in Germany, there were around forty-five smaller mosques, reflecting various ethnic backgrounds and sectarian orientations.[69] The mosque would be located in Cologne-Ehrenfeld, a district with a high percentage of Turkish residents. Reviewing the entries of their competition for the contract, DITIB chose the plans of German church architects Gottfried and Paul Böhm. Endeavoring to blend traditional Islamic architectural

[67] Central Mosque, Cologne. Photograph by Rolf Vennenbernd / AFP / Getty Images.
[68] A representative mosque is one with a traditional architectural design, including a dome and minarets.
[69] Miriam Bunjes, "Erstes Minarett über Köln," *die tageszeitung*, 3 March 2006, www.taz.de/?id=archivseite6dig=2006/03/03/a0012 (accessed 11 July 2011).

forms with modern style, the Böhms designed a building with a large central dome, constructed with nonconjoined pieces to give the impression of transparency and openness, flanked by two minarets.[70] Glass walls reinforced DITIB's efforts to communicate the mosque's – and the community's – transparency, and the size of the mosque was calculated to avoid overshadowing its neighboring buildings.[71] Receiving the city's approval for their plans, DITIB set out to construct the city's first representative mosque.

City government approval, however, did not equal universal acceptance. A coalition of city residents, calling themselves "pro Köln" (Pro-Cologne), formed in opposition to the mosque's construction and proceeded to agitate against the project, allying themselves with extreme-right political parties from across Europe, such as the Austrian Freedom Party and Belgian's Vlams Belaag. Yet it was the condemnation of writer Ralph Giordano, a Jewish German and Holocaust survivor, that propelled Cologne's local conflict into a countrywide controversy. Giordano entered the fray to protest the building of the mosque, which he describes in a 2005 article as evidence of a growing parallel society that oppresses women and refuses to bear the responsibilities of German society. The fact that it was to be a DITIB mosque – an organization that positions itself as dialogue friendly and pro-integration – only caused Giordano more concern. Although Germany's legal and political values protect religious diversity, the writer argued, Turkey's Ministry of Religious Affairs did not, and DITIB was an arm of that ministry.[72] While the positions of Giordano and Pro-Cologne were similar, Giordano considered the group a "local chapter of contemporary National Socialists" and resisted their efforts to co-opt him or his statements with their own.[73]

Pro-Cologne's demonstrations were matched by opposing protests from members of trade unions, political associations, and the general public, who argued that Muslims have the right to freedom of religion, which should include the construction of places of worship.[74] When

---

[70] Helmut Frangenberg, "Moderner Kuppelbau mit zwei Minaretten," *Kölner Stadt-Anzeiger*, 21 September 2006.

[71] Mark Landler, "Germans Split Over a Mosque and the Role of Islam," *The New York Times*, 5 July 2007, www.nytimes.com/2007/07/05/world/europe/05cologne.html?_r=1& pagewanted=all (accessed 11 July 2011).

[72] Ralph Giordano, "Nicht die Moschee, der Islam ist das Problem," in Franz Sommerfeld, ed., *Der Moscheestreit: Eine exemplarische Debatte über Einwanderung und Integration* (Cologne: Kiepenheuer & Witsch, 2005), 37–51.

[73] Landler, "Germans Split Over a Mosque and the Role of Islam."

[74] Anna Reimann, "'We Want the Cathedral, Not Minarets': Far-Right Mobilizes against Cologne Mega-Mosque," *Spiegel Online*, 19 June 2007, www.spiegel.de/international/germany/0,1518,489275,00.html (accessed 11 July 2011).

Pro-Cologne attempted to host an International Anti-Islamization Congress in September 2008, members from all levels of society demonstrated against the forum and the organization to such an extent that the event had to be canceled.[75] Despite the heated controversy, construction on DITIB's Central Mosque continued, and in February 2011 the organization celebrated its roofing ceremony.[76]

This clash over the construction of Cologne's Central Mosque grew from its local origins to a countrywide controversy and ultimately became part of the broader international discourse on the place of Islam in Western societies. At the center of this debate is the distinction between making a place for oneself in society and remaking that society. For those who oppose its construction, the Cologne mosque and others like it constitute a symbol of Muslim difference and separatism. Whereas the existence of the courtyard mosques, and the *Koranschulen* they contained, represented the withdrawal and secrecy of the Muslim community, purpose-built mosques have, for many Germans, come to stand for a blatant rejection of German values and a refusal to integrate. More than that, they are evidence of what some have termed the "Islamization of Europe," a foothold of Muslim infiltration into "Fortress Europe."[77] Through such media representations, political debates, and public demonstrations, the mosque has become a discursive space of separation, antagonism, and threat.

On the other side of this argument are those who contend that the move from private courtyards to public visibility reveals not a hostile separation from the host society but rather a deliberate effort to make a permanent place for oneself within it. In the words of DITIB member Kılıç Iqbal, purpose-built mosques, in this case the Cologne Central Mosque, "will show we are a part of society."[78] Returning to his study of mosques in Duisburg-Hochfeld, Ceylan finds that mosques improve the quality of life for their members as well as encourage them to identify more strongly with their neighborhood.[79] In addition, by bringing

---

[75] Yasemin Schooman and Riem Spielhaus, "The Concept of the Muslim Enemy in the Public Discourse," in Jocelyne Cesari, ed., *Muslims in the West After 9/11: Religion, Politics, and Law* (New York: Routledge, 2010), 208–209.

[76] Bildergalerie Bauphase, Dachverband Türkisch-Islamische Union der Anstalt für Religion, e.V., www.zentralmoschee-koeln.de/default.php?id=14&lang=de (accessed 14 July 2011).

[77] This term, while certainly not restricted to one organization, has been used by Pro-Cologne. See Reimann, "We Want the Cathedral, Not Minarets."

[78] Jason Burke, "Mosque Stirs Racial Passion in Germany," *The Observer*, 15 July 2007.

[79] Rauf Ceylan, *Ethnische Kolonien: Entstehung, Funktion und Wandel am Beispiel türkischer Moscheen und Cafes* (Wiesbaden: VS Verlag für Sozialwissenschaften, 2006), 149.

Muslim centers of worship onto the street front in representative mosques, the broader public is able to have more direct experiences with Muslims and Islamic worship. This interaction, an imam from Duisburg-Hochfeld contends, acts as a deterrent to prejudice through a fuller understanding of Muslims' beliefs and practices.[80] On the side of the Muslim community, building a representative mosque can be a concrete demonstration of their desire to put down permanent roots in the host society. As Ömer Alan concludes, "Whoever builds mosques wants to stay."[81] Representative mosques can be and have been spaces that anchor their members in their local environment and encourage better understanding between the mosque community and the host society.

Ceylan's position on mosques as integrative agents supports earlier research by geographer Thomas Schmitt. In his study on the conflicts surrounding the construction and use of mosques in Germany, Schmitt concludes that, in addition to acting as a visible representation of the Islamic community's recognition in German society, the mosque has served as a bridge and facilitator between Muslims and non-Muslims. The building itself has provided the physical space for interactions between Turkish Muslims and Germans, and the mosque has also allowed Turkish immigrants and their children to communicate and work with other German associations as a united group. From the platform of the mosque, Turkish Muslims have entered into interreligious dialogue, given their input on neighborhood issues, and consulted with local groups regarding construction projects.[82] This cooperation at an institutional level puts Turkish immigrants and their children on more equal footing with their German counterparts and has allowed Turkish Muslims to positively participate in German society as they work to make a space for themselves within it.

Cooperation between mosque communities and German associations has resulted in successful mosque construction projects that avoided the bulk of the controversy that plagued the more well-known examples. One of the earlier instances of such cooperation is Mannheim's Yavuz Sultan Selim mosque (Figure 14).[83] In 1984, the Islamischer Bund (Islamic Coalition) Mannheim started talking with city officials about the possibility of

[80] Ibid., 175.
[81] Ömer Alan, "Muslime im Ruhrgebiet: Wer Moscheen baut, möchte bleiben," in *Kommunalverband Ruhrgebiet (Hrsg): Standorte Ruhrgebiet 1999/2000* (Essen: Kommunalverband Ruhrgebiet, 1999).
[82] Thomas Schmitt, *Moscheen in Deutschland: Konflikte um ihre Errichtung und Nutzung* (Flensburg: Deutsches Akademie für Landeskunde, 2003).
[83] Yavuz Sultan Selim Mosque, Mannheim. Photograph by Sabine Simon / Ullstein Bild / Getty Images.

Figure 14. Yavuz Sultan Selim mosque, Mannheim

building a large mosque in the center of the city. During the next seven years, the Muslim group worked with local churches and the Office of Foreigner Affairs to garner support for their efforts. The Catholic priest of the church across the street from the proposed site organized an interfaith committee, the Christlich-Islamische Gesellschaft Mannheim (Christian-Islamic Association of Mannheim), that worked to calm the fears of local residents protesting against the building of the mosque. The collaborative effort paid off; in 1993 the city council gave its final approval, and two years later the mosque opened its doors. Similar to the construction of the Cologne Central Mosque, the Islamischer Bund chose a design for their mosque that reflected their commitment to openness and transparency, symbolized in the numerous small triangular windows that face the street front. Held up as an example for its contribution to social order and education, the mosque has offered classes for Germans to learn about Islam and operates an institute dedicated to interfaith cooperation and education.[84]

The 2008 construction of the Merkez Mosque in Duisburg-Marxloh is another example of the mosque as a space of interethnic and interreligious

---

[84] Joel S. Fetzer and J. Christopher Soper, *Muslims and the State in Britain, France, and Germany* (Cambridge, UK: Cambridge University Press, 2005), 118.

Figure 15. Merkez mosque, Duisburg-Marxloh

cooperation (Figure 15).[85] With space for up to twelve hundred worshippers, the Duisburg mosque was, at the time, the largest in Germany, and yet it attracted none of the controversy associated with the Cologne Central Mosque. Officials from DITIB entered into dialogue with local leaders and organizations early in the planning stages and made compromises in its design that made it more welcome to members of the broader community, such as keeping the minaret to half the height of the nearby Catholic church's spire. DITIB also decided from the start that the new mosque would not broadcast the call to prayer – a controversial tradition even in the best situations.[86] Although the construction project was not without its detractors,[87] many residents have developed a sense of civic pride concerning the local mosque, a feeling further encouraged by a corresponding rise in real estate prices.[88]

[85] Merkez Mosque, Duisburg-Marxloh. Photograph by Patrick Stollarz / AFP / Getty Images.

[86] Carolin Jenkner, "Why No One Protested against Germany's Biggest Mosque," *Der Spiegel International*, 27 October 2008, www.spiegel.de/international/germany/0,1518,586759,00.html (accessed 15 July 2011).

[87] Emily Harris, "Two Mosques, Two Different Reactions in Germany," NPR, 11 October 2007, www.npr.org/templates/story/story.php?storyId=15043704 (accessed 11 July 2011).

[88] Jenkner, "Why No One Protested against Germany's Biggest Mosque."

Apart from cooperation in construction projects, participation in local life also has brought the mosque and its community into German society. In Berlin-Wedding, Turkish and Turkish-German Muslims have hosted festivals aimed at creating shared space with the broader community within the mosque. Onur Korkmaz of the Yunus Emre mosque described such celebrations his mosque community has hosted in their courtyard: members prepare a wide variety of traditional Turkish foods and small gifts and invite their neighbors to join them for a meal. The goal is to start conversations, because when people talk with each other, Korkmaz explained, stereotypes break down. He insists that this is not only important for Germans but also for Turks, who have built a "capsule" around themselves and need to break out of it.[89] Some attempts at interreligious community activities, however, have not been as successful as others. Mehmet Asker remembered an instance when his mosque invited a local church to participate in an iftar meal with them, but nobody from the church came. While he did not feel that the lack of attendance was due to any animosity, it was clear that Asker was disappointed by the absence of a positive response and did not mention his mosque having attempted a similar event since then.[90] Despite such setbacks, both that effort at community involvement and other more successful attempts demonstrate the mosque's potential both as a space of openness and cooperation as well as a means for Turkish immigrants and their children to become a part of German society by making a space for themselves within it.

Mosque construction, however, constituted only one facet of the broader debate. As the visibility of observant Muslims increased, religious spaces began to extend beyond the mosque and the workplace (in the form of prayer rooms) and into new sites in the everyday landscape. One of the places into which religious spaces expanded was the school. Initially, school officials paid relatively little attention to the religious backgrounds of their "foreign" students. In the 1990s, however, teachers and principals in Wedding started to note an increased observance among the children with Turkish background, a devotion marked by larger numbers of young women wearing a *Kopftuch*. Two principals of Wedding secondary schools recalled that one hardly ever saw the headscarf in the 1970s and 1980s; it was not until the mid- to late 1990s that they first showed up in their schools. Although neither principal suggested the headscarf itself was a problem, both were concerned that some of their

---

[89] Onur Korkmaz (pseudonym), interview by author, 6 June 2009, Berlin.
[90] Mehmet Asker (pseudonym), interview by author, 8 June 2009, Berlin.

Turkish students felt pressured – both by families and by other students – to wear the headscarf as well.[91] Some administrators and teachers also used the headscarf as a measure of students' integration, viewing those who wore it as "aggressive" about their religion, to use the word of a Sprengelkiez primary school principal.[92] In addition, some Turkish-German students in secondary schools observed Ramadan, fasting during the course of the school day. Again, for one secondary school principal, the issue was not that students chose to fast but rather that some of those began to pressure others into fasting as well.[93] Both the secondary school principals and the primary school principal tied the increased religious observance and the pressure to conform to the growth of the Turkish immigrant community and the continual influx of new members from Turkey.

Whereas some religious spaces in school developed organically as a result of the growing Turkish-German population, the introduction of another such space was deliberate and engineered. Concerns and anxieties about what was being transmitted to Turkish children in *Koranschule* prompted many to call for transfer of Islamic religious education from the mosques to public schools. The trend continued through the 1990s until it became nearly universal across the political spectrum following the September 11, 2001, attacks in the United States. At this point, however, *Islamunterricht* (Islam instruction) advocates were confronted with the practical obstacles of implementing such a course. No single Islamic umbrella organization could legitimately claim to represent all Muslims in Germany, thus German politicians and education officials faced the dilemma of which organization they should partner with. Another significant sticking point was the almost complete lack of properly trained instructors. In the words of one *Spiegel* reporter, "The states are searching for educators with a training that does not even exist."[94] Officials in some of the states, including Bavaria, North Rhine-Westphalia, and Lower Saxony, attempted to find suitable instructors among those who already taught Turkish.[95]

The situation in Berlin, however, was unique. A 2001 court decision ended a two-decades-long struggle by the Islamic Federation of Berlin to teach *Islamkundestunden* (Islamic studies periods) in Berlin's public

---

[91] Max Schulz (pseudonym), interview by author, 29 May 2009, Berlin; Erik Weber (pseudonym), interview by author, 25 May 2009, Berlin.
[92] Paul Hoch (pseudonym), interview by Ursula Trüper, 29 October 1993, audiocassette, DLSA, MMA.
[93] Weber interview.
[94] Cordula Meyer, "Wenn Allah möchte," *Der Spiegel*, 5 August 2002, p. 49.
[95] Ibid., 48–49.

schools. The organization brought a case to the city's administrative court, and the court found in its favor, saying that the city's school administration was required to provide classroom space for voluntary *Islamkundestunden* as part of the constitutionally protected freedom of religion. Yet, even though the case accomplished the spatial transition from the mosque to the school, it circumvented the intended purpose of the move. Because in Berlin religion courses are voluntary and their content is the responsibility of the religious community, school officials had no influence over what the courses would teach.[96] The class itself may have transitioned to the public schools, but its control was still centered in the mosque. The court's decision for the Islamic Federation proved particularly troubling to many involved because of the organization's affiliation with Millî Görüş and its perceived hostility toward non-Muslims.[97] Longtime Commissioner for Foreigner Affairs Barbara John was among those disappointed with the outcome, but she acknowledged to a reporter from *The New York Times* that the court's decision was "the result of our own failure to come up with a different solution earlier."[98] The city's lack of engagement in the overlapping religious and education spaces opened up a path for control of a significant part of those spaces in the hands of an organization viewed with distrust by many Muslims and non-Muslims alike.

The struggle over the location and content of religious education in Berlin has been one part of the larger battle over the character of Islam in Germany. Even before the September 11 terrorist attacks, German politicians and the broader public anxiously watched what they feared to be the growing radicalization of Muslims in Germany. The anti-German and anti-Semitic rhetoric of some imams affiliated with Millî Görüş, the organization's outreach to Turkish-German youth, and its political and financial connections to extreme rightist parties in Turkey caused many in Germany to conclude that, at the least, this particular brand of Islam was inimical to the country's cultural and political values.[99] These fears were confirmed when it was uncovered that the men who carried out the September 11 attacks in the United States had ties to a terrorist cell in Hamburg.

[96] Carolin Ströbele, "Islamunterricht an Berlins Schulen erlaubt," *Spiegel Online*, 25 October 2001, www.spiegel.de/politik/deutschland/0,1518,164474,00.html (accessed 25 July 2011).
[97] Mushaben, *The Changing Faces of Citizenship*, 291.
[98] Roger Cohen, "Long Dispute Ends as Berlin Court Backs Islamic School Lessons," *The New York Times*, 6 November 1998.
[99] "Der Islam ist der Weg," *Der Spiegel*, 12 February 1996, pp. 44–49.

Yet, at the same time, numerous Muslims in Germany were attempting to define and articulate their religious beliefs in a way that illustrated both their compatibility with German political values and their contribution to broader society. In 2004, DITIB's chairman, Rıdvan Çakir, sat down with a reporter from *Die Zeit* in an effort to publicize his organization's values and character. Çakir emphasized the distance between his group and self-identified Muslim terrorists, explaining that such groups misused Islam for political ends. "We condemned the attacks in New York, Istanbul, and Madrid immediately and in clear words – in German and in Turkish, by the way," Çakir reprimanded the reporter. "However, these were not transmitted through the German media." Çakir went on to describe the apolitical nature of Islam – in line with the tradition of Turkish secularism. DITIB's stance on the headscarf demonstrated this religious/political divide. Whether or not a woman wears a headscarf does not make her more or less religious, he argued. "The present debate [over the headscarf] is not religious, but political. And thus we do not take part." Additionally, Çakir posited that imams in Germany should speak German, but said there were currently no properly trained imams who could fulfill this role.[100] The DITIB chairman's position on the separation of the political and the religious, as well as his strong stance against terrorism, reflected the viewpoints of many Muslims in Germany, despite its lack of media coverage relative to that of more extreme perspectives.

Finally, some Muslim thinkers, German politicians, and academics suggested another religious space they considered more suited to life in Germany: Euro-Islam. This, advocates claimed, would be a form of Islam compatible with daily life, responsibilities, and privileges in Europe. Some of the definitions advocates of Euro-Islam laid out sounded similar to the values set forth by Çakir in the *Die Zeit* interview. Bundestag president Wolfgang Thierse, in response to a question from a *Spiegel* reporter about an "ideal Islam," defined Euro-Islam as recognizing the separation of church and state, embracing pluralism, and practicing religious tolerance.[101] Syrian-German political scientist Bassam Tibi went even further, calling for a reformation in Islam and Muslim renouncement of efforts to convert others to Islam.[102] Researchers have found evidence to support the presence of this type of Euro-Islam, particularly among the second

[100] "Das Kopftuch ist nicht so wichtig," *Die Zeit*, 3 June 2004, www.zeit.de/2004/24/ditib-interview (accessed 29 July 2011).
[101] "Thierses Traum vom Euro-Islam," *Spiegel Online*, 23 December 2001, www.spiegel.de/politik/debatte/0,1518,174243,00.html (accessed 29 July 2011).
[102] Cordula Meyer and Caroline Schmidt, "Europeans Have Stopped Defending Their Values," *Spiegel Online*, 10 February 2006, www.spiegel.de/international/spiegel/0,1518,440340,00.html (accessed 25 July 2011).

generation. Scholars point to more open and tolerant attitudes toward religious difference, personal study and interpretation of the Qur'an, and the hybridization of modesty with fashion as indicators of the growth and viability of European-influenced Islam.[103]

The German government took a step toward encouraging a Euro-Islam in 2006 when it invited Muslims from a broad spectrum of religious, cultural, and political backgrounds to take part in open dialogue aimed at creating and promoting a German Islam. The participants – who ranged from a representative of the conservative Verband Islamischer Kultur-zentren (VIKZ) to Islam critic and feminist Necla Kelek – joined the government in forming the Deutsche Islam Konferenz (German Islam Conference, DIK), headed by Minister of the Interior Wolfgang Schäu-ble (CDU). On the agenda for the first meeting were the long-standing issues of training German-speaking imams and religious instruction in public schools.[104] Although it is difficult to gauge the impact of such an organization on the local level, a survey conducted by the DIK in 2009 does illuminate some aspects of Muslim daily life in Germany. Whereas it reaffirmed well-known information, such as the predominance of Turks among Muslims in Germany, the survey also turned up new data that challenged common stereotypes, particularly in regard to women and girls. For example, approximately 70 percent of Muslim women in Ger-many answered that they did not wear a headscarf. In addition, 90 percent of Muslim girls participated in class trips, swimming lessons, and sexual education classes.[105] These results suggest, if not a German Islam, then at least one that conforms more to German social customs than previ-ously assumed.[106] In other words, many German Muslims participate fully and readily in everyday social spaces, forging belonging and com-munity alongside and with their German peers.

It is difficult to ascertain the extent to which the Muslims from the first and second generation have remained active in the life of the mosque

---

[103] For example, see Peter P. Mandaville, "Muslim Youth in Europe," in Shireen T. Hunter, ed., *Islam, Europe's Second Religion: The New Social, Cultural, and Political Landscape* (Westport: Praeger Publishers, 2002), 219–229.

[104] "Lowering the Wall between Mosque and State," *Spiegel Online*, 27 September 2006, www.spiegel.de/international/0,1518,439410,00.html (accessed 20 August 2011).

[105] Deutsche Islam Konferenz, Summary: "Muslim Life in Germany," (2009), www.deutsche-islam-konferenz.de/cln_170/nn_1883412/SubSites/DIK/EN/BisherigeErgebnisse/Dokumente/dokumente-inhalt.html?__nnn=true (accessed 20 August 2011), 7–8.

[106] Bassam Tibi's own experience is a cautionary tale against declaring Euro-Islam's total victory over the public identity of Islam in Germany. Despite being a longtime German resident and citizen, Tibi felt that he was unable to be seen as a German by Germans or a Muslim by Muslims. He called his a "failed integration," and took a position at Cornell University in Ithaca, New York, in 2006.

over the course of Turkish immigrant settlement in the Federal Republic. Researchers have attempted to measure the degree of religiosity in the Turkish immigrant population and determine the impact of generational belonging and length of time in Germany on that aspect of community life. In October 2000, Germany's Center for Studies on Turkey, headed by Faruk Şen, conducted a survey on the influence of religion in the daily lives of "two thousand immigrants of Turkish origin." Generally, the majority defined themselves as "religious" (64.6 percent), and just over a quarter of respondents described themselves as "not religious."[107] Yet, despite the majority identifying as religious, only about 36 percent of respondents claimed membership with a mosque organization,[108] and a minority from each age group – with the exception of those over sixty – replied that they visited a mosque on a regular basis.[109]

Among Şen's survey respondents, generational differences quickly become apparent. The older generation tended to be more religious than the younger, with levels of religious observance (individual as well as corporate activities) increasing with age. Younger respondents, however, despite considering themselves not very religious, still participated in traditions related to religion, such as observing dietary restrictions and giving to the poor. Şen suggests that this pattern reflects a separation in the minds of the second generation of religious observance and cultural practice.[110] A 2004–2005 study conducted in Kiel focused on the second and third generations, examining the importance of religion and degree of religious observance. As in the Şen survey, the Kiel study found that observance of religious customs was not necessarily tied to membership in a mosque organization or even regular visits to a mosque. In addition, the Kiel study measured the importance of religion in comparison to the amount of time participants, their parents, and their grandparents had been living in Germany, finding that, in general, the longer the stay in Germany, the less central religion became.[111]

Taking these two studies together demonstrates why one should be wary of postulating the existence of a secularization versus increased religiosity dichotomy. Although religion and mosque attendance appear to be of more importance to the first generation than those who followed, it is also apparent that, although religion may not be the dominating aspect of their identity, it has continued to play an important role in the

---

[107] Faruk Şen, "Euro-Islam: Some Empirical Evidences," in Ala Al-Hamarneh and Jörn Thielmann, eds., *Islam and Muslims in Germany* (Leiden: Brill, 2008), 39.

[108] Ibid., 42.   [109] Ibid., 40.   [110] Ibid., 40.

[111] Kea Eilers, Clara Seitz, and Konrad Hirschler, "Religiousness among Young Muslims in Germany," in Ala Al-Hamarneh and Jörn Thielmann, eds., *Islam and Muslims in Germany* (Leiden: Brill, 2008), 83–115.

lives of many in the second generation. The importance of religion to their identity, it seems, is in many cases not connected to participation in the life of the mosque. Instead, many in the second generation have created spaces for themselves outside the realm of the mosque where they explore, redefine, and practice Islam.

Conclusion

This brief examination of developments in the Turkish-German community demonstrates some of the significant challenges facing that population since reunification in 1990, most of which reflected a continuation of difficulties faced in earlier decades. Economic instability and high unemployment affected workers with a Turkish background disproportionately. As jobs emigrated from the city and a new surge of ethnic German workers flooded the labor market, the first generation in particular found themselves bereft of the inducement that had brought and anchored them to living in Germany. Economic hardship took its toll on homes and neighborhoods, as many small businesses closed their doors and more financially secure residents moved away. Members of the second generation, many coming to an age at which they should have been entering the workplace, were faced with a situation very different from the one their parents had previously enjoyed. For a minority of young men, their decline in socioeconomic status coupled with rising anti-foreigner sentiment motivated them to seek their own solutions through gang membership and illicit activities. Their lack of economic opportunity was tied in part to a school system that still grappled with the challenges of educating a diverse student body for social and economic success. At the same time, school officials, German policy makers, and Islamic organizations – although largely in agreement on where Islamic studies classes should take place – had yet to arrive at a consensus as to how they should be conducted. The broader German public had become even more anxious about the Muslims living among them, who had in the intervening years grown more visible and vocal. This combination of factors led to more deliberate efforts at creating and defining (and, to an extent, controlling) religious spaces intended to fit into mainstream German society rather than develop at the margins.

Despite these many challenges, the postreunification decades were not wholly negative ones for the Turkish-German community. Indeed, several noteworthy developments further rooted that population both in their everyday landscapes as well as German society more broadly. The number of Turkish-owned businesses increased markedly, tying their proprietors to the customers they served and giving a segment of the

Turkish-German community an opportunity to influence the character and economic conditions of their environment. In the neighborhood, local activists from diverse backgrounds worked together to improve the economic and social conditions of their neighbors. Building and expanding on the foundations set in the 1980s, their efforts at intercultural and interreligious dialogue and cooperation created new spaces for open discussion and debate. Although they may not have resulted in agreement, such spaces did promote understanding and common cause, which participants considered a fundamental part of building a multicultural society. Finally, the expansion of religious spaces into other aspects of daily life, as well as public discourse, has given Muslim members of the Turkish-German community the chance to integrate their religious beliefs with their daily lives even as it has enabled them to redefine what it means to be Muslim in the face of one-dimensional media portrayals. By choosing to invest significant time, energy, and resources into mosque construction, the Turkish Muslim community made the strong statement that they considered the Federal Republic their home. Rather than looking back to a homeland they knew mainly through their parents' stories and from summer vacations, the second generation was building a physical and lasting space of belonging in the place they saw as their future.

Thus, the two decades after German reunification witnessed continuations of developments that began as far back as the 1970s as well as new situations prompted by the fall of the Wall and the political, economic, and social restructuring that followed. Although these developments had conflicting influences on the sense of belonging among Turkish immigrants and their children, one thing was clear – members of the Turkish-German community were taking an increasingly active role in articulating the challenges they faced and creating spaces through which they could seek solutions from the local to the national and transnational level. That their approaches to addressing these challenges could be very different reflected the growth and diversification the community had experienced during its more than fifty years of existence.

Conclusion
Integration as History, Reciprocity, and Space

Born in West Berlin to Turkish *Gastarbeiter*, Filiz Güler spent her childhood playing in Wedding's parks, attending its public schools, and wandering its streets with friends. Motivated by her parents' encouragement, a teacher's support, and her own ambition, she excelled at her studies. Despite being discouraged by well-meaning but misguided instructors, Güler opted to continue her schooling at the *Gymnasium*, and ultimately earned a university degree. Now an adult with a family of her own, Güler lives and works in Wedding as an elementary school teacher, specializing in English-language instruction. She speaks flawless German, considers religion a private matter, sees Germany as her home, and has a successful career that required advanced education. By most measures, Güler is the poster child for a well-integrated Turkish German.

At one point in her life, however, Güler wanted to leave Germany. While discussing some of the difficulties she encountered growing up with a different language and culture, Güler admitted, "Beginning at twenty, I really wanted to live in Turkey, I wanted to study there. I had this drive, this desire. It was pretty bad." With time, that desire diminished, and at present she cannot imagine relocating to Turkey or what her life would have been like had she made the move.[1] Despite embodying in so many ways the traditional markers of successful integration, the fact that she did not feel at home in the place she had been born and raised calls into question the ways in which the relationship between immigrant communities and host societies is understood and measured.

From the viewpoint of the host society, the process of integration has two possible outcomes: success or failure. Although more precise boundaries of integration are delineated by its particular context, the definitions of success and failure often include a set of basic standards. Success has been measured by language acquisition, financial independence, and cultural "passing." Failure to achieve these benchmarks has

---

[1] Filiz Güler (pseudonym), interview by author, 27 May 2009, transcription by Perrin Saylan, Berlin, 2.

consigned immigrants to living a parallel existence, holding on to traditions and customs foreign to German society. This bare equation obscures the complex relationship of interconnected, contending, and conflicting experiences and identities that Güler's reflections suggest. To better understand the dynamics of integration, it is necessary to take into account its basic elements: one, a historical process built on everyday experience and shaped by its contexts; two, a reciprocal relationship between immigrant community and host society; and three, an ongoing practice that is spatial in nature.

The immigration of Turkish workers, their coalescence into an immigrant community, and the increasing diversification of that community cannot be understood in isolation from broader German history, nor can Germany's postwar history be complete without acknowledgment of the role played by the *Gastarbeiter* and subsequent ethnic minority populations. At each step in its development, events, situations, and ideas unfolding in Germany affected the Turkish-German community. The thousands of Turkish citizens who left their homes in search of well-paying jobs did so in response to West Germany's demand for labor – a demand fueled by the Economic Miracle and the halt of resettlers (*Übersiedler*) from East Germany. The Federal Republic's use of foreign labor was grounded in the past experiences of Imperial Germany, the Weimar Republic, and even Nazi Germany.[2] In addition, the choice to utilize foreign workers was influenced by a political and social desire to enable German women to remain in the home.[3] In West Berlin, the construction of the Berlin Wall both halted the influx of East German émigrés – an important source of labor – and rendered the city that much more inhospitable and unattractive to West Germans. Turkish workers, men and women, came to the city, drawn by employment opportunities and potentially higher wages, and settled in the districts bordering the Wall to take advantage of lower rents.

Family reunification was also in large part directly tied to a specific historical situation. Throughout the 1970s and into the 1980s, federal and city governments made policy decisions that attempted to make it more difficult for immigrants to enter the Federal Republic. The Brandt government issued the official recruitment halt in 1973, while

---

[2] Ulrich Herbert, *A History of Foreign Labor in Germany, 1880–1980: Seasonal Workers, Forced Laborers, Guest Workers.* Translated by William Templer (Ann Arbor: University of Michigan Press, 1990), 1–7.
[3] Monika Mattes, *"Gastarbeiterinnen" in der Bundesrepublik: Anwerbepolitik, Migration, und Geschlecht in den 50er bis 70er Jahren* (Frankfurt am Main: Campus Verlag, 2005), 9–11.

the Schmidt and Kohl governments offered conflicting incentive programs to encourage repatriation that indirectly motivated the opposite.
Similarly, the West Berlin government attempted to block the immigration of older youth that it considered unlikely or unable to successfully
integrate. These political choices both forced guest workers to choose
between leaving permanently or committing to a longer stay and encouraged them to bring their families to be with them before the opportunity
was lost through future policy decisions. Family reunification set into
motion a series of developments that resulted in the creation of a new
community of Turkish Germans and introduced a set of practical and
ideological challenges to German society.

The economic downturn in the 1980s, the flight of businesses out
of West Berlin, and the upheaval caused by German reunification left
many Turkish immigrants without work and threw their belonging in a
nation of "one people" into question. The Wall had precipitated and, in
no small way, shaped Turkish and Turkish-German residents' presence
and employment in West Berlin, and the dissolution of that border
directly affected both. Rising unemployment and uncertainty among
ethnic Germans opened space for right-wing populists and extremists,
who blamed "foreigners" for the country's ills. The response of some in
the Turkish-German community to this perceived and real hostility was
to revalorize or even create new religious identities, forcing German
society to address the consequences of religious differences in public
and private spheres.

As these broad historical changes were taking place, the Turkish-
German community was undergoing change on a basic, everyday level.
The types of workplaces that Turkish immigrants, and eventually their
children, inhabited became more varied. Although unskilled or low-
skilled positions in manufacturing largely drew Turkish workers to West
Germany (and West Berlin especially), over the years they increasingly
found work in the service sector, including as small business owner-
operators. Yet with each economic downturn, Turkish and Turkish-
German workers were reminded how unstable their workplaces could
be, particularly in the manufacturing and service sectors. However insecure, by the 1990s Turkish Germans were present as both owners
and employees in all levels of the economy, from banks to *Imbisse* and
school teachers to housekeepers. Immigrant-owned businesses not only
changed people's shopping options, they contributed to a redefining of
neighborhoods and even entire districts, giving Berlin a new image and a
new reputation.

Whereas the diversification of the workplace happened gradually over
the course of the past four decades, the first major development in the

home and neighborhood occurred more quickly. For many Turkish *Gastarbeiter*, "home" in West Germany originally meant the company dormitory, and it was not until family reunification in the mid-1970s that they moved out of the *Wohnheim* and into neighborhoods. Homes became an early center of the Turkish community's social life but were also a site of familial obligations and required constant labor, particularly from women. Most interestingly, we see the home as a nexus, a site of connection that evolved based on its participants' relationships and experiences beyond its walls. Work, the neighborhood, school, and mosque – the influences of these spaces were felt and negotiated within the home, making it crowded, contested, and, ultimately, connected.

Similarly, the neighborhood evolved in response to outside events and local initiative. Even as Wedding's location on a Cold War fault line contributed to the degradation of its infrastructure and housing, Turkish men, women, and children moved to the district and began to populate and reshape its public spaces. Men and women created separate spaces for themselves away from the responsibilities of the home, although men generally moved their socializing indoors as Turkish-owned teahouses and *Kneipen* opened their doors. As the youth grew closer to adulthood, the expectations and social control of their neighbors, who kept watch for improper behavior, tempered the freedom of the neighborhood. Young women especially felt this pressure increase as the neighborhood grew more "Turkish" in the 1980s. At this time, however, formal sites were opening up with the intent of engaging the youth, and young women in particular. While Katrin Mayer's Sparrladen offered space for children and young women to socialize and receive help with schoolwork, the Ostergemeinde youth group, with the guidance of Hans-Peter Meyendorf, hosted neighborhood parties and less boisterous events with the goal of getting to know one another and having a good time. Such spaces provided social and educational spaces, which the local youth both took advantage of and reshaped to suit their purposes.

The formalization of social spaces for youth in the neighborhood was followed in the 1990s by the organized efforts of residents as well as city government to improve the local quality of life. Integration became not only a process through which Turkish immigrants and their children made themselves at home but also a project that both locals and outsiders sought to carry out within the boundaries of the neighborhood. The federal government may have lost interest in promoting the concept of a more multicultural German identity in the wake of reunification[4], but

[4] Rita Chin, *The Guest Worker Question in Postwar Germany* (Cambridge, UK: Cambridge University Press, 2007), 252–262.

Berliners – as individuals and through institutions – continued to pursue creating a society that understood and incorporated diverse cultures.

Even more than for the neighborhood, the school came to be viewed as a site where integration could be facilitated. When the second generation entered West German schools, administrators and teachers were unprepared and inconsistent in their approach to the children's education. Initially, government and education policy makers considered the education of foreign children a temporary situation that would end with their assumed *Rückkehr*. Yet by the early 1970s, West Berlin officials had decided that, in theory, foreign children must be educated for success in West Germany and instituted guidelines for language instruction and class composition. Although the prevailing political and administrative opinions focused on schools as a tool for immigrant integration, they lacked a clearly articulated policy for immigrant integration and failed to provide training for educators to prepare them for the challenges of diverse classrooms. Teachers in schools with high percentages of students with immigrant backgrounds, such as Wedding, grappled with how to implement this integration within the classroom. Some developed innovative ways to bring the backgrounds of all of their students into the learning process, and some of these approaches were formalized in teacher training programs. As in the neighborhood, grassroots programs developed into or were eventually superseded by formalized, top-down approaches.

While politicians, administrators, teachers, and parents debated the purposes and methods of education, Turkish-German youth attended classes, formed friendships, pushed the boundaries of "acceptable" behavior, and struggled with discrimination and the challenges of a new language. They used the school as a place that was at least partially independent of parental and neighborhood oversight to create new spaces of belonging where they could explore their own interests. Turkish-German youth also used their time at school to prepare themselves for life outside the building's walls. Yet, the challenge of language acquisition, lack of experience with the West German school system, indifferent or ill-prepared teachers, and difficulties with the formalized transition from school to workplace proved significant obstacles to many. For some of the second generation, such obstacles outweighed the potential benefits of school, and they left, seeking belonging and success elsewhere.

Perhaps more than any other, the evolution of religious spaces reflects the development and diversification of the Turkish-German community over time. Neither the Turkish nor the West German government took the religious needs of Turkish Muslim workers into account, leaving a void that the workers themselves filled. Initially, these sites were confined to whatever free spaces Turkish *Gastarbeiter* could carve out of their everyday landscape: attics or basements in the *Wohnheim*, a break room in the factory, a hall in a sympathetic local church. With the *Anwerbestopp* and the acceleration of family reunification, these more impromptu spaces no longer fit the needs of the growing and diversifying community. In addition, the relative openness of West German religious spaces and the persecution of certain religious organizations in Turkey, particularly the tumultuous late 1970s and early 1980s, led to the growth of religious organizations in West Germany at best apathetic to and at worst vehemently against the Turkish state. At the local level, this confluence of developments led to new and more established spaces for worship in former workshops, office buildings, and apartments in *Hinterhäuser*. Within these new spaces, mosques in function if not form, Turkish Muslims facilitated religious instruction for the youth and brought the faithful together for daily prayer as well as holiday celebrations. In so doing, they sought to sustain the religious community as well as preserve and practice Turkish culture – a source of comfort for the first generation and education for the second. At the same time, West German media coverage of the Iranian Revolution and the emergence of the Islamic Republic framed what "Islam" meant for West Germans, contributing to the conflation of Turkish Muslims with Iranian Islamists and then all Turks with Muslims. At the local level, this conflation fanned German residents' anxieties about the inner workings of neighborhood mosques and the perceived differences of their Turkish neighbors. Many German neighbors connected members of the local Turkish residents and their children with Islam, regardless of whether they were actually Muslim.

Mosque communities became increasingly organized and centralized over time. Although the move from impromptu prayer rooms to rented halls initially resulted in a diversification of mosques based on political, cultural, theological, and ethnic backgrounds, those different communities forged ties to like-minded mosques and, eventually, formed umbrella organizations at the national level. Such connections provided the administrative and financial support necessary for religious communities to begin constructing purpose-built mosques. The visibility (or, in some cases, the proposed visibility) of these mosques brought Islamic organizations in direct dialogue – and, at times, conflict – with German institutions and the public, providing Turkish-German Muslims with a platform from which they could engage with German society on a more equal basis.

The development of the Turkish-German community reveals the nature of integration as a historical process. Situated within and influenced by specific historical contexts, integration was an incremental and variable process driven by the needs, wants, and experiences of those in the immigrant community. The factor of generation played a particularly significant role in this regard. The first generation, brought to West Germany solely for work, carved out of their everyday landscape the basics that they needed to form a community within which they could work, raise children, fulfill religious obligations, and feel at home. Theirs was an integration, or space-making, largely defined by their relationship to the workplace and the factors that influenced it. The second generation built on the foundation their parents laid, even when they sometimes rebelled against it, and sought to understand and make a place for themselves within West German society. For the second generation, the school and the neighborhood, then, were key sites whose spaces reflected broad political and public opinion as well as their own activities. In both cases, the specific historical context played a pivotal role in their experiences, their ability to create spaces of belonging, and, ultimately, their overall sense of belonging in Germany.

At this point, it is helpful to take a step back from the results and reconsider the sources. Although this book draws on examples from across the Federal Republic, the core of its analysis focuses on the relationships between belonging, daily experience, and space in the daily lives of residents of Berlin-Wedding, and, more specifically, in Sprengelkiez. Comparison with similar studies has demonstrated how the dynamics of integration in this relatively narrow geographic place resonate in other neighborhoods across the country.[5] At the same time, this study reveals the specifically local nature of integration. What other neighborhoods had a Sparrladen, a *Volkshochschule* director interested in multicultural theater, and a resident-led initiative to counter and restructure the city's housing renovation plans? The spaces of belonging created by Turkish immigrants and their children in and around Sprengelkiez in the 1970s and 1980s were significantly rooted in and influenced by local conditions. Thus, whereas their experiences are relatable to and reflected in Turkish-German communities across the country, they also demonstrate integration as a process that takes place in the context of local history.

Just as the story of the Turkish-German community reveals the nature of integration as a historical process, it also illustrates the centrality of the

[5] In particular: Rauf Ceylan, *Ethnische Kolonien: Entstehung, Funktion und Wandel am Beispiel türkischer Moscheen und Cafes* (Wiesbaden: VS Verlag für Sozialwissenschaften, 2006); Esin Bozkurt, *Conceptualising "Home": The Question of Belonging Among Turkish Families in Germany* (Frankfurt: Campus Verlag, 2009); and Patricia Ehrkamp, "Placing Identities: Transnational Practices and Local Attachments of Turkish Immigrants in Germany," *Journal of Ethnic and Migration Studies* 31, no. 5 (March 2005): 345–364.

reciprocal relationship inherent in that process. That is, what we call "integration" happened not only within the immigrant community but also between that community and the host society, causing the perceived boundaries between them to grow more indistinct. During their integration process, the Turkish immigrant population came into contact with preexisting German spaces, learning either to operate within them or to change them to suit their needs. Immigrants became active users rather than solely passive consumers.[6] Concurrently, in some cases the German spaces responded to the presence of Turkish users, adapting to meet their needs and take advantage of their contributions. One of the clearest examples of this is the Wedding *Volkshochschule*, discussed in Chapter 4, which began with offering German-language classes and grew to foster a wide range of cross-cultural courses and events. Thus, the line between the groups (or, perhaps, the perception of difference and separateness) blurred, and something new formed at the borders.

Perspectives that focus solely on the ways immigrants adapt to the host society miss this reciprocal element of integration. They fail to see that integration was not only Turkish children learning to speak German in schools but also teachers becoming aware of their new students' cultural backgrounds and using them as a teaching aid in the classroom. Instead, the reciprocal influences highlighted are often characterized by conflict and violence, such as fights between Turkish street gangs and skinheads, or so-called honor killings of young women by male relatives. Recognition of joint influences and reactions reveals how Germans and immigrants acclimated to each other, and further acknowledges the role of Turkish immigrants in shaping German society in the postwar period.

This reciprocal acclimation resulted in the creation of new identities at three levels: (1) the individual, (2) the immigrant community, and (3) the host society. As we have seen, residents of West Berlin – mainly those with Turkish background but also some West Germans – molded their own identities and perspectives by incorporating elements from and attributing behaviors to different cultures. Some young women of Turkish background, for example, expressed the desire to be free of certain religious and cultural restrictions in order to pursue their own personal and professional interests. They attributed their ambition for independence and success to the "German" part of their identity and were frustrated when their parents' and the community's "Turkish" values stymied their efforts. At the same time, few expressed a wish to be "German"; rather, they viewed a synthesis of what they perceived as the best part of both cultures to be their key to success. The Turkish-German community itself is also a synthesis formed by the interaction of myriad experiences, ideas, and backgrounds. As such, it is hardly uniform, only loosely connecting the diverse and contradictory identities with which it is affiliated. Finally, the reciprocal influences at work in integration have led to the reshaping of the host society as well. Not monolithic to begin with, German society has been pushed – sometimes subtly, sometimes more dramatically – to change in response to the presence and activities of Turkish immigrants and their children. From local efforts at cross-cultural understanding to national discussions about mosque construction and the place of Islam, German society has, at all levels, come to engage with and respond to its changing composition.

It is important to note, however, that the amount of influence different actors exerted on each other was not balanced. The nature of the relationship between an immigrant community and the host society, with the relative power that each wields given size and degree of establishment, makes an equal degree of reciprocal influence highly unlikely, if not impossible. Immigrants are required to do more to conform to a host society than that society must alter to accept them. Despite the relative inequality, the first and second generations prompted changes in German society: politically, culturally, and economically. In incorporating immigrants – however slowly or reluctantly – the host society itself changes, and begins to reflect the identities of its newest members.

Recognizing this reciprocal aspect of integration also highlights its spatial nature. Indeed, the language of integration is full of spatial references: center versus margin, insider versus outsider, bridges and borders, to name a few. The public discourse concerning Turkish immigrants in the Federal Republic often reflected the relationship between integration and space. Politicians and the media, for example, described the *Koranschulen* as sequestered in courtyards, outside the oversight and control of state governments. Immigrant neighborhoods became ethnic ghettos, located within but closed off from the rest of the community. Turkish-owned teahouses, restaurants, travel agencies and the like were (and are) labeled part of a "parallel society," existing alongside but never intersecting with German society.[7] The discursive link between space

---

[7] Scholars have noted that this discursive positioning has been used to exclude Turkish immigrants and their children from being considered full members of society. Ayse S. Çağlar examines the use of the ghetto trope, arguing that it "simplifies the complexities of immigrants' presence in society" and restricts their incorporation into the city by defining them as a potential danger to "the national and social cohesion of German society" (Ayse S. Çağlar, "Constraining Metaphors and the Transnationalisation of Spaces in Berlin," *Journal of Ethnic and Migration Studies* 27, no. 4 [October 2001]:

and integration is often employed to exclude immigrants from belonging to the host society by demonstrating difference or revealing a potential threat. This was particularly evident in West German press coverage of the Iranian Revolution and how that coverage colored public perspective on Muslims and Muslim communities within the FRG. In that case, immigrant space-making was seen not only as a threat to integration but also to the well-being of the West German state itself.

Immigrant settlement and integration, however, are directly connected to immigrants' ability to make spaces for themselves in the host society. The spaces constructed by Turkish immigrants and their children could work to connect them to German society, mediate their interactions with Germans, or attempt to separate them entirely. Examining the process of integration through the framework of space brings together larger historical events with the more mundane aspects of daily life. It highlights the blurring of borders and helps us to see and make sense of overlapping and even conflicting belongings – what Ruth Mandel calls the "multilayered diversity of Turkish German lives."[8] Immigrant space-making creates the context in which individuals and communities make themselves a part of broader society: learning languages, seeking financial stability, acquiring cultural literacy. To understand that process, we must understand the contexts – the spaces – in which it takes place.

The process of space-making is directly tied to immigrants' efforts to create a new home for themselves and their families – to construct a sense of belonging in a new and challenging environment. Belonging, as we have seen, is related to integration, but it is also distinct from it. It is a measure not necessarily of how "successful" Turkish immigrants and their children were at the process of integration but rather of the relationships they had with the people and places in their daily lives. Forged as part of their space-making practice, belonging linked the first and second generations to the sites in their daily lives, to each other, and to their neighbors. It made them feel at home. Yet a sense of belonging is not static; it is affected by its environment. Consequently, as dynamics within their daily spaces shifted, the first and second generations could feel more or less rooted. In addition, although it grounded immigrants and their children in their daily lives, belonging to one thing could

602, 603). Similarly, John S. Brady focuses on how the discourse of immigrants as dangerous is constructed with references to threatening ideas and activities festering in separate and unregulated spaces, such as mosques (John S. Brady, "Dangerous Foreigners: The Discourse of Threat and the Contours of Inclusion and Exclusion in Berlin's Public Sphere," *New German Critique*, no. 92 [April 1, 2004]: 194–224).

[8] Ruth Mandel, *Cosmopolitan Anxieties: Turkish Challenges to Citizenship and Belonging in Germany* (Durham, NC: Duke University Press, 2008), 312.

alienate someone from another. The members of street gangs, for example, experienced an intense connection to place and to their particular group. Together, they constructed a space of belonging whose central purpose was to separate them from what they considered German society. In addition, the events leading up to and the repercussions of German reunification – highlighted by the rallying cry, "We are *one* people" – served to estrange many Turkish Germans both from the physical sites in their everyday landscapes, such as the workplace, and from the more abstract sense of belonging they constructed over years of life in West Berlin neighborhoods. Through no intention of their own but rather as a consequence of the changing context, Turkish Germans became perceived as more foreign and less a part of German society.

And yet, some of the spaces understood as separate could play a role in aiding their sense of belonging with German society. The home and neighborhood are often sites deemed part of the *Parallelgesellschaft*, but consider Sprengelkiez during the *Sanierung* (discussed in Chapter 3). The Turkish residents, faced with the disappearance of their homes and neighborhood, joined ranks with local German activists to preserve those spaces. They were rooted in these spaces – some considered distinctly "Turkish" by residents – and that sense of belonging brought them into common cause with their German neighbors and into contact with the city government. In addition, one of the consequences of their successful efforts was the renovation of the park at the center of Sparrplatz. Not just an example of local activism, the park gave the second generation opportunities to interact with other children from different backgrounds and served as the site of organized play for the group that would form the Sparrladen.

Just as separate spaces in the neighborhood troubled those concerned about Turkish integration, so, too, did the immigrant community's transnational ties to Turkey appear to pose a stumbling block to their complete incorporation into German society. Certainly there were and are numerous and strong connections between Germany's Turkish population and the Republic of Turkey: the Ministry of Religious Affairs in Turkey has staffed DITIB mosques with imams for decades, political and religious organizations banned in Turkey have found Germany to be a useful base, and numerous Turkish "foreign residents" in the Federal Republic own property and businesses in Turkey.[9] In addition, the advent and proliferation of satellite television have brought contemporary Turkish media and entertainment into homes in Berlin, Cologne, and Stuttgart. Indeed,

[9] Betigül Ercan Argun, *Turkey in Germany: The Transnational Sphere of Deutschkei* (New York: Routledge, 2003). See chapters 7–10.

several interview subjects – both ethnic Germans and Turkish Germans – pointed to the ability to "switch on" Turkey on a daily basis as one of the most significant challenges to integration.[10]

Yet a continuing practical and emotional attachment to Turkey has not precluded those with a Turkish background from creating a home for themselves in Germany. Nor is it surprising that Turkish immigrants and their children would maintain such connections to their and their parents' homeland. What would be more surprising, and more unusual historically, would be a complete break with their past lives and the experiences of their families. Immigration prompts a renegotiation of belongings, a shift in the nature and hierarchy of the aspects of one's personal identity. One facet might come to the fore as a more operative identity, whereas another aspect of identity – belonging to one's "homeland" – grows more abstract. In other words, the connection to the country of origin remains an important aspect of immigrants' identities, but it becomes renegotiated and redefined in the host society. As is common with many immigrant groups, the familial, religious, social, and cultural links Turkish immigrants shared with those in Turkey were, to greater and lesser degrees, a part of their lives and identities in Germany. The challenge has been for Turkish immigrants and their children to incorporate those roots and transnational spaces into their daily lives and spaces of belonging in the Federal Republic. Their sense of belonging hinged on the success of their efforts to construct such spaces, which depends on numerous factors – individual agency, responses of others inhabiting those sites, the historical context, and so on. As such, these spaces of belonging have been neither stagnant nor consistent across the different sites in the everyday landscapes. Turkish immigrants and their children have felt more at home in certain places and at certain times than others.

This last point leads directly to what is possibly the most significant development in the Turkish-German population during the fifty years since the first Turkish *Gastarbeiter* came to the Federal Republic: the steady and continuing diversification of that community. It is difficult to make general statements regarding the integration of Turkish Germans

[10] In addition to the consumption of contemporary Turkish media, Turkish immigrant populations have fallen under the purview of the recently created Ministry of Turks Abroad and Related Communities. This government agency, formed in 2010, is tasked with fostering and sustaining close ties between the Turkish government and its citizens abroad as well as utilizing those communities as a way to exercise soft power. See Kemal Yurtnaç, "Turkey's New Horizon: Turks Living Abroad and Related Communities," SAM Papers no. 3 (October 2012), http://sam.gov.tr/wp-content/uploads/2012/10/SAM_paper_ing_03.pdf (accessed 29 July 2014).

precisely because that population has grown so diverse. What began as a group of single and unaccompanied workers came to consist of spouses and children, asylum seekers and refugees, Turks and Kurds, secularists and political Islamists, leftists and conservative nationalists. Just as in any society, extremes exist at both ends with the majority of the population falling somewhere in the middle. For people with a Turkish background in Germany, this has meant the presence of a *Parallelgesellschaft* in which some residents of Turkish background conduct their daily lives with little connection to German spaces and society. At the other end are those whose only connection to the immigrant community is a name that "sounds Turkish." The majority of Turkish Germans, however, inhabit a more complicated space – less easily defined, less present in discourse on integration, but more reflective of their broader belonging in German society.

Leyla Sezer, forty-seven years old at the time of her interview with a German historian in 1993, summed up the development of her sense of belonging in this way. "Within ten days we came here – boarded the train and came here. It was interesting. With a small suitcase," she added, indicating the small size of the suitcase with her hands. "And now, like a stamp, we stuck here." She named the items in her suitcase: two sweaters, two skirts, two dresses. We arrived, she continued, "rented an apartment, bought stuff, settled ourselves in.... And now – we can't just return within another ten days. We couldn't return within another ten years. Look, how the years have passed, we just didn't notice it. Today, tomorrow, today, tomorrow, we said: how many years!"[11] Sezer's succinct description lays bare the complicated process of integration, from its beginning with the move itself to settling in to a day when one looks around and realizes they are at home. She and her family invested their lives in Germany, her suitcase now only being brought out for trips to Turkey on vacation. The fact that Sezer had, only a few sentences previously, somewhat ironically described herself as a "foreigner" reveals that integration does not find its conclusion in a permanent and irrevocable sense of belonging. Removing the imaginary endpoint allows us to see the changes the Turkish-German population has already made and to recognize Sezer as a member of the society in which she has lived and worked her entire adult life. For her and more than three million others, Turkey may continue to be the "homeland," but Germany is where they are at home.

[11] Leyla Sezer (pseudonym), interview by Hatice Renç and Ursula Trüper, 28 January 1993, transcription by Hatice Renç, p. 15, DLSA, MMA.

Appendix

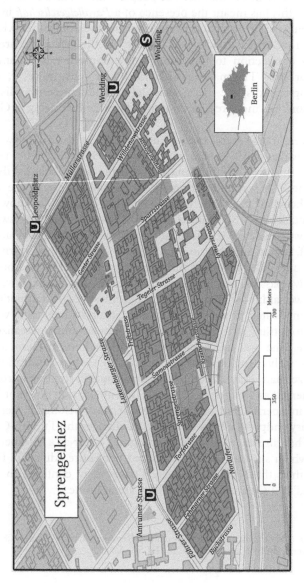

Map 1 Map of Sprengelkiez

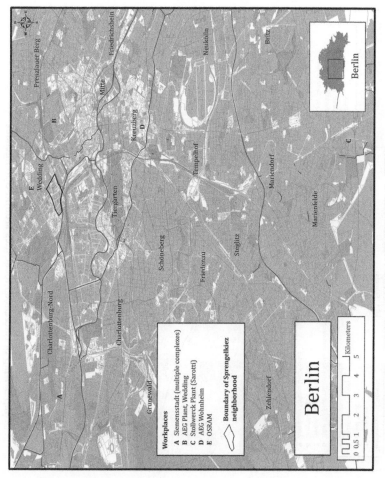

Map 2 Map of Sprengelkiez in relation to referenced workplaces

Workplaces
A Siemensstadt (multiple complexes)
B AEG Plant, Wedding
C Stollwerck Plant (Sarotti)
D AEG Wohnheim
E OSRAM

Boundary of Sprengelkiez neighborhood

Berlin

Kilometers
0 0.5 1   2   3   4   5

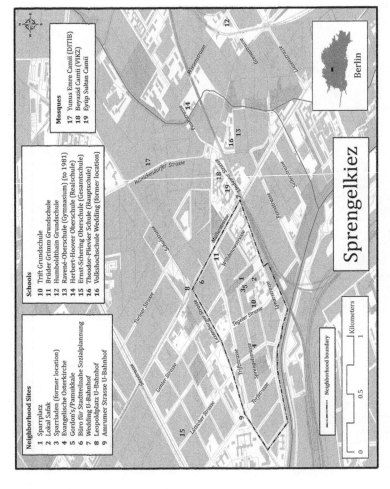

Neighborhood Sites

1 Sparrplatz
2 Lokal Safak
3 Sparrladen (former location)
4 Evangelische Osterkirche
5 Gordon's/Pamukkale
6 Büro für Stadtteilnahe Sozialplannung
7 Wedding U-Bahnhof
8 Leopoldplatz U-Bahnhof
9 Amrumer Strasse U-Bahnhof

Schools

10 Trift Grundschule
11 Brüder Grimm Grundschule
12 Humboldthain Grundschule
13 Ravené-Oberschule (Gymnasium) (to 1981)
14 Herbert-Hoover Oberschule (Realschule)
15 Ernst-Schering Oberschule (Gesamtschule)
16 Theodor-Plievier Schule (Hauptschule)
16 Volkshochschule Wedding (former location)

Mosques

17 Yunus Emre Camii (DİTİB)
18 Beyazid Camii (VIKZ)
19 Eyüp Sultan Camii

Berlin

Sprengelkiez

Neighborhood boundary

Kilometers

0   0.5   1

Map 3 Map of referenced local sites around Sprengelkiez

Bibliography

Archives and Collections

Amt für Statistik Berlin-Brandenburg, Berlin.
Bezirksmuseum Friedrichshain-Kreuzberg Archiv, Berlin
Bundespresseamt Archiv, Berlin
Deutsches Technikmuseum Historisches Archiv, Berlin
Dokumentationszentrum und Museum über die Migration in Deutschland, e.V., Cologne
Dr. Eduard Ditschek, personal files pertaining to Volkshochschule Wedding, Berlin
Museum Neukölln, (formerly Heimatmuseum Neukölln), Berlin
Herbert-Hoover-Schule (Realschule), Berlin
Landesarchiv Berlin
Mitte Museum Archiv und Bibliothek, Berlin
Siemens Corporate Archives, Munich
Staatsbibliothek zur Berlin, Zeitungsabteilung, Berlin
Theodor Plievier Oberschule (Hauptschule), Berlin

Interviews Conducted by Author

Asker, Mehmet (pseudonym). Berlin, Germany, 8 June 2009.
Ditschek, Eduard. Digital recording. Transcription by Perrin Saylan. Berlin, 11 May 2009.
Fischer, Margaret (pseudonym). Digital recording. Transcription by Perrin Saylan. Berlin, 20 May 2009.
Güler, Filiz (pseudonym). Digital recording. Transcription by Perrin Saylan. Berlin, 27 May 2009.
Günükutlu, Engin. Berlin, Germany, 9 May 2009.
Kayman, Erol (pseudonym). Digital recording. Transcription by Perrin Saylan. Berlin, 29 May 2009.
Korkmaz, Onur (pseudonym). Berlin, 6 June 2009.
Meyendorf, Hans-Peter. Digital Recording. Berlin, 20 July 2009.
Müller, Sabine (pseudonym). Digital recording. Transcription by Perrin Saylan. Berlin, 14 May 2009.
Özel, Sevim (pseudonym). Digital recording. Transcription by Perrin Saylan. Berlin, 30 June 2009.

Schmidt, Ute (pseudonym). Digital recording. Transcription by Perrin Saylan. Berlin, 29 June 2009.
Schulz, Max (pseudonym). Berlin, 29 May 2009.
Weber, Erik (pseudonym). Berlin, 25 May 2009.
Wolfermann, Klaus. Digital recording. Transcription by Perrin Saylan. Berlin, 10 June 2009.
Yılmaz, Bilge (pseudonym). Digital recording. Transcription by Perrin Saylan. Berlin, 2 June 2009.
Zimmermann, Andreas and Christine. Digital recording. Transcription by Perrin Saylan. Berlin, 18 May 2009.

Interviews Cited from Mitte Museum's "Die Leute vom Sparrplatz" Exhibit

Aylin (pseudonym). Interview and transcription by Ursula Trüper. Berlin, 22 December 1992.
Demir, Azra (pseudonym). Interview, translation, and transcription by Hatıce Renç. Berlin, 9 March 1993.
Deniz (pseudonym). Interview and transcription by Ursula Trüper. Berlin, 12 December 1992.
Elif (pseudonym). Interview and transcription by Ursula Trüper. Berlin, 11 December 1992.
Emre and Erkan (pseudonyms). Interview by Ursula Trüper. Audiocassette. Berlin, 7 December 1993.
Erdem, Nimet (pseudonym). Interview by Fatos Topac and Ursula Trüper. Translation and transcription by Fatos Topac. Berlin, 8 January 1993.
Hahn, Beate (pseudonym), cofounder of the Sparrladen. Interview by Ursula Trüper. Audiocassette. Berlin, 7 July 1993.
Herbert, Maja (pseudonym). Interview by Ursula Trüper. Audiocassette. Berlin, 16 June 1993.
Hoch, Paul (pseudonym), principal of a Grundschule. Interview by Ursula Trüper. Audiocassette. Berlin, 29 October 1993.
Kaplan, Bülent (pseudonym). Interview by Ursula Trüper. Audiocassette. Berlin, 14 June 1993.
Kaya, Beyhan (pseudonym). Interview. Translation and transcription by Hatıce Renç Berlin, 9 March 1993.
Keskin, Eren (pseudonym), "Wirt einer Kneipe am Sparrplatz." Interview by Ursula Trüper. Audiocassette, side A. Berlin, 1993.
Krause, Peter (pseudonym). Interview by Ursula Trüper. Audiocassette. Berlin, 21 July 1993.
Lale (pseudonym). Interview by Ursula Trüper. Transcription. Berlin, 28 May and 4 June 1992.
Lange, Christine, Viola Werner, and Thomas Hofmann (pseudonyms). Interview by Ursula Trüper. Audiocassette. Berlin, July 1994.
Mayer, Katrin (pseudonym), cofounder of the Sparrladen. Interview by Ursula Trüper. Audiocassette. Berlin, 6 July 1992.

Polat, Soner (pseudonym). Interview by Ursula Trüper and Kemal Kurt. Transcription. Berlin, 18 June 1993.

Sezer, Leyla (pseudonym). Interview by Hatıce Renç and Ursula Trüper. Translation and transcription by Hatıce Renç. Berlin, 28 January 1993.

Sezer, Sanem (pseudonym). Interview and transcription by Ursula Trüper. Berlin, 4 March 1993.

Timur (pseudonym). Interview by Ursula Trüper. Audiocassette. Berlin, 22 June 1993.

Turan, Zafer (pseudonym). Interview by Ursula Trüper. Audiocassette. Berlin, 11 October 1993.

Vogel, Anja (pseudonym). Interview by Ursula Trüper. Audiocassette. Berlin, 29 June 1993.

Unpublished Interviews

Korkmaz, Mehmet (pseudonym). Interview by Rita Klages. Transcript. "Projekt Migrantenbiographien," Heimatmuseum Neukölln, Berlin, 25 June 1998.

Yıldırım, Alev. Interview with Murat Güngör. Digital recording. "A, Aziza-Interview – 20040272.mp3," DOMiD, Cologne, 27 July 2004.

Published Memoirs and Interviews

Akyün, Hatıce. *Einmal Hans mit scharfer Soße: Leben zwischen zwei Welten*. Munich: Goldmann Verlag, 2005.

"Altona ist mein Dorf: Der Friseur Behçet Algan." In *Gekommen und Geblieben: Deutsch-türkische Lebensgeschichten*, edited by Michael Richter, 55–76. Hamburg: Edition Körber Stiftung, 2003.

Ateş, Seyran. *Grosse Reise ins Feuer: Die Geschichte einer deutschen Türkin*. Berlin: Rowohlt Taschenbuch Verlag, 2003.

Ayşe, and Renate Eder. *Mich hat keiner gefragt: Zur Ehe gezwungen – eine Türkin in Deutschland erzählt*. Munich: Blanvalet, 2005.

"Die Geschichte über Deutschland gefielen mir – Der Bauarbeiter Kazım Arslan." In *Gekommen und Geblieben: Deutsch-türkische Lebensgeschichten*, edited by Michael Richter, 77–96. Hamburg: Edition Körber Stiftung, 2003.

"Ich bin, wie ich bin: Die Lehrerin Hadiye Akın." In *Gekommen und Geblieben: Deutsch-türkische Lebensgeschichten*, edited by Michael Richter, 33–54. Hamburg: Edition Körber Stiftung, 2003.

"In Uhlenhorst kennt mich jeder – Der Kaufmann Erdem Dilşen." In *Gekommen und Geblieben: Deutsch-türkische Lebensgeschichten*, edited by Michael Richter, 97–118. Hamburg: Edition Körber Stiftung, 2003.

"Ohne Jazz kann ich nicht leben – Der Künstler Demir Gökgöl." In *Gekommen und Geblieben: Deutsch-türkische Lebensgeschichten*, edited by Michael Richter, 139–158. Hamburg: Edition Körber Stiftung, 2003.

Özdemir, Cem, and Hans Engels. *Ich bin Inländer: ein anatolischer Schwabe im Bundestag.* Munich: DTV, 1997.

Richter, Michael. *Gekommen und Geblieben: Deutsch-tuerkische Lebensgeschichten.* Hamburg: Edition Körber-Stiftung, 2003.

"Wird sind hier, um zu bleiben – Der Moscheegründer Hayrullah Şenay." In *Gekommen und Geblieben: Deutsch-türkische Lebensgeschichten,* edited by Michael Richter, 201–222. Hamburg: Edition Körber Stiftung, 2003.

Yeğenoğlu, Gülen. *Almanya'daki Yirmi Yılım.* Istanbul: Milliyet Yayınları, 1988.

Periodicals

AEG-Telefunken Report (1971–1981)
Berliner Morgenpost (1974–1982, 1998)
Berliner Zeitung (1999)
Der Nord-Berliner (1990)
Der Spiegel (1973, 1989–1998)
Der Spiegel International (2008)
Der Tagesspiegel (1986–1999)
die tageszeitung (1983, 2006)
Die Welt (1979, 1981)
Die Zeit (1978–2004)
Frankfurter Allgemeine Zeitung (1981)
Frankfurter Rundschau (1985, 1986)
Handelsblatt (1981)
Hannoverische Allgemeine (1982)
Hürriyet (1977–1986)
Kölner Stadt-Anzeiger (2006)
Lokal-Anzeiger (1991)
Milliyet (1987)
Münchener Merkur (1979)
NPR Online (2007)
Rheinische Post (1982)
Rheinischer Merkur (1981)
Saarbrücker Zeitung (1979)
Siemens Mitteilungen (1971–1991)
Sozialdemokratischer Pressedienst (1982)
Spiegel Online (2001–2009)
Süddeutsche Zeitung (1979–1983)
Tercüman-Berlin Ilavesi (1986)
The New York Times (1998, 2007)
The Observer (2007)
Vis-à-Vis (1987–1990)
Vorwärts (1982)
Welt am Sonntag (1979)

Online Resources

Deutsche Islam Konferenz, www.deutsche-islam-konferenz.de
Kommunales Forum Wedding, www.kommunales-forum-wedding
.de/cms/
Quartiersmanagement Sparrplatz, www.sparrplatz-quartier.de
SprengelHaus Wedding, www.sprengelhaus-wedding.de
Verband der islamischen Kulturzentren, e.V., www.vikz.de

Secondary Sources

Abadan-Unat, Nermin. "Identity Crisis of Turkish Migrants: First and Second Generation." In *Turkish Workers in Europe: An Interdisciplinary Study*, edited by Ilhan Başgöz and Norman Furniss, 3–22. Bloomington: Indiana University Turkish Studies, 1985.
"Implications of Migration on Emancipation and Pseudo-Emancipation of Turkish Women." *International Migration Review* 11, no. 1 (Spring 1977): 31–57.
Abicht, Ludo. *Islam & Europe: Challenges and Opportunities*. Leuven: Leuven University Press, 2008.
Akgündüz, Ahmet. *Labour Migration from Turkey to Western Europe, 1960–1974: A Multidisciplinary Analysis*. Aldershot: Ashgate, 2008.
Al-Ali, Nadje, and Khalid Koser, eds. *New Approaches to Migration? Transnational Communities and the Transformation of Home*. London: Routledge, 2002.
Alan, Ömer. "Muslime im Ruhrgebiet: Wer Moscheen baut, möchte bleiben." In *Standorte Ruhrgebiet 1999/2000*. Essen: Kommunalverband Ruhrgebiet, 1999.
Alamdar-Niemann, M., D. Bergs-Winkels, and H. Merkens. "Educational Conditions of Turkish Migrant Children in German Schools." *Anthropology & Education Quarterly* 22, no. 2 (June 1991): 154–161.
Al-Azmeh, Azīz. *Islam in Europe: Diversity, Identity and Influence*. Cambridge, UK: Cambridge University Press, 2007.
Al-Hamarneh, Ala, and Jörn Thielmann. *Islam and Muslims in Germany*. Leiden: Brill, 2008.
Andall, Jacqueline. *Gender and Ethnicity in Contemporary Europe*. 1st ed. Oxford: Berg Publishers, 2003.
Argun, Betigül Ercan. *Turkey in Germany: The Transnational Sphere of Deutschkei*. Middle East Studies: History, Politics, and Law Series. New York: Routledge, 2003.
Atabay, Ilhami. *Zwischen Tradition und Assimilation: Die zweite Generation türkischer Migranten in der Bundesrepublik Deutschland*. Freiburg im Breisgau: Lambertus-Verlag, 1998.
Bade, Klaus. *Europa in Bewegung: Migration vom späten 18: Jahrhundert bis zur Gegenwart*. Munich: C. H. Beck, 2000.

Bade, Klaus, ed. *Auswanderer – Wanderarbeiter – Gastarbeiter: Bevölkerung, Arbeitsmarkt und Wanderung in Deutschland seit der Mitte des 19 Jarhundert*. Ostfildern: Scripta Mercaturae, 1984.

Başer, Tevfik. *40 m² Deutschland*. Videocassette. Hamburg: Tevfik Başer Filmproduktion, 1986.

Başgöz, Ilhan, and Norman Furniss, eds. *Turkisher Workers in Europe: An Interdisciplinary Study*. Bloomington: Indiana University Turkish Studies, 1985.

Baumgartner-Karabak, Andrea and Gisela Landesberger. *Die verkauften Bräute: türkische Frauen zwischen Kreuzberg und Anatolien*. Reinbek bei Hamburg: Rowohlt, 1983.

Bergerson, Andrew Stuart, Paul Steege, Maureen Healy, and Pamela Swett. "The History of Everyday Life: A Second Chapter." *The Journal of Modern History* 80, no. 2 (June 2008): 358-378.

Berlin Amt für Statistik. *Statistisches Jahrbuch Berlin 1991*. Berlin-Wilmersdorf: Statistisches Landesamt Berlin, 1991.

Berlin (West) Statistisches Landesamt. *Statistisches Jahrbuch Berlin 1973*. Berlin-Wilmersdorf: Statistisches Landesamt Berlin, 1974.

Statistisches Jahrbuch Berlin 1977. Berlin-Wilmersdorf: Statistisches Landesamt Berlin, 1977.

Statistisches Jahrbuch Berlin 1981. Berlin-Wilmersdorf: Statistisches Landesamt Berlin, 1981.

Bezirksamt Wedding, ed. *Der Wedding im Wandel der Zeit*. Berlin: Bezirksamt Wedding, 1985.

Blaschke, Jochen, and Ahmet Ersöz. *Herkunft und Geschäftsaufnahme türkischer Kleingewerbetreibender in Berlin*. Berlin: Express-Edition, 1987.

Boos-Nünning, Ursula, and Manfred Hohmann. "The Educational Situation of Migrant Workers' Children in the Federal Republic of Germany." In *Different Cultures, Same School: Ethnic Minority Children in Europe*, edited by Lotty Eldering and Jo Kloprogge, 39-60. Berwyn: Swets North America, 1989.

Bozkurt, Esin. *Conceptualising "Home": The Question of Belonging among Turkish Families in Germany*. Frankfurt: Campus Verlag, 2009.

Brady, John S. "Dangerous Foreigners: The Discourse of Threat and the Contours of Inclusion and Exclusion in Berlin's Public Sphere." *New German Critique*, no. 92 (April 1, 2004): 194-224.

Brettell, Carolina B. and Patricia A. de Berjeois. "Anthropology and the Study of Immigrant Women." In *Seeking Common Ground: Multidisciplinary Studies of Immigrant Women in the United States*, edited by Donna Gabaccia, 3-63. Westport: Greenwood Press, 1992.

Brunn, Christine. *Moscheebau-Konflikte in Deutschland: Eine räumlich-semantische Analyse auf der Grundlage der Theorie der Produktion des Raumes von Henri Lefebvre*. Berlin: Wissenschaftlicher Verlag, 2006.

Bundesamt, Germany (West). *Statistisches Jahrbuch für die Bundesrepublik Deutschland*. Stuttgart: W. Kohlhammer, 1952.

Bundesargentur für Arbeit. "Arbeitslose Ausländer im Bundesgebiet nach ausgewählten Staatsangehörigkeiten." *Jahreszahlen 1980*. Nuremberg: Bundesargentur für Arbeit, 1980.

"Arbeitslose Ausländer im Bundesgebiet nach ausgewählten Staatsangehörigkeiten." *Jahreszahlen 1985.* Nuremberg: Bundesargentur für Arbeit, 1985.

"Arbeitslose Ausländer im Bundesgebiet nach ausgewählten Staatsangehörigkeiten." *Jahreszahlen 1990.* Nuremberg: Bundesargentur für Arbeit, 1990.

Bundesministerium für Bildung und Wissenschaft. *Arbeiterkinder im Bindungssystem.* Bad Honnef: Bock, 1981.

Grundlagen, Perspektiven, Bildung, Wissenschaft: Berufsbildungbericht 1990. Bad Honnef: 1990.

Büro für stadtteilnahe Sozialplannung. *Vorbereitende Untersuchungen Berlin-Wedding: Untersuchungsabschnitt C, Neue Hochstraße – Sparrplatz.* West Berlin: Der Senator für Bau- und Wohnungswesen, 1983.

Butler, Judith, and Joan W. Scott. *Feminists Theorize the Political.* 1st ed. New York: Routledge, 1992.

Çağlar, Ayşe S. "Constraining Metaphors and the Transnationalisation of Spaces in Berlin." *Journal of Ethnic and Migration Studies* 27, no. 4 (October 2001): 601–613.

Canning, Kathleen. "Feminist History after the Linguistic Turn: Historicizing Discourse and Experience." *Signs* 19, no. 2 (Winter 1994): 368–404.

Castles, Stephen. "The Guests Who Stayed – The Debate on 'Foreigners Policy' in the German Federal Republic." *International Migration Review* 19, no. 3 (Autumn 1985): 517–534.

"Migrants and Minorities in Post-Keynesian Capitalism: The German Case." In *Ethnic Minorities and Industrial Change in Europe and North America,* edited by Malcolm Cross, 36–54. Cambridge, UK: Cambridge University Press, 1992.

Castles, Stephen, and Godula Kosack. *Immigrant Workers and Class Structure in Western Europe.* 2nd ed. Oxford, UK: Oxford University Press, 1985.

Castles, Stephen, and Mark J. Miller. *The Age of Migration: International Population Movements in the Modern World.* London: MacMillan Press, 1998.

Certeau, Michel de. *The Practice of Everyday Life.* 2nd ed. Berkeley: University of California Press, 2002.

Ceylan, Rauf. *Ethnische Kolonien: Entstehung, Funktion und Wandel am Beispiel türkischer Moscheen und Cafes.* Wiesbaden: VS Verlag für Sozialwissenschaften, 2006.

Islamische Religionspädagogik in Moscheen und Schulen – Ein sozialwissenschaftlicher Vergleich der Ausgangslage, Inhalte und Ziele unter besonderer Berücksichtigung der Auswirkungen auf den Integrationsprozess der muslimischen Kinder und Jugendlichen. Hamburg: Verlag Kovac, 2008.

Chauncey, George. *Gay New York: Gender, Urban Culture, and the Making of the Gay Male World, 1890–1940.* New York: Basic Books, 1995.

Chin, Rita. *The Guest Worker Question in Postwar Germany.* Cambridge, UK: Cambridge University Press, 2007.

"Rewriting the 'Guest Worker': Turkish-German Artists and the Emergence of Multiculturalism in the Federal Republic of Germany, 1961–1989." PhD *dissertation*, University of California, Berkeley, 1999.

Chourabi, Hamza, and Riem El-Solami. "Moscheenräume, Räume für Frauen?" In *Moscheen und islamisches Leben in Berlin*, edited by Gerdien Jonker and Andreas Kapphan, 35–40. Berlin: Ausländerbeauftragte des Senats, 1999.

Çil, Nevim. *Topographie des Außenseiters: Türkische Generationen und der deutsch-deutsche Wiedervereinigungsprozess.* Berlin: Schiler, 2007.

"Türkische Migranten und der Mauerfall." *Aus Politik und Zeitgeschichte*, 21–22 (May 2009): 40–46.

Clarkson, Alexander. "Circling the Wagons: Immigration and the Battle for Space in West Berlin, 1970–1990." In *Dirty Cities: Towards a Political Economy of the Underground in Global Cities*, edited by Leila Simona Talani, Alexander Clarkson, and Ramon Pacheco Pardo, 110–134. New York: Palgrave Macmillan, 2013.

Fragmented Fatherland: Immigration and Cold War Conflict in the Federal Republic of Germany, 1945–1980. New York: Berghahn Books, 2013.

Cleveland, William and Martin Bunton. *A History of the Modern Middle East.* 5th edition. Boulder: Westview Press, 2015.

Dalaman, Serpil. "Türkischer Frauenkreis," in *Kunstvoller Alltag: Kommunale Kulturarbeit der Volkshochschule Berlin-Wedding*, edited by Ursula Diehl, Gisela Weimann, and Eduard Ditschek, 122. Berlin: FAB-Verlag, 1990.

Dettmer, Klaus. *Wedding: Geschichte der Berliner Verwaltungsbezirke.* Berlin: Colloquium Verlag, 1988.

Deutsch, Sarah. *Women and the City: Gender, Space, and Power in Boston, 1870–1940.* Oxford: Oxford University Press, 2002.

Deutschland (Bundesrepublik). *Arbeiterkinder im Bildungssystem.* Bad Honnef: Bock, 1981.

Diehl, Ursula, Gisela Weimann, and Eduard Ditschek. *Kunstvoller Alltag: Kommunale Kulturarbeit der Volkshochschule Berlin-Wedding.* Berlin: FAB-Verlag, 1990.

Ditschek, Eduard, and Sigrid Schulze, eds. *Volksbildung im Wedding: 50 Jahre Volkshochschule im Bezirk Wedding von Berlin 1945–1995.* Berlin: Verlag Joachim Mackensen, 1995.

Ehrkamp, Patricia. "Placing Identities: Transnational Practices and Local Attachments of Turkish Immigrants in Germany." *Journal of Ethnic and Migration Studies* 31, no. 5 (March 2005): 345–364.

Eilers, Kea, Clara Seitz, and Konrad Hirschler. "Religiousness among Young Muslims in Germany." In *Islam and Muslims in Germany*, edited by Ala Al-Hamarneh and Jörn Thielmann, 83–115. Leiden: Brill, 2008.

Eldering, Lotty, and Jo Kloprogge. *Different Cultures, Same School: Ethnic Minority Children in Europe.* Amsterdam: Swets & Zeitlinger, 1989.

Eley, Geoff. "Labor History, Social History, 'Alltagsgeschichte': Experience, Culture and the Politics of the Everyday – A New Direction for German Social History." *The Journal of Modern History* 61, no. 2 (June 1989): 297-343.

Erel, Umut. "Gendered and Racialized Experiences of Citizenship in the Life Stories of Women of Turkish Background in Germany." In *Gender and*

Ethnicity in Contemporary Europe, edited by Jacqueline Andall, 155–176. Oxford: Berg Publishers, 2003.

Ewing, Katherine Pratt. *Stolen Honor: Stigmatizing Muslim Men in Berlin*. Stanford: Stanford University Press, 2008.

Faist, Thomas, and Eyuep Oezveren, eds. *Transnational Social Spaces: Agents, Networks and Institutions*. Aldershot, UK: Ashgate Publishing Limited, 2004.

Fallon, Steve, Anthony Haywood, Andrea Schulte-Peevers, and Nick Selby. *Lonely Planet: Germany*. Hawthorn: Lonely Planet, 1998.

Fassman, Heinz, and Rainer Münz, eds. *European Migration in the Late Twentieth Century: Historical Patterns, Actual Trends and Social Implications*. Cornwall: IIASA, 1994.

Fetzer, Joel S., and J. Christopher Soper. *Muslims and the State in Britain, France, and Germany*. Cambridge, UK: Cambridge University Press, 2005

Fortier, Anne-Marie. *Migrant Belongings: Memory, Space, Identity*. Oxford: Berg, 2000.

Frisch, Max. *Überfremdung: Offentlichkeit als Partner*. Frankfurt am Main: Suhrkamp, 1967.

Fullbrook, Mary. *The Divided Nation: A History of Germany, 1918–1990*. New York: Oxford University Press, 1991.

Gabaccia, Donna. *From the Other Side: Women, Gender, and Immigrant Life in the U.S., 1820–1990*. Bloomington: Indiana University Press, 1995.

Seeking Common Ground: Multidisciplinary Studies of Immigrant Women in the United States. Westport: Greenwood Press, 1992.

Gitmez, Ali, and Czarina Wilpert. "A Micro-Society or an Ethnic Community? Social Organization and Ethnicity amongst Turkish Migrants in Berlin." In *Immigrant Associations in Europe*, edited by John Rex, Daniele Joy, and Czarina Wilpert, 86–125. Brookfield: Grower, 1987.

Göktürk, Deniz. "Beyond Paternalism: Turkish German Traffic in Cinema." In *The German Cinema Book*, edited by Tim Berfelder, Eric Carter, and Deniz Göktürk, 248–256. London: British Film Institute, 2002.

"Turkish Women on German Streets: Closure and Exposure in Transnational Cinema." In *Spaces in European Cinema*, edited by Mytro Konstantarakos, 64–76. Portland, OR: Intellect Books, 2000.

Göktürk, Deniz, David Gramling, and Anton Kaes. *Germany in Transit: Nation and Migration, 1955–2005*. Berkeley: University of California Press, 2007.

Goldberg, Andreas. "Islam in Germany." In *Islam, Europe's Second Religion: The New Social, Cultural and Political Landscape*, edited by Shireen T. Hunter, 29–50. Westport: Praeger Publishers, 2002.

Goldberg, Andreas, Dirk Halm, and Faruk Şen. *Die Deutschen Türken*. Münster: LIT Verlag, 2004.

Greve, Martin, and Tülay Çınar. *Das Türkische Berlin*. Miteinander Leben in Berlin. Berlin: Die Ausländerbeauftragte des Senats, 1998.

Hackett, Sarah. *Foreigners, Minorities and Integration: The Muslim Immigrant Experience in Britain and Germany*. Manchester: Manchester University Press, 2016.

Haddad, Yvonne Yazbeck, ed. *Muslims in the West: From Sojourners to Citizens*. Oxford: Oxford University Press, 2002.

Hagemann, Karen. "A West-German 'Sonderweg'? Gender, Work, and the Half-Day-Time Policy of Child Care and Primary Education." In *Children, Families and States: Time Policies of Child Care, Preschool and Primary Schooling in Europe*, edited by Karen Hagemann, Konrad H. Jarausch, and Cristina Allemann-Ghionda, 275–300. Oxford: Berghahn Books, 2011.

Hagemann, Karen, Donna Harsch, and Friederike Bruenhoefner, eds. *Gendering Post-1945 German History: Entanglements*. Oxford: Berghahn Books, 2018.

Haug, Sonja. *Muslimisches Leben in Deutschland: im Auftrag der Deutschen Islam-Konferenz*. 1st ed. Nuremberg: Bundesamt für Migration und Flüchtlinge, 2009.

Herbert, Ulrich. *A History of Foreign Labor in Germany, 1880–1980: Seasonal Workers, Forced Laborers, Guest Workers*. Translated by William Templer. Ann Arbor: University of Michigan Press, 1990.

Herbert, Ulrich, and Karin Hunn. "Guest Workers and Policy on Guest Workers in the Federal Republic: From the Beginning of Recruitment in 1955 until Its Halt in 1973." In *The Miracle Years: A Cultural History of West Germany, 1949–1968*, edited by Hanna Schissler, 187–218. Princeton: Princeton University Press, 2001.

Hoffmeyer-Zlotnik, Jürgen. *Gasterbeiter im Sanierungsgebiet: Das Beispiel Berlin-Kreuzberg*. Hamburg: Christian Verlag, 1977.

Horrocks, David, and Eva Kolinsky, eds. *Turkish Culture in German Society Today*. Providence: Berghahn Books, 1996.

Hunn, Karin. *"Naechstes Jahr kehren wir zurueck ...": Die Geschichte der tuerkischen "Gastarbeiter" in der Bundesrepublik*. Göttingen: Wallstein Verlag, 2005.

Hunter, Shireen. *Islam, Europe's Second Religion: The New Social, Cultural and Political Landscape*. Westport: Praeger Publishers, 2002.

Hüttermann, Jörg. *Das Minarett: zur politischen Kultur des Konflikts um islamische Symbole*. Weinheim: Juventa, 2006.

Jarausch, Konrad H. "Towards a Social History of Experience: Postmodern Predicaments in Theory and Interdisciplinarity." *Central European History* 22, no. 3/4, German Histories: Challenges in Theory, Practice, Technique (September–December 1989): 427–443.

———. "Unsettling German Society: Mobility and Migration." In *Shattered Past: Reconstructing German History*, edited by Konrad H. Jarausch and Michael Geyer, 197–220. Princeton: Princeton University Press, 2003.

Jonker, Gerdien. "The Mevlana Mosque in Berlin-Kreuzberg: An Unsolved Conflict." *Journal of Ethnic and Migration Studies* 31, no. 6 (November 2005): 1067–1081.

———. *Moscheen und islamisches Leben in Berlin*. Berlin: Die Ausländerbeauftragte des Senats, 1999.

———. *Politics of Visibility: Young Muslims in European Public Spaces*. Bielefeld: Transcript, 2006.

Karakaşoğlu, Yasemin. "Turkish Cultural Orientations in Germany and the Role of Islam." In *Turkish Culture in German Society Today*, edited by David Horrocks and Eva Kolinsky, 157–180. Providence: Berghahn Books, 1996.

Kaya, Ayhan. *Islam, Migration and Integration: The Age of Securitization.* New York: Palgrave Macmillan, 2009.

"Sicher in Kreuzberg" – Constructing Diasporas: Turkish Hip-Hop Youth in Berlin. Bielefeld: Transcript Verlag, 2001.

Kayser, P., F. Preusse, J. Riedel, and B. Umbreit. *Ethnische Ökonomie als Chance der Standortenentwicklung.* Berlin: Fachhochschule für Technik und Wirtschaft Berlin und Institut IKO, 2008.

Kelek, Necla. *Die fremde Braut: ein Bericht aus dem Inneren des türkischen Lebens in Deutschland.* Cologne: Kiepenheuer & Witsch, 2005.

Klee, Ernst. "Ein neues Wort für Gastarbeiter." In *Gastarbeiter: Analysen und Berichte,* edited by Ernst Klee, 149-157. Frankfurt am Main: Suhrkamp, 1981.

ed. *Gastarbeiter: Analysen und Berichte.* Frankfurt am Main: Suhrkamp, 1981.

Klopp, Brett. *German Multiculturalism: Immigrant Integration and the Transformation of Citizenship.* Westport: Praeger Publishers, 2002.

Knortz, Heike. *Diplomatische Tauschgeschäfte: "Gastarbeiter" in der westdeutschen Diplomatie und Beschäftigungspolitik 1953-1973.* Cologne: Böhlau Verlag, 2008.

Koch, Herbert. *Gastarbeiterkinder in deutschen Schulen.* Königswinter am Rhein: Verlag für Sprachmethodik, 1970.

Kofmann, Eleonore, Annie Phizacklea, Parvati Raghuram, and Rosemary Sales. *Gender and International Migration in Europe: Employment, Welfare and Politics.* London: Routledge, 2000.

Kolinsky, Eva. *Deutsch und türkisch leben: Bild und Selbstbild der türkischen Minderheit in Deutschland.* Bern: Peter Lang, 2000.

Women in Contemporary German: Life, Work, and Politics. Oxford: Berg, 1993.

Korte, Hermann. "Guestworker Question or Immigration Issue? Social Sciences and Public Debate in the Federal Republic of Germany." In *Population, Labour and Migration in 19th and 20th Century Germany,* 163–188. New York: Berg Publishers Limited, 1987.

Kosnick, Kira. *Migrant Media: Turkish Broadcasting and Multicultural Politics in Berlin.* Bloomington: Indiana University Press, 2007.

Kudat, Ayse. "Personal, Familial, and Societal Impacts of Turkish Women's Migration to Europe." In *Living in Two Cultures: The Socio-Cultural Situation of Migrant Workers and Their Families,* edited by Unesco, 291–305. Paris: Unesco Press, 1982.

Kuhlmann, Michael, and Alwin Meyer, eds. *Ayse und Devrim: Wo gehören wir hin?* Göttingen: Lamuv Verlag, 1983.

Kurt, Kemal, and Erika Meyer. *... weil wir Türken sind/ ...Türk oldugumuz için: Bilder und Texte von Türken/ Türklerin resim ve öyküleri.* Berlin: express-Edition, 1981.

Lanz, Stephen. "Inclusion and Segregation in Berlin, the 'Social City'." In *Transnationalism and the German City,* edited by Jeffry M. Diefendorf and Janet Ward, 55–72. New York: Palgrave MacMillan, 2014.

Lefebvre, Henri. *The Production of Space.* Translated by Donald Nicholson-Smith. Oxford: Blackwell, 1991.

Leffers, Irina, and Christholde Thielcke. "Zwischen Religion und Jugendarbeit: Angebote und Aktivitäten." In *Moscheen und islamisches Leben in Berlin*, edited by Gerdien Jonker and Andreas Kapphan, 30–34. Berlin: Die Ausländerbeauftragte des Senats, 1999.

Leggewie, Claus, and Zafer Senocak, eds. *Deutsche Türken/Türk Almanlar: Das Ender der Geduld/Sabrin sonu*. Hamburg: Rowohlt Taschenbuch Verlag, 1993.

Lehman, Brittany. "Teaching Migrant Children: Debates, Policies, and Practices in West Germany and Europe, 1949–1992." PhD dissertation, The University of North Carolina at Chapel Hill, 2015.

Linkiewicz, Günter, ed. *Ernst-Schering-Oberschule, Gesamtschule, 12. März 1986*. Berlin: Ernst-Schering-Oberschule, 1986.

Lüdtke, Alf. *The History of Everyday Life: Reconstructing Historical Experiences and Ways of Life*. Translated by William Templer. Princeton: Princeton University Press, 1995.

Lutz, Helma. "Hard Labour: The 'Biographical Work' of a Turkish Migrant Woman in Germany." *The European Journal of Women's Studies* 7 (2000): 301–319.

Lutz, Helma, Ann Phoenix, and Nira Yuval-Davis, eds.. *Crossfires: Nationalism, Racism and Gender in Europe*. London: Pluto Press, 1996.

MacDougall, Carla Elizabeth. "Cold War Capital: Contested Urbanity in West Berlin, 1963–1989," PhD dissertation, Rutgers, The State University of New Jersey, New Brunswick, 2011.

Mandaville, Peter P. "Muslim Youth in Europe." In *Islam, Europe's Second Religion: The New Social, Cultural, and Political Landscape*, edited by Shireen T. Hunter, 219–229. Westport: Praeger Publishers, 2002.

Mandel, Ruth. *Cosmopolitan Anxieties: Turkish Challenges to Citizenship and Belonging in Germany*. Durham: Duke University Press, 2008.

"A Place of Their Own: Contesting Spaces and Defining Places in Berlin's Migrant Community." In *Making Muslim Space in North America and Europe*, edited by Barbara Daly Metcalf, 147–166. Berkeley: University of California Press, 1996.

"Turkish Headscarves and the 'Foreigner Problem': Constructing Difference Through Emblems of Identity." *New German Critique* 16, no. 1 (1989): 27–46.

Massey, Doreen. *Space, Place, and Gender*. Minneapolis: University of Minnesota Press, 1994.

Massey, Douglas S., Joaquin Arango, Graeme Huge, Ali Kouaouci, and Adela Pellegrino. "Theories of International Migration: A Review and Appraisal." *Population and Development Review* 19, no. 3 (September 1993): 431–466.

Mattes, Monika. *"Gastarbeiterinnen" in der Bundesrepublik: Anwerbepolitik, Migration, und Geschlecht in den 50er bis 70er Jahren*. Frankfurt am Main: Campus Verlag, 2005.

Melk-Koch, Marion. *Schulen im Wedding, 1821–1992: Materialien zur Schulgeschichte des Bezirks Wedding von Berlin*. Berlin: Bezirksamt Wedding, Abteilung Volksbildung, 1993.

Michels, Marcel. *"Ausländische Arbeitnehmer bei Siemens Berlin in den 1960er/70er Jahren."* Master's thesis. Munich: Ludwig-Maximilian-Universität, 2001.

Miller, Brian Joseph-Keysor. "Reshaping the Turkish Nation-State: The Turkish-German Guest Worker Program and Planned Development, 1961–1985." PhD Dissertation, The University of Iowa, Iowa City, 2015.

Miller, Jennifer. "Her Fight Is Your Fight: 'Guest Worker' Labor Activism in the Early 1970s West Germany." *International Labor and Working-Class History*, no. 84 (Fall 2013): 226–247.

"On Track for West Germany: Turkish 'Guest-worker' Rail Transportation to West Germany in the Postwar Period." *German History* 30, no. 4 (December 2012): 528–549.

Modood, Tariq. *The Politics of Multiculturalism in the New Europe: Racism, Identity, and Community.* London: St. Martin's Press, 1997.

Morokvasic, Mirjana. "Birds of Passage Are also Women ..." *International Migration Review* 18, no. 4 (Winter 1984): 886–907.

Müller, Bernhard, ed. *Wedding: Wege zu Geschichte und Alltag eines Berliner Arbeiterbezirkes.* Berlin: Stattbuch Verlag, 1990.

Mushaben, Joyce Marie. *The Changing Faces of Citizenship: Integration and Mobilization Among Ethnic Minorities in Germany.* New York: Berghahn Books, 2008.

"From Ausländer to Inlander: The Changing Faces of Citizenship in Post-Wall Germany." *German Politics and Society* 94, vol. 28, no. 1 (Spring 2010): 141–164.

Mushaben, Joyce Marie, Ilyan Başgöz, and Norman Furniss. "A Crisis of Culture: Isolation and Integration among Turkish Guestworkers in the German Federal Republic." In *Turkish Workers in Europe: An Interdisciplinary Study*, edited by Ilyan Başgöz and Norman Furniss, 125–150. Bloomington: Indiana University Turkish Studies, 1985.

O'Brien, Peter. "Continuity and Change in Germany's Treatment of Non-Germans." *International Migration Review* 22, no. 3 (Autumn 1988): 109–134.

Ohliger, Rainer, and Ulrich Raiser. *Integration und Migration in Berlin: Zahlen – Daten – Fakten.* Berlin: Der Beauftragte des Sentas von Berlin für Integration und Migration, 2005.

Özcan, Ertekin. *Türkische Immigrantenorganisationen in der Bundesrepublik Deutschland: Die Entwicklung politischer Organisationen unter türkischen Arbeitsimmigranten in der Bundesrepublik Deutschland und Berlin West.* West Berlin: Hitit Verlag, 1989.

Pauly, Robert. *Islam in Europe: Integration or Marginalization?* Aldershot: Ashgate, 2004.

Phizacklea, Annie. "Gendered Actors in Migration." In *Gender and Ethnicity in Contemporary Europe*, edited by Jacqueline Andall, 23–37. Oxford: Berg, 2003.

Pugh, Emily. *Architecture, Politics, and Identity in Divided Berlin.* Pittsburgh: University of Pittsburgh Press, 2014.

Rex, John, Daniele Joy, and Czarina Wilpert, eds. *Immigrant Associations in Europe.* Brookfield: Grower, 1987.

Richie, Alexandra. *Faust's Metropolis: A History of Berlin.* New York: Carroll & Graf Publishers, Inc., 1998.

Rist, Ray C. *Guestworkers in Germany: The Prospects for Pluralism.* New York: Praeger Publishers, 1978.

Rosenow, Kerstin. *Organizing Muslims and Integrating Islam in Germany: New Developments in the 21st Century.* Boston: Brill, 2013.

Rudolph, Hedwig. "Dynamics of Immigration in a Nonimmigrant Country: Germany." In *European Migration in the Late Twentieth Century: Historical Patterns, Actual Trends, and Social Implications,* edited by Heinz Fassman and Rainer Münz, 113–126. Cornwall: IIASA, 1994.

Rudolph, Hedwig, and Felicitas Hillmann. "Döner contra Boulette – Döner und Boulette: Berliner türkischer Herkunft als Arbeitskräfte und Unternehmer im Nahrungsgütersektor." In *Zuwanderung und Stadtentwicklung,* edited by Hartmut Häußermann and Ingrid Oswald, 85–105. Opladen/Wiesbaden: Leviathan, 1997.

Schiffauer, Werner. *Die Gottesmänner: türkische Islamisten in Deutschland, eine Studie zur Herstellung religiöser Evidenz.* Frankfurt: Suhrkamp, 2000.

Die Migranten aus Subay: Türken in Deutschland, eine Ethnographie. Stuttgart, Germany: Klett-Cotta, 1991.

Nach dem Islamismus: Die Islamische Gemeinschaft Milli Görüş. Eine Ethnographie. Frankfurt: Suhrkamp Verlag, 2010.

Schmitt, Thomas. *Moscheen in Deutschland: Konflikte um ihre Errichtung und Nutzung.* Flensburg: Deutsches Akademie für Landeskunde, 2003.

Schoenberg, Ulrike. "Participation in Ethnic Organizations: The Case of Immigrants in West Germany." *International Migration Review* 19, no. 3 (Autumn 1985): 416–437.

Schönpflug, Ute, Rainer K. Silbereisen, and Jörg Schulz. "Perceived Decision-Making Influence in Turkish Migrant Workers' and German Workers' Families: The Impact of Social Support." *Journal of Cross-Cultural Psychology* 21, no. 3 (September 1990): 261–282.

Schönwälder, Karen. *Einwanderung und ethnische Pluralität: Politische Entscheidungen und öffentliche Debatten in Grossbritannien und der Bundesrepublik von den 1950er bis zu den 1970er Jahren.* Essen: Klartext Verlag, 2001.

Schulte-Peevers, Andrea, Kerry Christiani, Marc Di Duca, Anthony Haywood, Catherine Le Nevez, Daniel Robinson, and Caroline Sieg. *Lonely Planet: Germany.* Footscray: Lonely Planet, 2010.

Scott, Joan. "Experiences." In *Feminists Theorize the Political,* edited by Judith Butler and Joan Scott, 22–40. London: Routledge, 1992.

Scott, Joan Wallach. *The Politics of the Veil.* Princeton: Princeton University Press, 2010.

Seidel-Pielen, Eberhard. *Aufgespießt: Wie der Döner über die Deutschen kam.* Berlin: Rotbuch, 1996.

Unsere Türken: Annäherungen an ein gespaltenes Verhältnis. Berlin: Elefanten Press, 1998.

Seidel-Pielen, Eberhard, and Klaus Farin. *Der Gewalt die Stirn bieten: Berliner Jugendliche auf der Suche nach neuen Normen und Umgangsformen im kulturübergreifenden Milieu.* Berlin: Ausländerbeauftragte des Senats, 1992.

Sekretariat der Kultusministerkonferenz. *Statistische Veröffentlichungen der Kultusministerkonferenz: Ausländische Schüler in der Bundesrepublik Deutschland, 1970 bis 1983.* Bonn: KMK, 1984.

Şen, Faruk. "Euro-Islam: Some Empirical Evidences." In *Islam and Muslims in Germany*, edited by Ala Al-Hamarneh and Jörn Thielmann, 33–48. Leiden: Brill, 2008.

Islam in Deutschland. Munich: C. H. Beck, 2002.

Şen, Faruk, and Martina Sauer. *Türkische Unternehmer in Berlin: Struktur – Wirthschaft – Problemlagen.* Berliner Beiträge zu Integration und Migration. Berlin: Der Beauftragte des Senats von Berlin für Integration und Migration, 2005.

Silvey, Rachel, and Victoria Lawson. "Placing the Migrant." *Annals of the Association of American Geographers* 89, no. 1 (March 1999): 121–132.

Sommerfeld, Franz. *Der Moscheestreit: Eine exemplarische Debatte über Einwanderung und Integration.* Cologne: Kiepenheuer & Witsch, 2008.

Spohn, Margret. *Türkische Männer in Deutschland: Familie und Identität. Migranten der ersten Generation erzählen ihre Geschichte.* Bielefeld: Transcript, 2002.

Stanley, David. *Lonely Planet: Eastern Europe on a Shoestring.* 2nd ed. Hawthorn: Lonely Planet Publications, 1991.

Statistisches Bundesamt (West). *Statistisches Jahrbuch für die Bundesrepublik Deutschland.* Stuttgart: W. Kohlhammer, 1968.

Statistisches Jahrbuch für die Bundesrepublik Deutschland. Stuttgart: W. Kohlhammer, 1974.

Statistisches Landesamt Berlin. *Berliner Statistik: Die Ausländer in Berlin (West) am 31. Dezember 1974.* Berlin: Statistisches Landesamt Berlin, 1975.

Berliner Statistik: Die Ausländer in Berlin (West) am 31. Dezember 1976. Berlin: Statistisches Landesamt Berlin, 1977.

Berliner Statistik: Die melderechtlich registrierten Ausländer in Berlin (West) am 31. Dezember 1978. Berlin: Statistisches Landesamt Berlin, 1979.

Berliner Statistik: Die melderechtlich registrierten Ausländer in Berlin (West) am 31. Dezember 1980. Berlin: Statistisches Landesamt Berlin, 1981.

Berliner Statistik: Melderechtlich registrierte Ausländer in Berlin (West) am 31. Dezember 1982. Berlin: Statistisches Landesamt Berlin, 1983.

Berliner Statistik: Melderechtlich registrierte Ausländer in Berlin (West) am 31. Dezember 1984. Berlin: Statistisches Landesamt Berlin, 1985.

Berliner Statistik: Melderechtlich registrierte Ausländer in Berlin (West) am 31. Dezember 1986. Berlin: Statistisches Landesamt Berlin, 1987.

Berliner Statistik: Melderechtlich registrierte Ausländer in Berlin (West) am 31. Dezember 1988. Berlin: Statistisches Landesamt Berlin, 1989.

Berliner Statistik: Melderechtlich registrierte Ausländer in Berlin (West) am 31. Dezember 1990. Berlin: Statistisches Landesamt Berlin, 1991.

Stowasser, Barbara Freyer. "The Turks in Germany: From Sojourners to Citizens." In *Muslims in the West: From Sojourners to Citizens*, edited by Yvonne Yazbeck Haddad, 52–71. Oxford: Oxford University Press, 2002.

Summers, Sarah. "Finding Feminism: Rethinking Activism in the West German Women's Movement." In *Gendering Post-1945 German History: Entanglments*, edited by Karen Hagemann, Donna Harsch, and Friederike Bruenhoefner. Oxford: Berghahn Books, 2018. In production.

Sunier, Thijl, and Nico Landman. *Transnational Turkish Islam: Shifting Geographies of Religious Activism and Community Building in Turkey and Europe.* Boston: Palgrave Macmillan, 2015.

Tan, Dursun, and Hans-Peter Waldhoff. "Turkish Everyday Culture in Germany and Its Prospects." In *Turkish Culture in German Society Today*, edited by David Horrocks and Eva Kolinsky, 137–156. Providence: Berghahn Books, 1996.

Trüper, Ursula. "Die Leute vom Sparrplatz: Eine Ausstellung im Heimatmuseum Wedding, März 1995." *Die Leute vom Sparrplatz Exhibit Manuscript.* Berlin: Mitte Museum, 1995.

UNESCO. *Living in Two Cultures: The Socio-Cultural Situation of Migrant Workers and Their Families.* Paris: UNESCO Press, 1982.

Van Tubergen, Frank. *Immigrant Integration: A Cross-National Study.* New York: LFB Scholarly Publishers LLC, 2006.

Vermeulen, Floris Freek. *The Immigrant Organising Process: The Emergence and Persistence of Turkish Immigrant Organisations in Amsterdam and Berlin and Surinamese Organisations in Amsterdam, 1960–2000.* Amsterdam: Amsterdam University Press, 2006.

Von Oertzen, Christina. *Teilzeitarbeit und die Lust am Zuverdienen: Geschlechterpolitik und gesellschaftlicher Wandel in Westdeutschland 1948–1969.* Göttingen: Vandenhoeck & Ruprecht, 1999.

Walter, Bronwen. *Outsiders Inside: Whiteness, Place and Irish Women.* New York: Routledge, 2000.

Wilpert, Czarina. "Children of Foreign Workers in the Federal Republic of Germany." *International Migration Review* 11, no. 4 (Winter 1977): 473–485.

"Identity Issues in the History of the Postwar Migration from Turkey to Germany." *German Politics and Society* 107, vol. 31, no. 2 (Summer 2013): 108–131.

Worbs, Susanne. "The Second Generation in Germany: Between School and Labor Market." *International Migration Review* 37, no. 4 (Winter 2003): 1011–1038.

Yasin, Mehmet. "Gather Up the Bales, We Are Going Back: Lost-Generation, Runaway Girls are Speaking." In *Turkish Workers in Europe: An Interdisciplinary Study*, edited by Ilhan Başgöz and Norman Furniss, translated by Sabri M. Akural, 175–191. Bloomington: Indiana University Turkish Studies, 1985.

Yurdakul, Gökçe. "State, Political Parties, and Immigrant Elites: Turkish Immigrant Associations in Berlin." *Journal of Ethnic and Migration Studies* 32, no. 3 (April 2006): 435–453.

Yurdakul, Gökçe, and Ahmet Yükleyen. "Islam, Conflict, and Integration: Turkish Religious Associations in Germany." *Turkish Studies* 10, no. 2 (June 2009): 217–231.

Zentrum für Türkeistudien. *Türkische Unternehmer in Bremen und Bremerhaven. Eine Analyse ihrer Struktur, ihrer wirtschaftlichen Situation sowie ihrer Integration in das deutsche Wirthschaftsgefüge – Ergebnisse einer standardisierten telefonischen Befragung im Auftrag der Ausländerbeauftragten des Bundeslandes Bremen.* Essen: 2001.

Index

264   Index

266   Index